# studysync®

## Reading & Writing Companion

# GRADE 8 UNITS

Suspense! • In Time of War
A Moral Compass • The Civil War

**studysync**®

**studysync.com**

Send all inquiries to:
BookheadEd Learning, LLC
610 Daniel Young Drive
Sonoma, CA 95476

8 9 10 11 12 13 LMN 25 24 23 22 E

# studysync®

# Table of Contents

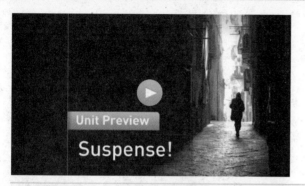

# STUDENT GUIDE

# GETTING STARTED

Welcome to the StudySync Reading and Writing Companion! In this booklet, you will find a collection of readings based on the theme of the unit you are studying. As you work through the readings, you will be asked to answer questions and perform a variety of tasks designed to help you closely analyze and understand each text selection. Read on for an explanation of each section of this booklet.

## CORE ELA TEXTS

In each Core ELA Unit you will read texts and text excerpts that share a common theme, despite their different genres, time periods, and authors. Each reading encourages a closer look with questions and a short writing assignment.

### 1 INTRODUCTION

An Introduction to each text provides historical context for your reading as well as information about the author. You will also learn about the genre of the excerpt and the year in which it was written.

### 2 FIRST READ

During your first reading of each excerpt, you should just try to get a general idea of the content and message of the reading. Don't worry if there are parts you don't understand or words that are unfamiliar to you. You'll have an opportunity later to dive deeper into the text.

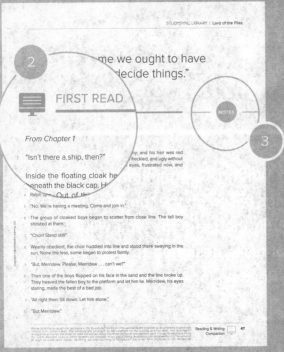

### 3 NOTES

Many times, while working through the activities after each text, you will be asked to **annotate** or **make annotations** about what you are reading. This means that you should highlight or underline words in the text and use the "Notes" column to make comments or jot down any questions you may have. You may also want to note any unfamiliar vocabulary words here.

### 4 | THINK QUESTIONS

These questions will ask you to start thinking critically about the text, asking specific questions about its purpose, and making connections to your prior knowledge and reading experiences. To answer these questions, you should go back to the text and draw upon specific evidence that you find there to support your responses. You will also begin to explore some of the more challenging vocabulary words used in the excerpt.

### 5 | CLOSE READ & FOCUS QUESTIONS

After you have completed the First Read, you will then be asked to go back and read the excerpt more closely and critically. Before you begin your Close Read, you should read through the Focus Questions to get an idea of the concepts you will want to focus on during your second reading. You should work through the Focus Questions by making annotations, highlighting important concepts, and writing notes or questions in the "Notes" column. Depending on instructions from your teacher, you may need to respond online or use a separate piece of paper to start expanding on your thoughts and ideas.

### 6 | WRITING PROMPT

Your study of each excerpt or selection will end with a writing assignment. To complete this assignment, you should use your notes, annotations, and answers to both the Think and Focus Questions. Be sure to read the prompt carefully and address each part of it in your writing assignment.

# ENGLISH LANGUAGE DEVELOPMENT TEXTS

The English Language Development texts and activities take a closer look at the language choices that authors make to communicate their ideas. Individual and group activities will help develop your understanding of each text.

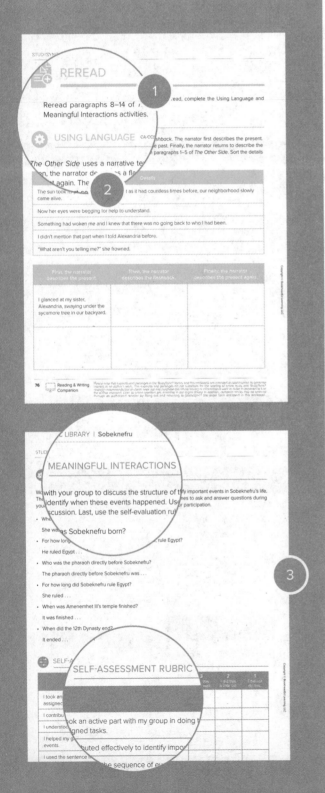

## 1 REREAD

After you have completed the First Read, you will have two additional opportunities to revisit portions of the excerpt more closely. The directions for each reread will specify which paragraphs or sections you should focus on.

## 2 USING LANGUAGE

These questions will ask you to analyze the author's use of language and conventions in the text. You may be asked to write in sentence frames, fill in a chart, or you may simply choose between multiple-choice options. To answer these questions, you should read the exercise carefully and go back in the text as necessary to accurately complete the activity.

## 3 MEANINGFUL INTERACTIONS & SELF-ASSESSMENT RUBRIC

After each reading, you will participate in a group activity or discussion with your peers. You may be provided speaking frames to guide your discussions or writing frames to support your group work. To complete these activities, you should revisit the excerpt for textual evidence and support. When you finish, use the Self-Assessment Rubric to evaluate how well you participated and collaborated.

# EXTENDED WRITING PROJECT

The Extended Writing Project is your opportunity to explore the theme of each unit in a longer written work. You will draw information from your readings, research, and own life experiences to complete the assignment.

## 1 WRITING PROJECT

After you have read all of the unit text selections, you will move on to a writing project. Each project will guide you through the process of writing an argumentative, narrative, informative, or literary analysis essay. Student models and graphic organizers will provide guidance and help you organize your thoughts as you plan and write your essay. Throughout the project, you will also study and work on specific writing skills to help you develop different portions of your writing.

## 2 WRITING PROCESS STEPS

There are five steps in the writing process: **Prewrite**, **Plan**, **Draft**, **Revise**, and **Edit, Proofread, and Publish**. During each step, you will form and shape your writing project so that you can effectively express your ideas. Lessons focus on one step at a time, and you will have the chance to receive feedback from your peers and teacher.

## 3 WRITING SKILLS

Each Writing Skill lesson focuses on a specific strategy or technique that you will use during your writing project. The lessons begin by analyzing a student model or mentor text, and give you a chance to learn and practice the skill on its own. Then, you will have the opportunity to apply each new skill to improve the writing in your own project.

# studysync®

## Reading & Writing Companion

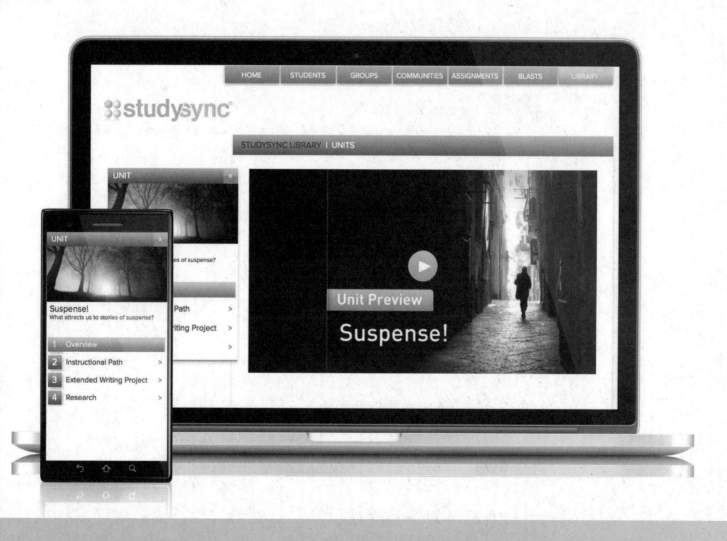

What attracts us to stories of suspense?

# Suspense!

# Suspense!

## TEXTS

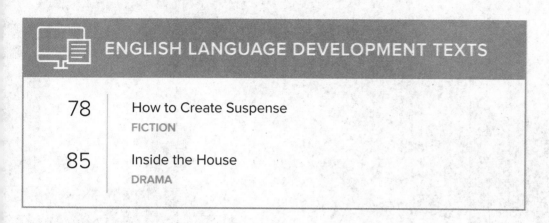

## ENGLISH LANGUAGE DEVELOPMENT TEXTS

## EXTENDED WRITING PROJECT

501

Text Fulfillment
through
StudySync

# LET 'EM PLAY GOD

**NON-FICTION**
Alfred Hitchcock
1948

# INTRODUCTION

With films that consistently put viewers on the edge of their seats, British film director Alfred Hitchcock earned the nickname "The Master of Suspense." In the following excerpt from a 1948 essay, Hitchcock describes how he creates suspense by letting the audience "play God"—by providing them with certain information not known to characters in a movie—and illustrates how he used the technique to create dramatic tension in his 1948 thriller, *Rope*.

# "You have suspense when you let the audience play God."

## FIRST READ

1   Every maker of mystery movies aims at getting the audience on the edge of their seats. The **ingredient** to keep them there is called "suspense." Producers cry for it, writers cry in agony to get it, and actors cry for joy when they do get it. I've often been asked what it is.

2   As far as I'm concerned, you have suspense when you let the audience play God.

3   Suppose, for instance, you have six characters involved in a mystery. A man has been murdered and all six are possible **suspects** but no one is sure including the audience.

4   One of the characters, a young man, is standing in a shadowy room with his back to the door when an unidentified character in a cloak and black hat sneaks in and slugs him into **insensibility.** It's a brutal act, but if the audience does not know whether the young man is a killer or a hero they will not know whether to cheer or weep.

5   If the audience does know, if they have been told all the secrets that the characters do not know, they'll work like the devil for you because they know what fate is facing the poor actors. That is what is known as "playing God." That is suspense.

6   For 17 years I have been making pictures described alternately as thriller, dark mysteries, and chillers, yet I have never actually directed a whodunit or a puzzler. Offhand this may sound like **debunking,** but I do not believe that puzzling the audience is the essence of suspense.

7   Take, for instance, the drama I recently filmed at Warner Bros. called *Rope*. It stars James Stewart with Joan Chandler, our new discovery, in the feminine lead.

8    John Dall and Farley Granger strangle a young man in the opening shot. They put his body in a chest, cover the chest with a damask cloth and silver service, then serve *hors d'oeuvres* and drinks from it at a party for the victim's father, mother, sweetheart, and assorted friends. Everyone is gay and charming. When Stewart begins to suspect foul play late in the film John Dall puts a gun in his pocket in case things get too hot.

9    The audience knows everything from the start, the players know nothing. There is not a single detail to puzzle the audience. It is certainly not a whodunit for the simple reason that everyone out front knows who did it. No one on the screen knows except the two murderers. The fact that the audience watches actors go blithely through an atmosphere that is loaded with evil makes for real suspense.

10   These are the questions, now, that constantly pop up. Will the murderers break and give themselves away? When the victim does not show up for the party will his father suspect? Will Jimmy get killed before he discovers the actual crime? How long will that body lie in its wooden grave at a champagne party without being discovered? If we are successful we'll have the audience at such a pitch that they want to shout every time one of the players goes near that chest.

11   In order to achieve this, one of the necessary ingredients of the formula is a series of **plausible** situations with people that are real. When characters are unbelievable you never get suspense, only surprise.

12   Just because there is a touch of murder and an air of mystery about a story it is not necessary to see transoms opening, clutching fingers, hooded creatures, and asps on the Chinese rug.

13   Spellbound was based on complete psychiatric truth. *Foreign Correspondent* was simply the story of a man hammering away at events with a woman who was not much help. *Notorious* concerned a woman caught in a web of world events from which she could not extricate herself and *The Paradine Case* was a love story embedded in the emotional quicksand of a murder trial.

14   In none of these was the house filled with shadows, the weather dull and stormy throughout, the moor windswept, and the doors creaky. In fact, it is important in a story with sinister implications to use counterpoint, great contrast between situation and background, as we did in *Rope*.

Copyright © BookheadEd Learning, LLC

15 John Dall is guilty of a bestial crime which the audience sees him perform with young Granger. But throughout the film he is grace and charm itself and his apartment is gay and beautifully appointed. And when Granger plays the piano he picks a light and childish piece, a minuet. Suspense involves contrast.

 THINK QUESTIONS  CA-CCSS: CA.RI.8.1, CA.L.8.4a, CA.L.8.4b, CA.L.8.5b

1.  From his examples, it's clear that Alfred Hitchcock expects readers to be familiar with his films. However, some readers may not have seen many or any of Hitchcock's movies. What do the examples that Hitchcock uses in paragraphs 3 and 4 tell you about the kinds of movies he made? How does paragraph 6 support your inferences? Use evidence from the text to explain your answer.

2.  Based on the first five paragraphs, what is Alfred Hitchcock discussing in this essay? Hitchcock says, "I do not believe that puzzling the audience is the essence of suspense." What kinds of examples does he use to help him support that statement?

3.  How does Alfred Hitchcock explain creating suspense in a film by using the example of his movie, *Rope*, starring James Stewart? Refer to one or more details from the text to support your answer.

4.  Use context to determine the meaning of the word **plausible** as it is used in paragraph 11 of "Let 'Em Play God." Write your definition of *plausible* here and explain how you figured it out.

5.  The Latin prefix *in-* means "not," and the word "sense" comes from the Latin root *sensus*, meaning "to feel or perceive." Use your knowledge of Latin roots and affixes, as well as context clues provided in the passage, to determine the meaning of **insensibility** in paragraph 4. Write your definition of *insensibility* and explain how you figured it out.

# CLOSE READ
CA-CCSS: CA.RI.8.1, CA.RI.8.4, CA.RI.8.6, CA.L.8.4a, CA.W.8.4, CA.W.8.5, CA.W.8.6, CA.W.8.10

Reread the excerpt from "Let 'Em Play God." As you reread, complete the Focus Questions below. Then use your answers and annotations from the questions to help you complete the Writing Prompt.

 FOCUS QUESTIONS

1. In paragraph 2, the author states that in a movie, "you have suspense when you let the audience play God." Highlight text evidence and make annotations that explain how the author, film director Alfred Hitchcock, allows the audience to "play God" in his films.

2. In paragraph 5, Hitchcock says that an audience "will work like the devil" for him if he tells them all the secrets his characters do not know. What can you infer about Hitchcock's attitude toward the people who watch his movies? How does this phrase relate, or connect, to Hitchcock's purpose for writing? Highlight context clues to define the phrase, as well as text evidence that tells you how Hitchcock and his actors will know they have succeeded in engaging the audience for *Rope*.

3. How does Hitchcock feel about what he describes as "whodunit or puzzler" movies? Highlight the sentences that explain Hitchcock's point of view toward these kinds of films, and annotate to explain what Hitchcock believes is the difference between suspense and surprise.

4. In paragraph 10, Hitchcock asks a series of questions. What purpose do these questions serve in the article? What does Hitchcock mean when he says that the questions "constantly pop up"? Annotate your answer to explain your reasoning.

5. Discuss Alfred Hitchcock's article and his movie *Rope* in relation to the essential question for this unit: *What attracts us to stories of suspense?* Make annotations and highlight textual evidence that supports your ideas.

## WRITING PROMPT

What does the author mean by the phrase "letting the audience play God"? Is the plot of the movie *Rope* that Hitchcock describes a good example of letting the audience "play God"? Why or why not? How does Hitchcock use the film as an illustration of his point of view? Be sure to cite textual evidence to develop your essay and support your ideas.

# THE MONKEY'S PAW

**FICTION**

W.W. Jacobs
1902

## INTRODUCTION

I n "The Monkey's Paw," W.W. Jacob's cautionary tale from 1902, a well-to-do family in Victorian England is presented with a dubious opportunity to increase their fortunes. A magical monkey's paw from India has the power to make three wishes come true, but what will be the price?

# "...it's just an ordinary little paw dried to a mummy."

 **FIRST READ**

I.

1 Without, the night was cold and wet, but in the small parlour of Laburnam Villa the blinds were drawn and the fire burned brightly. Father and son were at chess, the former, who possessed ideas about the game involving radical changes, putting his king into such sharp and unnecessary perils that it even provoked comment from the white-haired old lady knitting placidly by the fire.

2 "Hark at the wind," said Mr. White, who, having seen a fatal mistake after it was too late, was amiably desirous of preventing his son from seeing it.

3 "I'm listening," said the latter, grimly surveying the board as he stretched out his hand. "Check."

4 "I should hardly think that he'd come to-night," said his father, with his hand poised over the board.

5 "Mate," replied the son.

6 "That's the worst of living so far out," bawled Mr. White, with sudden and unlooked-for violence; "of all the beastly, slushy, out-of-the-way places to live in, this is the worst. Pathway's a bog, and the road's a torrent. I don't know what people are thinking about. I suppose because only two houses in the road are let, they think it doesn't matter."

7 "Never mind, dear," said his wife, soothingly; "perhaps you'll win the next one."

8 Mr. White looked up sharply, just in time to intercept a knowing glance between mother and son. The words died away on his lips, and he hid a guilty grin in his thin grey beard.

9   "There he is," said Herbert White, as the gate banged to loudly and heavy footsteps came toward the door.

10  The old man rose with hospitable haste, and opening the door, was heard condoling with the new arrival. The new arrival also condoled with himself, so that Mrs. White said, "Tut, tut!" and coughed gently as her husband entered the room, followed by a tall, burly man, beady of eye and rubicund of visage.

11  "Sergeant-Major Morris," he said, introducing him.

12  The sergeant-major shook hands, and taking the **proffered** seat by the fire, watched contentedly while his host got out whiskey and tumblers and stood a small copper kettle on the fire.

13  At the third glass his eyes got brighter, and he began to talk, the little family circle regarding with eager interest this visitor from distant parts, as he squared his broad shoulders in the chair and spoke of wild scenes and doughty deeds; of wars and plagues and strange peoples.

14  "Twenty-one years of it," said Mr. White, nodding at his wife and son. "When he went away he was a slip of a youth in the warehouse. Now look at him."

15  "He don't look to have taken much harm," said Mrs. White, politely.

16  "I'd like to go to India myself," said the old man, "just to look round a bit, you know."

17  "Better where you are," said the sergeant-major, shaking his head. He put down the empty glass, and sighing softly, shook it again.

18  "I should like to see those old temples and **fakirs** and jugglers," said the old man. "What was that you started telling me the other day about a monkey's paw or something, Morris?"

19  "Nothing," said the soldier, hastily. "Leastways nothing worth hearing."

20  "Monkey's paw?" said Mrs. White, curiously.

21  "Well, it's just a bit of what you might call magic, perhaps," said the sergeant-major, offhandedly.

22  His three listeners leaned forward eagerly. The visitor absent-mindedly put his empty glass to his lips and then set it down again. His host filled it for him.

23  "To look at," said the sergeant-major, fumbling in his pocket, "it's just an ordinary little paw, dried to a mummy."

NOTES

24   He took something out of his pocket and proffered it. Mrs. White drew back with a grimace, but her son, taking it, examined it curiously.

25   "And what is there special about it?" inquired Mr. White as he took it from his son, and having examined it, placed it upon the table.

26   "It had a spell put on it by an old fakir," said the sergeant-major, "a very holy man. He wanted to show that fate ruled people's lives, and that those who interfered with it did so to their sorrow. He put a spell on it so that three separate men could each have three wishes from it."

27   His manner was so impressive that his hearers were conscious that their light laughter jarred somewhat.

28   "Well, why don't you have three, sir?" said Herbert White, cleverly.

29   The soldier regarded him in the way that middle age is wont to regard presumptuous youth. "I have," he said, quietly, and his blotchy face whitened.

30   "And did you really have the three wishes granted?" asked Mrs. White.

31   "I did," said the sergeant-major, and his glass tapped against his strong teeth.

32   "And has anybody else wished?" persisted the old lady.

33   "The first man had his three wishes. Yes," was the reply; "I don't know what the first two were, but the third was for death. That's how I got the paw."

34   His tones were so grave that a hush fell upon the group.

35   "If you've had your three wishes, it's no good to you now, then, Morris," said the old man at last. "What do you keep it for?"

36   The soldier shook his head. "Fancy, I suppose," he said, slowly. "I did have some idea of selling it, but I don't think I will. It has caused enough mischief already. Besides, people won't buy. They think it's a fairy tale; some of them, and those who do think anything of it want to try it first and pay me afterward."

37   "If you could have another three wishes," said the old man, eyeing him keenly, "would you have them?"

38   "I don't know," said the other. "I don't know."

39   He took the paw, and dangling it between his forefinger and thumb, suddenly threw it upon the fire. White, with a slight cry, stooped down and snatched it off.

40   "Better let it burn," said the soldier, solemnly.

41   "If you don't want it, Morris," said the other, "give it to me."

42   "I won't," said his friend, doggedly. "I threw it on the fire. If you keep it, don't blame me for what happens. Pitch it on the fire again like a sensible man."

43   The other shook his head and examined his new possession closely. "How do you do it?" he inquired.

44   "Hold it up in your right hand and wish aloud," said the sergeant-major, "but I warn you of the **consequences.**"

45   "Sounds like the Arabian Nights," said Mrs. White, as she rose and began to set the supper. "Don't you think you might wish for four pairs of hands for me?"

46   Her husband drew the **talisman** from pocket, and then all three burst into laughter as the sergeant-major, with a look of alarm on his face, caught him by the arm.

47   "If you must wish," he said, gruffly, "wish for something sensible."

48   Mr. White dropped it back in his pocket, and placing chairs, motioned his friend to the table. In the business of supper the talisman was partly forgotten, and afterward the three sat listening in an enthralled fashion to a second installment of the soldier's adventures in India.

49   "If the tale about the monkey's paw is not more truthful than those he has been telling us," said Herbert, as the door closed behind their guest, just in time for him to catch the last train, "we sha'nt make much out of it."

50   "Did you give him anything for it, father?" inquired Mrs. White, regarding her husband closely.

51   "A trifle," said he, colouring slightly. "He didn't want it, but I made him take it. And he pressed me again to throw it away."

52   "Likely," said Herbert, with pretended horror. "Why, we're going to be rich, and famous and happy. Wish to be an emperor, father, to begin with; then you can't be henpecked."

53   He darted round the table, pursued by the maligned Mrs. White armed with an antimacassar.

Copyright © BookheadEd Learning, LLC

54   Mr. White took the paw from his pocket and eyed it dubiously. "I don't know what to wish for, and that's a fact," he said, slowly. "It seems to me I've got all I want."

55   "If you only cleared the house, you'd be quite happy, wouldn't you?" said Herbert, with his hand on his shoulder. "Well, wish for two hundred pounds, then; that 'll just do it."

56   His father, smiling shamefacedly at his own credulity, held up the talisman, as his son, with a solemn face, somewhat marred by a wink at his mother, sat down at the piano and struck a few impressive chords.

57   "I wish for two hundred pounds," said the old man distinctly.

58   A fine crash from the piano greeted the words, interrupted by a shuddering cry from the old man. His wife and son ran toward him.

59   "It moved," he cried, with a glance of disgust at the object as it lay on the floor.

60   "As I wished, it twisted in my hand like a snake."

61   "Well, I don't see the money," said his son as he picked it up and placed it on the table, "and I bet I never shall."

62   "It must have been your fancy, father," said his wife, regarding him anxiously.

63   He shook his head. "Never mind, though; there's no harm done, but it gave me a shock all the same."

64   They sat down by the fire again while the two men finished their pipes. Outside, the wind was higher than ever, and the old man started nervously at the sound of a door banging upstairs. A silence unusual and depressing settled upon all three, which lasted until the old couple rose to retire for the night.

65   "I expect you'll find the cash tied up in a big bag in the middle of your bed," said Herbert, as he bade them good-night, "and something horrible squatting up on top of the wardrobe watching you as you pocket your ill-gotten gains."

66   He sat alone in the darkness, gazing at the dying fire, and seeing faces in it. The last face was so horrible and so simian that he gazed at it in amazement. It got so vivid that, with a little uneasy laugh, he felt on the table for a glass containing a little water to throw over it. His hand grasped the monkey's paw, and with a little shiver he wiped his hand on his coat and went up to bed.

II.

67 In the brightness of the wintry sun next morning as it streamed over the breakfast table he laughed at his fears. There was an air of prosaic wholesomeness about the room which it had lacked on the previous night, and the dirty, shrivelled little paw was pitched on the sideboard with a carelessness which betokened no great belief in its virtues.

68 "I suppose all old soldiers are the same," said Mrs. White. "The idea of our listening to such nonsense! How could wishes be granted in these days? And if they could, how could two hundred pounds hurt you, father?"

69 "Might drop on his head from the sky," said the frivolous Herbert.

70 "Morris said the things happened so naturally," said his father, "that you might if you so wished attribute it to coincidence."

71 "Well, don't break into the money before I come back," said Herbert as he rose from the table. "I'm afraid it'll turn you into a mean, avaricious man, and we shall have to disown you."

72 His mother laughed, and following him to the door, watched him down the road; and returning to the breakfast table, was very happy at the expense of her husband's credulity. All of which did not prevent her from scurrying to the door at the postman's knock, nor prevent her from referring somewhat shortly to retired sergeant-majors of bibulous habits when she found that the post brought a tailor's bill.

73 "Herbert will have some more of his funny remarks, I expect, when he comes home," she said, as they sat at dinner.

74 "I dare say," said Mr. White, pouring himself out some beer; "but for all that, the thing moved in my hand; that I'll swear to."

75 "You thought it did," said the old lady soothingly.

76 "I say it did," replied the other. "There was no thought about it; I had just— What's the matter?"

77 His wife made no reply. She was watching the mysterious movements of a man outside, who, peering in an undecided fashion at the house, appeared to be trying to make up his mind to enter. In mental connection with the two hundred pounds, she noticed that the stranger was well dressed, and wore a silk hat of glossy newness. Three times he paused at the gate, and then walked on again. The fourth time he stood with his hand upon it, and then with sudden resolution flung it open and walked up the path. Mrs. White at

Please note that excerpts and passages in the StudySync® library and this workbook are intended as touchstones to generate interest in an author's work. The excerpts and passages do not substitute for the reading of entire texts, and StudySync® strongly recommends that students seek out and purchase the whole literary or informational work in order to experience it as the author intended. Links to online resellers are available in our digital library. In addition, complete works may be ordered through an authorized reseller by filling out and returning to StudySync® the order form enclosed in this workbook.

Reading & Writing Companion  **15**

the same moment placed her hands behind her, and hurriedly unfastening the strings of her apron, put that useful article of apparel beneath the cushion of her chair.

78    She brought the stranger, who seemed ill at ease, into the room. He gazed at her furtively, and listened in a preoccupied fashion as the old lady apologized for the appearance of the room, and her husband's coat, a garment which he usually reserved for the garden. She then waited as patiently as her sex would permit, for him to broach his business, but he was at first strangely silent.

79    "I—was asked to call," he said at last, and stooped and picked a piece of cotton from his trousers. "I come from 'Maw and Meggins.'"

80    The old lady started. "Is anything the matter?" she asked, breathlessly. "Has anything happened to Herbert? What is it? What is it?"

81    Her husband interposed. "There, there, mother," he said, hastily. "Sit down, and don't jump to conclusions. You've not brought bad news, I'm sure, sir;" and he eyed the other wistfully.

82    "I'm sorry—" began the visitor.

83    "Is he hurt?" demanded the mother, wildly.

84    The visitor bowed in assent. "Badly hurt," he said, quietly, "but he is not in any pain."

85    "Oh, thank God!" said the old woman, clasping her hands. "Thank God for that! Thank—"

86    She broke off suddenly as the sinister meaning of the assurance dawned upon her and she saw the awful confirmation of her fears in the other's averted face. She caught her breath, and turning to her slower-witted husband, laid her trembling old hand upon his. There was a long silence.

87    "He was caught in the machinery," said the visitor at length in a low voice.

88    "Caught in the machinery," repeated Mr. White, in a dazed fashion, "yes."

89    He sat staring blankly out at the window, and taking his wife's hand between his own, pressed it as he had been wont to do in their old courting-days nearly forty years before.

90    "He was the only one left to us," he said, turning gently to the visitor. "It is hard."

NOTES

91  The other coughed, and rising, walked slowly to the window. "The firm wished me to convey their sincere sympathy with you in your great loss," he said, without looking round. "I beg that you will understand I am only their servant and merely obeying orders."

92  There was no reply; the old woman's face was white, her eyes staring, and her breath inaudible; on the husband's face was a look such as his friend the sergeant might have carried into his first action.

93  "I was to say that 'Maw and Meggins' disclaim all responsibility," continued the other. "They admit no liability at all, but in consideration of your son's services, they wish to present you with a certain sum as compensation."

94  Mr. White dropped his wife's hand, and rising to his feet, gazed with a look of horror at his visitor. His dry lips shaped the words, "How much?"

95  "Two hundred pounds," was the answer.

96  Unconscious of his wife's shriek, the old man smiled faintly, put out his hands like a sightless man, and dropped, a senseless heap, to the floor.

III.

97  In the huge new cemetery, some two miles distant, the old people buried their dead, and came back to a house steeped in shadow and silence. It was all over so quickly that at first they could hardly realize it, and remained in a state of expectation as though of something else to happen—something else which was to lighten this load, too heavy for old hearts to bear.

98  But the days passed, and expectation gave place to **resignation**—the hopeless resignation of the old, sometimes miscalled, apathy. Sometimes they hardly exchanged a word, for now they had nothing to talk about, and their days were long to weariness.

99  It was about a week after that the old man, waking suddenly in the night, stretched out his hand and found himself alone. The room was in darkness, and the sound of subdued weeping came from the window. He raised himself in bed and listened.

100  "Come back," he said, tenderly. "You will be cold."

101  "It is colder for my son," said the old woman, and wept afresh.

102  The sound of her sobs died away on his ears. The bed was warm, and his eyes heavy with sleep. He dozed fitfully, and then slept until a sudden wild cry from his wife awoke him with a start.

NOTES

103    "The paw!" she cried wildly. "The monkey's paw!"

104    He started up in alarm. "Where? Where is it? What's the matter?"

105    She came stumbling across the room toward him. "I want it," she said, quietly. "You've not destroyed it?"

106    "It's in the parlour, on the bracket," he replied, marvelling. "Why?"

107    She cried and laughed together, and bending over, kissed his cheek.

108    "I only just thought of it," she said, hysterically. "Why didn't I think of it before? Why didn't you think of it?"

109    "Think of what?" he questioned.

110    "The other two wishes," she replied, rapidly. "We've only had one."

111    "Was not that enough?" he demanded, fiercely.

112    "No," she cried, triumphantly; "we'll have one more. Go down and get it quickly, and wish our boy alive again."

113    The man sat up in bed and flung the bedclothes from his quaking limbs. "Good God, you are mad!" he cried, aghast.

114    "Get it," she panted; "get it quickly, and wish—Oh, my boy, my boy!"

115    Her husband struck a match and lit the candle. "Get back to bed," he said, unsteadily. "You don't know what you are saying."

116    "We had the first wish granted," said the old woman, feverishly; "why not the second?"

117    "A coincidence," stammered the old man.

118    "Go and get it and wish," cried his wife, quivering with excitement.

119    The old man turned and regarded her, and his voice shook. "He has been dead ten days, and besides he—I would not tell you else, but—I could only recognize him by his clothing. If he was too terrible for you to see then, how now?"

120    "Bring him back," cried the old woman, and dragged him toward the door. "Do you think I fear the child I have nursed?"

121    He went down in the darkness, and felt his way to the parlour, and then to the mantelpiece. The talisman was in its place, and a horrible fear that the unspoken wish might bring his mutilated son before him ere he could escape

from the room seized upon him, and he caught his breath as he found that he had lost the direction of the door. His brow cold with sweat, he felt his way round the table, and groped along the wall until he found himself in the small passage with the unwholesome thing in his hand.

122 Even his wife's face seemed changed as he entered the room. It was white and expectant, and to his fears seemed to have an unnatural look upon it. He was afraid of her.

123 "Wish!" she cried, in a strong voice.

124 "It is foolish and wicked," he faltered.

125 "Wish!" repeated his wife.

126 He raised his hand. "I wish my son alive again."

127 The talisman fell to the floor, and he regarded it fearfully. Then he sank trembling into a chair as the old woman, with burning eyes, walked to the window and raised the blind.

128 He sat until he was chilled with the cold, glancing occasionally at the figure of the old woman peering through the window. The candle-end, which had burned below the rim of the china candlestick, was throwing pulsating shadows on the ceiling and walls, until, with a flicker larger than the rest, it expired. The old man, with an unspeakable sense of relief at the failure of the talisman, crept back to his bed, and a minute or two afterward the old woman came silently and apathetically beside him.

129 Neither spoke, but lay silently listening to the ticking of the clock. A stair creaked, and a squeaky mouse scurried noisily through the wall. The darkness was oppressive, and after lying for some time screwing up his courage, he took the box of matches, and striking one, went downstairs for a candle.

130 At the foot of the stairs the match went out, and he paused to strike another; and at the same moment a knock, so quiet and stealthy as to be scarcely audible, sounded on the front door.

131 The matches fell from his hand and spilled in the passage. He stood motionless, his breath suspended until the knock was repeated. Then he turned and fled swiftly back to his room, and closed the door behind him. A third knock sounded through the house.

132 "What's that?" cried the old woman, starting up.

133 "A rat," said the old man in shaking tones—"a rat. It passed me on the stairs."

Please note that excerpts and passages in the StudySync® library and this workbook are intended as touchstones to generate interest in an author's work. The excerpts and passages do not substitute for the reading of entire texts, and StudySync® strongly recommends that students seek out and purchase the whole literary or informational work in order to experience it as the author intended. Links to online resellers are available in our digital library. In addition, complete works may be ordered through an authorized reseller by filling out and returning to StudySync® the order form enclosed in this workbook.

Reading & Writing Companion    **19**

134 His wife sat up in bed listening. A loud knock resounded through the house.

135 "It's Herbert!" she screamed. "It's Herbert!"

136 She ran to the door, but her husband was before her, and catching her by the arm, held her tightly.

137 "What are you going to do?" he whispered hoarsely.

138 "It's my boy; it's Herbert!" she cried, struggling mechanically. "I forgot it was two miles away. What are you holding me for? Let go. I must open the door."

139 "For God's sake don't let it in," cried the old man, trembling.

140 "You're afraid of your own son," she cried, struggling. "Let me go. I'm coming, Herbert; I'm coming."

141 There was another knock, and another. The old woman with a sudden wrench broke free and ran from the room. Her husband followed to the landing, and called after her appealingly as she hurried downstairs. He heard the chain rattle back and the bottom bolt drawn slowly and stiffly from the socket. Then the old woman's voice, strained and panting.

142 "The bolt," she cried, loudly. "Come down. I can't reach it."

143 But her husband was on his hands and knees groping wildly on the floor in search of the paw. If he could only find it before the thing outside got in. A perfect fusillade of knocks reverberated through the house, and he heard the scraping of a chair as his wife put it down in the passage against the door. He heard the creaking of the bolt as it came slowly back, and at the same moment he found the monkey's paw, and frantically breathed his third and last wish.

144 The knocking ceased suddenly, although the echoes of it were still in the house. He heard the chair drawn back, and the door opened. A cold wind rushed up the staircase, and a long loud wail of disappointment and misery from his wife gave him courage to run down to her side, and then to the gate beyond. The street lamp flickering opposite shone on a quiet and deserted road.

# THINK QUESTIONS

CA-CCSS: CA.RL.8.1, CA.L.8.4a, CA.L.8.4c, CA.L.8.4d, CA.SL.8.1a, CA.SL.8.1c, CA.SL.8.1d

1. What is "the monkey's paw"? What is Herbert White's attitude toward the monkey's paw? Cite textual evidence from the selection to support your answer.

2. Foreshadowing is a literary device in which a writer gives an advance hint of what is to come later in the story. How does the author of "The Monkey's Paw" use foreshadowing in the first chapter to suggest that the spell placed on the paw might not bring happiness to whomever possesses it? Cite textual evidence from the selection to support your answer.

3. Compare Mr. White's feelings about the monkey's paw when he makes the first wish, second wish, and third wish. How does his attitude change? Cite textual evidence from the selection to support your answer.

4. Use context to determine the meaning of the word **fakirs** as it is used in paragraph 18 of "The Monkey's Paw." The singular form is used in paragraph 26. Write your definition of *fakirs* and explain how you figured it out. How can you check the word's precise meaning as well as its pronunciation?

5. Find the word **consequences** in paragraph 44. Use context clues in the surrounding sentences, as well as the sentence in which *consequences* appears, to determine the word's meaning. Write your definition of *consequences* and explain how you figured it out. Then check the meaning in a dictionary.

## CLOSE READ   CA-CCSS: CA.RL.8.1, CA.RL.8.2, CA.RL.8.3, CA.W.8.4, CA.W.8.5, CA.W.8.6, CA.W.8.10

Reread the short story "The Monkey's Paw." As you reread, complete the Focus Questions below. Then use your answers and annotations from the questions to help you complete the Writing Prompt.

## FOCUS QUESTIONS

1. How does Mr. White approach the game of chess that he plays with his son Herbert? What does this reveal about his personality, and how he will react when he learns about the monkey's paw later in the story? Support your answer with textual evidence.

2. How does Mrs. White's attitude, as well as her circumstances, create a problem for both her and Mr. White at the end of the story? How does the setting add to the suspense? Cite textual evidence to support your answer.

3. What causes the downfall of the White family, and how is it related to the theme of "The Monkey's Paw"? Cite textual evidence to support your answer.

4. The entire story is set in the Whites' home, yet it seems different in each of the three parts of the story. Why are these changes significant? How do they contribute to the theme of the story? Highlight evidence to support your ideas and write annotations to explain your choices.

5. What elements of "The Monkey's Paw" might attract people to this story? Cite textual evidence from the selection to support your answer.

## WRITING PROMPT

How do the story elements of character, setting, and plot contribute to the theme of "The Monkey's Paw"? Use your understanding of story elements to determine the theme of the short story. Then discuss how the elements combine to contribute to that theme. Support your writing with evidence from the text.

# SORRY, WRONG NUMBER

DRAMA
Lucille Fletcher
1948

## INTRODUCTION

**studysync tv**

Lucille Fletcher's play from the 1940s (famously produced for radio audiences only as well) relies on voices and sound effects to create a world of increasing fear for a neurotic woman alone in her New York apartment. The excerpt is from the opening scene.

# "Make it quick.
# As little blood as possible."

 FIRST READ

*EXCERPT FROM ACT ONE*

1　[SCENE: *As curtain rises, we see a divided stage, only the center part of which is lighted and furnished as* MRS. STEVENSON'S *bedroom. Expensive, rather* **fussy** *furnishings. A large bed, on which* MRS. STEVENSON, *clad in bed jacket, is lying. A night-table close by, with phone, lighted lamp, and pill bottles. A mantle, with clock, right. A closed door, right. A window, with curtains closed, rear. The set is lit by one lamp on a night-table. It is enclosed by three flats. Beyond this central set, the stage, on either side, is in darkness.*

2　MRS. STEVENSON *is dialing a number on the phone, as curtain rises. She listens to phone, slams down receiver in irritation. As she does so, we hear sound of a train roaring by in the distance. She reaches for her pill bottle, pours herself a glass of water, shakes out pill, swallows it, then reaches for the phone again, dials number nervously.]*

3　[SOUND: *Number being dialed on phone: Busy signal.]*

4　MRS. STEVENSON [*a* **querulous,** *self-centered* **neurotic**]: Oh—dear! [*Slams down receiver, dials* OPERATOR.]

5　[SCENE: *A spotlight, left of side flat, picks up out of* **peripheral** *darkness, figure of* 1st OPERATOR, *sitting with headphones at small table. If spotlight not available, use flashlight, clicked on by* 1st OPERATOR, *illuminating her face.]*

6　OPERATOR: Your call, please?

7　MRS. STEVENSON: Operator? I've been dialing Murray Hill 4-0098 now for the last three-quarters of an hour, and the line is always busy. But I don't see how it *could* be busy that long. Will you try it for me please?

Copyright © BookheadEd Learning, LLC

8   OPERATOR: Murray Hill 4-0098? One moment, please.

9   [SCENE: *She makes gesture of plugging in call through switchboard.*]

10  MRS. STEVENSON: I don't see how it could be busy all this time. It's my husband's office. He's working late tonight, and I'm all alone here in this house. My health is very poor—and I've been feeling so nervous all day—

11  OPERATOR: Ringing Murray Hill 4-0098.

12  [SOUND: *Phone buzz. It rings three times. Receiver is picked up at other end.*]

13  MAN: Hello.

14  MRS. STEVENSON: Hello? *[A little puzzled.]* Hello. Is Mr. Stevenson there?

15  MAN *[into phone, as though he had not heard]*: Hello. *[Louder.]* Hello.

16  SECOND MAN *[slow, heavy quality, faintly foreign accent]*: Hello.

17  FIRST MAN: Hello. George?

18  GEORGE: Yes, sir.

19  MRS. STEVENSON *[louder and more **imperious,** to phone]*: Hello. Who's this? What number am I calling, please?

20  FIRST MAN: We have heard from our client. He says the coast is clear for tonight.

21  GEORGE: Yes, sir.

22  FIRST MAN: Where are you now?

23  GEORGE: In a phone booth.

24  FIRST MAN: Okay. You know the address. At eleven o'clock the private patrolman goes around to the bar on Second Avenue for a beer. Be sure that all the lights downstairs are out. There should be only one light visible from the street. At eleven fifteen a subway train crosses the bridge. It makes a noise in case her window is open and she should scream.

25  MRS. STEVENSON [shocked]: Oh—*hello!* What number is this, please?

26  GEORGE: Okay. I understand.

27 FIRST MAN: Make it quick. As little blood as possible. Our client does not wish to make her suffer long.

28 GEORGE: A knife okay, sir?

29 FIRST MAN: Yes. A knife will be okay. And remember—remove the rings and bracelets, and the jewelry in the bureau drawer. Our client wishes it to look like a simple robbery.

30 [SOUND: *A bland buzzing signal.*]

31 MRS. STEVENSON [*clicking phone*]: Oh! [*Bland buzzing signal continues. She hangs up.*] How awful! How unspeakably—

---

Excerpted from *Sorry, Wrong Number* by Lucille Fletcher, published by Dramatists Play Service, Inc.

## THINK QUESTIONS CA-CCSS: CA.RL.8.1, CA.L.8.4a, CA.L.8.4b, CA.SL.8.1a, CA.SL.8.1b, CA.SL.8.1c, CA.SL.8.1d

1. How is Mrs. Stevenson feeling as the scene begins? How do we know she is feeling that way? Cite details from the text to explain her condition.

2. How does the setting help emphasize that Mrs. Stevenson is alone? Cite evidence from the stage directions to explain.

3. Why do you think Mrs. Stevenson explains her health condition to the operator? Use textual evidence to explain your inference.

4. Use context to determine the meaning of the word **imperious** as it is used in paragraph 19 of "Sorry, Wrong Number." Write your definition of *imperious* and explain how you figured it out.

5. Knowing that the Greek prefix *peri-* means "about" or "around," you can use this knowledge and context to help you determine the meaning of **peripheral** in paragraph 5. Write your definition of *peripheral* and explain how you figured it out.

# CLOSE READ
CA-CCSS: CA.RL.8.1, CA.RL.8.3, CA.W.8.4, CA.W.8.5, CA.W.8.6, CA.W.8.10

Reread the short drama "Sorry, Wrong Number." As you reread, complete the Focus Questions below. Then use your answers and annotations from the questions to help you complete the Writing Prompt.

 FOCUS QUESTIONS

1. How do Mrs. Stevenson's character traits affect the plot of the play? What can you infer about her situation based on her short exchange with the telephone operator? Cite specific evidence from the text in your response.

2. From the information the author provides about the setting, and the details she reveals about the murder plot Mrs. Stevenson overhears, what inferences can you make that suggest Mrs. Stevenson herself might be the intended victim? Support your answer with evidence from the text.

3. How does the author use the stage directions in the play to reveal aspects of Mrs. Stevenson's character? Cite text evidence to support your answer.

4. Use your understanding of plot development to help you summarize the exposition of the drama. Highlight evidence from the text that will help support your answer.

5. Mrs. Stevenson cannot be heard by the other callers, and she slowly realizes that she is hearing something she obviously was not intended to hear. Highlight the part of the text where Mrs. Stevenson and the reader know for sure that the callers are planning a crime. What draws the reader into the story's suspense?

## WRITING PROMPT

Analyze the ways in which fear and suspense is introduced and maintained during this play's developing plot. Consider how the suspense naturally causes the reader to make predictions about what may happen in the text. Consider the sound effects, the content and structure of the lines, and the way the characters' voices may sound when the lines are spoken aloud on a stage. Use textual evidence from *Sorry, Wrong Number* to support your analysis.

Please note that excerpts and passages in the StudySync® library and this workbook are intended as touchstones to generate interest in an author's work. The excerpts and passages do not substitute for the reading of entire texts, and StudySync® strongly recommends that students seek out and purchase the whole literary or informational work in order to experience it as the author intended. Links to online resellers are available in our digital library. In addition, complete works may be ordered through an authorized reseller by filling out and returning to StudySync® the order form enclosed in this workbook.

Reading & Writing Companion  **27**

# VIOLENCE IN THE MOVIES

NON-FICTION
2014

## INTRODUCTION

In these two articles the writers make arguments for and against the use of violence in the movies. This debate has been going on since people began to gather together to watch cinematic performances like "The Great Train Robbery" in 1903. Both writers present strong arguments and support their claims with evidence. Which of the writers does the better job in convincing you that his or her view is correct?

# "The typical American child will view more than 200,000 acts of violence..."

## FIRST READ

1   **Violence in the Movies: Cinematic Craft or Hollywood Gone Too Far?**

2   **Point:** Hollywood, Stop Exposing Our Kids to Violence!

3   Violence in Hollywood movies has become excessive and is putting our youth and our entire society at risk for violent behaviors. In the golden age of Hollywood, filmmakers relied on solid storytelling techniques to entertain audiences. Unfortunately, today's film industry often draws audiences to movie theaters with promotional promises of action-packed violence, brutal murders, and mass destruction.

4   Violence in movies is on the rise. A recent study published by researchers at the Annenberg Public Policy Center (APPC) of the University of Pennsylvania found that "the amount of gun violence shown in PG-13 films has more than tripled since 1985." Children are being exposed to high levels of violence in movies, television, and other media throughout the span of childhood. According to media violence research published by the American Academy of Child and Adolescent Psychiatry, "The typical American child will view more than 200,000 acts of violence, including more than 16,000 murders, before age 18."

5   Researchers have found tremendous evidence supporting a link between exposure to violence in media and violent behavior in children. In 2000, researchers from six leading professional medical organizations, including the American Medical Association and the American Psychiatric Association, reviewed hundreds of scholarly studies on media violence and its influence on **aggressive** behavior in children. They reported their conclusions to Congress, stating that "viewing entertainment violence can lead to increases in aggressive attitudes, values, and behavior, particularly in children."

6   Another 2005 review of such studies, published by *The Lancet* and reported by the *New York Times,* found that "exposure to media violence leads to aggression, **desensitization** toward violence and lack of sympathy for victims of violence, particularly in children." How can anyone deny the existence of a link between media violence and violent behavior in children when it is being proven and supported by our country's top researchers? "The evidence is overwhelming," stated Jeffrey McIntyre of the American Psychological Association. "To argue against it is like arguing against gravity."

7   What Hollywood filmmakers must understand is that children model what they see in movies. When a hero exhibits violent behaviors to defeat an enemy, children learn that violence is an acceptable form of problem solving and conflict resolution. Those who see themselves as victims may be more likely to act out in violent behaviors, whether against peers, parents, teachers, or other authority figures. According to the U.S. Bureau of Justice Statistics, in 2011, students ages 12-18 were victims of 597,500 violent victimizations at school.

8   "Violence in the media has been increasing and reaching proportions that are dangerous," Emanuel Tanay, MD, former Wayne State University professor and forensic psychiatrist, reported to *Psychiatric Times.* "What we call entertainment is really propaganda for violence. If you manufacture guns, you don't need to advertise, because it is done by our entertainment industry." Do we really want to teach our children that guns and violence are the answers to our problems?

9   Some people do not believe that exposure to violence in movies is a risk factor for violent behavior because they themselves have not been affected by the exposure. However, no one would reasonably argue, "I've always ridden my bicycle without a helmet, and I have never incurred a head injury. Therefore, there is no link between not wearing a bicycle helmet and increasing your risk of getting a head injury." Why apply such flawed reasoning when it comes to violence in Hollywood movies?

10   Others suggest that it is up to parents to protect their children from violence in films by following the rating guidelines set by the Motion Picture Association of America (MPAA). However, APPC researchers report that PG-13 movies portray the same amount of violence as is shown in R-rated movies. Parents can no longer rely on MPAA's film ratings to help determine which movies are suitable for children of different ages.

11   Of course, media violence is not the only risk factor for violent behavior in children, but it is certainly a large threat. Screenwriters and moviemakers do not need to resort to depictions of sensational violence that put children and the society at large at risk in order to entertain audiences. Good storytelling

NOTES

creates suspense and keeps an audience engaged with the suggestion that something terrible is about to happen. Playwrights of Ancient Greece included violent elements such as murder and suicide in their stories, but these violent actions happened offstage, and audiences remained emotionally engaged just the same. Movies should present scenarios in which conflict is resolved through nonviolent behaviors, without weapons. It's time to hold filmmakers accountable for the violent messages they are sending out to society and to our children.

12  **Counterpoint:** Hollywood Filmmakers Should Not be Villainized for Movie Violence

13  Hollywood filmmakers include violence in movies as part of the craft of storytelling, to create an enjoyable movie-going experience for the audience. It is not right to restrict their abilities to tell stories through film, nor is it right to limit entertainment options for people who enjoy watching action and horror movies and have no tendency toward violence.

14  Some people feel that violence in media causes people to act violently in real life.

15  This just isn't true. I watch violent movies on a regular basis, and I have never engaged in violent behavior. I'm not the only one, either. Millions of Americans see violent imagery in films and on TV every day, but very few commit violent crimes.

16  Violent behavior is an extremely complex issue that cannot be reduced to a simple cause-effect relationship. According to the Center for Disease Control and Prevention (CDC), risk factors for youth violence include history of early aggressive behavior, exposure to violence in the family, low parental involvement, association with delinquent peers, low IQ, poor academic performance, low socioeconomic status, and many others. Exposure to violence in movies does not appear on the CDC's list.

17  Although some psychological studies seem to prove a connection between media violence and violent behavior, those links are not significant enough to justify restrictions on movies. Jonathan L. Freedman, a professor of psychology at the University of Toronto, reported "a very small **correlation**" between media violence and aggressive behavior in children. Freedman suggested that violent behavior is most likely present in children who lack regular adult supervision. How can we hold filmmakers responsible for putting children at risk for violence and aggression when it's a parental duty to monitor what children are watching? Parents must teach their children appropriate behaviors and help their children interpret the violence they encounter in movies as fantasy, not reality.

NOTES

18  Opponents of movie violence claim that crime is on the rise. According to the U.S. Bureau of Justice Statistics, crime rates have dropped steadily since 1993, when 80 of every 1,000 people reported being victims of violent crime. The homicide rate declined 48% from 1993 to 2011. In fact, violent movies may actually play a part in this reduction in violent crime. Children who are watching a movie are taking part in a nonviolent activity. Movie watching provides time for entertainment and takes away from the time in which these children might engage in violent behaviors. According to Gordon Dahl and Stefano DellaVigna, research associates of the National Bureau of Economic Research, "estimates suggest that in the short-run violent movies deter almost 1,000 assaults on an average weekend." Because watching violent movies provides those who might otherwise engage in violent behaviors with an alternative, nonviolent activity, it turns out to be a beneficial activity to those with aggressive tendencies. Do we really want to restrict violence in movies and risk an increase in violent crime?

19  Violence has existed in entertainment for centuries, starting with the epic literature and mythology of ancient civilizations through the sixteenth century esteemed works of William Shakespeare. Yet human societies have actually become less violent over time. The violence we see in movies does not **dictate** how we act toward one another in real life. It exists as a storytelling tool to engage an audience, much like the tools of suspense and humor, and is an effective aid to teach morality through stories of good and evil. We must leave filmmakers to their artistry and allow them to contribute to our culture without censoring their craft.

## THINK QUESTIONS    CA-CCSS: CA.RI.8.1, CA.L.8.4a, CA.L.8.4b, CA.L.8.4c

1. What is the author's position about violence in the movies in the Point selection, "Hollywood, Stop Exposing Our Kids to Violence!"? Cite textual evidence to explain your understanding.

2. Why does the author of the Point text include a quote from Jeffrey McIntyre in paragraph 4? Cite an example from the text to explain your answer.

3. How does the author of the Counterpoint text, "Hollywood Filmmakers Should Not Be Villainized for Movie Violence," respond to the first author's viewpoint?

4. The author of the second passage writes that one professor reported "'a very small **correlation**' between media violence and aggressive behavior in children." Remember that the Latin prefix *co-* means "together with." Use your knowledge of the prefix along with context clues to determine the meaning of the word *correlation*. Write the definition and explain how you figured it out.

5. Use a print or online dictionary to determine the meaning of the word **aggressive**. Write your definition of *aggressive*, along with its part of speech, and tell how you figured out the meaning.

# CLOSE READ   CA-CCSS: CA.RI.8.1, CA.RI.8.6, CA.W.8.4, CA.W.8.5, CA.W.8.6, CA.W.8.10

Reread the debate about violence in the movies. As you reread, complete the Focus Questions below. Then use your answers and annotations from the questions to help you complete the Writing Prompt.

 FOCUS QUESTIONS

1. In paragraph 2 of the article, the author states, "Children are being exposed to high levels of violence in movies, television, and other media throughout the span of childhood." What textual evidence does the author give to support this point of view?

2. In the eleventh and twelfth paragraphs of the article, the author states, "Some people feel that violence in media causes people to act violently in real life. This just isn't true. I watch violent movies on a regular basis, and I have never engaged in violent behavior." Does this statement alone provide strong support for the author's point of view? Why or why not? What factual evidence does the author present to back up this statement?

3. In both the "Point" and "Counterpoint" sections of the article, the authors cite entertainment created hundreds and even thousands of years ago in order to support their specific points of view. How does each author make use of these older forms of entertainments in the article as supporting evidence? Which do you think is more successful? Cite textual evidence to support your answer.

4. The authors often ask questions of the reader in both the "Point" and "Counterpoint" sections of the article, knowing that readers will not be able to answer them directly. Why might an author choose to express a point of view in the form of a question? Highlight the question the author asks in the fourth paragraph of the "Point" section. Then make annotations rewriting the question in the form of a statement expressing the author's point of view.

5. How do you think the author of the second article might answer the question "What attracts people to stories of suspense?" Use details and evidence from the text to support your answer.

## WRITING PROMPT

The authors of these articles hold different points of view on whether or not violence in Hollywood movies has a negative effect on society. Which author is more convincing? Which author best supports his or her points with strong evidence? Use your understanding of point of view and supporting evidence to defend one of the two claims. Support your writing with evidence from the text and additional media evidence support.

Please note that excerpts and passages in the StudySync® library and this workbook are intended as touchstones to generate interest in an author's work. The excerpts and passages do not substitute for the reading of entire texts, and StudySync® strongly recommends that students seek out and purchase the whole literary or informational work in order to experience it as the author intended. Links to online resellers are available in our digital library. In addition, complete works may be ordered through an authorized reseller by filling out and returning to StudySync® the order form enclosed in this workbook.

Reading & Writing Companion    **33**

# A NIGHT TO REMEMBER

### NON-FICTION
Walter Lord
1955

## INTRODUCTION

**studysync tv**

Walter Lord interviewed scores of *Titanic* survivors to create a powerful account of the ship's sinking in the calm, frigid North Atlantic on April 14, 1912. In this passage, we hear a variety of reactions at the beginning of the disaster, from the first sighting of an iceberg by the ship's lookout to the mysterious jolt heard and felt by crew members and passengers alike, each observer interpreting the impact differently.

# "He felt sure the ship had struck something but he didn't know what."

## FIRST READ

Copyright © BookheadEd Learning, LLC

*From Chapter: "Another Belfast Trip"*

1    High in the crow's-nest of the New White Star Liner *Titanic,* Lookout Frederick Fleet peered into a dazzling night. It was calm, clear and bitterly cold. There was no moon, but the cloudless sky blazed with stars. The Atlantic was like polished plate glass; people later said they had never seen it so smooth.

2    This was the fifth night of the *Titanic's* maiden voyage to New York, and it was already clear that she was not only the largest but also the most glamorous ship in the world. Even the passengers' dogs were glamorous. John Jacob Astor had along his Airedale Kitty. Henry Sleeper Harper, of the publishing family, had his prize Pekingese Sun Yat-sen. Robert W. Daniel, the Philadelphia banker, was bringing back a champion French bulldog just purchased in Britain. Clarence Moore of Washington also had been dog-shopping, but the 50 pairs of English foxhounds he bought for the Loudoun Hunt weren't making the trip.

3    That was all another world to Frederick Fleet. He was one of six lookouts carried by the *Titanic,* and the lookouts didn't worry about passenger problems. They were the "eyes of the ship," and on this particular night Fleet had been warned to watch especially for icebergs.

4    So far, so good. On duty at 10 o'clock . . . a few words about the ice problem with Lookout Reginald Lee, who shared the same watch . . . a few more words about the cold ... but mostly just silence, as the two men stared into the darkness.

5    Now the watch was almost over, and still there was nothing unusual. Just the night, the stars, the biting cold, the wind that whistled through the rigging as the *Titanic* raced across the calm, black sea at 22 1/2 knots. It was almost 11:40 P.M. on Sunday, the 14th of April, 1912.

6   Suddenly Fleet saw something directly ahead, even darker than the darkness. At first it was small (about the size, he thought, of two tables put together), but every second it grew larger and closer. Quickly Fleet banged the crow's-nest bell three times, the warning of danger ahead. At the same time he lifted the phone and rang the bridge.

7   "What did you see?" asked a calm voice at the other end.

8   "Iceberg right ahead," replied Fleet.

9   "Thank you," acknowledged the voice with curiously **detached** courtesy. Nothing more was said.

10   For the next 37 seconds, Fleet and Lee stood quietly side by side, watching the ice draw nearer. Now they were almost on top of it, and still the ship didn't turn. The berg towered wet and glistening far above the forecastle deck, and both men braced themselves for a crash. Then, miraculously, the bow began to swing to port. At the last second the stem shot into the clear, and the ice glided swiftly by along the starboard side. It looked to Fleet like a very close shave.

11   At this moment Quartermaster George Thomas Rowe was standing watch on the after bridge. For him too, it had been an uneventful night—just the sea, the stars, the biting cold. As he paced the deck, he noticed what he and his mates called "Whiskers 'round the Light"—tiny splinters of ice in the air, fine as dust, that gave off **myriads** of bright colors whenever caught in the glow of the deck lights.

12   Then suddenly he felt a curious motion break the steady rhythm of the engines. It was a little like coming alongside a dock wall rather heavily. He glanced forward—and stared again. A windjammer, sails set, seemed to be passing along the starboard side. Then he realized it was an iceberg, towering perhaps 100 feet above the water. The next instant it was gone, drifting astern into the dark.

13   Meanwhile, down below in the First Class dining saloon on D Deck, four other members of the *Titanic's* crew were sitting around one of the tables. The last diner had long since departed, and now the big white Jacobean room was empty except for this single group. They were dining-saloon **stewards,** indulging in the time-honored pastime of all stewards off duty—they were gossiping about their passengers.

14   Then, as they sat there talking, a faint grinding jar seemed to come from somewhere deep inside the ship. It was not much, but enough to break the conversation and rattle the silver that was set for breakfast next morning.

15    Steward James Johnson felt he knew just what it was. He recognized the kind of shudder a ship gives when she drops a propeller blade, and he knew this sort of mishap meant a trip back to the Harland & Wolff Shipyard at Belfast—with plenty of free time to enjoy the hospitality of the port.

16    Somebody near him agreed and sang out cheerfully, "Another Belfast trip!"

17    In the galley just to the stern, Chief Night Baker Walter Belford was making rolls for the following day. (The honor of baking fancy pastry was reserved for the day shift.) When the jolt came, it impressed Belford more strongly than Steward Johnson—perhaps because a pan of new rolls clattered off the top of the oven and scattered about the floor.

18    The passengers in their cabins felt the jar too, and tried to connect it with something familiar. Marguerite Frolicher, a young Swiss girl accompanying her father on a business trip, woke up with a start. Half-asleep, she could think only of the little white lake ferries at Zurich making a sloppy landing. Softly she said to herself, "Isn't it funny … we're landing!"

19    Major Arthur Godfrey Peuchen, starting to undress for the night, thought it was like a heavy wave striking the ship. Mrs. J. Stuart White was sitting on the edge of her bed, just reaching to turn out the light, when the ship seemed to roll over "a thousand marbles." To Lady Cosmo Duff Gordon, waking up from the jolt, it seemed "as though somebody had drawn a giant finger along the side of the ship." Mrs. John Jacob Astor thought it was some mishap in the kitchen.

20    It seemed stronger to some than to others. Mrs. Albert Caldwell pictured a large dog that had a baby kitten in its mouth and was shaking it. Mrs. Walter B. Stephenson recalled the first **ominous** jolt when she was in the San Francisco earthquake—then decided this wasn't that bad. Mrs. E. D. Appleton felt hardly any shock at all, but she noticed an unpleasant ripping sound … like someone tearing a long, long strip of **calico.**

21    The jar meant more to J. Bruce Ismay, Managing Director of the White Star Line, who in a festive mood was going along for the ride on the *Titanic's* first trip. Ismay woke up with a start in his deluxe suite on B Deck—he felt sure the ship had struck something, but he didn't know what.

Excerpted from *A Night to Remember* by Walter Lord, published by Bantam Books.

## THINK QUESTIONS    CA-CCSS: CA.RI.8.1, CA.L.8.4a, CA.L.8.4c, CA.SL.8.1a, CA.SL.8.1c, CA.SL.8.1d, CA.SL.8.2

1. The author states that it was clear the *Titanic* was "the most glamorous ship in the world." What made the ship so glamorous? Cite evidence from the text to support your answer.

2. How do various people on board experience the impact of the iceberg? Why does Walter Lord, in this chapter, show how different people on board the *Titanic* experience the impact? Cite textual evidence to support your inference.

3. What were some of the fundamental, or main, differences between crew members and their various jobs on the *Titanic?* Why do you think Lord includes these descriptions? Cite textual evidence to explain your inference.

4. Use context to determine the meaning of the word **myriads** as it is used in paragraph 11 of *A Night to Remember.* Write your definition of *myriads* and tell how you arrived at it.

5. Use context to determine the meaning of the word **stewards** as it is used in paragraph 13 of *A Night to Remember.* Write your definition of *stewards* and tell how you found it. Finally, follow up by consulting a dictionary to clarify the precise meaning of the word.

## CLOSE READ
CA-CCSS: CA.RI.8.1, CA.RI.8.3, CA.RI.8.6, CA.W.8.4, CA.W.8.5, CA.W.8.6, CA.W.8.10

Reread the excerpt from *A Night to Remember*. As you reread, complete the Focus Questions below. Then use your answers and annotations from the questions to help you complete the Writing Prompt.

## FOCUS QUESTIONS

1. How might the weather on the fifth night of *Titanic*'s maiden voyage to New York have caught the crew and the passengers off-guard, both thinking there was little reason to think anything would happen? Cite textual evidence to support your answer.

2. At certain points in the narrative, the author uses specific times and even measurements to describe what is happening, using an almost scientific approach or point of view. What purpose might the author have for supplying readers with this information? How does it contrast with the more descriptive or personal parts of the narrative? Use textual evidence to support your answer.

3. In paragraphs 18-20, Walter Lord describes the reactions various passengers had to the "faint grinding jar" that was felt throughout the ship when *Titanic* passed too close to an iceberg. Then, in the final paragraph of the excerpt, he describes the reaction of another passenger. How and why is his reaction to the impact different from the others, and how does this lend an element of suspense to the text?

4. *A Night to Remember* was written in 1955, many years after the 1912 tragedy, but the author interviewed many people who had experienced it firsthand. In this excerpt, how does the author use information from those interviews to create a story that reads almost like fiction? Cite evidence from the text that shows how Walter Lord seems to get inside the heads of both passengers and crew. How does this help develop the element of suspense?

5. Given that *Titanic* sank more than a century ago, why do many readers still feel suspense when reading about it in *A Night to Remember*? Highlight examples of suspenseful details in the text.

### WRITING PROMPT

How do the reactions of the *Titanic* passengers affect your knowledge and your feelings about the collision? How is the experience different from reading a straight description by Walter Lord? Explain what this shows about the importance of point of view in texts. In your explanation, refer to specific connections among individuals, ideas, or events. Use quotations from the text to support your ideas.

# CUJO

## FICTION

Stephen King
1981

## INTRODUCTION

In Stephen King's thriller, *Cujo*, Donna Trenton and her four-year-old boy barely manage to get their broken-down car to a familiar, but remote, repair shop. Before long, they discover that the shop owner's beloved dog, a huge St. Bernard named Cujo, has turned rabid and is out for blood. Stuck in an immobile car during the middle of a heat wave, and with help nowhere to be found, the mother and son fight desperately to stay alive.

# "Cujo's growl rose to a shattering roar of rage and he charged at her."

## FIRST READ

1   She reached the front of the hood and started to cross in front of the Pinto, and that was when she heard a new sound. A low, thick growling.

2   She stopped, her head coming up at once, trying to pinpoint the source of that sound. For a moment she couldn't and she was suddenly terrified, not by the sound itself but by its seeming directionlessness. It was nowhere. It was everywhere. And then some internal radar—survival equipment, perhaps—turned on all the way, and she understood that the growling was coming from inside the garage.

3   "Mommy?" Tad poked his head out his open window as far as the seatbelt harness would allow. "I can't get this damn old—"

4   *"Shhhh!"*

5   *(growling)*

6   She took a tentative step backward, her right hand resting lightly on the Pinto's low hood, her nerves on tripwires as thin as filaments, not panicked but in a state of heightened alertness, thinking: *It didn't growl before.*

7   Cujo came out of Joe Camber's garage. Donna stared at him, feeling her breath come to a painless and yet complete stop in her throat. It was the same dog. It was Cujo. But—

8   *But oh my*

9   *(oh my God)*

10  The dog's eyes settled on hers. They were red and **rheumy.** They were leaking some **viscous** substance. The dog seemed to be weeping gummy tears. His tawny coat was caked and matted with mud and—

Copyright © BookheadEd Learning, LLC

11   *Blood. is that*

12   *(it is it's blood Christ Christ)*

13   She couldn't seem to move. No breath. Dead low tide in her lungs. She had heard about being paralyzed with fear but had never realized it could happen with such totality. There was no contact between her brain and her legs. That twisted gray filament running down the core of her spine had shut off the signals. Her hands were stupid blocks of flesh south of her wrists with no feeling in them. Her urine went. She was unaware of it save for some vague sensation of distant warmth.

14   And the dog seemed to know. His terrible, thoughtless eyes never left Donna Trenton's wide blue ones. He paced forward slowly, almost **languidly.** Now he was standing on the barnboards at the mouth of the garage. Now he was on the crushed gravel twenty-five feet away. He never stopped growling. It was a low, purring sound, soothing in its menace. Foam dropped from Cujo's snout. And she couldn't move, not at all.

15   Then Tad saw the dog, recognized the blood which streaked its fur, and shrieked—a high piercing sound that made Cujo shift his eyes. And that was what seemed to free her.

16   She turned in a great shambling drunk's pivot, slamming her lower leg against the Pinto's fender and sending a steely bolt of pain up to her hip. She ran back around the hood of the car. Cujo's growl rose to a shattering roar of rage and he charged at her. Her feet almost skidded out from under her in the loose gravel, and she was only able to recover by slamming her arm down on the Pinto's hood. She hit her crazybone and uttered a thin shriek of pain.

17   The car door was shut. She had shut it herself, automatically, after getting out. The chromed button below the handle suddenly seemed dazzlingly bright, winking arrows of sun into her eyes. *I'll never be able to get that door open and get in and get it shut,* she thought, and the choking realization that she might be about to die rose up in her. *Not enough time. No way.*

18   She raked the door open. She could hear her breath sobbing in and out of her throat. Tad screamed again, a shrill, breaking sound.

19   She sat down, almost falling into the driver's seat. She got a glimpse of Cujo coming at her, hindquarters tensing down for the leap that would bring all two hundred pounds of him right into her lap.

20   She yanked the Pinto's door shut with both hands, reaching over the steering wheel with her right arm, honking the horn with her shoulder. She was just in time. A split second after the door slammed closed there was a heavy, solid

thud, as if someone had swung a chunk of stovewood against the side of the car. The dog's barking roars of rage were cut off cleanly, and there was silence.

21  *Knocked himself out,* she thought hysterically. *Thank God, thank God for that—*

22  And a moment later Cujo's foam-covered, twisted face popped up outside her window, only inches away, like a horror-movie monster that has decided to give the audience the ultimate thrill by coming right out of the screen. She could see his huge, heavy teeth. And again there was that swooning, terrible feeling that the dog was looking at *her,* not at a woman who just happened to be trapped in her car with her little boy, but at *Donna Trenton,* as if he had just been hanging around, waiting for her to show up.

23  Cujo began to bark again, the sound incredibly loud even through the Saf-T-Glas. And suddenly it occurred to her that if she had not automatically rolled her window up as she brought the Pinto to a stop (something her father had insisted on: stop the car, roll up the windows, set the brake, take the keys, lock the car), she would now be minus her throat. Her blood would be on the wheel, the dash, the windshield. That one action, so automatic she could not even really remember performing it.

24  She screamed.

25  The dog's terrible face dropped from view.

26  She remembered Tad and looked around. When she saw him, a new fear invaded her, drilling like a hot needle. He had not fainted, but he was not really conscious, either. He had fallen back against the seat, his eyes dazed and blank. His face was white. His lips had gone bluish at the corners.

27  "Tad!" She snapped her fingers under his nose, and he blinked sluggishly at the dry sound. "Tad!"

28  "Mommy," he said thickly. "How did the monster in my closet get out? Is it a dream? Is it my nap?"

29  "It's going to be all right," she said, chilled by what he had said about his closet nonetheless. "It's—"

30  She saw the dog's tail and the top of its broad back over the hood of the Pinto. It was going around to Tad's side of the car—

31  And Tad's window wasn't shut.

Reading & Writing Companion

32 She jackknifed across Tad's lap, moving with such a hard muscular spasm that she cracked her fingers on the window crank. She turned it as fast as she could, panting, feeling Tad squirming beneath her.

33 It was three quarters of the way up when Cujo leaped at the window. His muzzle shot in through the closing gap and was forced upward toward the ceiling by the closing window. The sound of his snarling barks filled the small car. Tad shrieked again and wrapped his arms around his head, his forearms crossed over his eyes. He tried to dig his face into Donna's belly, reducing her leverage on the window crank in his blind efforts to get away.

34 "Momma! Momma! Momma! *Make it stop! Make it go away!*"

35 Something warm was running across the backs of her hands. She saw with mounting horror that it was mixed slime and blood running from the dog's mouth. Using everything that she had, she managed to force the window crank through another quarter turn . . . and then Cujo pulled back. She caught just a glimpse of the Saint Bernard's features, twisted and crazy, a mad **caricature** of a friendly Saint Bernard's face. Then it dropped back to all fours and she could only see its back.

36 Now the crank turned easily. She shut the window, then wiped the backs of her hands on her jeans, uttering small cries of **revulsion.**

Excerpted from *Cujo* by Stephen King, published by Signet.

 **THINK QUESTIONS** CA-CCSS: CA.RL.8.1, CA.L.8.4a, CA.L.8.4d

1. Based on the descriptions and events in this excerpt, what can you infer about the title character, Cujo? Use textual evidence to explain your inferences.

2. Think about how Donna handles this situation with Cujo. What do Donna's actions and thoughts reveal about her character? Give examples from the text to support your thinking.

3. What is one way the author increases the sense of horror and suspense in this excerpt? Cite textual evidence to explain your ideas.

4. What words in the excerpt help you understand the meaning of the word **languidly** in paragraph 14? Explain the context clues and then write your definition of *languidly*.

5. Read this passage from the text: "She caught just a glimpse of the Saint Bernard's features, twisted and crazy, a mad caricature of a friendly Saint Bernard's face." What can you infer about meaning of the word **caricature** in this passage? Write the definition based on the context, and then verify your inferred meaning by using a print or online dictionary.

# CLOSE READ
CA-CCSS: CA.RL.8.1, CA.RL.8.3, CA.RL.8.7, CA.W.8.4, CA.W.8.5, CA.W.8.6, CA.W.8.10

Reread the excerpt from *Cujo*. As you reread, complete the Focus Questions below. Then use your answers and annotations from the questions to help you complete the Writing Prompt.

 FOCUS QUESTIONS

1. In the paragraph 24, after all Donna has been through—hearing the dog growl, catching her first glimpse of Cujo's blood soaked fur, getting into the car and securing the door—Stephen King writes simply that "she screamed." Use text evidence to explain why Donna finally lets loose with this expression of terror, even though she is now in relative safety inside the car.

2. At several points in the passage, the author describes how Donna hurts herself. At one point, for example, she hits her leg on the car's fender. Reread the text that describes each of these details. What inference can you make about Donna from this text evidence? How does Stephen King use these incidents to build suspense? Highlight your evidence and annotate to explain your ideas.

3. The characters in this excerpt are Donna Trenton and her son Tad. Readers experience both of them reacting to a frightening situation. What details does the author, Stephen King, include that describe Tad's reaction to the dog? What can you infer about Tad and his fears? Highlight evidence to support your ideas, and write annotations to explain your assessment.

4. What inferences can you make about the situation at the end of the passage? Can you use these inferences to predict what will happen next in the story? Highlight evidence from the text that will help support your prediction.

5. What details hold the reader's attention, creating suspense in the story? Use details from the selection to describe why people are attracted to stories of suspense.

## WRITING PROMPT

Ask your teacher for the link needed to view a movie clip. Then respond to the prompt.
Watch the 1983 film version of this scene. Then reread the excerpt. How did director Lewis Teague stay true to the original novel? What liberties did he take with the script? What inferences did you make in the text passage that are retained or abandoned in the film version? In about 300 words, analyze the choices the film director made and the effects these changes have on your perception of the characters as well as the film's level of suspense.

Please note that excerpts and passages in the StudySync® library and this workbook are intended as touchstones to generate interest in an author's work. The excerpts and passages do not substitute for the reading of entire texts, and StudySync® strongly recommends that students seek out and purchase the whole literary or informational work in order to experience it as the author intended. Links to online resellers are available in our digital library. In addition, complete works may be ordered through an authorized reseller by filling out and returning to StudySync® the order form enclosed in this workbook.

Reading & Writing Companion  **45**

# LORD OF THE FLIES

**FICTION**
William Golding
1954

## INTRODUCTION

studysync tv

When a plane carrying British schoolboys crash-lands on a remote island, the youths' attempt to govern themselves turns into an increasingly brutal struggle for power in William Golding's *Lord of the Flies*. Golding served in the Royal Navy during World War II, and claimed his depiction of the boys' behavior was influenced by his experiences watching how men reacted in the heat of battle. In this excerpt from early in the novel, a group of choir boys has followed the sound of a conch shell to a second group. After a wary sorting out, they decide to elect a leader.

# "Seems to me we ought to have a chief to decide things."

 FIRST READ

 NOTES

*From Chapter 1*

1   "Isn't there a ship, then?"

2   Inside the floating cloak he was tall, thin, and bony; and his hair was red beneath the black cap. His face was crumpled and freckled, and ugly without silliness. Out of this face stared two light blue eyes, frustrated now, and turning, or ready to turn, to anger.

3   "Isn't there a man here?"

4   Ralph spoke to his back.

5   "No. We're having a meeting. Come and join in."

6   The group of cloaked boys began to scatter from close line. The tall boy shouted at them.

7   "Choir! Stand still!"

8   Wearily obedient, the choir huddled into line and stood there swaying in the sun. None the less, some began to protest faintly.

9   "But, Merridew. Please, Merridew . . . can't we?"

10  Then one of the boys flopped on his face in the sand and the line broke up. They heaved the fallen boy to the platform and let him lie. Merridew, his eyes staring, made the best of a bad job.

11  "All right then. Sit down. Let him alone."

12  "But Merridew."

13    "He's always throwing a faint," said Merridew. "He did in Gib.; and Addis; and at **matins** over the precentor."

14    This last piece of shop brought sniggers from the choir, who perched like black birds on the criss-cross trunks and examined Ralph with interest. Piggy asked no names. He was intimidated by this uniformed superiority and the offhand authority in Merridew's voice. He shrank to the other side of Ralph and busied himself with his glasses.

15    Merridew turned to Ralph.

16    "Aren't there any grownups?"

17    "No."

18    Merridew sat down on a trunk and looked round the circle.

19    "Then we'll have to look after ourselves."

20    Secure on the other side of Ralph, Piggy spoke timidly.

21    "That's why Ralph made a meeting. So as we can decide what to do. We've heard names. That's Johnny. Those two—they're twins, Sam 'n Eric. Which is Eric—? You? No—you're Sam—"

22    "I'm Sam—"

23    "'n I'm Eric."

24    "We'd better all have names," said Ralph, "so I'm Ralph."

25    "We got most names," said Piggy. "Got 'em just now."

26    "Kids' names," said Merridew. "Why should I be Jack? I'm Merridew."

27    Ralph turned to him quickly. This was the voice of one who knew his own mind.

28    "Then," went on Piggy, "that boy—I forget—"

29    "You're talking too much," said Jack Merridew. "Shut up, Fatty."

30    Laughter arose.

31    "He's not Fatty," cried Ralph, "his real name's Piggy!"

32    "Piggy!"

33    "Piggy!"

34   "Oh, Piggy!"

35   A storm of laughter arose and even the tiniest child joined in. For the moment the boys were a closed circuit of sympathy with Piggy outside: he went very pink, bowed his head and cleaned his glasses again.

36   Finally the laughter died away and the naming continued. There was Maurice, next in size among the choir boys to Jack, but broad and grinning all the time. There was a slight, furtive boy whom no one knew, who kept to himself with an inner intensity of avoidance and secrecy. He muttered that his name was Roger and was silent again. Bill, Robert, Harold, Henry; the choir boy who had fainted sat up against a palm trunk, smiled **pallidly** at Ralph and said that his name was Simon.

37   Jack spoke.

38   "We've got to decide about being rescued."

39   There was a buzz. One of the small boys, Henry, said that he wanted to go home.

40   "Shut up," said Ralph absently. He lifted the conch. "Seems to me we ought to have a chief to decide things."

41   "A chief! A chief!"

42   "I ought to be chief," said Jack with simple arrogance, "because I'm chapter chorister and head boy. I can sing C sharp."

43   Another buzz.

44   "Well then," said Jack, "I—"

45   He hesitated. The dark boy, Roger, stirred at last and spoke up.

46   "Let's have a vote."

47   "Yes!"

48   "Vote for chief!"

49   "Let's vote—"

50   This toy of voting was almost as pleasing as the conch. Jack started to protest but the clamor changed from the general wish for a chief to an election by acclaim of Ralph himself. None of the boys could have found good reason for this; what intelligence had been shown was traceable to Piggy while the most

Please note that excerpts and passages in the StudySync® library and this workbook are intended as touchstones to generate interest in an author's work. The excerpts and passages do not substitute for the reading of entire texts, and StudySync® strongly recommends that students seek out and purchase the whole literary or informational work in order to experience it as the author intended. Links to online resellers are available in our digital library. In addition, complete works may be ordered through an authorized reseller by filling out and returning to StudySync® the order form enclosed in this workbook.

Reading & Writing
Companion

**49**

obvious leader was Jack. But there was a stillness about Ralph as he sat that marked him out: there was his size, and attractive appearance; and most obscurely, yet most powerfully, there was the conch. The being that had blown that, had sat waiting for them on the platform with the delicate thing balanced on his knees, was set apart.

51   "Him with the shell."

52   "Ralph! Ralph!"

53   "Let him be chief with the trumpet-thing."

54   Ralph raised a hand for silence.

55   "All right. Who wants Jack for chief?"

56   With dreary obedience the choir raised their hands.

57   "Who wants me?"

58   Every hand outside the choir except Piggy's was raised immediately. Then Piggy, too, raised his hand grudgingly into the air.

59   Ralph counted.

60   "I'm chief then."

61   The circle of boys broke into applause. Even the choir applauded; and the freckles on Jack's face disappeared under a blush of **mortification.** He started up, then changed his mind and sat down again while the air rang. Ralph looked at him, eager to offer something.

62   "The choir belongs to you, of course."

63   "They could be the army—"

64   "Or hunters—"

65   "They could be—"

66   The **suffusion** drained away from Jack's face.

· · ·

67   The three boys walked briskly on the sand. The tide was low and there was a strip of weed-strewn beach that was almost as firm as a road. A kind of glamour was spread over them and the scene and they were conscious of

the glamour and made happy by it. They turned to each other, laughing excitedly, talking, not listening. The air was bright. Ralph, faced by the task of translating all this into an explanation, stood on his head and fell over. When they had done laughing, Simon stroked Ralph's arm shyly; and they had to laugh again.

68    "Come on," said Jack presently, "we're explorers."

---

Excerpted from *Lord of the Flies* by William Golding, published by The Berkley Publishing Group.

 ## THINK QUESTIONS    CA-CCSS: CA.RL.8.1, CA.L.8.4a, CA.L.8.4b, CA.SL.8.1a, CA.SL.8.1c

1.  What has happened that has caused the boys to be where they are? Explain your inferences about where they are and what happened using textual evidence.

2.  Why must the boys choose a leader, and what role does the conch shell play? Explain your answer using evidence from the text.

3.  What can you infer about the characters of Ralph and Jack? Use textual evidence to explain your inferences.

4.  The Latin root of the word **furtive** is *fur,* meaning "thief." Using this knowledge and context clues, determine the meaning of the word *furtive* as it is used in paragraph 36 of *Lord of the Flies*. Write your definition of furtive and tell how you figured it out.

5.  Remembering that the Latin root *mort* means "death," use your knowledge of the Latin root and the context clues provided in the passage to determine the meaning of **mortification**. Write your definition of *mortification* and tell how you figured it out.

Please note that excerpts and passages in the StudySync® library and this workbook are intended as touchstones to generate interest in an author's work. The excerpts and passages do not substitute for the reading of entire texts, and StudySync® strongly recommends that students seek out and purchase the whole literary or informational work in order to experience it as the author intended. Links to online resellers are available in our digital library. In addition, complete works may be ordered through an authorized reseller by filling out and returning to StudySync® the order form enclosed in this workbook.

Reading & Writing Companion    **51**.

# CLOSE READ   CA-CCSS: CA.RL.8.1, CA.RL.8.2, CA.RL.8.3, CA.W.8.4, CA.W.8.6, CA.W.8.10

Reread the excerpt from *Lord of the Flies*. As you reread, complete the Focus Questions below. Then use your answers and annotations from the questions to help you complete the Writing Prompt.

 FOCUS QUESTIONS

1. As you reread the excerpt from *The Lord of the Flies*, focus on the character of Jack Merridew. What do his words and actions reveal about his character? Why do you think he wants to be called Merridew instead of Jack? Ask and answer your own question about Jack's character.

2. Analyze the character of Piggy in the novel excerpt. How do his words and actions, as well as the narrator's descriptions, reveal aspects of his character? How do the other boys treat Piggy, and how and why does this treatment reflect negatively on human nature?

3. In this excerpt, the boys choose a leader. Why do they choose Ralph? Is it because they think he will be the best leader or for some other reason? What possible theme might Golding be exploring through the election and its results?

4. What might the mysterious conch symbolize? Why might it hold such a strange power over the boys? What possible theme in the novel might Golding be exploring through the conch?

5. In *The Lord of the Flies,* Golding explores the theme of civilization. Based on evidence throughout the excerpt, what tension exists between the boys' ideas about civilization and their behavior toward one another?

6. The story is a classic in literature as well as being very popular. Summarize the events that take place in this excerpt from the story. What do you think has attracted readers to the story's conflicts and suspense? Use text evidence to describe how the reader is drawn into the story's plot.

## WRITING PROMPT

Think about the relationship between the characters of Ralph and Piggy as revealed in this excerpt. How does Jack Merridew affect this relationship? Use your understanding of character and theme to examine the relationship between Ralph and Piggy and what it might suggest about the rules and challenges of friendship.

# TEN DAYS IN A MAD-HOUSE
## (CHAPTER IV)

**NON-FICTION**
Nellie Bly
1887

## INTRODUCTION

In 1887, reporter Nellie Bly went on an undercover assignment for a New York newspaper, the *World*, for which she feigned insanity in order to get committed to the Blackwell's Island Insane Asylum. Her exposé of the conditions inside the Women's Lunatic Asylum launched a criminal investigation that later led to an $850,000 budget increase from the Department of Public Charities and Corrections. *Ten Days in a Mad-House* began as a series of newspaper articles and was eventually published as a book.

# "At last the question of my sanity or insanity was to be decided."

## FIRST READ

*Chapter IV: Judge Duffy and the Police*

1   "Are you Nellie Brown?" asked the officer. I said I supposed I was. "Where do you come from?" he asked. I told him I did not know, and then Mrs. Stanard gave him a lot of information about me—told him how strangely I had acted at her home; how I had not slept a wink all night, and that in her opinion I was a poor unfortunate who had been driven crazy by inhuman treatment. There was some discussion between Mrs. Standard and the two officers, and Tom Bockert was told to take us down to the court in a car.

2   "Come along," Bockert said, "I will find your trunk for you." We all went together, Mrs. Stanard, Tom Bockert, and myself. I said it was very kind of them to go with me, and I should not soon forget them. As we walked along I kept up my refrain about my trunks, injecting occasionally some remark about the dirty condition of the streets and the curious character of the people we met on the way. "I don't think I have ever seen such people before," I said. "Who are they?" I asked, and my companions looked upon me with expressions of pity, evidently believing I was a foreigner, an emigrant or something of the sort. They told me that the people around me were working people. I remarked once more that I thought there were too many working people in the world for the amount of work to be done, at which remark Policeman P. T. Bockert eyed me closely, evidently thinking that my mind was gone for good. We passed several other policemen, who generally asked my sturdy guardians what was the matter with me. By this time quite a number of ragged children were following us too, and they passed remarks about me that were to me original as well as amusing.

3   "What's she up for?" "Say, kop, where did ye get her?" "Where did yer pull 'er?" "She's a daisy!"

NOTES

4   Poor Mrs. Stanard was more frightened than I was. The whole situation grew interesting, but I still had fears for my fate before the judge.

5   At last we came to a low building, and Tom Bockert kindly volunteered the information: "Here's the express office. We shall soon find those trunks of yours."

6   The entrance to the building was surrounded by a curious crowd and I did not think my case was bad enough to permit me passing them without some remark, so I asked if all those people had lost their trunks.

7   "Yes," he said, "nearly all these people are looking for trunks."

8   I said, "They all seem to be foreigners, too." "Yes," said Tom, "they are all foreigners just landed. They have all lost their trunks, and it takes most of our time to help find them for them."

9   We entered the courtroom. It was the Essex Market Police Courtroom. At last the question of my sanity or insanity was to be decided. Judge Duffy sat behind the high desk, wearing a look which seemed to indicate that he was dealing out the **milk of human kindness** by wholesale. I rather feared I would not get the fate I sought, because of the kindness I saw on every line of his face, and it was with rather a sinking heart that I followed Mrs. Stanard as she answered the summons to go up to the desk, where Tom Bockert had just given an account of the affair.

10   "Come here," said an officer. "What is your name?"

11   "Nellie Brown," I replied, with a little accent. "I have lost my trunks, and would like if you could find them."

12   "When did you come to New York?" he asked.

13   "I did not come to New York," I replied (while I added, mentally, "because I have been here for some time.")

14   "But you are in New York now," said the man.

15   "No," I said, looking as **incredulous** as I thought a crazy person could, "I did not come to New York."

16   "That girl is from the west," he said, in a tone that made me tremble. "She has a western accent."

17   Someone else who had been listening to the brief dialogue here asserted that he had lived south and that my accent was southern, while another officer

Please note that excerpts and passages in the StudySync® library and this workbook are intended as touchstones to generate interest in an author's work. The excerpts and passages do not substitute for the reading of entire texts, and StudySync® strongly recommends that students seek out and purchase the whole literary or informational work in order to experience it as the author intended. Links to online resellers are available in our digital library. In addition, complete works may be ordered through an authorized reseller by filling out and returning to StudySync® the order form enclosed in this workbook.

Reading & Writing Companion   55

NOTES

was positive it was eastern. I felt much relieved when the first spokesman turned to the judge and said:

18 "Judge, here is a peculiar case of a young woman who doesn't know who she is or where she came from. You had better attend to it at once."

19 I commenced to shake with more than the cold, and I looked around at the strange crowd about me, composed of poorly dressed men and women with stories printed on their faces of hard lives, abuse and poverty. Some were consulting eagerly with friends, while others sat still with a look of utter hopelessness. Everywhere was a sprinkling of well-dressed, well-fed officers watching the scene passively and almost indifferently. It was only an old story with them. One more unfortunate added to a long list which had long since ceased to be of any interest or concern to them.

20 "Come here, girl, and lift your veil," called out Judge Duffy, in tones which surprised me by a harshness which I did not think from the kindly face he possessed.

21 "Who are you speaking to?" I inquired, in my stateliest manner.

22 "Come here, my dear, and lift your veil. You know the Queen of England, if she were here, would have to lift her veil," he said, very kindly.

23 "That is much better," I replied. "I am not the Queen of England, but I'll lift my veil."

24 As I did so the little judge looked at me, and then, in a very kind and gentle tone, he said: "My dear child, what is wrong?"

25 "Nothing is wrong except that I have lost my trunks, and this man," indicating Policeman Bockert, "promised to bring me where they could be found."

26 "What do you know about this child?" asked the judge, sternly, of Mrs. Stanard, who stood, pale and trembling, by my side.

27 "I know nothing of her except that she came to the home yesterday and asked to remain overnight."

28 "The home! What do you mean by the home?" asked Judge Duffy, quickly.

29 "It is a temporary home kept for working women at No. 84 Second Avenue."

30 "What is your position there?"

31 "I am assistant **matron.**"

Copyright © BookheadEd Learning, LLC

NOTES

32    "Well, tell us all you know of the case."

33    "When I was going into the home yesterday I noticed her coming down the avenue. She was all alone. I had just got into the house when the bell rang and she came in. When I talked with her she wanted to know if she could stay all night, and I said she could. After awhile she said all the people in the house looked crazy, and she was afraid of them. Then she would not go to bed, but sat up all the night."

34    "Had she any money?"

35    "Yes," I replied, answering for her, "I paid her for everything, and the eating was the worst I ever tried."

36    There was a general smile at this, and some murmurs of "She's not so crazy on the food question."

37    "Poor child," said Judge Duffy, "she is well dressed, and a lady. Her English is perfect, and I would stake everything on her being a good girl. I am positive she is somebody's darling."

38    At this announcement everybody laughed, and I put my handkerchief over my face and endeavored to choke the laughter that threatened to spoil my plans, in despite of my resolutions.

39    "I mean she is some woman's darling," hastily amended the judge. "I am sure someone is searching for her. Poor girl, I will be good to her, for she looks like my sister, who is dead."

40    There was a hush for a moment after this announcement, and the officers glanced at me more kindly, while I silently blessed the kind-hearted judge, and hoped that any poor creatures who might be afflicted as I pretended to be should have as kindly a man to deal with as Judge Duffy.

41    "I wish the reporters were here," he said at last. "They would be able to find out something about her."

42    I got very much frightened at this, for if there is anyone who can **ferret out** a mystery it is a reporter. I felt that I would rather face a mass of expert doctors, policemen, and detectives than two bright specimens of my craft, so I said:

43    "I don't see why all this is needed to help me find my trunks. These men are **impudent,** and I do not want to be stared at. I will go away. I don't want to stay here."

Please note that excerpts and passages in the StudySync® library and this workbook are intended as touchstones to generate interest in an author's work. The excerpts and passages do not substitute for the reading of entire texts, and StudySync® strongly recommends that students seek out and purchase the whole literary or informational work in order to experience it as the author intended. Links to online resellers are available in our digital library. In addition, complete works may be ordered through an authorized reseller by filling out and returning to StudySync® the order form enclosed in this workbook.

Reading & Writing Companion    **57**

44  So saying, I pulled down my veil and secretly hoped the reporters would be detained elsewhere until I was sent to the asylum.

45  "I don't know what to do with the poor child," said the worried judge. "She must be taken care of."

46  "Send her to the Island," suggested one of the officers.

47  "Oh, don't!" said Mrs. Stanard, in evident alarm. "Don't! She is a lady and it would kill her to be put on the Island."

48  For once I felt like shaking the good woman. To think the Island was just the place I wanted to reach and here she was trying to keep me from going there! It was very kind of her, but rather provoking under the circumstances.

## THINK QUESTIONS   CA-CCSS: CA.RI.8.1, CA.L.8.4a, CA.L.8.4b, CA.L.8.4c

1.  What can you infer about what Nellie Bly is like as a reporter and a person? Write a response in which you describe Nellie based on what you learn about her from the passage. Cite evidence from the text to support your inferences.

2.  What is the main point Nellie Bly makes in this chapter as she tries to get into the asylum? Cite textual evidence to support your ideas.

3.  When Nellie Bly describes the people around her as having "stories printed on their faces of hard lives, abuse and poverty," and that it is "only an old story" to the court, what does she mean? Cite evidence from the text to support your response.

4.  Use context to determine the meaning of the word **impudent** as it is used in *Ten Days in a Mad-House*. Write your definition of *impudent* and tell how you figured it out.

5.  Remembering that the Latin prefix *in-* means "not," and the Latin root *cred* means "believe or trust," use this knowledge to determine the meaning of **incredulous**. Write your definition of *incredulous* and tell how you figured it out. Use a print or digital dictionary to verify your meaning.

# CLOSE READ   CA-CCSS: CA.RI.8.1, CA.RI.8.6, CA.W.8.4, CA.W.8.6, CA.W.8.10

Reread the excerpt from *Ten Days in a Mad-House*. As you reread, complete the Focus Questions below. Then use your answers and annotations from the questions to help you complete the Writing Prompt.

## FOCUS QUESTIONS

1. Reread the first eight paragraphs of *Ten Days in a Mad-House*. Based on details in Nellie Bly's description of her journey to the courthouse, what is her point of view about how society perceives and treats those taken into custody by the police?

2. In paragraph 19, the author describes the officers in the courtroom. What words does she use to describe them? What do these words reveal about her point of view toward the court officials?

3. In paragraph 40, the author says that she "silently blessed the kind-hearted judge." Why does she do so? What does this tell you about her point of view about the way that the poor, particularly those who are mentally ill, are treated in the legal system?

4. Based on details throughout the passage, how would you describe Nellie's Bly's overall reporting style? How might this style have encouraged readers to share her point of view and have contributed to the impact *Ten Days in a Mad-House* had on changing New York City's treatment of the mentally ill?

5. The excerpt contains dramatic irony. Dramatic irony occurs when the reader or audience knows something that the characters or subjects do not know. Dramatic irony can be used to create effects such as humor or suspense. Write a response in which you explain the use of dramatic irony in the passage. Use your understanding of point of view to explain how the author uses dramatic irony to reveal her point of view and to develop suspense that keeps the reader interested.

## WRITING PROMPT

What is Nellie Bly's point of view about the plight of the poor and mentally ill and the attitudes of officials toward these people? How does she use humor, dramatic irony, and descriptive adjectives to reveal her opinions? What do Bly's opinions and actions tell you about her as a person? Support your writing with evidence from the text.

# THE TELL-TALE HEART

FICTION

Edgar Allan Poe
1843

## INTRODUCTION

Edgar Allan Poe's short story "The Tell-Tale Heart" sets the standard for Gothic fiction. Convinced that officers at his house can hear the dead man's heart beating through the floorboard, Poe's narrator confesses to killing an old man in his care, despite the fact he bore the man no grudge. In a dramatic monologue of increasing volume and intensity—as well as mental disintegration-- the "perfectly sane" murderer painstakingly describes how the "vulture eye" of his victim drove him to commit the horrible act.

# "His eye would trouble me no more."

 FIRST READ

Copyright © BookheadEd Learning, LLC

NOTES

1   TRUE! nervous, very, very dreadfully nervous I had been and am; but why WILL you say that I am mad? The disease had sharpened my senses, not destroyed, not dulled them. Above all was the sense of hearing acute. I heard all things in the heaven and in the earth. I heard many things in hell. How then am I mad? Hearken! and observe how healthily, how calmly, I can tell you the whole story.

2   It is impossible to say how first the idea entered my brain, but, once conceived, it haunted me day and night. Object there was none. Passion there was none. I loved the old man. He had never wronged me. He had never given me insult. For his gold I had no desire. I think it was his eye! Yes, it was this! One of his eyes resembled that of a vulture -- a pale blue eye with a film over it. Whenever it fell upon me my blood ran cold, and so by degrees, very gradually, I made up my mind to take the life of the old man, and thus rid myself of the eye forever.

3   Now this is the point. You fancy me mad. Madmen know nothing. But you should have seen me. You should have seen how wisely I proceeded—with what caution—with what foresight, with what **dissimulation,** I went to work! I was never kinder to the old man than during the whole week before I killed him. And every night about midnight I turned the latch of his door and opened it oh, so gently! And then, when I had made an opening sufficient for my head, I put in a dark lantern all closed, closed so that no light shone out, and then I thrust in my head. Oh, you would have laughed to see how cunningly I thrust it in! I moved it slowly, very, very slowly, so that I might not disturb the old man's sleep. It took me an hour to place my whole head within the opening so far that I could see him as he lay upon his bed. Ha! would a madman have been so wise as this? And then when my head was well in the room I undid the lantern cautiously— oh, so cautiously—cautiously (for the hinges creaked), I undid it just so much that a single thin ray fell upon the vulture eye. And this I did for seven long nights, every night just at midnight, but I found the eye

NOTES

always closed, and so it was impossible to do the work, for it was not the old man who **vexed** me but his Evil Eye. And every morning, when the day broke, I went boldly into the chamber and spoke courageously to him, calling him by name in a hearty tone, and inquiring how he had passed the night. So you see he would have been a very profound old man, indeed, to suspect that every night, just at twelve, I looked in upon him while he slept.

4   Upon the eighth night I was more than usually cautious in opening the door. A watch's minute hand moves more quickly than did mine. Never before that night had I felt the extent of my own powers, of my **sagacity.** I could scarcely contain my feelings of triumph. To think that there I was opening the door little by little, and he not even to dream of my secret deeds or thoughts. I fairly chuckled at the idea, and perhaps he heard me, for he moved on the bed suddenly as if startled. Now you may think that I drew back—but no. His room was as black as pitch with the thick darkness (for the shutters were close fastened through fear of robbers), and so I knew that he could not see the opening of the door, and I kept pushing it on steadily, steadily.

5   I had my head in, and was about to open the lantern, when my thumb slipped upon the tin fastening, and the old man sprang up in the bed, crying out, "Who's there?"

6   I kept quite still and said nothing. For a whole hour I did not move a muscle, and in the meantime I did not hear him lie down. He was still sitting up in the bed, listening; just as I have done night after night hearkening to the death watches in the wall.

7   Presently, I heard a slight groan, and I knew it was the groan of mortal terror. It was not a groan of pain or of grief—oh, no! It was the low stifled sound that arises from the bottom of the soul when overcharged with awe. I knew the sound well. Many a night, just at midnight, when all the world slept, it has welled up from my own bosom, deepening, with its dreadful echo, the terrors that distracted me. I say I knew it well. I knew what the old man felt, and pitied him although I chuckled at heart. I knew that he had been lying awake ever since the first slight noise when he had turned in the bed. His fears had been ever since growing upon him. He had been trying to fancy them causeless, but could not. He had been saying to himself, "It is nothing but the wind in the chimney, it is only a mouse crossing the floor," or, "It is merely a cricket which has made a single chirp." Yes he has been trying to comfort himself with these suppositions; but he had found all in vain. ALL IN VAIN, because Death in approaching him had stalked with his black shadow before him and enveloped the victim. And it was the mournful influence of the unperceived shadow that caused him to feel, although he neither saw nor heard, to feel the presence of my head within the room.

8   When I had waited a long time very patiently without hearing him lie down, I resolved to open a little—a very, very little crevice in the lantern. So I opened it—you cannot imagine how stealthily, stealthily—until at length a single dim ray like the thread of the spider shot out from the crevice and fell upon the vulture eye.

9   It was open, wide, wide open, and I grew furious as I gazed upon it. I saw it with perfect distinctness—all a dull blue with a hideous veil over it that chilled the very marrow in my bones, but I could see nothing else of the old man's face or person, for I had directed the ray as if by instinct precisely upon the damned spot.

10  And now have I not told you that what you mistake for madness is but over-acuteness of the senses? now, I say, there came to my ears a low, dull, quick sound, such as a watch makes when enveloped in cotton. I knew that sound well too. It was the beating of the old man's heart. It increased my fury as the beating of a drum stimulates the soldier into courage.

11  But even yet I refrained and kept still. I scarcely breathed. I held the lantern motionless. I tried how steadily I could maintain the ray upon the eye. Meantime the hellish tattoo of the heart increased. It grew quicker and quicker, and louder and louder, every instant. The old man's terror must have been extreme! It grew louder, I say, louder every moment! —do you mark me well? I have told you that I am nervous: so I am. And now at the dead hour of the night, amid the dreadful silence of that old house, so strange a noise as this excited me to uncontrollable terror. Yet, for some minutes longer I refrained and stood still. But the beating grew louder, louder! I thought the heart must burst. And now a new anxiety seized me—the sound would be heard by a neighbour! The old man's hour had come! With a loud yell, I threw open the lantern and leaped into the room. He shrieked once—once only. In an instant I dragged him to the floor, and pulled the heavy bed over him. I then smiled gaily, to find the deed so far done. But for many minutes the heart beat on with a muffled sound. This, however, did not vex me; it would not be heard through the wall. At length it ceased. The old man was dead. I removed the bed and examined the corpse. Yes, he was stone, stone dead. I placed my hand upon the heart and held it there many minutes. There was no pulsation. He was stone dead. His eye would trouble me no more.

12  If still you think me mad, you will think so no longer when I describe the wise precautions I took for the concealment of the body. The night waned, and I worked hastily, but in silence.

13  I took up three planks from the flooring of the chamber, and deposited all between the scantlings. I then replaced the boards so cleverly so cunningly, that no human eye—not even his—could have detected anything wrong.

I had been too wary for that. There was nothing to wash out—no stain of any kind—no blood-spot whatever.

14 When I had made an end of these labours, it was four o'clock—still dark as midnight. As the bell sounded the hour, there came a knocking at the street door. I went down to open it with a light heart, —for what had I now to fear? There entered three men, who introduced themselves, with perfect suavity, as officers of the police. A shriek had been heard by a neighbour during the night; suspicion of foul play had been aroused; information had been lodged at the police office, and they (the officers) had been deputed to search the premises.

15 I smiled, —for what had I to fear? I bade the gentlemen welcome. The shriek, I said, was my own in a dream. The old man, I mentioned, was absent in the country. I took my visitors all over the house. I bade them search—search well. I led them, at length, to his chamber. I showed them his treasures, secure, undisturbed. In the enthusiasm of my confidence, I brought chairs into the room, and desired them here to rest from their fatigues, while I myself, in the wild audacity of my perfect triumph, placed my own seat upon the very spot beneath which reposed the corpse of the victim.

16 The officers were satisfied. My MANNER had convinced them. I was singularly at ease. They sat and while I answered cheerily, they chatted of familiar things. But, ere long, I felt myself getting pale and wished them gone. My head ached, and I fancied a ringing in my ears; but still they sat, and still chatted. The ringing became more distinct: I talked more freely to get rid of the feeling: but it continued and gained definitiveness—until, at length, I found that the noise was NOT within my ears.

17 No doubt I now grew VERY pale; but I talked more fluently, and with a heightened voice. Yet the sound increased -- and what could I do? It was A LOW, DULL, QUICK SOUND -- MUCH SUCH A SOUND AS A WATCH MAKES WHEN ENVELOPED IN COTTON. I gasped for breath, and yet the officers heard it not. I talked more quickly, more vehemently but the noise steadily increased. I arose and argued about trifles, in a high key and with violent gesticulations; but the noise steadily increased. Why WOULD they not be gone? I paced the floor to and fro with heavy strides, as if excited to fury by the observations of the men, but the noise steadily increased. O God! what COULD I do? I foamed—I raved—I swore! I swung the chair upon which I had been sitting, and grated it upon the boards, but the noise arose over all and continually increased. It grew louder—louder—louder! And still the men chatted pleasantly, and smiled. Was it possible they heard not? Almighty God! —no, no? They heard! —they suspected! —they KNEW! —they were making a mockery of my horror! —this I thought, and this I think. But anything was better than this agony! Anything was more tolerable than this derision! I could bear

those hypocritical smiles no longer! I felt that I must scream or die! —and now —again —hark! louder! louder! louder! LOUDER! —

18 "Villains!" I shrieked, **"dissemble** no more! I admit the deed! —tear up the planks! —here, here! —it is the beating of his hideous heart!"

## THINK QUESTIONS CA-CCSS: CA.RL.8.1, CA.L.8.4a, CA.L.8.4b, CA.SL.8.1c, CA.SL.8.1d

1. Citing evidence from the story, briefly explain how the narrator feels about the old man and why he decides to murder him. What can you infer about the narrator? Explain your inference.

2. Is the first-person narrator trustworthy as he gives his account of the events in the story? Cite textual evidence to explain your opinions.

3. What sound does the narrator hear at the end of the story that causes him to confess to the murder? What effect does the narration have on the story? Provide textual evidence to support your inference.

4. Use context to determine the meaning of the word **vexed** as it is used in *The Tell-Tale Heart*. Write your definition of *vexed* and explain how you figured it out.

5. Remembering that the Latin prefix *dis-* means "not," use your knowledge of the prefix and the context clues in the passage to determine the meaning of **dissemble.** Write your definition of *dissemble* and explain how you arrived at it.

# CLOSE READ

CA-CCSS: CA.RL.8.1, CA.RL.8.2, CA.RL.8.3, CA.L.8.4b, CA.W.8.4, CA.W.8.6, CA.W.8.9a, CA.W.8.10

Reread the short story "The Tell-Tale Heart." As you reread, complete the Focus Questions below. Then use your answers and annotations from the questions to help you complete the Writing Prompt.

## FOCUS QUESTIONS

1. What central ideas about the narrator of "The Tell-Tale Heart" does Edgar Allan Poe intend readers to infer, based on textual evidence throughout the story? Based on what he does, what he says, and what he doesn't say, describe the narrator's state of mind in the aftermath of committing murder and what this suggests about his character. Use the strategies you learned about making inferences. First, find facts, details, and examples that can help make a reasonable guess. Second, use your own knowledge, experiences, and observations to figure out things the author doesn't directly state. Third, read closely and critically, thinking about why the author provides certain details and information but not others. Cite textual evidence and write annotations to explain your understanding.

2. What motivation for his actions does the narrator offer in paragraph 2? How does the narrator likely intend his audience to react to his motivation for murder? What actual reaction will readers likely have, based on the details he provides? Use textual evidence to explore the contrast between what the narrator intends to demonstrate about his character and what he ends up revealing in this paragraph.

3. Poe's narrator twice uses the word *corpse,* in paragraphs 11 and 15. *Corpse* comes from the Latin root *corpus,* meaning "body." Using your knowledge of this Latin root, as well as context clues and any prior knowledge, define the word *corpse.* Why do you think the narrator uses this specific word in his narrative of events? Cite textual evidence to explain your ideas.

4. The particular character of the narrator in this story may affect what details are presented directly, as well as those the readers are intended to infer. Based on the details in the first paragraph, how is the narrator relating these events? In paragraphs 3 and 4, how does this narration affect readers' impression of the narrator and interpretation of the events that have taken place?

5. Authors of Gothic tales such as "The Tell-Tale Heart" often use symbols to help develop the theme of a story. The "vulture eye" and "the beating heart" are examples of two key symbols used in this way. Highlight several instances of the author's use of these symbols. Make annotations to interpret the significance of these symbols and describe how they contribute to the story's theme.

6. There's no denying that "The Tell-Tale Heart" is a gruesome story. A mentally and emotionally unstable narrator gets an insane idea in his head and savagely murders an innocent old man who trusts him. Yet the story is among Poe's most popular works, and is read with pleasure by every succeeding generation. Why do people enjoy suspense and horror stories like this one? Is it despite—or because of—their dreadful details? Use evidence from the story to support your answer.

## WRITING PROMPT

Suppose you are the narrator's attorney, assigned to defend him in the aftermath of the murder he committed. Since the narrator freely admitted to the police that he committed the crime, you have decided to have him enter a plea of "not guilty by reason of insanity." First, identify evidence in the text that you believe most strongly illustrates the narrator's psychological state before, during, and after the murder. Then, identify details that you would advise the narrator to leave out during his testimony, as they reflect poorly on his character and might alienate or offend the jury. Finally, based on text evidence, construct a brief "closing argument" to the jury that makes the case that the narrator is not guilty by reason of insanity for the crime of murder.

# ANNABEL LEE

**POETRY**
Edgar Allen Poe
1849

## INTRODUCTION

Edgar Allan Poe's last complete poem, "Annabel Lee," follows a familiar Poe storyline—the death of a beautiful woman. Poe lost many women close to him over the course of his life, and there has been much speculation and debate about who served as the inspiration for "Annabel Lee". Most people believe that Poe wrote the poem about his late wife, Virginia Clemm, who died of tuberculosis in 1847.

# "But we loved with a love that was more than love—"

## FIRST READ

1    It was many and many a year ago,
2        In a kingdom by the sea
3    That a maiden there lived whom you may know
4        By the name of Annabel Lee;
5    And this maiden she lived with no other thought
6        Than to love and be loved by me.

7    She was a child and I was a child,
8        In this kingdom by the sea,
9    But we loved with a love that was more than love—
10       I and my Annabel Lee—
11   With a love that the wingèd **seraphs** of heaven
12       **Coveted** her and me.

13   And this was the reason that, long ago,
14       In this kingdom by the sea,
15   A wind blew out of a cloud by night
16       Chilling my Annabel Lee;
17   So that her high-born **kinsmen** came
18       And bore her away from me,
19   To shut her up in a **sepulchre**
20       In this kingdom by the sea.

21   The angels, not half so happy in heaven,
22       Went envying her and me—
23   Yes!—that was the reason (as all men know,
24       In this kingdom by the sea)
25   That the wind came out of the cloud, chilling
26       And killing my Annabel Lee.

NOTES

27  But our love it was stronger by far than the love
28      Of those who were older than we—
29      Of many far wiser than we—
30  And neither the angels in heaven above,
31      Nor the demons down under the sea,
32  Can ever **dissever** my soul from the soul
33      Of the beautiful Annabel Lee:

34  For the moon never beams, without bringing me dreams
35      Of the beautiful Annabel Lee,
36  And the stars never rise, but I see the bright eyes
37      Of the beautiful Annabel Lee:
38  And so, all the night-tide, I lie down by the side
39  Of my darling—my darling—my life and my bride,
40      In the sepulchre there by the sea—
41      In her tomb by the side of the sea.

## THINK QUESTIONS  CA-CCSS: CA.RL.8.1, CA.L.8.4a, CA.L.8.4d

1.  What is the relationship between the speaker of the poem and Annabel Lee? What happens during the course of the poem to change that relationship? Use ideas that are directly stated and ideas that you have inferred from clues in the text to explain your answer.

2.  Using what the text explicitly says, as well as what you have inferred, is the speaker reliable? Do you believe everything he says? Is there anything in the poem that would give you reason to doubt what he says?

3.  Think about the words, sounds, and rhythms that Poe uses throughout the poem. What kinds of images do the words create? What sort of feeling does the author create at the beginning, and does it change? Cite textual examples to explain your ideas.

4.  Use context to determine the meaning of the word **seraphs** as it is used in line 11 of "Annabel Lee." Write your definition of *seraphs* and explain how you figured it out.

5.  Find the word **dissever** in the poem. Identify the context clues that support its meaning. Write the definition of *dissever* based on the context clues and explain how you figured it out. Then use a dictionary to verify the meaning. Was your meaning correct?

# CLOSE READ
CA-CCSS: CA.RL.8.1, CA.RL.8.3, CA.RL.8.4, CA.W.8.4, CA.W.8.6, CA.W.8.10

Reread the poem "Annabel Lee." As you reread, complete the Focus Questions below. Then use your answers and annotations from the questions to help you complete the Writing Prompt.

 FOCUS QUESTIONS

1. As you reread the poem "Annabel Lee," highlight examples of interesting rhyming words within the lines and at the ends of lines. In addition, highlight examples of words and phrases that are repeated. In an annotation, explain the effect of these rhymes and repetitions, expressed in a repetitive rhythm, on the subject of the poem. What tone or feeling does Poe create through his word choice?

2. The speaker of the poem believes that the loss of his love, Annabel Lee, is an event worth sharing with the world. In what figurative terms does the speaker frame his love and his loss, and how is this intended to heighten readers' sense of their importance? Highlight relevant words, phrases, and lines in the first two stanzas. Annotate to explain how the speaker's feelings about his love and loss are revealed in this section of the poem.

3. Highlight the various words the speaker uses to refer to Annabel Lee. How much does the reader learn about who Annabel Lee was a person? How does the speaker see Annabel Lee? Explain what the speaker's characterization of Annabel Lee reveals about his own character.

4. Highlight words and phrases that strike you as unusual or unsettling in the poem. What makes this poem different from a simple love poem? Explain how this love poem contains elements of a horror story.

5. How does Poe build suspense in the poem as the stanzas progress from beginning to end? In what way does this suspense continue even after the "climax," or turning point in the story the poem tells, compelling readers to keep going—even if they fear what lies ahead?

## WRITING PROMPT

Identify those lines in the poem that most clearly allow you to follow the "story" of the poem. Then retell the story of the poem in prose. Finally, explain what the poem loses when it becomes a prose story rather than a poem. How does the poem's rhythm and rhyme, as well as other poetic elements, support its theme or message? Use evidence from the text, as well as from comparing your retelling with that of the poem itself, to support your response.

# THE BELLS

POETRY
Edgar Allan Poe
1849

## INTRODUCTION

Not published until shortly after his death in 1849, Edgar Allan Poe is said to have been inspired to write "The Bells" by a comment from the woman who cared for his dying wife, Virginia. Living near enough to hear Fordham University's bell tower, Poe asked the nurse for a poem topic, and Mrs. Shew suggested the ringing bells for a starting point. The heavily onomatopoeic poem has been interpreted in different ways.

# "Keeping time, time, time..."

## FIRST READ

I

1    Hear the sledges with the bells—
2    Silver bells!
3    What a world of merriment their melody foretells!
4    How they tinkle, tinkle, tinkle,
5    In the icy air of night!
6    While the stars that oversprinkle
7    All the heavens, seem to twinkle
8    With a crystalline delight;
9    Keeping time, time, time,
10   In a sort of **Runic** rhyme,
11   To the **tintinnabulation** that so musically wells
12   From the bells, bells, bells, bells,
13   Bells, bells, bells—
14   From the jingling and the tinkling of the bells.

II

15   Hear the mellow wedding bells—
16   Golden bells!
17   What a world of happiness their harmony foretells!
18   Through the balmy air of night
19   How they ring out their delight!—
20   From the **molten**-golden notes,
21   And all in tune,
22   What a liquid **ditty** floats
23   To the turtle-dove that listens, while she gloats
24   On the moon!
25   Oh, from out the sounding cells,
26   What a gush of **euphony voluminously** wells!

NOTES

27   How it swells!
28   How it dwells
29   On the Future!—how it tells
30   Of the rapture that impels
31   To the swinging and the ringing
32   Of the bells, bells, bells—
33   Of the bells, bells, bells, bells,
34   Bells, bells, bells—
35   To the rhyming and the chiming of the bells!

III

36   Hear the loud **alarum** bells—
37   Brazen bells!
38   What a tale of terror, now, their turbulency tells!
39   In the startled ear of night
40   How they scream out their affright!
41   Too much horrified to speak,
42   They can only shriek, shriek,
43   Out of tune,
44   In a clamorous appealing to the mercy of the fire,
45   In a mad expostulation with the deaf and frantic fire,
46   Leaping higher, higher, higher,
47   With a desperate desire,
48   And a resolute endeavor
49   Now—now to sit, or never,
50   By the side of the pale-faced moon.
51   Oh, the bells, bells, bells!
52   What a tale their terror tells
53   Of Despair!
54   How they clang, and clash and roar!
55   What a horror they outpour
56   On the bosom of the palpitating air!
57   Yet the ear, it fully knows,
58   By the twanging,
59   And the clanging,
60   How the danger ebbs and flows;
61   Yet the ear distinctly tells,
62   In the jangling,
63   And the wrangling,
64   How the danger sinks and swells,
65   By the sinking or the swelling in the anger of the bells—
66   Of the bells—
67   Of the bells, bells, bells, bells,

NOTES

68  Bells, bells, bells—
69  In the clamor and the clanging of the bells!

IV

70  Hear the tolling of the bells—
71  Iron bells!
72  What a world of solemn thought their monody compels!
73  In the silence of the night,
74  How we shiver with affright
75  At the melancholy menace of their tone!
76  For every sound that floats
77  From the rust within their throats
78  Is a groan.
79  And the people—ah, the people—
80  They that dwell up in the steeple,
81  All alone,
82  And who, tolling, tolling, tolling,
83  In that muffled monotone,
84  Feel a glory in so rolling
85  On the human heart a stone—
86  They are neither man nor woman—
87  They are neither brute nor human—
88  They are Ghouls:—
89  And their king it is who tolls:—
90  And he rolls, rolls, rolls,
91  Rolls
92  A paean from the bells!
93  And his merry bosom swells
94  With the paean of the bells!
95  And he dances, and he yells;
96  Keeping time, time, time,
97  In a sort of Runic rhyme,
98  To the paean of the bells:—
99  Of the bells:
100  Keeping time, time, time
101  In a sort of Runic rhyme,
102  To the throbbing of the bells—
103  Of the bells, bells, bells:—
104  To the sobbing of the bells:—
105  Keeping time, time, time,
106  As he knells, knells, knells,
107  In a happy Runic rhyme,
108  To the rolling of the bells—
109  Of the bells, bells, bells—

110 To the tolling of the bells—
111 Of the bells, bells, bells, bells,
112 Bells, bells, bells,—
113 To the moaning and the groaning of the bells.

## THINK QUESTIONS   CA-CCSS: CA.RL.8.1, CA.L.8.4a, CA.L.8.4b, CA.L.8.4d

1. Think about the poem's title. Why do you think the poet created a four-part poem about bells? What seems to happen to the speaker as he expresses the ideas in each part of the poem? Cite textual evidence to explain your ideas.

2. What are the subjects of the first two sections of the poem? How are they connected? Cite textual evidence to explain your insights.

3. What are some examples of different rhyming words, and what emotions do the rhymes suggest? How do the rhymes in this poem add to its meaning?

4. Use context to determine the meaning of the word **tintinnabulation** as it is used in "The Bells." Write your definition and explain how you figured it out. Use a dictionary or other resource to verify your preliminary determination of the word's meaning. Was your definition correct?

5. Remember that *eu* is the Greek root meaning "good," and *phon* is the Greek root meaning "sound," combine this knowledge with the context clues provided in the passage to determine the meaning of **euphony.** Write your definition of *euphony* and explain how you figured it out.

# CLOSE READ

CA-CCSS: CA.RL.8.1, CA.RL.8.2, CA.RL.8.4, CA.L.8.5a, CA.W.8.4, CA.W.8.6, CA.W.8.10

Reread the poem "The Bells." As you reread, complete the Focus Questions below. Then use your answers and annotations from the questions to help you complete the Writing Prompt.

## FOCUS QUESTIONS

1. *Onomatopoeia* is the use of words to represent specific sounds. As you reread "The Bells," highlight examples of onomatopoeia that you see in the first and third stanzas. How do the examples of onomatopoeia change from stanza to stanza? How do the sounds of the words create a feeling or mood? Write annotations to explain your ideas.

2. In his poem, Poe includes a great deal of alliteration, which is the repetition of consonant sounds at the beginnings of words—such as the *w* and the *m* in "What a world of merriment their melody foretells" in the first stanza. Highlight a few examples of alliteration in the third stanza of the poem. Annotate to describe the effect the consonant sounds create.

3. Poe has arranged the poem in four stanzas. What is the theme or central idea in each stanza? Write an annotation by each stanza, highlighting textual evidence to support your ideas. Finally,

what do you think the poem is about? Summarize the poem's ideas in another annotation.

4. Highlight the line that includes the word *euphony* in the second stanza. Reread the definition of *euphony* and annotate to explain why the author would think this is a good word to use in this poem. How does the idea of euphony contrast with the way the bells change in the poem? Highlight text that seems to contrast to euphony. Annotate to explain your understanding.

5. Personification is representing an inanimate thing or an idea as a person. Highlight examples of personification in the third and fourth stanzas and annotate to explore how these examples affect the poem's meaning and tone.

6. How does Poe use word choice, sound devices, imagery, and other poetic elements to give the poem a feeling of terror and suspense? Use evidence from the text to support your answer.

## WRITING PROMPT

An alternate reading of "The Bells" is that the poem's theme is about the changing of the seasons, as opposed to the story of a tragic loss and subsequent grief. Choose one theme and use text evidence, including examples of specific word choices, as well as personal experience and inference, to defend your interpretation of the poem's theme.

Please note that excerpts and passages in the StudySync® library and this workbook are intended as touchstones to generate interest in an author's work. The excerpts and passages do not substitute for the reading of entire texts, and StudySync® strongly recommends that students seek out and purchase the whole literary or informational work in order to experience it as the author intended. Links to online resellers are available in our digital library. In addition, complete works may be ordered through an authorized reseller by filling out and returning to StudySync® the order form enclosed in this workbook.

Reading & Writing Companion  77

# HOW TO CREATE SUSPENSE

English Language
Development

FICTION

## INTRODUCTION

A tingling on the back of your neck, a sinking feeling in the pit of your stomach—nothing grabs a reader's attention quite like suspense. The following article, "How to Create Suspense," is written from the point of view of a horror novelist and explores several elements of suspense. The essay explains how the information that you add to a story, and the details that you choose to leave out, can keep readers on the edge of their seats.

# "Becca thinks it is the pizza she ordered, but the reader knows the man is standing on the porch."

 **FIRST READ**

 NOTES

1 The feeling of **excitement** or nervousness people feel when they do not know what is going to happen is called **suspense**. People feel suspense when watching a scary movie.

2 I am an author of horror stories. When I write, I use several methods to create suspense. First of all, the author needs to give the reader the whole story, not only one side. The reader needs to know what both the hero and the villain are doing in order to understand their actions. Readers need to care about the characters. Also, the characters and their actions need to be **plausible**, or believable. For suspense to happen, readers need to **anticipate** what is going to happen. Readers can't guess what unbelievable characters will do.

3 Another way to build suspense is to have a time limit. For example, some stories might have a bomb that is going to explode in 60 minutes or an **asteroid** that will hit Earth in 24 hours.

4 Finally, the stakes have to be high. The main character must be willing to do anything to stop the bad thing from happening.

5 To explain how I create suspense, let's explore my novel *Alone in the Dark*. In *Alone in the Dark,* a woman named Becca is babysitting her sister's baby for the first time. Becca has just put the baby to sleep when the power goes out. She is **frustrated**, but not scared. In the next chapter, the reader learns why the lights went out. A man is standing outside near the electrical wires.

6 At that moment, you as the reader should start to feel suspense. You do not know what the man will do, but you do know something is wrong. You want to read on to find out what happens. Later in the book, the doorbell rings. Becca thinks it is the pizza she ordered, but the reader knows the man is standing on the porch. He holds something behind his back. Becca walks toward the door.

Copyright © BookheadEd Learning, LLC

NOTES

7 At this point, you are on the edge of your seat, yelling at Becca to not open the door. You feel this suspense because I, the writer, told you a stranger is outside. If I had not written that, Becca would simply be a woman who ordered pizza. Suspense happens when you know an action is dangerous.

8 Since you know Becca will be safe when her sister returns, the story has a time limit. Because Becca needs to protect her sister's baby, the stakes are high. You care what happens to Becca because you like her and admire her for protecting the baby. All of these elements create a suspenseful story that encourages the reader to keep reading.

 ## USING LANGUAGE   CA-CCSS: ELD.PI.8.6.a.Ex

Write the key idea from the text in the blank for each sentence below.

1.  **What is suspense?**

    Suspense is the feeling of _____ people feel when _____
    _____.

2.  **What does the author need to tell the reader in order to create suspense?**

    The author needs to tell the reader _____.

3.  **What must the main character need to be willing to do for suspense to happen?**

    The main character must be willing to _____.

4.  **Why do readers of *Alone in the Dark* want to tell Becca not to open the door?**

    Readers of *Alone in the Dark* want to tell Becca not to open the door because _____
    _____.

5.  **What three elements of suspense does *Alone in the Dark* have?**

    *Alone in the Dark* has a _____, a _____, and
    _____.

MEANINGFUL INTERACTIONS  CA-CCSS: ELD.PI.8.6.a.Ex

With your partner or group, identify the author's process when creating suspense in a novel and complete the writing frames below. Then use the self-assessment rubric to evaluate your participation in the activity.

First, the author needs to _____.

Another thing the author does is _____.

Finally, the author creates a main character who _____.

Work with your partner or group to identify the sequence of events in the novel *Alone in the Dark* and complete the writing frames below.

1.  At the beginning, a woman named Becca is _____ her sister's baby for the first time.

2.  Becca has just put the baby to sleep when _____ suddenly goes out.

3.  The lights went out because a _____ stands outside near the electrical wires.

4.  The suspense builds as the _____ rings.

5.  Becca thinks it is the _____ she ordered, but _____ is standing on the porch, holding something behind his back.

6.  Then Becca reaches for the _____.

 SELF-ASSESSMENT RUBRIC  CA-CCSS: ELD.PI.8.4.Ex

|  | 4<br>I did this well. | 3<br>I did this pretty well. | 2<br>I did this a little bit. | 1<br>I did not do this. |
|---|---|---|---|---|
| I took an active part with others in doing the activity. |  |  |  |  |
| I contributed effectively to the group's decisions. |  |  |  |  |
| I understood the author's process in the selection. |  |  |  |  |
| I helped others understand the sequence of events in the selection. |  |  |  |  |
| I completed the process and sequence activities carefully and accurately. |  |  |  |  |

Please note that excerpts and passages in the StudySync® library and this workbook are intended as touchstones to generate interest in an author's work. The excerpts and passages do not substitute for the reading of entire texts, and StudySync® strongly recommends that students seek out and purchase the whole literary or informational work in order to experience it as the author intended. Links to online resellers are available in our digital library. In addition, complete works may be ordered through an authorized reseller by filling out and returning to StudySync® the order form enclosed in this workbook.

Reading & Writing Companion

81

# REREAD

Reread paragraphs 1–4 in "How to Create Suspense." After you reread, complete the Using Language and Meaningful Interactions activities.

## USING LANGUAGE  CA-CCSS: ELD.PI.8.6.b.Ex

Complete the sentences by filling in the blanks.

1. Why do scary movies make people feel suspense?

   Scary movies make people feel suspense because _____
   _____.

2. What can you infer that the author's books have, based on the second paragraph?

   I can infer that _____.

3. How does understanding a character's actions help build suspense?

   Understanding a character's actions helps a reader _____.

4. How does a time limit help create suspense?

   A time limit helps create suspense by making the hero work quickly to stop the _____
   _____.

## MEANINGFUL INTERACTIONS  CA-CCSS: ELD.PI.8.3.Ex, ELD.PI.8.6.b.Ex

Based on what you have read in "How to Create Suspense," make an inference about the author or how she builds suspense. Find evidence in the text to support your inference. Work with partners to practice convincing each other that your inference is valid. Use the speaking frames to support your discussion. Then, use the self-assessment rubric to evaluate your participation in the discussion.

- In my opinion, the author . . . because . . .

- My inference is correct because . . .

- Why do you think the author said . . . ?

- I think . . . said that . . .

- I agree with . . . but . . .

## SELF-ASSESSMENT RUBRIC  CA-CCSS: ELD.PI.8.4.Ex

|  | 4<br>I did this well. | 3<br>I did this pretty well. | 2<br>I did this a little bit. | 1<br>I did not do this. |
|---|---|---|---|---|
| I expressed my opinion clearly. | | | | |
| I listened carefully to others' opinions. | | | | |
| I spoke respectfully when disagreeing with others. | | | | |
| I was courteous when persuading others to share my view. | | | | |

# REREAD

Reread paragraphs 5–8 of "How to Create Suspense." After you reread, complete the Using Language and Meaningful Interactions activities.

## USING LANGUAGE   CA-CCSS: ELD.PII.8.1.Ex

In "How to Create Suspense," the author describes the sequence of events in the novel *Alone in the Dark*. Sort the statements into the correct order of events in the story.

| Statements | | |
|---|---|---|
| A man is standing outside. | The doorbell rings. | The power goes out. |

| First | Then | Last |
|---|---|---|
|  |  |  |

## MEANINGFUL INTERACTIONS   CA-CCSS: ELD.PI.8.9.Ex, ELD.PII.8.7.Ex

What are the author's main ideas in "How to Create Suspense"? Write a short summary of the text and present it to the class. Work with partners in small groups to practice writing and presenting your summary. Use the writing frames to support your summary.

The author starts by saying _____

_____.

Then the author explains _____

_____.

The author ends by _____

_____.

# INSIDE THE HOUSE

English Language
Development

DRAMA

## INTRODUCTION

❝ "Inside the House" tells the story of two teenage siblings who spend a stormy night alone telling scary stories. In this scene from the play, Cristina and Fernando learn just how scary a story can be when their real life starts to match a tale they've told. The author uses dialogue, sound effects, and foreshadowing to build suspense.

# "I heard something. A scratching. Over there. By the window."

## FIRST READ

1 [SCENE: *A teenager's bedroom on a stormy night. Thunder rumbles. Lightning flashes outside the window. Fifteen-year-old twins* CRISTINA *and* FERNANDO *sit together on the floor. Their only light is a flashlight. They are home alone. The power is out because of the storm. They have been telling scary stories. As the scene opens,* CRISTINA *finishes her story.*]

2 CRISTINA [*speaking quickly*]: Suddenly the knocking stopped and the bedroom door flew open. They reached for the phone, but it was too late. The killer was already inside the house! [*She smiles proudly.*]

3 FERNANDO [*coldly*]: Yawn! That wasn't scary at all. Of course the killer was already inside the house. The killer is always already inside the house! Nice try, Tina. But that ending was so **predictable.**

4 CRISTINA: You think you could do better?

5 FERNANDO: In my sleep! [*acts like he is thinking*] Okay. [*eager to tell a scarier tale*] Once there was this guy camping alone in the woods. . .

6 CRISTINA [*looks at her watch and **interrupts***]: Speaking of sleep, it's bedtime. Mom and Dad will be home from their party soon, and I promised we would be asleep by 10:00. School tomorrow.

7 FERNANDO: Whatever. You're just too scared to hear my terrifying story.

8 CRISTINA [***sarcastic***]: Yeah, that's it. I am just too scared—and too tired. [*stands*] Go to bed, Fernando.

9 [CRISTINA *leaves the room. She closes the door.* FERNANDO *stands and gets into bed. The sound of the rain gets louder. Then we hear a persistent scratching on the window.*]

NOTES

10  FERNANDO [*jumping up*]: Cristina! Get in here!

11  CRISTINA [*rushing in*]: What's wrong?

12  FERNANDO [**anxious** *and* **embarrassed**]: I don't know. I heard something. A **scratching**. Over there. By the window.

13  CRISTINA [**suspicious**]: You did not. You are trying to scare me. We're twins. I know how you think. Stop being silly and go to bed. We have that big test in the morning.

14  [CRISTINA leaves again. She slams the door. There are three loud knocks against the window.]

15  FERNANDO: Tina!

16  CRISTINA [*entering again, annoyed*]: What?

17  FERNANDO [*terrified*]: Tell me you heard that.

18  CRISTINA: Heard what?

19  FERNANDO: That knocking! On the window!

20  CRISTINA: There is nobody knocking on the window. You are not going to scare me, so just get some sleep. Good night. [*turns to go*]

21  FERNANDO: Wait a second, and you might hear it. I heard it when you closed my door. Close the door again.

22  CRISTINA: Fine. But this isn't funny.

23  FERNANDO: You're right. It's not. There is somebody out there.

24  [CRISTINA *closes the door. She turns back to face her brother.* FERNANDO *waits to hear another noise.* CRISTINA *is impatient to end the game. Three loud knocks break the silence. This time they sound against the bedroom door. Slowly, the doorknob begins to turn.*]

## USING LANGUAGE  CA-CCSS: ELD.PII.8.1.Ex

Complete the chart by filling in the correct sequence of events from the options below.

| Then Options | Last Options |
|---|---|
| Cristina comes in and asks what's wrong. | There is a knock on the door. |
| The power goes out. | Fernando tells Cristina what he heard. |
| Fernando asks Cristina to be quiet. | Fernando hears knocking on the window. |
| Cristina leaves to go to bed. | Fernando hears scratching on the window. |
| Cristina leaves the room again. | Cristina and Fernando tell each other stories. |

| First | Then | Last |
|---|---|---|
| Cristina and Fernando's parents go out. | | |
| Cristina checks her watch. | | |
| Fernando calls Cristina's name. | | |
| Cristina does not believe Fernando. | | |
| Cristina comes back a second time. | | |

## MEANINGFUL INTERACTIONS CA-CCSS: ELD.PI.8.5.Ex

Use the speaking frames below to support your discussion after your group has finished reading aloud the excerpt of "Inside the House." Then, use the self-assessment rubric to evaluate your participation in the discussion.

- How is Cristina feeling when she says . . . ?

- I think Cristina is feeling . . . because . . .

- How is Fernando feeling when he says . . . ?

- I think Fernando is feeling . . . because . . .

- What emotion do you think (group member) . . . showed with his or her voice?

- (group member) . . . showed that emotion with her or her voice by . . . ?

- I showed emotion with my voice by . . .

- How would the scene be different if the line . . . was read in a more/less . . . voice?

- The scene would be different because . . .

## SELF-ASSESSMENT RUBRIC CA-CCSS: ELD.PI.8.4.Ex

|  | 4<br>I did this well. | 3<br>I did this pretty well. | 2<br>I did this a little bit. | 1<br>I did not do this. |
|---|---|---|---|---|
| I took an active part with others in doing the assigned task. |  |  |  |  |
| I contributed effectively to the group's discussion. |  |  |  |  |
| I identified the emotion my group members portrayed while reading. |  |  |  |  |
| I helped others understand the emotions the characters felt in the scene. |  |  |  |  |
| I used my voice well to show emotion while reading. |  |  |  |  |

# REREAD

Reread paragraphs 1–8 of "Inside the House." After you reread, complete the Using Language and Meaningful Interactions activities.

 **USING LANGUAGE**  CA-CCSS: ELD.PI.8.8.Ex

In "Inside the House," the author uses word choice to develop each character's unique voice. Sort the quotations and stage directions from the text into those that correspond to Cristina and those that correspond to Fernando.

| Quotations and Stage Directions |
|---|
| Whatever. You're just too scared to hear my terrifying story.   *Eager to tell a scarier tale.* |
| Yeah, that's it. I am just too scared—and too tired.   But that ending was so predictable. |
| I promised we would be asleep by 10:00. School tomorrow.   *... smiles proudly.* |

| Cristina | Fernando |
|---|---|
|  |  |
|  |  |
|  |  |

## MEANINGFUL INTERACTIONS   CA-CCSS: ELD.PI.8.1.Ex

Based on what you have read in "Inside the House," how does the author use word choice to develop different voices and character traits for Cristina and Fernando? Work with a small group to practice sharing and discussing your opinions, using the speaking frames. Then, use the self-assessment rubric to evaluate your participation in the discussion.

- In my opinion, Cristina seems . . . because . . .

- In my opinion, Fernando seems . . . because . . .

- I can tell when each character is speaking because . . .

- I think . . . said that . . .

- I agree / don't agree with . . . that . . .

## SELF-ASSESSMENT RUBRIC   CA-CCSS: ELD.PI.8.4.Ex

|  | 4<br>I did this well. | 3<br>I did this pretty well. | 2<br>I did this a little bit. | 1<br>I did not do this. |
|---|---|---|---|---|
| I expressed my opinion clearly. |  |  |  |  |
| I listened carefully to others' opinions. |  |  |  |  |
| I spoke respectfully when disagreeing with others. |  |  |  |  |
| I was courteous when persuading others to share my view. |  |  |  |  |

Please note that excerpts and passages in the StudySync® library and this workbook are intended as touchstones to generate interest in an author's work. The excerpts and passages do not substitute for the reading of entire texts, and StudySync® strongly recommends that students seek out and purchase the whole literary or informational work in order to experience it as the author intended. Links to online resellers are available in our digital library. In addition, complete works may be ordered through an authorized reseller by filling out and returning to StudySync® the order form enclosed in this workbook.

Reading & Writing Companion   **91**

# REREAD

Reread paragraphs 9–24 of "Inside the House." After you reread, complete the Using Language and Meaningful Interactions activities.

## USING LANGUAGE   CA-CCSS: ELD.PI.8.8.Ex

Complete the sentences by filling in the blanks.

1.  Find the stage directions in paragraph 9 that tell what Fernando is doing.

    FERNANDO stands and _____.

2.  Find the stage directions in paragraph 9 that tell what is happening outside.

    Then we hear a _____ on the window.

3.  Find the stage directions in paragraph 12 that tell how Fernando is feeling.

    FERNANDO [ _____ embarrassed]: I don't know. I heard something. A scratching. Over there. By the window.

4.  Find the stage directions in paragraph 24 that tell what Cristina is doing.

    CRISTINA _____. She _____ to face her brother.

5.  Find the stage directions in paragraph 24 that tell how the scene ends.

    Three loud knocks break the silence. This time they sound against _____. Slowly, _____.

MEANINGFUL INTERACTIONS   CA-CCSS: ELD.PI.8.9.Ex

Imagine that you are a director who is planning a performance of "Inside the House." What would you want the actors to do? Which lines of dialogue would you want them to emphasize? What stage directions would you add? Reread the end of the scene. Then use the blank lines to write notes for the actors who will play Fernando and Cristina. The first line has been done for you.

FERNANDO: Tina!

Fernando shouts. He looks around the room quickly. He reaches for the door.

CRISTINA [*entering again, annoyed*]: What?

FERNANDO [*terrified*]: Tell me you heard that.

CRISTINA: Heard what?

FERNANDO: That knocking! On the window!

CRISTINA: There is nobody knocking on the window. You are not going to scare me, so just get some sleep. Good night. [*turns to go*]

FERNANDO: Wait a second, and you might hear it. I heard it when you closed my door. Close the door again.

CRISTINA: Fine. But this isn't funny.

FERNANDO: You're right. It's not. There is somebody out there.

[CRISTINA *closes the door. She turns back to face her brother.* FERNANDO *waits to hear another noise.* CRISTINA *is impatient to end the game. Three loud knocks break the silence. This time they sound against the bedroom door. Slowly, the doorknob begins to turn.*]

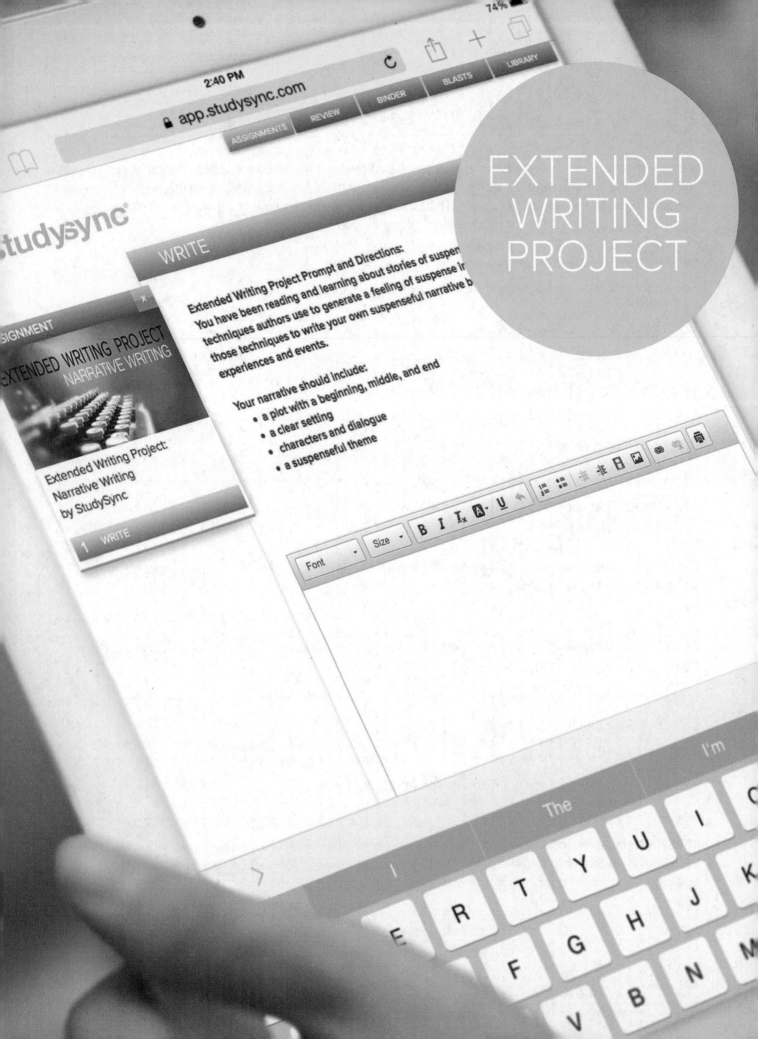

# NARRATIVE WRITING

## WRITING PROMPT

You have been reading and learning about stories of suspense, in addition to studying techniques authors use to generate a feeling of suspense in readers. Now you will use those techniques to write your own suspenseful narrative based on real or imagined experiences and events.

**Your essay should include:**

- a plot with a beginning, middle, and end
- a clear setting
- characters and dialogue
- a suspenseful theme

**Narrative writing** tells a story of real or imagined experiences or events. Narratives can be fiction, such as stories and poems, or non-fiction, such as memoirs and personal essays. Good narrative writing uses effective techniques, relevant descriptive details, and well-structured event sequences to convey a story to readers.

**The features of narrative writing include:**

- setting
- characters
- plot
- theme
- point of view

As you continue with this extended writing project, you'll receive more instruction and practice crafting each of the elements of narrative writing to create your own suspenseful narrative.

## STUDENT MODEL

Before you get started on your own suspenseful narrative, read this excerpt from the beginning of a narrative that one student wrote in response to the writing prompt. As you read the model, highlight and annotate the features of narrative writing that this student included in her story.

### The Silver Box

The night was so clear that if the Carey family had been standing in the front yard, beneath the clear dome that separated them from the atmosphere beyond, they would have seen the usual pools of dull light that had replaced bright stars since The Pollution. Beneath the dome, in the concrete structure that had become their new home, Finn and his father, Patrick Carey, played Robot Wars on the main screen of the family quarters, while Mrs. Caitlin Carey constructed solar garments on the table in the corner.

"I'll beat you yet!" shouted Mr. Carey, clicking frantically on his controller as the boy did the same, eyes glued to the screen. Caitlin sighed and applied new glue to the seams of the garment in front of her.

"You should stop this silliness and get to bed," she warned. "The sun will be coming up in just a few hours. I'll be turning in soon myself."

"I've got you!" shouted Finn, pressing one final button on his controller. The screen exploded in victory lights and then went dark. Finn grinned at his father, ignoring his mother's warning of imminent danger.

"We can't turn in yet," Patrick grumbled, tossing his controller to the floor. "He's still on his way."

Just then a chime sang from the dome, and the old man rose to open the hatch.

"He's here," breathed Finn, scrambling to stand near the entryway. The visitor entered and removed his shiny outer garments just inside the dome. He then stepped into the family quarters and introduced himself as Captain Burns.

"The solar rays are getting hotter," he told them, over a rare and refreshing glass of ice water. "I've been told there's a way to survive outside the domes, but no one has tried it yet."

"Tell us what it is!" Mr. Carey said eagerly, and then began coughing. The visitor waited until he'd stopped.

"The answer lies here," the captain said, pulling a small, silver box from his pocket. "But as I said, no one has tried it yet. Well—without eluding the rays entirely." He coughed as well, and Mrs. Carey let out a barely audible giggle.

"How does it work?" asked Finn, eyes wide as he stared at the glistening box.

"It's designed to act as a personal shield. But, I'm not sure it's feasible. As I believe I've said, I wouldn't recommend trying it, even with the food supplies running so low."

Patrick reached for the box, and Finn's eyes followed as his father held it up in his palm.

"We're very hungry, captain," Mr. Carey said, flipping open the lid of the box to examine the buttons below. "Please, tell us how it works."

As the family gathered around, Captain Burns carefully explained to Mr. Carey how the device worked. Finn could feel both excitement and apprehension as Captain Burns methodically described what each button was for, and the consequences of making the wrong choice.

"I know this is asking a lot," Mr. Carey said nervously, "but let me try this device. I realize it's never worked successfully before, but I'm willing to take the risk. My family will soon need food, and this is our only chance."

Avoiding Mr. Carey's eyes, Captain Burns reluctantly shook his head, yes. Holding the box in his hands, Mr. Carey pulled it tightly to his chest. He prayed that he had made a sensible decision.

THINK QUESTIONS

1. What is the setting of this narrative? Identify two or more textual details that help identify the setting, and explain why you think the student included them. What does the setting tell you about the kind of story this is?

2. Describe the conflict, or main problem, of this story. Explain which details reveal the conflict, and explain why you think the student has chosen to include these details.

3. What suspenseful elements do you detect in this first reading of the student model narrative? How do these elements add to your interest in the story?

4. As you consider the writing prompt, which selections or other resources would you like to examine to help you create your own narrative?

5. Based on what you have read, listened to, or researched, how would you answer the question, *What attracts us to stories of suspense?*

SKILL:
ORGANIZE
NARRATIVE
WRITING

##  DEFINE

Every narrative plot contains a **conflict,** or problem the characters must face. The conflict in a narrative is often developed throughout the story and revealed over time. A story's conflict builds to a climax or turning point, when the **characters**—the people or players in the narrative—are forced to take action.

This problem is presented by a **narrator,** who serves as the voice of the story. The narrator can tell the story in the first-person point of view (as a participant in the story) or in the third-person point of view (as an outside observer). The narrator serves as the reader's eyes, allowing readers to view the actions of the story.

Through the narrator, authors introduce characters and reveal details about their relationships to one another as the story unfolds. Characters are the driving force of a story. Their actions, thoughts, and dialogue move the plot forward as they encounter conflict and seek a resolution. Characters develop throughout a story and often undergo a significant change by the story's end.

##  IDENTIFICATION AND APPLICATION

- A story's narrator helps to orient readers with the details of the story, such as where and when the story takes place and who the story is about.

- Writers reveal information about characters over time, to help readers know and understand the players in the story.

- Writers build stories around a conflict that is interesting to readers. The conflict may be internal (within a character) or external (the character faces an outside force).

- As the story unfolds, writers introduce more details to develop the problem and keep the reader engaged with the characters.

- Narrative writers often introduce elements of suspense to keep a reader guessing about what will happen next. In many suspense stories, writers add a detail that creates an additional problem, or conflict, for a character already facing one problem. This is called heightened conflict, and it works to intensify and increase the tension in the story.

- The sequence of events in a story builds to climax, the point at which the characters are forced to take action or make a decision.

 ## MODEL

*Cujo* is a fictional narrative, so the author is able to invent the situation in which the characters will face a conflict or problem. In this excerpt from the novel, author Stephen King has placed a mother and son in a closed garage with a rabid dog that is ready to attack. The story begins:

> She reached the front of the hood and started to cross in front of the Pinto, and that was when she heard a new sound. A low, thick growling.
>
> She stopped, her head coming up at once, trying to pinpoint the source of that sound. For a moment she couldn't and she was suddenly terrified, not by the sound itself, but by its seeming directionlessness. It was nowhere. It was everywhere. And then some internal radar—survival equipment, perhaps—turned on all the way, and she understood that the growling was coming from inside the garage.
>
> "Mommy?" Tad poked his head out his open window as far as the seatbelt harness would allow.
>
> "I can't get this damn old—"
>
> *"Shhh!"*
>
> *(growling)*

Here, the author has introduced two characters, a woman and her son, Tad. He has also introduced the problem: a growling noise alerts the woman that she and her son are in danger. The reader can also determine that the narrator of this story holds a third-person point of view. The narrator describes the woman's thoughts and actions not as a participant in the story, but as an outside observer. The narrator also reveals details about the scene that heighten the problem: When Tad pokes his head out of the car, the reader learns that the child is inside of the car, while his mother is outside. King writes that the mother "reached the front of the hood, and started to cross in front of the Pinto," which is the name of a car made by the Ford Motor Company in the 1970s. The story then continues:

> She took a tentative step backward, her right hand resting lightly on the Pinto's low hood, her nerves on tripwires as thin as filaments, not

panicked but in a state of heightened alertness, thinking: *It didn't growl before.*

Cujo came out of Joe Camber's garage. Donna stared at him, feeling her breath come to a painless and yet complete stop in her throat. It was the same dog. It was Cujo. But—

*But oh my*

*(oh my God)*

The dog's eyes settled on hers. They were red and rheumy. They were leaking some viscous substance. The dog seemed to be weeping gummy tears. His tawny coat was caked and matted with mud and—

*Blood. is that*

*(it is it's blood . . .)*

Now the author has given the woman a name, Donna. He has also introduced another character—Cujo, the source of the conflict.

The author includes Donna's thoughts, in italics, to disclose what she is thinking as she stares at Cujo. She is shocked, and her terror grows as she begins to understand the severity of her problem. The thought "It didn't growl before" lets the reader know that Donna has encountered Cujo in the past, and the dog did not present a problem at that time. However, the dog has changed, and Donna and her son are now in danger.

Readers can also infer that Cujo's owner, Joe Camber, is dead, although the narrator does not directly state this as a fact. Cujo "came out of Joe Camber's garage," and Donna soon realizes that Cujo's coat is "caked and matted with mud and—*blood.*" The reader can now assume that the dog is a killer, and he is growling at Donna as she stands outside of her car. As you read on, you will see that certain events cause the conflict between Donna and Cujo to heighten, or intensify, at different points in the story.

 ## PRACTICE

Name your three favorite suspenseful stories. For each story, identify what conflict or problem the character or characters face and what narrative point of view the story uses to introduce, develop, and heighten this conflict. Describe any trends or patterns you notice in what kinds of conflicts and which type of narrator you find most interesting or engaging as a reader. Doing so may help you identify the kind of suspenseful story you want to tell. Exchange your work with a partner to give and receive feedback about your ideas.

# PREWRITE

CA-CCSS: CA.RL.8.1, CA.RL.8.3, CA.RL.8.6, CA.W.8.3a, CA.W.8.4, CA.W.8.5, CA.W.8.6, CA.W.8.10, CA.SL.8.1a

## WRITING PROMPT

You have been reading and learning about stories of suspense, in addition to studying techniques authors use to generate a feeling of suspense in readers. Now you will use those techniques to write your own suspenseful narrative based on real or imagined experiences and events.

**Your essay should include:**

- a plot with a beginning, middle, and end
- a clear setting
- characters and dialogue
- a suspenseful theme

In addition to studying techniques authors use to entertain readers, you have been reading and learning about stories that contain elements of suspense. In the extended writing project, you will use those narrative writing techniques to compose your own suspenseful narrative.

Writers often take notes about story ideas before they sit down to write. Often, writers like to work in a specific genre, such as science fiction. Some writers list ideas about characters, plot, and setting, and then choose the ones that will be most entertaining for readers. Others start with a conclusion and then map out situations that will lead the characters to the predetermined end of the story.

- Think about what you've learned so far about organizing narrative writing to help you begin prewriting.
  › In what sort of genre would you like to write? Genres include science fiction, horror, romance, fantasy, adventure and detective fiction, to name some examples. Most any genre can include suspense.

NOTES

› What types of characters would you like to write about in your suspenseful narrative?

› What kinds of problems might these characters face? How might the setting of your story affect the characters and problem?

› What events will lead to the resolution of the conflict while keeping a reader in suspense?

› From which point of view should your story be told, and why?

• Make a list of answers to these questions by completing the "Prewrite: Narrative Writing" graphic organizer. Record your brainstorming ideas about character, conflict, setting, and narrator on the chart. Then examine your ideas and choose the details that you think will work best for your suspenseful narrative. Here is the chart below, completed by the writer of the student model narrative. Make a fresh chart to help guide your prewriting:

Please note that excerpts and passages in the StudySync® library and this workbook are intended as touchstones to generate interest in an author's work. The excerpts and passages do not substitute for the reading of entire texts, and StudySync® strongly recommends that students seek out and purchase the whole literary or informational work in order to experience it as the author intended. Links to online resellers are available in our digital library. In addition, complete works may be ordered through an authorized reseller by filling out and returning to StudySync® the order form enclosed in this workbook.

Reading & Writing Companion

**103**

NOTES

| PREWRITE – NARRATIVE WRITING | | | |
|---|---|---|---|
| **Characters** *What types of characters would I like to write about?* | **Conflict** *What types of problems might these characters face?* | **Setting** *How might the setting affect the characters and the problem?* | **Narrator** *From which point of view should this story be told? Why?* |
| A family—mother, father, ~~daughter,~~ and son ~~Teenage friends~~ ~~An elderly man~~ A mysterious stranger (good for element of suspense—potential for conflict) | Parents struggling to provide for a family ~~Children getting along with one another~~ Outside forces threatening the characters' well-being ("man versus environment"—good for suspense because the outcome is unpredictable; room to create engaging character experiences) ~~Friends who aren't seeing eye to eye~~ ~~A man who discovers something he thought was true is not true after all~~ | A futuristic setting could create an interesting "man versus environment" conflict—maybe the family can't go outside because the environment is too unstable (the sun is getting hotter? ~~no more oxygen to breathe?)~~ (good for suspense—readers will wonder what will happen to my characters in this setting; good basis for creating interesting imagined experiences) ~~A modern setting could bring modern issues/a current conflict into play~~ | Third-person narrator, so that 1) I can reveal character thoughts if I think it will add to the suspense of the story; and 2) I can more easily discuss the setting details to help describe a science fiction plot. |

# SKILL:
# INTRODUCTIONS

 **DEFINE**

The **introduction** is the opening of the story, which sets the stage for the events that follow. Because the introduction of a narrative is the reader's first experience with a particular story, writers often include elements of **exposition**—essential information such as character, setting, and problem—in the opening paragraphs of the story. A story's introduction should capture a reader's attention and tempt the reader to move forward into the story with interest. After reading a story's introduction, a reader should think, "I wonder what will happen in this story. I'd like to keep reading and discover more about these characters." A good introduction hooks a reader with precise language and sensory details that transport a reader into the world of the story.

 **IDENTIFICATION AND APPLICATION**

- The beginning, or introduction of a narrative includes **exposition.** The exposition introduces and establishes the setting, the narrator, and the characters. It frequently provides clues about the genre. For example, a science fiction story could include details that let readers know that the narrative is set in the future.

- As in other forms of writing, authors of narrative fiction often use a "hook" to grab a reader's interest. In a narrative, a hook can be an exciting moment, a detailed description, or a surprising or thoughtful comment made by the narrator or the main character.

- The beginning of a narrative also establishes the story structure an author intends to use. For example, some suspense stories begin with a flashback. This strategy "grabs" the reader's attention and builds suspense by making the reader wonder what's going on. Most stories, however, start at the beginning, introduce a conflict, and relate the events in time order. They use descriptive supporting details, engaging characters, and unexpected plot twists to keep readers interested.

NOTES

##  MODEL

In the opening paragraphs of a narrative, a writer aims to engage and orient, or familiarize, readers with specific details. These details often reveal important information about the characters and setting of the story, and a hint of what the conflict or problem might be. The author of "The Monkey's Paw," W.W. Jacobs, introduces the story as follows:

> Without, **the night was cold and wet,** but in the **small parlour of Laburnam Villa** the **blinds were drawn** and the **fire burned brightly. Father and son** were at chess, the former, who **possessed ideas about the game involving radical changes, putting his king into such sharp and unnecessary perils** that it even **provoked comment** from **the white-haired old lady** knitting placidly by the fire.

Here the author introduces the setting—a "small parlour of Laburnam Villa"—and gives the reader sensory details to help place the reader in the opening scene. The reader knows that it is a "cold and wet" night outside, but in contrast, the family has created a cozy atmosphere inside with "drawn" blinds and a "bright" fire. These sensory details help the reader see the scene in his or her mind and draw the reader into the story.

The author also introduces the characters—"father and son," and "the white-haired old lady"—though he does not name them. Jacobs also gives the reader clues about the personalities of these characters. The father "possessed ideas about the game [of chess] involving radical changes" and put "his king into such sharp and unnecessary perils" that it prompts the old woman to comment. These details reveal to readers that the father is a bit reckless and headstrong, while the old woman is more cautious. These hints are meant to tempt the reader to wonder, "Who are these characters?" and "How will these character traits play into the plot of the story?" A reader might also think, "This setting is peaceful. When will the conflict arise?" The author hopes the reader will want to read on to find out the answers to these questions.

## ⚡ PRACTICE

Write an introduction for your suspenseful narrative that reveals information about the story's setting and characters. When you are finished, trade with a partner and offer each other feedback. How precise is the language used in your partner's introduction? Do the details help you to picture the setting and characters? What information about the characters is revealed in the introduction? Were you interested in what would happen next? Offer each other suggestions, and remember that they are most helpful when they are constructive.

Copyright © BookheadEd Learning, LLC

SKILL:
NARRATIVE
TECHNIQUES AND
SEQUENCING

 DEFINE

When writing a story, authors use a variety of narrative techniques to develop both the plot and the characters, explore the setting, and engage the reader. These techniques include dialogue, a sequencing of events, pacing, and description. **Dialogue,** what the characters say to one another, is often used to develop characters and move the events of the plot forward. Every narrative contains a **sequence of events,** which is carefully planned and controlled by the author as the story unfolds. Writers often manipulate the **pacing** of a narrative, or the speed with which events occur, to slow down or speed up the action at certain points in a story. This can create tension and suspense. Writers use **description** to build story details and reveal information about the characters, setting, and plot.

The beginning of a story is called the **introduction** or **exposition.** This is the part of the story in which the writer provides the reader with essential information, introducing the characters, the time and place in which the action occurs, and the problem or conflict the characters must face and attempt to solve.

As the story continues, the writer includes details and events to develop the conflict and move the story forward. These events—known as the **rising action** of the story—build until the story reaches its **climax.** This is a turning point in the story, where the most exciting and intense action usually occurs. It is also the point at which the characters begin to find a solution to the problem or conflict in the plot.

The writer then focuses on details and events that make up the **falling action** of the story. This is everything that happens after the climax, leading to a **resolution.** These elements make up a story's **conclusion,** which often contains a message or final thought for the reader.

NOTES

## IDENTIFICATION AND APPLICATION

- A narrative outline can help writers organize a sequence of events before they begin writing a story.
- A narrative outline should follow this framework:
  › exposition, rising action (conflict), climax, falling action, resolution

- The exposition contains essential information for the reader, such as characters, setting, and the problem or conflict the characters will face.
  › Settings are shown in descriptions and can influence events.
  › Writers often include details to reveal the elements of the exposition without directly stating these elements for the reader.
  › Readers should feel interested during the exposition and wonder "What will happen in this story?"

- In the rising action, a writer begins to develop plot and character.
  › Characters are developed through dialogue, action, and description.
  › The rising action introduces and builds on the conflict until the story reaches the climax.
  › During the rising action, readers should feel invested in the story and care about what is going to happen next.

- The climax is the turning point in the story, often where the most exciting action takes place.
  › Pacing is a technique writers use to control the speed of the way events are revealed.
  › The events that take place during the climax often force characters into action.
  › Readers should feel tense or excited during the climax and wonder, "How will the characters move forward?"

- The details and events that follow the climax make up the falling action of the story.
  › The events that take place during the climax should lead to the resolution.
  › During the falling action, readers should feel anxious to know how the story will end and wonder, "How will the conflict be resolved?"

- The story must end in resolution of the conflict.
  › The way the problem and developed and moves toward resolution should be logical and feel natural to the story.
  › The resolution should explain—with no room for doubt—how the characters resolved the conflict.

Copyright © BookheadEd Learning, LLC

STUDYSYNC LIBRARY | **Extended Writing Project**

> By the end of the story, readers should feel satisfied and entertained and think, "That was a great story!"

 ## MODEL

In the story "The Monkey's Paw," author W.W. Jacobs uses narrative techniques and sequencing to develop both the characters in the story and the events of the plot. Look at this excerpt, which occurs just after Sergeant-Major Morris has left the White family home:

> "Did you give him anything for it, father?" inquired Mrs. White, **regarding her husband closely.**

> "A trifle," said he, **colouring slightly.** "He didn't want it, but I made him take it. And he pressed me again to throw it away."

> "Likely," said Herbert, **with pretended horror.** "Why, we're going to be rich, and famous, and happy. Wish to be an emperor, father, to begin with; then you can't be henpecked."

> He darted round the table, pursued by the maligned Mrs. White armed with an antimacassar.

> Mr. White took the paw from his pocket and eyed it **dubiously.** "I don't know what to wish for, and that's a fact," he said slowly. **"It seems to me I've got all I want."**

In this exchange of dialogue, the author provides many key details that reveal character traits. When Mrs. White asks her husband if he has paid for the monkey's paw, she is "regarding him closely." This signals her worry that her husband has foolishly spent the family's money, and that perhaps he has done so before. It also lets readers know that the family is not wealthy, and that money is a concern in the White household. Mr. White tells his wife that he has paid a small amount, "colouring slightly." Mr. White's flushed face indicates that his wife's concern is justified, and that he has probably paid too much for the paw after all.

Herbert's "pretended horror" as he mocks the power of the monkey's paw shows that he is good-humored—and perhaps foolish. As Herbert teases his parents, the scene becomes light and playful. Then Mr. White takes the paw from his pocket and eyes it "dubiously," revealing his uncertainty about its powers. "I don't know what to wish for, and that's a fact," Mr. White says, and the author notes that he says this slowly, as he considers whether he should bother wishing at all. White's statement "It seems to me I've got all I want" not

Please note that excerpts and passages in the StudySync® library and this workbook are intended as touchstones to generate interest in an author's work. The excerpts and passages do not substitute for the reading of entire texts, and StudySync® strongly recommends that students seek out and purchase the whole literary or informational work in order to experience it as the author intended. Links to online resellers are available in our digital library. In addition, complete works may be ordered through an authorized reseller by filling out and returning to StudySync® the order form enclosed in this workbook.

Reading & Writing Companion 109

only reveals the fact that, basically, he is satisfied with his life, but it also sets up the events to come in the story. Will he or won't he make a wish? The author draws out the suspense.

As the rising action of the story continues, Mr. White makes his first wish:

> "I wish for two hundred pounds," said the old man distinctly.
>
> **A fine crash from the piano** greeted the words, interrupted by **a shuddering cry** from the old man. **His wife and son ran toward him.**
>
> "It moved," he cried, with a glance of **disgust** at the object as it lay on the floor. "As I wished **it twisted in my hands like a snake.**"

Here the pacing of the story quickens as the author changes the tone of the scene and presents readers with sensory details and character action. "A fine crash from the piano" and the old man's "shuddering cry" are jarring to both characters and readers, who are eager to see what will happen after Mr. White makes his wish. Herbert and his mother spring into action and rush toward Mr. White, who—once "dubious"—now looks at the paw with "disgust." His revelation that the paw "twisted" in his hands "like a snake" suggests to the characters—and to readers—that the paw might have powers after all. The author then slows the pacing of the story again as the scene continues:

> "Well, I don't see the money," said his son, as he picked it up and placed it on the table, "and I bet I never shall."
>
> "It must have been your fancy, father," said his wife, regarding him **anxiously.**
>
> He shook his head. "Never mind, though; there's no harm done, but it gave me a shock all the same."
>
> They sat down by the fire again while the two men finished their pipes. Outside, **the wind was higher than ever,** and the old man **started nervously at the sound of a door banging upstairs. A silence unusual and depressing** settled upon all three, which lasted until the old couple rose to retire for the night.

Though the pacing of the action has slowed, the author includes details that reveal the characters' oppression as they attempt to convince themselves that the paw holds no formidable power. The characters act "anxiously" and "nervously" as they settle into an "unusual and depressing" silence. The wind, "higher than ever," and the sound of a banging door upstairs are sensory details, often associated with spooky houses, which set both readers and the characters in the story on edge as the scene comes to a close. By using

Copyright © Bookheaded Learning, LLC

these narrative techniques, the author has crafted a suspenseful scene that points the story toward its climax. A outline of the story's rising action might look as follows:

I. Rising Action
  A. Mrs. White asks what her husband spent on paw, suggesting her fear that he has spent too much.
  B. Mr. White blushes, which suggests that he did and feels somewhat sheepish about it.
  C. Herbert teases his parents to show that that he does not take the paw seriously.
  D. Mr. White muses aloud that he is basically content and does not have anything to wish for.
  E. At last, Mr. White wishes for 200 pounds.
  F. Mr. White cries out that the paw moved, which startles and alarms his family.
  G. The pleasant mood of the evening is destroyed; Mr. and Mrs. White feel anxious.

 PRACTICE

Create an outline of the sequence of events that might make up the rising action in your suspenseful narrative. As you create your outline, consider the characters, conflict, setting, and narrative point of view you identified in the Prewrite stage and the exposition you began to develop in your introduction. What events will follow this introduction and form your story's rising action? How might you use pacing to propel the action and advance the plot in this part of the narrative? When you are finished, exchange outlines with a partner to offer and receive feedback.

Please note that excerpts and passages in the StudySync® library and this workbook are intended as touchstones to generate interest in an author's work. The excerpts and passages do not substitute for the reading of entire texts, and StudySync® strongly recommends that students seek out and purchase the whole literary or informational work in order to experience it as the author intended. Links to online resellers are available in our digital library. In addition, complete works may be ordered through an authorized reseller by filling out and returning to StudySync® the order form enclosed in this workbook.

Reading & Writing Companion  **111**

NOTES

PLAN

CA-CCSS: CA.W.8.3a, CA.W.8.3b, CA.W.8.5, CA.W.8.6, CA.W.8.10, CA.SL.8.1a, CA.SL.8.1b, CA.SL.8.1c, CA.SL.8.1d

## WRITING PROMPT

You have been reading and learning about stories of suspense, in addition to studying techniques authors use to generate a feeling of suspense in readers. Now you will use those techniques to write your own suspenseful narrative based on real or imagined experiences and events.

**Your essay should include:**

• a plot with a beginning, middle, and end

• a clear setting

• characters and dialogue

• a suspenseful theme

In preparing to write your suspenseful narrative, you have learned about organizing narrative writing. This helped you brainstorm ideas to complete your prewriting. Now you will consider the elements of a narrative outline that you explored in the Narrative Techniques and Sequencing lesson to help plan your writing.

To begin planning the main action of your own suspenseful narrative, review your prewriting and ask yourself the following questions:

• What details and events are most important in the exposition of a story?

• What story developments should take place during the rising action of a story?

• What is the purpose of a story's climax? What might my own story's climax be?

• What can I do to lead readers toward the resolution of a story? How do I want my story to resolve?

- What narrative techniques would be most effective in creating a feeling of suspense?

Use the StudySync "Narrative Writing Plot Diagram" to plan a complete sequence of events for your suspenseful narrative. You may include or revise the rising action events you brainstormed earlier. The plot diagram below was completed by the writer of the student model narrative. Use a blank version of the model to help guide your planning:

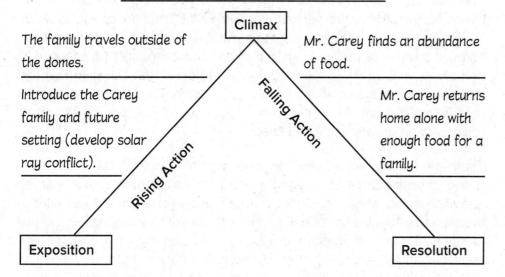

They discover that the silver box can only protect one family member. Caitlin and Finn are zapped by solar rays and disappear.

**Climax**

The family travels outside of the domes.

Mr. Carey finds an abundance of food.

Introduce the Carey family and future setting (develop solar ray conflict).

Mr. Carey returns home alone with enough food for a family.

*Rising Action*

*Falling Action*

**Exposition**

**Resolution**

Please note that excerpts and passages in the StudySync® library and this workbook are intended as touchstones to generate interest in an author's work. The excerpts and passages do not substitute for the reading of entire texts, and StudySync® strongly recommends that students seek out and purchase the whole literary or informational work in order to experience it as the author intended. Links to online resellers are available in our digital library. In addition, complete works may be ordered through an authorized reseller by filling out and returning to StudySync® the order form enclosed in this workbook.

Reading & Writing Companion    **113**

# SKILL:
# WRITING
# DIALOGUE

 **DEFINE**

Dialogue is a written verbal exchange between two or more characters, and it is one of the primary tools of narrative writing. It is used not only to show an interaction between characters, but to provide readers with important details. Through the use of dialogue, an author can show aspects of a character's personality and advance the plot, revealing details that can give readers information about the conflict or problem in the story. Dialogue can even give readers hints about where the story is set if the characters speak with a regional or historically accurate dialect.

There are two different types of dialogue: direct and indirect. Direct dialogue is speech within a narrative using a character's *exact* words. In this case, quotation marks are used. Direct dialogue allows characters to speak for themselves without relying on a narrator to express their feelings and ideas for them. Indirect dialogue, however, is a summary of a dialogue or conversation. Writers use indirect dialogue to indicate that a conversation took place, but the exact words that were spoken are unimportant. Readers only need to know that the conversation occurred and, generally, what it was about.

No matter what type of dialogue a writer uses, however, it is important that punctuation is used appropriately so that the reader understands who is speaking.

 **IDENTIFICATION AND APPLICATION**

**Here are a few basic guidelines to follow when using dialogue in your narrative:**

- Use open (") and closed (") quotation marks to indicate the words that are spoken by the characters.
- Always begin a new paragraph when the speaker changes.

Copyright © BookheadEd Learning, LLC

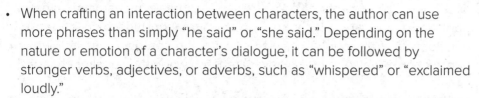

NOTES

- Make sure the reader knows who is saying what.
- When crafting an interaction between characters, the author can use more phrases than simply "he said" or "she said." Depending on the nature or emotion of a character's dialogue, it can be followed by stronger verbs, adjectives, or adverbs, such as "whispered" or "exclaimed loudly."
- Use correct punctuation marks and capitalization. Periods and commas always go inside quotation marks.

Writers can use both direct and indirect dialogue to develop characters by showcasing the characters' opinions, reactions, emotions, experiences, personalities, and even appearances through:

- What the characters say (direct or indirect speech)
- How the characters say it (their speech patterns; the expressions and language they use)
- The way the characters say it (angrily, happily, etc.)
- The characters' body language, actions, and thoughts as they are speaking

 ## MODEL

Read the following excerpt from "The Monkey's Paw," by W.W. Jacobs to see how the author effectively uses direct dialogue:

> **"Hark at the wind," said Mr. White,** who, having seen a fatal mistake after it was too late, was amiably desirous of preventing his son from seeing it.

> **"I'm listening," said the latter, grimly surveying the board as he stretched out his hand. "Check."**

> "I should hardly think that he'd come to-night," said his father, with his hand poised over the board.

> "Mate," replied the son.

> **"That's the worst of living so far out," bawled Mr. White, with sudden and unlooked-for violence; "of all the beastly, slushy, out-of-the-way places to live in, this is the worst. Pathway's a bog, and the road's a torrent.** I don't know what people are thinking about. I suppose because only two houses in the road are let, they think it doesn't matter."

> **"Never mind, dear," said his wife, soothingly; "perhaps you'll win the next one."**

In this excerpt the author has followed all of the technical guidelines regarding direct dialogue. He sets off the direct speech of each character with open quotation marks and places the closed quotation mark outside the end punctuation of the quote, while the rest of the sentence has its own end punctuation. He also begins a new paragraph when the speaker changes.

But notice what else the author does with dialogue. When his son wins the chess game, Mr. White suddenly explodes "with sudden and unlooked for violence," complaining about living "so far out" in a "beastly, slushy, out-of-the-way place." His wife, however, knows that though her husband is complaining about the location of their house and the weather, he "explodes" because he is really angry about losing the game. So she responds, "Never mind, dear, perhaps you'll win the next one." It is through dialogue, then, that the author reveals one of Mr. White's character traits. He is very competitive, and he does not like to lose at chess.

Now let's look at another excerpt to see how the author uses indirect dialogue:

> The sergeant-major shook hands, and taking the proffered seat by the fire, watched contentedly while his host got out whiskey and tumblers and stood a small copper kettle on the fire.
>
> **At the third glass his eyes got brighter, and he began to talk,** the little family circle regarding with eager interest this visitor from distant parts, as he squared his broad shoulders in the chair **and spoke of wild scenes and doughty deeds; of wars and plagues and strange peoples.**

Within this excerpt, the author uses indirect dialogue to introduce readers to the character Sergeant-Major Morris. We can see that he is lively and enjoys being social and telling stories. Though he has known Mr. White for many years, he now seems exotic to the White family as "a visitor from distant parts." It is Sergeant-Major Morris who will pass the monkey's paw onto the White family, but first he speaks of "wild scenes" and the "strange peoples" he has met in his travels. Readers need to know that this conversation took place to set the scene for what is to follow, but it is not important to know the exact words that were spoken.

Finally, let's explore the third excerpt to see how the author uses dialogue, as well as verbs, adverbs, and adjectives, to help develop character.

> **"Nothing,"** said the soldier, hastily. "Leastways nothing worth hearing."
>
> "Monkey's paw?" **said Mrs. White, curiously.**

Copyright © BookheadEd Learning, LLC

"Well, it's **just a bit of what you might call magic, perhaps,"** said the sergeant-major, offhandedly.

His three listeners **leaned forward eagerly.** The visitor absent-mindedly put his empty glass to his lips and then set it down again. His host filled it for him.

"To look at," **said the sergeant-major, fumbling in his pocket** "it's just an ordinary little paw, dried to a mummy."

Readers can tell that Sergeant-Major Morris does not wish to talk about the monkey's paw—they can tell because the author uses the words "hastily" and "offhandedly" to describe Morris's manner of speaking. He knows how powerful and dangerous the monkey's paw can be and he is trying to protect the White family from the temptation. The Whites, however, are fascinated. Mrs. White asks her question in a curious tone of voice, and the entire family "leans forward eagerly" to listen to the sergeant-major's tale. Though it is clear that Morris is uncomfortable talking about it, Mr. White fills his glass as soon as he sets it down. This indicates that he is encouraging Morris to stay and continue talking. The sergeant-major fumbles for the monkey's paw in his pocket as he speaks, indicating a nervousness to continue.

Through the use of dialogue in these excerpts from "The Monkey's Paw" readers learn not only what the characters discussed, but also what they are like and how they feel at different points in the story.

 PRACTICE

Write a scene for your suspenseful narrative in which two or more characters engage in both direct and indirect dialogue. When you are finished, trade with a partner and offer each other feedback. Has the writer followed the technical guidelines relating to direct dialogue? Are there areas where the indirect dialogue can be improved? How does the dialogue help develop the characters? Does the dialogue reveal information about the plot? Offer each other suggestions, and remember that they are most helpful when they are constructive.

Please note that excerpts and passages in the StudySync® library and this workbook are intended as touchstones to generate interest in an author's work. The excerpts and passages do not substitute for the reading of entire texts, and StudySync® strongly recommends that students seek out and purchase the whole literary or informational work in order to experience it as the author intended. Links to online resellers are available in our digital library. In addition, complete works may be ordered through an authorized reseller by filling out and returning to StudySync® the order form enclosed in this workbook.

Reading & Writing Companion    117

# SKILL: CONCLUSIONS

 **DEFINE**

At the climax of a story, the main character or characters figure out a way to solve the problem or conflict in the plot. But the story isn't over yet. The falling action in a work of literature is the sequence of events that follow the climax and end in the conclusion of the story. The **conclusion** ends all action within the plot, and provides a resolution of the conflict or problem in the story. A story's conclusion often communicates a lesson that the characters have learned—one that will benefit a reader to learn as well. This is the theme of the story. Because the conclusion is the author's farewell to the reader, an author must consider how the conclusion will affect the reader, as well as how to leave him or her with a lasting impression of the story.

 **IDENTIFICATION AND APPLICATION**

- A narrative conclusion includes the last events in the story, including:
  › A final interaction between characters who have faced the main problem or conflict in the story.
  › The final thoughts of the character(s) and/or narrator.

- An effective narrative conclusion presents a resolution of the conflict in the story. It should tell clearly how the characters resolved the conflict or problem or how it was resolved for them.

- The way a problem is resolved can be a surprise to the reader, particularly in a suspense story, but it should still be logical and feel like a natural part of the plot.

- At the end of the story, the reader should be able to think about the narrator's role–how his or her point of view affected the way the story was told.

- A strong narrative conclusion leaves the reader with a lasting impression, and often wraps up the theme of the story.

MODEL

In Edgar Allan Poe's story "The Tell-Tale Heart" the narrator describes his sensitivity to the old man with whom he lives, and particularly to his "evil eye," which has kept the narrator awake night after night. The story builds to a moment of climax when the narrator murders the old man and buries his body beneath the floorboards of the house.

Though the narrator now believes he has resolved his problem, the falling action of the story takes place afterward. As the narrator entertains the police officers who have come to investigate the old man's shriek, Poe presents the falling action that will lead to the actual resolution of the conflict:

> No doubt I now grew **VERY pale;** but I talked more fluently, and with a **heightened voice.** Yet the sound increased — and what could I do? It was **A LOW, DULL, QUICK SOUND — MUCH SUCH A SOUND AS A WATCH MAKES WHEN ENVELOPED IN COTTON.** I gasped for breath, and yet the officers heard it not. I talked more quickly, more vehemently but the noise steadily increased. I arose and argued about trifles, in a **high key** and with **violent gesticulations;** but the noise steadily increased. Why WOULD they not be gone? I paced the floor to and fro with **heavy strides,** as if excited to fury by the observations of the men, but the noise steadily increased. O God! what COULD I do? I foamed — I raved — I swore! **I swung the chair upon which I had been sitting, and grated it upon the boards,** but the noise arose over all and continually increased. It grew **louder — louder — louder!** And still the men chatted pleasantly, and smiled. Was it possible they heard not? Almighty God! — no, no? They heard! — they suspected! — they KNEW! — they were making a mockery of my **horror!** — this I thought, and this I think. But anything was better than this **agony!** Anything was more tolerable than this **derision!** I could bear those hypocritical smiles no longer! I felt that I must scream or die! — and now — again — hark! **louder! louder! louder! LOUDER! —**

In this part of the story, Poe shows readers that the narrator's mental unrest is now greater than ever, despite his claims of sanity. Poe uses descriptive details such as the narrator's "very pale" face and "heightened voice" in a "high key" to help readers understand how the narrator is feeling. He uses strong verbs and adjectives such as "violent gesticulations" and "heavy strides" to convey the narrator's increasingly wild actions, until he has reached the point where he has "swung" the chair he was sitting in and "grated" the floorboards to drown out the noise of the beating heart.

Poe also creates a sensory experience for readers in his description of the heartbeat, which begins as "a low, dull, quick sound—much as a sound a watch makes when enveloped in cotton" and grows increasingly "louder! louder! louder!" within the narrator's mind. As the heartbeat grows and the narrator comes undone in front of the police, readers may find their own heartbeats quickened with anxiety over the narrator's situation. Poe then brings the action and narrative to a halt, frightening in its suddenness, with a final statement made by the narrator:

> **"Villains!" I shrieked,** "dissemble no more! I admit the deed! — **tear up the planks!** — here, here! — it is **the beating of his hideous heart!"**

Though the officers have been calmly chatting with the narrator, unaware of his guilt, the narrator has convinced himself that they are scheming "villains" who are waiting for a confession. When the unexpected confession comes—with the narrator's emotional request to "tear up the planks" and rid him of the burden he carries—the narrative comes to a halt. The conflict has been resolved; the narrator has confessed to the crime and will no longer be tortured by the beating heart. *Or will he?* a reader might ask after reading the story. Will the narrator's conscience continue to haunt him?

"The Tell-Tale Heart" contains one of the most memorable conclusions of all-time. The author's pacing—crafted carefully through repetition and the narrator's frantic thoughts—and rich descriptions of the narrator's building mental distress allow readers to journey into madness. Anxious, excited, shaken, upset—no matter how an individual reader feels after reading the story's conclusion, Poe took care to ensure that his story left readers with a lasting impression of their reading experience. One theme in the story is that the human heart cannot endure the burden of guilt, especially in the case of murder. The guilty must confess somehow or be consumed by his or her conscience. The narrator might not learn anything in the story, but the reader does.

# DRAFT

CA-CCSS: CA.W.8.3a, CA.W.8.3b, CA.W.8.3d, CA.W.8.3e, CA.W.8.4, CA.W.8.5, CA.W.8.6, CA.W.8.10, CA.SL.8.1a, CA.SL.8.1c, CA.L.8.2c, CA.L.8.4b

## WRITING PROMPT

You have been reading and learning about stories of suspense, in addition to studying techniques authors use to generate a feeling of suspense in readers. Now you will use those techniques to write your own suspenseful narrative based on real or imagined experiences and events.

**Your essay should include:**

- a plot with a beginning, middle, and end
- a clear setting
- characters and dialogue
- a suspenseful theme

You have already made much progress toward writing your suspenseful narrative. You have planned your writing by identifying your characters, conflict, setting, and point of view and developing a sequence of events. You have considered about how writers use descriptive details to enhance and support a narrative. You have drafted your introductory paragraphs and paragraphs containing dialogue, and you have practiced writing the elements of a strong and effective conclusion. You have also considered the elements of suspense writing in relation to audience and purpose. Now it is time to write a draft of your suspenseful narrative.

Use your prewriting graphic organizer, plot diagram, and other prewriting materials to help you as you write. Remember that in the rising action of a narrative, writers introduce characters, setting, and conflict and begin to develop characters and plot. The rising action leads to the story's climax, the turning point in the story, where the most exciting action takes place. The falling action of a story occurs after the climax and leads to the resolution of

Please note that excerpts and passages in the StudySync® library and this workbook are intended as touchstones to generate interest in an author's work. The excerpts and passages do not substitute for the reading of entire texts, and StudySync® strongly recommends that students seek out and purchase the whole literary or informational work in order to experience it as the author intended. Links to online resellers are available in our digital library. In addition, complete works may be ordered through an authorized reseller by filling out and returning to StudySync® the order form enclosed in this workbook.

Reading & Writing Companion    **121**

the conflict and the story's conclusion. Keep readers in mind as you write, and aim to keep your audience engaged and in suspense.

When drafting, ask yourself these questions:

- What can I do to improve my introduction so that readers understand expository information—including character, conflict, setting, and point of view—early on in my story?
- How logical is the sequence of events I have established in my story?
- How can I use dialogue and description to reveal information about characters and advance the plot?
- How can I use pacing to build suspense in my story?
- What details can I improve and expand on to create a vivid experience for readers?
- How will I resolve the story's conflict in a way that is satisfying and memorable to readers?

Before you submit your draft, read it over carefully. You want to be sure that you've responded to all aspects of the prompt.

# SKILL: TRANSITIONS

## DEFINE

**Transitions** are words or phrases that help carry a thought from one sentence to another, from one idea to another, or from one paragraph to another. Good transitions can act as bridges, and turn disconnected, "choppy" writing into a unified whole that flows smoothly from one point or event to another. Transitions between events in a plot can help readers understand how certain events are related and work together in a story, building toward a climax. In narrative stories, transitional devices usually take the form of time order words and phrases that show the relationships between events. They can also signal a change in the setting, or where a story takes place.

## IDENTIFICATION AND APPLICATION

- Transitional devices link sentences and paragraphs together smoothly so that there are no sudden jumps or breaks between events or ideas. Writers can also use transitions to show the relationships between character experiences and story events.

- There are several types of transitional devices, and each category leads readers to make certain connections.

- Transitional words and phrases to indicate time has passed include *immediately, thereafter, soon, after a few hours* (or days, weeks, etc.), *finally, then, later, previously, formerly, first* (second, etc.), *next,* and *then.*

- To indicate a sequence of events, writers often use transitional words and phrases such as *next, following this, at this time, now, at this point, after, afterward, subsequently, finally, consequently, previously,* and *just then.*

- To show differences or exceptions between characters and events in a narrative, authors sometimes use transitional words and phrases such as *yet, still, however, nevertheless, in spite of, despite, of course, once in a while,* or *sometimes.*

NOTES

 MODEL

This excerpt from "The Monkey's Paw," contains transitions that help the reader understand the setting and sequence of events. Read the passages to identify the transitions the author used.

> **In the huge new cemetery,** some two miles distant, the old people buried their dead, and came back to a house steeped in shadow and silence. It was all over so quickly that at first they could hardly realize it, and remained in a state of expectation as though of something else to happen —something else which was to lighten this load, too heavy for old hearts to bear.
>
> **But the days passed,** and expectation gave place to resignation—the hopeless resignation of the old, sometimes miscalled, apathy. Sometimes they hardly exchanged a word, for now they had nothing to talk about, and their days were long to weariness.
>
> **It was about a week after that the old man, waking suddenly in the night, stretched out his hand and found himself alone.** The room was in darkness, and the sound of subdued weeping came from the window. He raised himself in bed and listened.

In the first paragraph from this excerpt, the author uses the transition "In the huge cemetery," to indicate that the action in the story has moved from its previous location (the home of the old couple) to the cemetery where they have just buried their son. In the next paragraph, the transition "But the days passed" helps the reader understand that some time has gone by since the burial, and the old man and woman have become hopeless, and hardly speak to one another. The author then moves the action to the present with the sentence "It was about a week after that the old man, waking suddenly in the night, stretched out his hand and found himself alone." The rest of the action, and the conclusion of the story, will take place that night, after the man wakes up.

 PRACTICE

Write one body paragraph for your suspenseful narrative that uses transition words and/or phrases. When you are finished, trade with a partner and offer each other feedback. How effective are the transitions at indicating the passage of time? How well do the transitions show relationships among character experiences and story events? Offer each other constructive, helpful suggestions for revision.

NOTES

# REVISE

CA-CCSS: CA.W.8.3a, CA.W.8.3b, CA.W.8.3c, CA.W.8.3d, CA.W.8.3e, CA.W.8.4, CA.W.8.5, CA.W.8.6, CA.W.8.10, CA.SL.8.1a, CA.SL.8.1c, CA.L.8.2c

## WRITING PROMPT

You have been reading and learning about stories of suspense, in addition to studying techniques authors use to generate a feeling of suspense in readers. Now you will use those techniques to write your own suspenseful narrative based on real or imagined experiences and events.

**Your essay should include:**

- a plot with a beginning, middle, and end
- a clear setting
- characters and dialogue
- a suspenseful theme

You have written a draft of your suspenseful narrative. You have also received input from your peers about how to improve it. Now you are going to revise your draft.

Here are some recommendations to help you revise:

- Review the suggestions made by your peers. Decide which ones you want to include.
- Examine the introduction to your narrative.
  - › Do your introductory paragraphs contain helpful expository information about your characters?
  - › Does the introduction establish a narrative point of view?
  - › Does your story's introduction orient the reader in the time and place of your story's setting?
  - › Have you introduced the conflict in the introductory paragraphs of your narrative?
  - › Does your introduction contain details that provide needed information?

- Evaluate the sequencing of events in your narrative.
  - › Do the events in your narrative follow a logical order?
  - › Have you used transition words and phrases to signal shifts in time or setting and show the relationships among experiences and events?
  - › Are your story events organized in a way that creates a sense of suspense for readers?
  - › Does the order of events in your narrative help build and develop the conflict in your story?
  - › Is the pacing appropriate? Should the pace be quickened or slowed at points to create a sense of urgency or suspense?

- Examine the prose you have used to tell your story.
  - › Have you included descriptive, sensory, and precise details that help readers visualize the characters, setting, and events in your narrative?
  - › Are there places where you need to add information or details, or where you can eliminate irrelevant details?
  - › Do your transitions show the relationships among character experiences and story events?
  - › Have you used language that is engaging and exciting for readers?

- Look at the dialogue in your story.
  - › Do your characters address one another in direct dialogue?
  - › What do details in the dialogue reveal about the characters?
  - › Does the dialogue help build the conflict and advance the plot?
  - › Does the dialogue reveal additional information about the setting of your narrative?
  - › Have you followed the technical guidelines for writing direct and indirect dialogue?
  - › Is it clear to readers who is speaking when characters converse in your story?

- Evaluate the conclusion of your story.
  - › Does the conclusion present a logical resolution of the conflict?
  - › Do you think readers will feel satisfied and entertained after reading your story's conclusion?
  - › Have you crafted a conclusion that will leave the reader with a lasting impression of your story?
  - › Does your conclusion contain any elements that might elicit an emotional response from a reader?

Use these questions to help you evaluate your suspenseful narrative to determine areas that should be strengthened or improved. Then revise these elements of your narrative.

NOTES

# EDIT, PROOFREAD, AND PUBLISH

CA-CCSS: CA.RL.8.7, CA.W.8.3a, CA.W.8.3b, CA.W.8.3c, CA.W.8.3d, CA.W.8.3e, CA.W.8.4, CA.W.8.5, CA.W.8.6, CA.W.8.10, CA.SL.8.1a, CA.SL.8.4a, CA.SL.8.5, CA.SL.8.6, CA.L.8.1a, CA.L.8.1b, CA.L.8.1c, CA.L.8.2c

## WRITING PROMPT

You have been reading and learning about stories of suspense, in addition to studying techniques authors use to generate a feeling of suspense in readers. Now you will use those techniques to write your own suspenseful narrative based on real or imagined experiences and events.

**Your essay should include:**

- a plot with a beginning, middle, and end
- a clear setting
- characters and dialogue
- a suspenseful theme

The final steps to complete your suspenseful narrative are to polish your piece by editing, proofreading, and publishing it. You should have the revised draft that you completed in a previous lesson. Think about all of the lessons in this sequence. As you reread your narrative, be sure to apply what you have learned about audience and purpose, organization of events, descriptive details, writing dialogue, introductions (with exposition), conclusions (with a resolution), and transitions. Review the suggestions that you received from the peer reviews during each step in the process and make sure you have applied them.

Here are some suggestions to guide you through the process of finalizing your essay:

- Now that you are satisfied with your work, proofread for grammar, punctuation, and spelling. Pay special attention to the parts of the essay that you just revised because it is easy to introduce new errors or to accidentally create unclear sentences when you are proofreading and making last-minute corrections.

› Check each sentence to make sure it is clearly written and punctuated. Check that your dialogue is formatted and punctuated correctly.

› Be sure you have included appropriate transitions between events or when introducing characters. Check that the transitions are punctuated correctly.

› Examine your use of verbs. Check to see that your verbs correctly express the intended mood and accurately show the actions or thoughts of the characters.

› Check the spelling of your work. Look at words that have suffixes to be sure you followed the rules for adding endings properly and that they represent the intended meaning. Check, too, for words whose meanings and spellings are often confused.

• Once your narrative has been proofread and edited, it is time to publish your work. You can add it to your classroom's website or blog, post it on a bulletin board, or share it with family and friends. Be sure to include a list of the works you used for sources, and if you publish online, add links to those resources so that interested readers can gather more information.

# studysync®

## Reading & Writing Companion

What does our response to conflict say about us?

# In Time of War

UNIT 2   What does our response to conflict say about us?

# In Time of War

## TEXTS

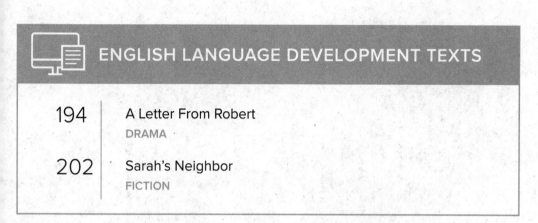

## ENGLISH LANGUAGE DEVELOPMENT TEXTS

## EXTENDED WRITING PROJECT

501

Text Fulfillment
through
StudySync

# BLOOD, TOIL, TEARS AND SWEAT

**NON-FICTION**
Winston Churchill
1940

## INTRODUCTION

I n 1939, Great Britain found itself at war with Germany after the Nazi invasion of Poland. Hitler's army was raging across Europe, and British Prime Minister Neville Chamberlain was forced to resign. The First Lord of the Admiralty, Winston Churchill, a soldier and longtime critic of Chamberlain, took over as Prime Minister. In this speech before Parliament in May 1940, his first as Prime Minister, Churchill resolves to win the war by whatever means necessary. Inspiring the people of the United Kingdom to fight on, he borrows words first uttered in English by Theodore Roosevelt, "I have nothing to offer but blood, toil, tears, and sweat."

# "We have before us many, many months of struggle and suffering."

## FIRST READ

1   On Friday evening last I received from His Majesty the mission to form a new **administration.** It was the evident will of Parliament and the nation that this should be conceived on the broadest possible basis and that it should include all parties. I have already completed the most important part of this task.

2   A war cabinet has been formed of five members, representing, with the Labour, Opposition, and Liberals, the unity of the nation. It was necessary that this should be done in one single day on account of the extreme urgency and rigor of events. Other key positions were filled yesterday. I am submitting a further list to the king tonight. I hope to complete the appointment of principal ministers during tomorrow.

3   The appointment of other ministers usually takes a little longer. I trust when Parliament meets again this part of my task will be completed and that the administration will be complete in all respects. I considered it in the public interest to suggest to the Speaker that the House should be summoned today. At the end of today's proceedings, the **adjournment** of the House will be proposed until May 21 with **provision** for earlier meeting if need be. Business for that will be notified to MPs at the earliest opportunity.

4   I now invite the House by a resolution to record its approval of the steps taken and declare its confidence in the new government.

5   The resolution:

6   "That this House welcomes the formation of a government representing the united and inflexible resolve of the nation to prosecute the war with Germany to a victorious conclusion."

7   To form an administration of this scale and complexity is a serious undertaking in itself. But we are in the preliminary phase of one of the greatest battles in

history. We are in action at many other points—in Norway and in Holland-and we have to be prepared in the Mediterranean. The air battle is continuing, and many preparations have to be made here at home.

8    In this crisis I think I may be pardoned if I do not address the House at any length today, and I hope that any of my friends and colleagues or former colleagues who are affected by the political reconstruction will make all allowances for any lack of ceremony with which it has been necessary to act.

9    I say to the House as I said to ministers who have joined this government, I have nothing to offer but blood, toil, tears, and sweat. We have before us an ordeal of the most grievous kind. We have before us many, many months of struggle and suffering.

10    You ask, what is our policy? I say it is to wage war by land, sea, and air. War with all our might and with all the strength God has given us, and to wage war against a monstrous tyranny never surpassed in the dark and lamentable catalogue of human crime. That is our policy.

11    You ask, what is our aim? I can answer in one word. It is victory. Victory at all costs—Victory in spite of all terrors—Victory, however long and hard the road may be, for without victory there is no survival.

12    Let that be realized. No survival for the British Empire, no survival for all that the British Empire has stood for, no survival for the urge, the impulse of the ages, that mankind shall move forward toward his goal.

13    I take up my task in **buoyancy** and hope. I feel sure that our cause will not be suffered to fail among men. I feel entitled at this **juncture,** at this time, to claim the aid of all and to say, "Come then, let us go forward together with our united strength."

THINK QUESTIONS CA-CCSS: CA.RI.8.1, CA.RI.8.4, CA.L.8.4a, CA.L.8.4b, CA.SL.8.1a, CA.SL.8.1b, CA.SL.8.1c, CA.SL.8.1d

1. According to the first three paragraphs of this excerpt of the speech, what has Winston Churchill been doing since becoming prime minister? Cite textual evidence to explain your understanding.

2. In the fourth paragraph, Churchill offers a "resolution" to the House of Commons in Parliament to "record its approval of the steps taken and declare its confidence in the new government." In paragraph six, Churchill states the resolution. What is he asking of the House? How important is this resolution? Explain your inference using evidence from the text.

3. What mood does Churchill convey as he moves through his speech? Use text evidence to explain how Churchill achieves it.

4. Use context to determine the meaning of the word **provision** as it is used in *Blood, Toil, Tears and Sweat*. Write your definition of *provision* and tell how you found it.

5. The Latin prefix *ad-* means "toward," and the root *jour* comes from the French, meaning "day." The Latin suffix *-ment* turns a word into a noun and has to do with an action or a process. Based on this knowledge of roots and affixes, write your definition of **adjournment** as it is used in the text, and tell how you got it. Use a dictionary to check its precise meaning.

Please note that excerpts and passages in the StudySync® library and this workbook are intended as touchstones to generate interest in an author's work. The excerpts and passages do not substitute for the reading of entire texts, and StudySync® strongly recommends that students seek out and purchase the whole literary or informational work in order to experience it as the author intended. Links to online resellers are available in our digital library. In addition, complete works may be ordered through an authorized reseller by filling out and returning to StudySync® the order form enclosed in this workbook.

Reading & Writing Companion | 135

# CLOSE READ

CA-CCSS: CA.RI.8.1, CA.RI.8.2, CA.W.8.4, CA.W.8.5, CA.W.8.6, CA.W.8.10

Reread the excerpt from *Blood, Toil, Tears and Sweat*. As you reread, complete the Focus Questions below. Then use your answers and annotations from the questions to help you complete the Writing Prompt.

 FOCUS QUESTIONS

1. Churchill asked the Speaker to summon the House today so he might deliver this speech. What makes the situation so important that this action must be taken right away? Highlight evidence from the text and make annotations to explain Churchill's main idea.

2. How does Churchill request that Parliament show its support for his actions? Highlight evidence from the text that shows Parliament's support of Churchill, as well as why it should continue its support. What do you think might have happened if the parliament had not given its full support? Use text evidence to support your inference.

3. Explain what Churchill means by the "monstrous tyranny never surpassed in the dark and lamentable catalogue of human crime." Cite textual evidence, as well as any of your own previous knowledge, to support your inference.

4. What is the central or main idea of Churchill's last five paragraphs? Highlight supporting details that help identify his central idea. State the central idea, and write a summary of the paragraphs.

5. Churchill is faced with an extremely difficult situation during his early days as prime minister. Compare the first half of his speech with the second half. What do both parts of the speech say about his strength as a leader in a time of war? Highlight textual evidence to support your answer.

## WRITING PROMPT

According to Churchill's speech, what will war mean for the British people, and why should England be involved? How does the main idea of Churchill's speech reveal his response to conflict, and what does this say about him? Support your writing with textual evidence from the speech.

# ANNE FRANK: THE DIARY OF A YOUNG GIRL

**NON-FICTION**
Anne Frank
1947

## INTRODUCTION

studysync tv

From a secret annex, Anne Frank wrote in her diary conveying the hopes and fears of an everyday teenager. But the times were anything but ordinary. The diary begins two days after Anne's 13th birthday, just 22 days before she and her family are forced into hiding, the occupying Nazi army scouring Amsterdam for Jewish people, loading them on trains to concentration camps. Her diary ends abruptly as she is betrayed and deported to Auschwitz. From there she is taken to Bergen-Belsen where she dies just two weeks before the concentration camp was liberated at the end of WWII. Of those who were in hiding with her, only her father Otto survived the war. He took on the task of editing and publishing Anne's unique journal, a perspective of a young girl amidst the unimaginable horrors of the holocaust.  In the following passages, Anne's words portray her life both before and after being forced into hiding.

# "...we're very afraid the neighbors might hear or see us..."

## FIRST READ

**WEDNESDAY, JUNE 24, 1942**

1 Dearest Kitty,

2 It's **sweltering.** Everyone is huffing and puffing, and in this heat I have to walk everywhere. Only now do I realize how pleasant a streetcar is, but we Jews are no longer allowed to make use of this luxury; our own two feet are good enough for us. Yesterday at lunchtime I had an appointment with the dentist on Jan Luykenstraat. It's a long way from our school on Stadstimmertuinen. That afternoon I nearly fell asleep at my desk. Fortunately, people automatically offer you something to drink. The dental assistant is really kind.

3 The only mode of transportation left to us is the ferry. The ferryman at Josef Israëlkade took us across when we asked him to. It's not the fault of the Dutch that we Jews are having such a bad time.

4 I wish I didn't have to go to school. My bike was stolen during Easter vacation, and Father gave Mother's bike to some Christian friends for safekeeping. Thank goodness summer vacation is almost here; one more week and our torment will be over.

5 Something unexpected happened yesterday morning. As I was passing the bicycle racks, I heard my name being called. I turned around and there was the nice boy I'd met the evening before at my friend Wilma's. He's Wilma's second cousin. I used to think Wilma was nice, which she is, but all she ever talks about is boys, and that gets to be a bore. He came toward me, somewhat shyly, and introduced himself as Hello Silberberg. I was a little surprised and wasn't sure what he wanted, but it didn't take me long to find out. He asked if I would allow him to accompany me to school. "As long as you're headed that way, I'll go with you," I said. And so we walked together. Hello is sixteen and good at telling all kinds of funny stories.

6   He was waiting for me again this morning, and I expect he will be from now on.

7   Anne

WEDNESDAY, JULY 8, 1942

8   Dearest Kitty,

9   It seems like years since Sunday morning. So much has happened it's as if the whole world had suddenly turned upside down. But as you can see, Kitty, I'm still alive, and that's the main thing, Father says. I'm alive all right, but don't ask where or how. You probably don't understand a word I'm saying today, so I'll begin by telling you what happened Sunday afternoon.

10  At three o'clock (Hello had left but was supposed to come back later), the doorbell rang. I didn't hear it, since I was out on the balcony, lazily reading in the sun. A little while later Margot appeared in the kitchen doorway looking very **agitated.** "Father has received a call-up notice from the SS," she whispered. "Mother has gone to see Mr. van Daan." (Mr. van Daan is Father's business partner and a good friend.)

11  I was stunned. A call-up: everyone knows what that means. Visions of concentration camps and lonely cells raced through my head. How could we let Father go to such a fate? "Of course he's not going," declared Margot as we waited for Mother in the living room. "Mother's gone to Mr. van Daan to ask whether we can move to our hiding place tomorrow. The van Daans are going with us. There will be seven of us altogether." Silence. We couldn't speak. The thought of Father off visiting someone in the Jewish Hospital and completely unaware of what was happening, the long wait for Mother, the heat, the suspense—all this reduced us to silence.

12  Suddenly the doorbell rang again. "That's Hello," I said.

13  "Don't open the door!" exclaimed Margot to stop me. But it wasn't necessary, since we heard Mother and Mr. van Daan downstairs talking to Hello, and then the two of them came inside and shut the door behind them. Every time the bell rang, either Margot or I had to tiptoe downstairs to see if it was Father, and we didn't let anyone else in. Margot and I were sent from the room, as Mr. van Daan wanted to talk to Mother alone.

14  When she and I were sitting in our bedroom, Margot told me that the call-up was not for Father, but for her. At this second shock, I began to cry. Margot is sixteen—apparently they want to send girls her age away on their own. But thank goodness she won't be going; Mother had said so herself, which must be what Father had meant when he talked to me about our going into hiding. Hiding . . . where would we hide? In the city? In the country? In a house? In a

Please note that excerpts and passages in the StudySync® library and this workbook are intended as touchstones to generate interest in an author's work. The excerpts and passages do not substitute for the reading of entire texts, and StudySync® strongly recommends that students seek out and purchase the whole literary or informational work in order to experience it as the author intended. Links to online resellers are available in our digital library. In addition, complete works may be ordered through an authorized reseller by filling out and returning to StudySync® the order form enclosed in this workbook.

Reading & Writing Companion   139

shack? When, where, how . . . ? These were questions I wasn't allowed to ask, but they still kept running through my mind.

15   Margot and I started packing our most important belongings into a schoolbag. The first thing I stuck in was this diary, and then curlers, handkerchiefs, schoolbooks, a comb and some old letters. **Preoccupied** by the thought of going into hiding, I stuck the craziest things in the bag, but I'm not sorry. Memories mean more to me than dresses. ...

16   Yours, Anne

SATURDAY, JULY 11, 1942

17   Dearest Kitty,

18   Father, Mother, and Margot still can't get used to the chiming of the Westertoren clock, which tells us the time every quarter of an hour. Not me, I liked it from the start; it sounds so reassuring, especially at night. You no doubt want to hear what I think of being in hiding. Well, all I can say is that I don't really know yet. I don't think I'll ever feel at home in this house, but that doesn't mean I hate it. It's more like being on vacation in some strange pension. Kind of an odd way to look at life in hiding, but that's how things are. The Annex is an ideal place to hide in. It may be damp and **lopsided,** but there's probably not a more comfortable hiding place in all of Amsterdam. No, in all of Holland.

19   Up to now our bedroom, with its blank walls, was very bare. Thanks to Father—who brought my entire postcard and movie-star collection here beforehand—and to a brush and a pot of glue, I was able to plaster the wall with pictures. It looks much more cheerful. When the Van Daans arrive, we"l be able to build cupboards and other odds and ends out of the wood piled in the attic.

20   Margot and Mother have recovered somewhat. Yesterday Mother felt well enough to cook split-pea soup for the first time, but then she was downstairs talking and forgot all about it. The beans were scorched black, and no amount of scraping could get them out of the pan.

21   Last night the four of us went down to the private office and listened to England on the radio. I was so scared someone might hear it that I literally begged Father to take me back upstairs. Mother understood my **anxiety** and went with me. Whatever we do, we're very afraid the neighbors might hear or see us...

22   Yours, Anne

Excerpted from *Anne Frank: The Diary of a Young Girl* by Anne Frank, published by Doubleday.

## THINK QUESTIONS
CA-CCSS: CA.RI.8.1, CA.L.8.4a, CA.L.8.4c, CA.SL.8.1a, CA.SL.8.1b, CA.SL.8.1c, CA.SL.8.1d

1. According to the text, what was one way Jews were discriminated against during the Nazi occupation of Amsterdam in the early 1940s? Cite details from the text to support your response.

2. What event takes place in the second entry of Anne Frank's diary? How does this event affect Anne's family? Cite details from the text to explain what takes place.

3. What does Anne pack to bring to the hiding place? Why does she pack these particular items? After she arrives, what does she do to make the hiding place feel more like home? Cite details from the text in your response.

4. Use context to determine the meaning of the word **agitated** as it is used within the text. Write your definition of *agitated*.

5. Look up the definition and part of speech of **lopsided** in a dictionary. Write the definition and part of speech that you found. Then rewrite the sentence in paragraph 18 in which *lopsided* appears, replacing this term with a synonym.

Please note that excerpts and passages in the StudySync® library and this workbook are intended as touchstones to generate interest in an author's work. The excerpts and passages do not substitute for the reading of entire texts, and StudySync® strongly recommends that students seek out and purchase the whole literary or informational work in order to experience it as the author intended. Links to online resellers are available in our digital library. In addition, complete works may be ordered through an authorized reseller by filling out and returning to StudySync® the order form enclosed in this workbook.

Reading & Writing Companion    **141**

# CLOSE READ
CA-CCSS: CA.RI.8.1, CA.RI.8.2, CA.RI.8.3, CA.W.8.3b, CA.W.8.4, CA.W.8.5, CA.W.8.6, CA.W.8.10

Reread the excerpt from *Anne Frank: The Diary of a Young Girl*. As you reread, complete the Focus Questions below. Then use your answers and annotations from the questions to help you complete the Writing Prompt.

## FOCUS QUESTIONS

1. In this excerpt of the diary, readers learn how Anne Frank responded to the frightening circumstances she faced as a Jewish girl during the Holocaust. What do her diary entries suggest about the kind of person she was? Highlight details that reveal Anne's character, and make annotations to explain your ideas.

2. What is the central or main idea of the first entry of this excerpt? How does paragraph 4 support the main idea? Highlight textual details. Make annotations to write the main idea and to explain how the details support it.

3. What is the central or main idea of the second entry of this excerpt? Highlight details, especially in paragraph 10, that support the main idea. Make annotations to write the main idea and to explain how the details support it.

4. What does Anne Frank describe in the third entry of this excerpt? Highlight Anne's details about her mother and sister in the last two paragraphs. What do the details reveal about them and the situation? Make annotations to explain your ideas.

5. Highlight the dates in each of the diary entries in this excerpt. How do Anne's circumstances change between each entry? Make annotations to summarize the changes. Highlight details that will help you write your summary.

## WRITING PROMPT

If Kitty were a person instead of a diary, Anne Frank might expect to receive a response. How might a friend respond to Anne in her time of crisis? Suppose you are Anne's friend and that the entries from her diary are letters to you. Choose one of the three entries and write a letter to Anne in response. Be sure to include an appropriate day, date, greeting, and signature. Refer to details from her letter, including Anne's central idea, in your response. If you wish, you may also include fictional details as if you lived during that time. Use narrative techniques, such as pacing, description, and reflection, to develop the experiences and events you describe in your letters.

# THE DIARY OF ANNE FRANK: A PLAY

**DRAMA**
Frances Goodrich and
Albert Hackett
1955

## INTRODUCTION

studysync tv

rances Goodrich and Albert Hackett's drama based on Anne Frank's *The Diary of Young Girl* provides a first-hand account of the persecution of the Jewish people by the Nazis during World War II. The excerpt below comes from early in the play, with Miep, one of the family's confidants, showing Mr. Frank the secret rooms that hid them.

# "Yesterday Father told me we were going into hiding."

NOTES

## FIRST READ

Act I, Scene 1

1   *The curtain rises on an empty stage. It is late afternoon November, 1945.*

2   *The rooms are dusty, the curtains in rags. Chairs and tables are overturned.*

3   *The door at the foot of the small stairwell swings open. MR. FRANK comes up the steps into view. He is a gentle,* **cultured** *European in his middle years. There is still a trace of a German accent in his speech.*

4   *He stands looking slowly around, making a supreme effort at self-control. He is weak, ill. His clothes are* **threadbare.**

5   *After a second he drops his* **rucksack** *on the couch and moves slowly about. He opens the door to one of the smaller rooms, and then abruptly closes it again, turning away. He goes to the window at the back, looking off at the Westertoren as its carillon strikes the hour of six, then he moves restlessly on.*

6   *From the street below, we hear the sound of a barrel organ and children's voices at play. There is a many-colored scarf hanging from a nail. MR. FRANK takes it, putting it around his neck. As he starts back for his rucksack, his eye is caught by something lying on the floor. It is a woman's white glove. He holds it in his hand and suddenly all of his self-control is gone. He breaks down, crying.*

7   *We hear footsteps on the stairs. MIEP GIES comes up, looking for MR. FRANK. MIEP is a Dutch girl of about twenty-two. She wears a coat and hat, ready to go home. She is pregnant. Her attitude toward MR. FRANK is protective, compassionate.*

8   MIEP: Are you all right, Mr. Frank?

9   MR. FRANK [*quickly controlling himself*]: Yes, Miep, yes.

10   MIEP: Everyone in the office has gone home... It's after six. [*then pleading*] Don't stay up here, Mr. Frank. What's the use of torturing yourself like this?

11   MR. FRANK: I've come to say good-bye... I'm leaving here, Miep.

12   MIEP: What do you mean? Where are you going? Where?

13   MR. FRANK: I don't know yet. I haven't decided.

14   MIEP: Mr. Frank, you can't leave here! This is your home! Amsterdam is your home. Your business is here, waiting for you... You're needed here... Now that the war is over, there are things that...

15   MR. FRANK: I can't stay in Amsterdam, Miep. It has too many memories for me. Everywhere there's something... the house we lived in... the school... that street organ playing out there... I'm not the person you used to know, Miep. I'm a bitter old man. [*breaking off*] Forgive me, I shouldn't speak to you like this... after all that you did for us... the suffering...

16   MIEP: No. No. It wasn't suffering. You can't say we suffered. [*As she speaks, she straightens a chair which is overturned.*]

17   MR. FRANK: I know what you went through, you and Mr. Kraler. I'll remember it as long as I live. [*He gives one last look around.*] Come, Miep. [*He starts for the steps, then remembers his rucksack, going back to get it.*]

18   MIEP [*hurrying up to a cupboard*]: Mr. Frank, did you see? There are some of your papers here. [*She brings a bundle of papers to him.*] We found them in a heap of rubbish on the floor after... after you left.

19   MR. FRANK: Burn them. [*He opens his rucksack to put the glove in it.*]

20   MIEP: But, Mr. Frank, there are letters, notes...

21   MR. FRANK: Burn them. All of them.

22   MIEP: Burn this? [*She hands him a paperbound notebook.*]

23   MR FRANK [*quietly*]: Anne's diary. [*He opens the diary and begins to read.*] "Monday, the sixth of July, nineteen forty-two." [*to* MIEP] Nineteen forty-two. Is it possible, Miep? ... Only three years ago. [*As he continues his reading, he sits down on the couch.*] "Dear Diary, since you and I are going to be great friends, I will start by telling you about myself. My name is Anne Frank. I am thirteen years old. I was born in Germany the twelfth of June, nineteen twenty-nine. As my family is Jewish, we **emigrated** to Holland when Hitler came to power."

24  [*As* MR. FRANK *reads, another voice joins his, as if coming from the air. It is* ANNE'S VOICE.]

25  MR. FRANK and ANNE: "My father started a business, importing spice and herbs. Things went well for us until nineteen forty. Then the war came, and the Dutch **capitulation,** followed by the arrival of the Germans. Then things got very bad for the Jews."

26  [MR. FRANK'S VOICE *dies out.* ANNE'S VOICE *continues alone. The lights dim slowly to darkness. The curtain falls on the scene.*]

27  ANNE'S VOICE: You could not do this and you could not do that. They forced Father out of his business. We had to wear yellow stars. I had to turn in my bike. I couldn't go to a Dutch school any more. I couldn't go to the movies, or ride in an automobile or even on a streetcar, and a million other things. But somehow we children still managed to have fun. Yesterday Father told me we were going into hiding. Where, he wouldn't say. At five o'clock this morning Mother woke me and told me to hurry and get dressed. I was to put on as many clothes as I could. It would look too suspicious if we walked along carrying suitcases. It wasn't until we were on our way that I learned where we were going. Our hiding place was to be upstairs in the building where Father used to have his business. Three other people were coming in with us—the Van Daans and their son Peter. Father knew the Van Daans but we had never met them.

28  [*During the last lines the curtain rises on the scene. The lights dim on.* ANNE'S VOICE *fades out.*]

---

Excerpted from *The Diary of Anne Frank: A Play* by Frances Goodrich and Albert Hackett, published by Nelson Thornes Ltd.

THINK QUESTIONS  CA-CCSS: CA.RL.8.1, CA.L.8.4a, CA.SL.8.1b, CA.SL.8.1c, CA.SL.8.1d

1. Why does Mr. Frank break down crying, as described in the stage direction that begins this passage? Use evidence from the text and your prior knowledge of Mr. Frank's history to support your answer.

2. Why is Mr. Frank grateful to Miep? Use evidence from the text and your prior knowledge of Mr. Frank's history to support your answer.

3. Did Anne Frank begin keeping a diary before or after she and her family went into hiding? Support your answer with textual evidence.

4. Use context to determine the meaning of the word **rucksack** as it is used in the passage. Write your definition of *rucksack* and tell how you found it.

5. Use context to determine the meaning of the word **emigrated** as it is used in the passage. Write your definition of *emigrated* and tell how you found it.

# CLOSE READ
CA-CCSS: CA.RL.8.1, CA.RL.8.2, CA.RL.8.3, CA.RL.8.7, CA.W.8.4, CA.W.8.5, CA.W.8.6, CA.W.8.10

Reread the excerpt from the drama *The Diary of a Young Girl: A Play.* As you reread, complete the Focus Questions below. Then use your answers and annotations from the questions to help you complete the Writing Prompt.

## FOCUS QUESTIONS

1. How to live with the pain of memory is one of the questions, and themes, in *The Diary of Anne Frank: A Play.* How is this theme revealed in the conflict Mr. Frank feels within himself when he returns to the attic rooms? Support your answer with evidence from the text.

2. The stage directions that open the play reveal that the rooms are dusty, the curtains are in rags, and tables and chairs are overturned. Mr. Frank walks onstage and finds a scarf and a woman's white glove. In the film, Mr. Frank arrives at the annex and stands on the street in front of the building. The viewer sees him through a window in the attic room as he looks up at the building. Later, as he walks through the dark rooms, Mr. Frank's face is mostly hidden, until he becomes a black silhouette. How does the camera make the attic setting seem almost like another character in the film? Support your answer with evidence from the film.

3. The stage directions in the play reveal a great deal about the characters, but much information about them is also revealed through the dialogue. Explain how the author uses dialogue to help readers understand the characters of Miep and Mr. Frank in this excerpt. Highlight dialogue that reveals information about each character, and make annotations to explain what you can infer about the characters from what they say.

4. Highlight the stage directions in the play that introduce and describe Anne. The stage directions indicate that as Mr. Frank reads from Anne's diary, "another voice joins his, as if coming from the air." Why do you think Anne is introduced in this way? Support your answer with evidence from the text.

5. What does Anne's monologue at the end of the excerpt, an entry from her diary, reveal about the difficulties the Frank family will face in the future? Highlight textual evidence and make annotations to explain your ideas.

## WRITING PROMPT

How does political or national conflict influence individual families? How does *The Diary of Anne Frank: A Play* explore this theme? What elements of the play help you understand this influence? Support your answer with text evidence from the selection.

# THE BOY IN THE STRIPED PAJAMAS: A FABLE

**FICTION**
John Boyne
2006

## INTRODUCTION

Written by Irish author John Boyne, *The Boy in the Striped Pajamas* has become a worldwide bestseller and has won numerous book awards. The novel tells the story of the friendship between two young boys—Bruno, the son of a high-ranking SS officer, and Shmuel, a Jewish boy who is a prisoner at Auschwitz concentration camp (called Out-With in the book). Though immensely popular, the book has not been without criticism. While many have praised it as a powerful tale of friendship amidst the horrors of war, others have criticized the book for trivializing the Holocaust.

# "The boy stared at the food in his hand for a moment and then looked up at Bruno..."

## FIRST READ

*Excerpt from Chapter Fifteen: Something He Shouldn't Have Done*

1   Bruno went into the kitchen and got the biggest surprise of his life. There, sitting at the table, a long way from the other side of the fence, was Shmuel. Bruno could barely believe his eyes.

2   "Shmuel!" he said. "What are you doing here?"

3   Shmuel looked up and his terrified face broke into a broad smile when he saw his friend standing there. "Bruno!" he said.

4   "What are you doing here?" repeated Bruno, for although he still didn't quite understand what took place on the other side of the fence, there was something about the people from there that made him think they shouldn't be here in his house.

5   "He brought me," said Shmuel.

6   "He?" asked Bruno. "You don't mean Lieutenant Kotler?"

7   "Yes. He said there was a job for me to do here."

8   And when Bruno looked down he saw sixty-four small glasses, the ones Mother used when she was having one of her medicinal sherries, sitting on the kitchen table, and beside them a bowl of warm soapy water and lots of paper napkins.

9   "What on earth are you doing?" asked Bruno.

10  "They asked me to polish the glasses," said Shmuel. "They said they needed someone with tiny fingers."

Copyright © BookheadEd Learning, LLC

11 As if to prove something that Bruno already knew, he held his hand out and Bruno couldn't help but notice that it was like the hand of the pretend skeleton that Herr Liszt had brought with him one day when they were studying human **anatomy.**

12 "I'd never noticed before," he said in a **disbelieving** voice, almost to himself.

13 "Never noticed what?" said Shmuel.

14 In reply, Bruno held his own hand out so that the tips of their middle fingers were almost touching. "Our hands," he said. "They're so different. Look!"

15 The two boys looked down at the same time and the difference was easy to see. Although Bruno was small for his age, and certainly not fat, his hand appeared healthy and full of life. The veins weren't visible through the skin, the fingers weren't little more than dying twigs. Shmuel's hand, however, told a very different story.

16 "How did it get like that?" he asked.

17 "I don't know," said Shmuel. "It used to look more like yours, but I didn't notice it changing. Everyone on my side of the fence looks like this now."

18 Bruno frowned. He thought about the people in their striped pajamas and wondered what was going on at Out-With and whether it wasn't a very bad idea if it made people look so unhealthy. None of it made any sense to him. Not wanting to look at Shmuel's hand any longer, Bruno turned round and opened the refrigerator, **rooting** about inside it for something to eat. There was half a stuffed chicken left over from lunch time, and Bruno's eyes sparkled in delight for there were very few things in life that he enjoyed more than cold chicken with **sage** and onion stuffing. He took a knife from the drawer and cut himself a few healthy slices and coated them with the stuffing before turning back to his friend.

19 "I'm very glad you're here," he said, speaking with his mouth full. "If only you didn't have to polish the glasses, I could show you my room."

20 "He told me not to move from this seat or there'd be trouble."

21 "I wouldn't mind him," said Bruno, trying to sound braver than he really was. "This isn't his house, it's mine, and when Father's away I'm in charge. Can you believe he's never even read *Treasure Island?*"

22 Shmuel looked as if he wasn't really listening; instead his eyes were focused on the slices of chicken and stuffing that Bruno was throwing casually into his

Copyright © BookheadEd Learning, LLC

mouth. After a moment Bruno realized what he was looking at and immediately felt guilty.

23 "I'm sorry Shmuel," he said quickly. "I should have given you some chicken too. Are you hungry?"

24 "That's a question you never have to ask me," said Shmuel who, although he had never met Gretel in his life, knew something about sarcasm too.

25 "Wait there, I'll cut some off for you," said Bruno, opening the fridge and cutting another three healthy slices.

26 "No, if he comes back—" said Shmuel, shaking his head quickly and looking back and forth towards the door.

27 "If who comes back? You don't mean Lieutenant Kotler?"

28 "I'm just supposed to be cleaning the glasses," he said, looking at the bowl of water in front of him in despair and then looking back at the slices of chicken that Bruno held out to him.

29 "He's not going to mind," said Bruno, who was confused by how anxious Shmuel seemed. "It's only food."

30 "I can't," said Shmuel, shaking his head and looking as if he was going to cry. "He'll come back, I know he will," he continued, his sentences running quickly together. "I should have eaten them when you offered them, now it's too late, if I take them he'll come in and—"

31 "Shmuel! Here!" said Bruno, stepping forward and putting the slices in his friend's hand. "Just eat them. There's lots left for our tea—you don't have to worry about that."

32 The boy stared at the food in his hand for a moment and then looked up at Bruno with wide and grateful but terrified eyes. He threw one more glance in the direction of the door and then seemed to make a decision, because he thrust all three slices into his mouth in one go and gobbled them down in twenty seconds flat.

33 "Well, you don't have to eat them so quickly," said Bruno. "You'll make yourself sick."

34 "I don't care," said Shmuel, giving a faint smile. "Thank you, Bruno."

35 Bruno smiled back and he was about to offer him some more food, but just at that moment Lieutenant Kotler reappeared in the kitchen and stopped when he saw the two boys talking. Bruno stared at him, feeling the atmosphere

grow heavy, sensing Shmuel's shoulders sinking down as he reached for another glass and began polishing. Ignoring Bruno, Lieutenant Kotler marched over to Shmuel and glared at him.

36 "What are you doing?" he shouted. "Didn't I tell you to polish these glasses?"

37 Shmuel nodded his head quickly and started to tremble a little as he picked up another napkin and dipped it in the water.

38 "Who told you that you were allowed to talk in this house?" continued Kotler. "Do you dare to disobey me?"

39 "No, sir," said Shmuel quietly. "I'm sorry, sir."

40 He looked up at Lieutenant Kotler, who frowned, leaning forward slightly and tilting his head as he examined the boy's face. "Have you been eating?" he asked him in a quiet voice, as if he could scarcely believe it himself.

41 Shmuel shook his head.

42 "You *have* been eating," insisted Lieutenant Kotler. "Did you steal something from that fridge?"

43 Shmuel opened his mouth and closed it. He opened it again and tried to find words, but there were none. He looked towards Bruno, his eyes pleading for help.

44 "Answer me!" shouted Lieutenant Kotler. "Did you steal something from that fridge?"

45 "No, sir. He gave it to me," said Shmuel, tears **welling** up in his eyes as he threw a sideways glance at Bruno. "He's my friend," he added.

46 "Your...?" began Lieutenant Kotler, looking across at Bruno in confusion. He hesitated. "What do you mean he's your friend?" he asked. "Do you know this boy, Bruno?"

47 Bruno's mouth dropped open and he tried to remember the way you used your mouth if you wanted to say the word "yes". He'd never seen anyone look so terrified as Shmuel did at that moment and he wanted to say the right thing to make things better, but then he realized that he couldn't; because he was feeling just as terrified himself.

*Excerpted from* The Boy in the Striped Pajamas: A Fable *by John Boyne, published by David Fickling Books.*

## THINK QUESTIONS
CA-CCSS: CA.RL.8.1, CA.RL.8.4, CA.L.8.4a, CA.L.8.4b

1. Before finding Shmuel in his house, Bruno had never noticed how thin Shmuel's fingers were, like "dying twigs." Why do Shmuel's and Bruno's hands look so different? Use evidence from the text to support your answer.

2. Why isn't Bruno afraid of Lieutenant Kotler at first? Use evidence from the text to support your response.

3. What additional evidence does the author provide that suggests Bruno has no idea what really goes on at "Out-With" as he calls it?

4. Use context to determine the meaning of the word **rooting** as it is used in *The Boy in the Striped Pajamas*. Write your definition of *rooting* and tell how you found it.

5. Remembering that the Latin prefix *dis-* can mean "not," use the context clues provided in the passage to determine the meaning of **disbelieving.** Write your definition of *disbelieving* and tell how you got it.

# CLOSE READ   CA-CCSS: CA.RL.8.1, CA.RL.8.2, CA.RL.8.3, CA.RL.8.6, CA.W.8.2

Reread the excerpt from *The Boy in the Striped Pajamas: A Fable.* As you reread, complete the Focus Questions below. Then use your answers and annotations from the questions to help you complete the Writing Prompt.

 FOCUS QUESTIONS

1. Explain how the author uses the first several paragraphs to establish the point of view in the story. Highlight evidence from the text and make annotations to explain your choices.

2. Reread paragraphs 18 and 19 that begin with the words "Bruno frowned" and end with "…. I could show you my room." What do Bruno's thoughts, actions, and dialogue reveal about his character?

3. Reread paragraphs 20 through 30 beginning with "He told me not to move" and ending with "…if I take them he'll come in and—." What can you infer about Shmuel's character from the dialogue in these paragraphs?

4. In the 18th paragraph that begins with "Bruno frowned," the term "Out-With" is mentioned. Who or what is "Out-With"? How is Lieutenant Kotler a symbol for this larger, although unseen, antagonist? Use evidence from the text to support your response.

5. In the last eight paragraphs of the story, all three characters have conflicts. Discuss these conflicts with a focus on the Essential Question for this unit: "What does our response to conflict say about us?" Use evidence from the text to support your response.

## WRITING PROMPT

How can point of view and character shape the overall theme of a text? Identify the theme of *The Boy in the Striped Pajamas: A Fable* and discuss how character and point of view contribute to the theme. Include textual evidence to support your writing.

# TEACHING HISTORY THROUGH FICTION

NON-FICTION

2015

## INTRODUCTION

Teaching history through fiction can capture the imaginations of young readers and bring history alive. But using historical fiction to teach history is not without risks. Authors of historical fiction are not always primarily concerned with teaching history. Such is the case with John Boyne, author of *The Boy in the Striped Pajamas*. Boyne subtitled his book "A Fable" to alert readers to the fact that he had altered some realities of the Holocaust. But is that enough? The writers in these two articles explore whether Boyne's desire to explore the moral issues of the Holocaust from the perspective of children outweighs the dangers of distorting the historical realities of this dark time in history.

# "Fiction can make history matter— make it irresistible—to young readers."

 FIRST READ

 NOTES

Teaching History Through Fiction: Valuable or Dangerous?

Point: There is Value in Teaching History Through Fiction

1 Every history teacher knows that making students believe that history is relevant to their lives is Challenge Number 1. The question is, how can this difficult feat be accomplished? One answer lies in a source we might least expect: fiction. As Valerie Tripp points out in her blog entry on the teachinghistory.org website, "Fiction can make history matter—make it irresistible—to young readers" (Tripp). This effect is achieved by John Boyne's *The Boy in the Striped Pajamas.* By approaching the Holocaust through the eyes of two nine-year-old boys, the book provides a unique perspective on this dark and horrible chapter in history. Fiction, including stories, novels, and films, is a great way to teach people about history, and John Boyne's *The Boy in the Striped Pajamas* is an excellent example.

2 Reviewers and readers alike praise the book. Boyne notes on his website that the novel has sold more than six million copies worldwide. In addition to reaching the top of the New York Times Best Seller list, *The Boy in the Striped Pajamas* has won many awards. Not surprisingly, it was made into a movie in 2008 (Boyne). Reviewers have offered equally high praise for the movie. Film critic Peter Rainer notes in his online movie review for the *Christian Science Monitor,* "The great conundrum of the Holocaust is that it was perpetrated by human beings, not monsters. Few movies have rendered this puzzle so powerfully" (Rainer, "Review: *The Boy in the Striped Pajamas*"). It is interesting to note that Rainer has also reviewed Richard Linklater's *Boyhood. Boyhood* is another child-centered movie.

3 Critics of the novel and movie argue that both are historically inaccurate. The premise of the story is the friendship between Bruno, the son of the German commandant at Auschwitz, and Shmuel, a Jewish boy imprisoned in the

concentration camp. Over the course of a year, the boys' friendship grows as they meet and talk for hours at the camp's fence. Innocent Bruno does not understand why his friend cannot leave the camp to play or why Shmuel must wear the striped pajamas. Critics, like David Cesarani, argue that Bruno's innocence is unrealistic. A nine-year-old boy in wartime Germany would clearly understand the purpose of the camp and why Shmuel was there. This would be particularly true for the son of a high-ranking Nazi (Cesarani). That may be true. But these critics are missing the point. As Claudia Moscovici notes in her literature blog, the subtitle clearly indicates that *The Boy in the Striped Pajamas* is a fable. "By its own admission," Moscovici argues, "this novel doesn't propose to offer a realistic historical account of the Holocaust" (Moscovici). Fables are not history. Fables are designed to explore moral lessons. Both the novel and movie do just that through their touching and thought-provoking exploration of the moral issues surrounding the Holocaust.

4   Reviewer Kathryn Hughes, writing in the online edition of the *Guardian* newspaper, sums up the value of *The Boy in the Striped Pajamas*. She writes, "For the older reader, of course, Bruno's innocence comes to stand for the willful refusal of all adult Germans to see what was going on under their noses in the first half of the 1940s." For younger readers, she argues, the story's slow release of details "becomes an education in real time of the horrors of 'Out-With,' known to the grown-ups as Auschwitz" (Hughes). This is exactly what we expect of the fiction we use to teach history.

5   As Joanne Brown notes in her article on writing historical fiction for young adults, "Any writer who tells a story set in the past must negotiate the fine line between history and fiction, between readers' contemporary sensibilities and historical accuracy." Admittedly, some of the literary devices in *The Boy in the Striped Pajamas* might require readers familiar with the Holocaust to accept some historical inaccuracy (Brown). For example, as Cesarani points out, the fences of the camps "were heavily guarded and frequently electrified" (Cesarani). Thus it is doubtful that Bruno and Shmuel could sit for hours and talk. But in the end, this is not important. Boyne's main purpose in writing this novel was not to teach young readers facts about the Holocaust. His main goal was to present a story that would move them to want to learn more about the subject (Boyne).

6   The goal of good fiction should be to move people. It should move them to laugh, to cry, to care, to think—or else why should they bother reading it? History too should move people—or else how will they learn from it? By exploring the moral issues of the Holocaust through the eyes of two innocent young boys, *The Boy in the Striped Pajamas* accomplishes what should be important aims of both fiction and history: it moves people to care and to think. Thus, the story is an excellent example of how to teach history through fiction.

Counterpoint: There is Danger in Fictionalizing History

NOTES

7   Teaching history through the use of fiction, including stories, novels, and films, is often misleading and can be dangerous, and John Boyne's *The Boy in the Striped Pajamas* shows why. By manipulating the historical realities of the Holocaust for the sake of a good story, Boyne runs the risk of giving readers a distorted view of the Holocaust.

8   No one would consider Valerie Tripp an opponent of using fiction to teach history. On the teachinghistory.org website, Tripp notes that "fiction can make history matter—make it irresistible—to young readers" (Tripp, "Vitamins in Chocolate Cake"). Yet Tripp, an author of youth fiction herself, also knows the dangers. She offers this warning to teachers: "When choosing historical fiction to use in the classroom as a way to interest students in history, I'd say: First, do no harm. That is, before it is used in a history classroom, historical fiction should be checked for bias, for anachronistic voice and views, and for shying away from honest presentation of the period. What is not said is as misleading as what is said!" (Tripp, "Neither Spinach Nor Potato Chip").

9   Judged according to Tripp's criteria, teachers should use *The Boy in the Striped Pajamas* with caution. Boyne's bias rests not in his personal beliefs about the Holocaust, but in his view of storytelling. In an interview with Alexis Burling on Teenreads.com, Boyne explains how he approached the story:

10          Considering the serious subject matter of this novel and the fact that I would be taking certain aspects of concentration camp history and changing them slightly in order to serve the story, I felt it was important not to pretend that a story like this was fully based in reality (which was also the reason why I chose never to use the word "Auschwitz" in the novel). My understanding of the term "fable" is a piece of fiction that contains a moral. I hope that the moral at the center of THE BOY IN THE STRIPED PAJAMAS is self-evident to readers. (Burling)

11  Personally, I don't like fables. But that aside, the problem with Boyne's premise is that writing a fable does not release him from an author's obligation not to distort history. This is particularly true when dealing with an event as serious as the Holocaust. The danger of "serving the story" over serving the facts is that young readers will not know enough Holocaust history to understand what has been changed. As critic David Cesarani notes, "Except for a few peculiar cases there were no Jewish children in the extermination camps: they were gassed on arrival" (Cesarani). Thus the very premise of the story is, in Cesarani's words, "utterly implausible." In his scathing review of the book, Cesarani explains why the implausibility matters: "Should this matter if the book is a 'fable' which is presumably intended by its author to warn against the evils of prejudice? Yes. Because there are people at large who contest

whether the systematic mass murder of the Jews occurred" (Cesarani). This is a serious charge, especially given that, according to Boyne's website, the book has sold more than six million copies worldwide and has been made into a movie (Boyne).

12   The critics of the book and the 2008 movie are many. One of their complaints is Boyne's use of clever word devices to avoid addressing the real facts of the Holocaust. Young Bruno mishears "Auschwitz" as "Out-With" and "the Führer" as "the Fury." As Cesarani points out, "Any normal German nine-year-old would have been able to pronounce Führer and Auschwitz correctly." Also, Bruno's word choices are culturally misplaced. As reviewer A. O. Scott notes, "There is something illogical about them, since Bruno's native language is presumably German in which the portentous puns would make no sense, not English, in which they do" (Scott).

13   More serious complaints involve what Tripp calls "shying away from honest presentation of the period." Most notably, even if there had been a lot of Jewish children at Auschwitz, the idea that the commandant's son and one of those children would meet repeatedly is beyond belief. As critics note, the two boys would not have had the opportunity. Guards patrolled the fences and prisoners did not have the freedom to move about at will. Boyne's literary device hides the ugly truth of the concentration camps: constant roll calls, slave labor, forced marches, and guards with vicious dogs (Cesarani; Moscovici).

14   For these reasons, I believe that *The Boy in the Striped Pajamas* is a perfect example of why using fiction to teach history can be dangerous. Teachers are wise to keep Valerie Tripp's warning in mind when presenting the book: "What is not said is as misleading as what is said!"

**THINK QUESTIONS**   CA-CCSS: CA.RI.8.1, CA.RI.8.4, CA.L.8.4a, CA.L.8.4b

1. The writer of the Point, "The Value of Teaching History Through Fiction," and the writer of the Counterpoint, "The Dangers of Fictionalizing History," share their views of using fiction to teach history. How do their ideas differ? Cite textual details to summarize the main points that each essay writer makes.

2. The Point writer cites Kathryn Hughes as a source to support her view. Summarize Hughes's view of the value of *The Boy in the Striped Pajamas*. How does what Hughes says help support the claim made in the Point essay? Support your answer with textual evidence and inferences.

3. One of the arguments the writer of the Counterpoint essays makes is that Boyne's clever wordplay is inappropriate. Identify what the wordplay is and the experts' arguments. How do the experts help the author support his claim? Support your answer with textual evidence.

4. Use context to determine the meaning of the word **conundrum** as it is used in the Point essay. Write your definition of *conundrum* and explain how you arrived at it.

5. Remembering that the Greek prefix *ana-* means "against," the Greek root *chron* means "time," and the suffix *-istic* means "characteristic of," use your knowledge of affixes and roots and the context clues in the Counterpoint essay to determine the meaning of **anachronistic.** Write your definition of *anachronistic* and explain how you arrived at it.

Please note that excerpts and passages in the StudySync® library and this workbook are intended as touchstones to generate interest in an author's work. The excerpts and passages do not substitute for the reading of entire texts, and StudySync® strongly recommends that students seek out and purchase the whole literary or informational work in order to experience it as the author intended. Links to online resellers are available in our digital library. In addition, complete works may be ordered through an authorized reseller by filling out and returning to StudySync® the order form enclosed in this workbook.

Reading & Writing Companion   **161**

# CLOSE READ
**CA-CCSS:** CA.RI.8.1, CA.RI.8.2, CA.RI.8.5, CA.RI.8.8, CA.RI.8.9, CA.W.8.4, CA.W.8.5, CA.W.8.6, CA.W.8.9b, CA.W.8.10, CA.SL.8.3

Reread the text "Teaching History Through Fiction." As you reread, complete the Focus Questions below. Then use your answers and annotations from the questions to help you complete the Writing Prompt.

## FOCUS QUESTIONS

1. Both writers provide bibliographies—lists of online sources they used to write their essays. As far as you can judge without actually consulting these links, are the sources reputable, and do they appear likely to provide accurate information? How does your analysis of the bibliography affect your opinion of the persuasiveness of each essay? Use specific details from the bibliographies and essays in your response.

2. Choose one example in either essay of weak, incomplete, or irrelevant evidence, and analyze what makes this evidence ineffective. How does the writer's choice to include this evidence affect your overall impression of the essay, and why? Use specific details and relevant textual evidence from the essay to support your answer.

3. Both writers base their arguments on *The Boy in the Striped Pajamas*. On the surface, this seems strange. How can a book be both a good example of using fiction to teach history and a good example of why using fiction to teach history can be dangerous? Cite evidence from both essays to explain how the writers structure their arguments to make this strategy work.

4. The two writers cite some of the same sources. Pick one of those sources and compare and contrast how the writers use the evidence in similar or different ways. Then evaluate whether one or both of the writers is twisting the evidence. Back up your ideas with text evidence.

5. Summarize the claims and key points of both essays. How effectively does each writer use evidence to support his or her position? What makes the evidence effective or ineffective? Which argument seems more convincing? Use specific details from both essays to support your answer.

## WRITING PROMPT

Both essays focus on *The Boy in the Striped Pajamas* in discussing the role of fiction in teaching history. But the writers approach the book from different perspectives. Compare and contrast the perspectives. Which argument is more effective and persuasive? How might you suggest making it even stronger? Use textual evidence from both passages to support your response.

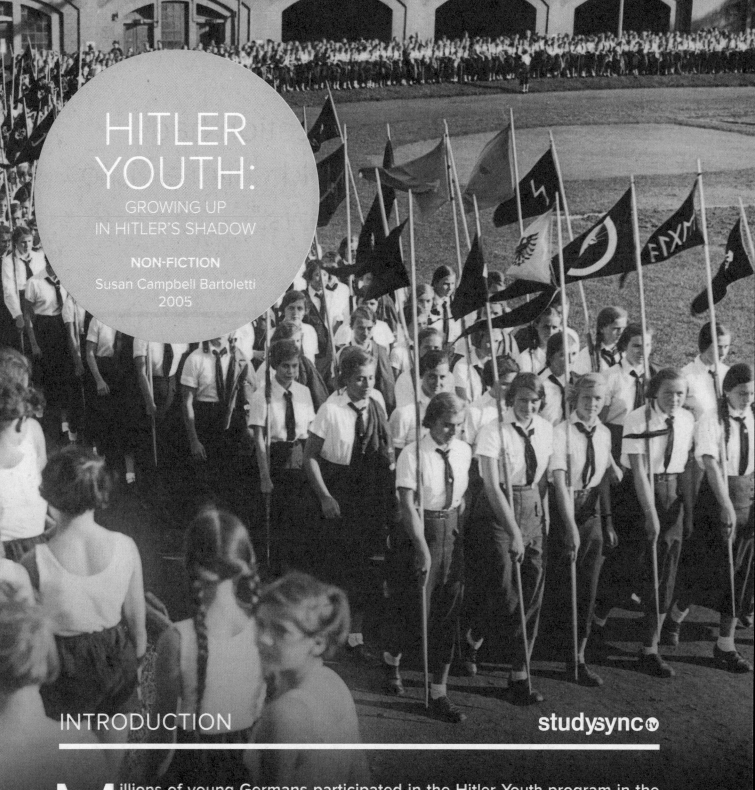

# HITLER YOUTH:

## GROWING UP
## IN HITLER'S SHADOW

**NON-FICTION**
Susan Campbell Bartoletti
2005

# INTRODUCTION

**studysync** tv

M illions of young Germans participated in the Hitler Youth program in the
years leading up to World War II, and those who resisted did so at their
peril. Through diaries, letters, photographs, oral histories, and interviews,
Susan Campbell Bartoletti's book illustrates what life was like for children growing
up under Hitler. The excerpt below describes the Nazis' use of schools to further
their goals. Sophie Scholl, a teenager discussed in the passage, was later beheaded
for distributing anti-Nazi leaflets.

# "For Hitler, education had one purpose: to mold children into good Nazis."

 **FIRST READ**

*Excerpt from Chapter Three: "Where One Burns Books" – A Nazi Education*

1   At fourteen, Sophie Scholl moved from the Jungmädel to the older Bund Deutscher Mädel. Just as her sister Inge and brother Hans did, she believed that Hitler would help Germany achieve greatness, fortune, and prosperity.

2   Deeply sensitive, Sophie was a talented artist. She loved music, and, like many teenagers, she longed for individuality and independence. Although a German motto said, "German girls wear braids," dark-haired Sophie wore her hair short.

3   During high school, Sophie began to grow away from the National Socialistic ideas about race, religion, and duty. She was beginning to form her own political views, which she often wrote about in her diary and letters.

4   But to Sophie's dismay, her Nazi teachers did not tolerate disagreement or discussion of other viewpoints. Though Sophie knew the correct National Socialist answer to every question, she soon found herself unwilling to give her teachers the answers they wanted but she felt were wrong.

5   Sophie measured herself against high standards and believed others should do the same. "We all have this yardstick inside ourselves, but it just isn't sought enough. Maybe because it is the most difficult yardstick," she explained in a letter to her boyfriend, Fritz Hartnagel. Four years older than Sophie, Fritz was a young officer in the German army.

6   In school, Sophie felt **alienated** because she could not confide in a classmate or teacher. She longed to graduate and join her older brother, Hans, whom she adored, at the University of Munich, where she planned to study biology and philosophy.

NOTES

7   But for now, Sophie was stuck in high school, feeling frustrated and stifled. One day, she stopped raising her hand to be called upon. Her silence frustrated her teachers. The principal warned Sophie that she might not graduate if she didn't participate and show more enthusiasm for National Socialism. The threat worked: Worried now, Sophie **buckled** and studied hard to pass the Abitur, a difficult graduation test, in order to receive her diploma. Her diploma was her ticket to the university.

8   Later, Sophie would not buckle again on her political views: In another letter to Fritz, she wrote, "I don't like to think about it, but soon there is going to be nothing left but politics, and as long as it's so confused and evil, it's cowardly to turn away from it."

9   Sophie's frustration during high school stemmed from the Nazis' new **standardized** school curriculum. It was important to Adolf Hitler that all Germans shared the same outlook on the world. This was called *Weltanschauung,* or "worldview."

10  Although a poor student himself, Hitler had definite ideas about education. For Hitler, education had one purpose: to mold children into good Nazis. As soon as the Nazis came to power, they took control of the public schools, called National Schools. They threw out old textbooks and **implemented** new ones. They rewrote the curriculum from the top to bottom, so that it only taught Nazi-approved ideas.

11  Soon, the Nazi flag and Hitler's portrait hung in every classroom. "In the morning, we stood at attention, and there was the Nazi flag," said Karl Schnibbe. "We always had to start class with 'HeilHitler!' There was no more, 'Good morning, children.'"

12  The Nazis wanted to ensure that the teachers were politically reliable and supported the National Socialist Party and its principles. To accomplish this end, teachers were given a choice: Either join the National Socialist Teacher's Alliance and train the students in National Socialism or be dismissed.

13  The Hitler Youth enjoyed the power they had over teachers and other authority figures. Dressed in full uniform, entire Hitler Youth squads—as many as one hundred boys—showed up at classroom doors to **intimidate** teachers who did not espouse the Nazi worldview.

14  In Munich, they broke up teachers' association meetings and even smashed out the apartment windows of a Latin teacher who had given out low grades. The police were called, but the Nazi Party wouldn't allow them to arrest the Hitler Youth. All the police could do was take down their names. Never before had students felt so much power over adults and school authority. But the

Please note that excerpts and passages in the StudySync® library and this workbook are intended as touchstones to generate interest in an author's work. The excerpts and passages do not substitute for the reading of entire texts, and StudySync® strongly recommends that students seek out and purchase the whole literary or informational work in order to experience it as the author intended. Links to online resellers are available in our digital library. In addition, complete works may be ordered through an authorized reseller by filling out and returning to StudySync® the order form enclosed in this workbook.

NOTES

leader of the Hitler Youth, Baldur van Schirach, was unhappy about the unfavorable publicity, and he told the Hitler Youth to obey the law.

15    The Nazi Party pressured teachers for 100 percent Hitler Youth membership, and the teachers, in turn, pressured the students to join. Henry Metelmann's teacher criticized a boy who held out. "You see, all your friends in class have become members," said the teacher. "Surely so many cannot be wrong in their choice while you are the only one who is right. Remember they are all determined to help the Fuhrer."

16    Some teachers quit rather than join the Nazis. Those who refused to quit were dealt with harshly. The Scholl children were upset when the Nazis arrested a young teacher and forced him to stand as Storm Troopers marched past and spat in his face. Afterward, the teacher was taken to a concentration camp.

Excerpted from *Hitler Youth: Growing up in Hitler's Shadow* by Susan Campbell Bartoletti, published by Scholastic Inc.

## THINK QUESTIONS    CA-CCSS: CA.RI.8.1, CA.RI.8.4, CA.L.8.4a, CA.L.8.5b, CA.SL.8.1a, CA.SL.8.1b, CA.SL.8.1d

1.  Were Sophie's political views in the majority or in the minority among her classmates? Provide textual evidence for your answer.

2.  How and why did Sophie's views change as she grew older? Cite evidence for your answer in the text.

3.  In addition to the ideas expressed by National Socialism, what motivated students to become active in the Hitler Youth? Support your answer with textual evidence.

4.  Use context to determine the meaning of the word **alienated** as it is used in *Hitler Youth: Growing up in Hitler's Shadow*. Write your definition of *alienated* and tell how you found it.

5.  Use context, word relationships, and word parts to help you understand the meaning of the word **standardized** in paragraph 9. Write the meaning of *standardized* and explain how you arrived at it.

# CLOSE READ   CA-CCSS: CA.RI.8.1, CA.RI.8.2, CA.RI.8.3, CA.RI.8.6, CA.RI.8.8, CA.W.8.4, CA.W.8.5, CA.W.8.6, CA.W.8.10

Reread the excerpt from *Hitler Youth: Growing Up in Hitler's Shadow*. Then use your answers and annotations from the questions to help you complete the Writing Prompt.

## FOCUS QUESTIONS

1.  What informational details does the second paragraph reveal that make Sophie seem special? Highlight evidence from the text and make annotations to explain your choices.

2.  Describe the conflict between Sophie and the school authorities. What were the reasons behind Sophie's point of view? Support your answer with textual evidence and make annotations to explain your answer choices

3.  What role did Adolf Hitler play in the education of Sophie and other German children at the time? Highlight specific textual details and make annotations to support your answer.

4.  What is the author's view of the Hitler Youth? How can you tell? In her evaluation of the Hitler Youth, does the author introduce evidence that you feel is irrelevant? Highlight evidence from the text and make annotations to support your explanation.

5.  What do Sophie's responses to the Nazis reveal about her? How did she handle the conflict she felt over National Socialism? Highlight textual evidence and make annotations to explain your ideas.

## WRITING PROMPT

What is the central or main idea in this excerpt from *Hitler Youth: Growing Up in Hitler's Shadow?* What details does the author use to support this central idea? Use your understanding of informational text elements as well as reasons and evidence to determine the central idea that emerges in this passage. Support your writing with evidence from the text.

Please note that excerpts and passages in the StudySync® library and this workbook are intended as touchstones to generate interest in an author's work. The excerpts and passages do not substitute for the reading of entire texts, and StudySync® strongly recommends that students seek out and purchase the whole literary or informational work in order to experience it as the author intended. Links to online resellers are available in our digital library. In addition, complete works may be ordered through an authorized reseller by filling out and returning to StudySync® the order form enclosed in this workbook.

Reading & Writing Companion   **167**

# PARALLEL JOURNEYS

FICTION
Eleanor Ayer
1995

## INTRODUCTION

*Parallel Journeys* weaves together the stories of two young Germans—Alfons Heck, an enthusiastic participant in the Hitler Youth, and Helen Waterford, a Jewish girl who flees to Holland to avoid persecution by the Nazis, only to be captured and sent to Auschwitz death camp. Partially narrated in the protagonists' own words, the book serves as a warning against hatred and discrimination and offers an uplifting message about peace and understanding. The excerpt here focuses on recollections of *Kristallnacht*, the Night of Broken Glass.

# "Jewish homes and businesses were destroyed and synagogues burned."

## FIRST READ

From Chapter 4: Kristallnacht: The Night of Broken Glass

1   On the afternoon of November 9, 1938, we were on our way home from school when we ran into small troops of SA and SS men, the Brownshirts and the Blackshirts. We watched open-mouthed as the men jumped off trucks in the marketplace, fanned out in several directions, and began to smash the windows of every Jewish business in Wittlich.

2   Paul Wolff, a local carpenter who belonged to the SS, led the biggest troop, and he pointed out the locations. One of their major targets was Anton Blum's shoe store next to the city hall. Shouting SA men threw hundreds of pairs of shoes into the street. In minutes they were snatched up and carried home by some of the town's nicest families—folks you never dreamed would steal anything.

3   It was *Kristallnacht,* the night of broken glass. For Jews all across Europe, the dark words of warning hurled about by the Nazis suddenly became very real. Just two weeks earlier, thousands of Polish Jews living in Germany had been arrested and shipped back to Poland in boxcars. Among them was the father of seventeen-year-old Herschel Grynszpan, a German Jew who was living in France. Outraged by the Nazis' treatment of his family, Herschel walked into the German Embassy in Paris and shot Ernst vom Rath, the secretary.

4   The murder spawned a night of terror. It was the worst **pogrom**—the most savage attack against the Jews of Germany—thus far in the twentieth century. Leading the attack was the brutal, boorish SS—the *Schutzstaffel*. On their uniforms, SS members wore emblems shaped like double lightening bolts, perfect symbols of the terror and suddenness with which they swooped from the night to arrest their frightened victims.

5 Heading the *Schutzstaffel* was Heinrich Himmler who worshipped Adolf Hitler. Himmler was a man of great organizational skills, with a passion for perfect record keeping and a heart as black as his *Schutzstaffel* uniform. His power in the Reich was tremendous; only Hitler **reigned** above him.

6 Working under Himmler to carry out the savagery of *Kristallnacht* was Reinhard Heydrich, the number-two man in the SS. His victims dubbed him "The Blond Beast." Even Hitler called him the man with the iron heart. On direct orders from Heydrich, Jewish homes and businesses were destroyed and **synagogues** burned. "Demonstrations," the SS called the violence, and they informed police that they were to do nothing to stop them.

7 "As many Jews, especially rich ones, are to be arrested as can be accommodated in the prisons," the orders read. Immediately officials at the concentration camps—the special prisons set up by the Nazis—were notified that Jews would be shipped there right away. SS men stormed the streets and searched the attics of Jewish homes, throwing their victim onto trucks to be hauled off to the camps.

8 Four or five of us boys followed Wolff's men when they headed up the *Himmeroder Strasse* toward the Wittlich synagogue. Seconds later the beautiful lead crystal window above the door crashed into the street, and pieces of furniture came flying through doors and windows. A shouting SA man climbed to the roof and waved the rolls of the Torah, the sacred Jewish religious scrolls. "Use it for toilet paper, Jews," he screamed. At that, some people turned shamefacedly away. Most of us stayed, as if **riveted** to the ground, some grinning evilly.

9 It was horribly brutal, but at the same time very exciting to us kids. "Let's go in and smash some stuff," urged my buddy Helmut. With shining eyes, he bent down, picked up a rock and fired it toward one of the windows. I don't know if I would have done the same thing seconds later, but at that moment my Uncle Franz grabbed both of us by the neck, turned us around and kicked us in the seat of the pants. "Get home, you two *Schweinhunde,*" he yelled. "What do you think this is, some sort of circus?"

10 Indeed, it was like a beastly, **bizarre** circus of evil. All across Germany the scene was the same. Terror rained down upon the Jews as Nazis took to the streets with axes, hammers, grenades, and guns. According to reports from high Nazi officials, some 20,000 Jews were arrested, 36 killed, and another 36 seriously injured. Thousands of Jews were hauled to concentration camps during *Kristallnacht.* There many died or were beaten severely by Nazi guards who used this chance to take revenge on a hated people.

• • •

11    Across Europe, Jews panicked as news of the horrors of *Kristallnacht* reached them. In Amsterdam, Helen and Siegfried got their first reports in a phone call from Helen's family.

12        My hometown of Frankfurt, with its 35,000 Jews, had four synagogues. The pogrom started with the burning of the synagogues and all their sacred contents. Jewish stores were destroyed and the windows shattered.

13        Nearly every house was searched for Jewish men. The SA, in plain clothes, came to my parents' apartment to arrest my father and eighteen-year-old brother. A "helpful" neighbor had shown them where in the roomy attic Jews might be hiding. My brother was deported to Buchenwald—a concentration camp near Weimar in eastern Germany—as was Siegfried's brother, Hans.

14    It was not enough for the Jews to suffer destruction of their homes and businesses, beatings and arrests by the SS, and deportation to concentration camps. The Nazis now ordered that the victims must pay for the loss of their own property. The bill for broken glass alone was five million marks. Any insurance money that the Jews might have claimed was taken by the government. And because many of the buildings where Jews had their shops were actually owned by Aryans, the Jews as a group had to pay an additional fine "for their abominable crimes, etc." So declared Hermann Goring, a high-ranking Nazi who was in charge of the German economy. He set their fine at one *billion* marks.

15    For the Jews still left in Germany, the future looked very grim. Many had fled, like Helen and Siegfried, after the first ominous rumblings from Hitler's government. But thousands still remained. These people simply refused to believe that conditions would get any worse. They thought the plight of the Jews would improve, if only they were patient. Helen's father was among them.

16        Although he had lost his business, he was still stubbornly optimistic about the future of the Jews in Germany. Earlier in the summer of 1938 he had been arrested, for no particular reason, and sent to Buchenwald. At that time it was still possible to get people out of a camp if they had a visa to another country. Siegfried and I got permission from the Dutch government for him to come to Holland, but he did not want to leave Germany without his wife and son. Since they had no visas, he stayed with them and waited—until it was almost too late.

*Excerpted from Parallel Journeys by Eleanor Ayer, published by Aladdin Paperbacks.*

## THINK QUESTIONS     CA-CCSS: CA.RI.8.1, CA.RI.8.4, CA.L.8.4a, CA.L.8.4b

1. What images does the word *Kristallnacht,* or its English translation, "night of broken glass," bring to mind? What words and phrases do the three narrators of the selection—Alfons, Helen, and the author—use that help you form mental pictures of the events happening across Germany on the night of November 9, 1938? Use specific details from the excerpt to support your response.

2. Use details from the text to explain what happened in Germany on *Kristallnacht.*

3. Why did *Kristallnacht* happen? Support your answer, including any inferences you make, with textual evidence.

4. Use context clues in the passage to determine the meaning of the word **bizarre.** Write your definition of *bizarre* and explain how you arrived at it.

5. Remembering that the Greek prefix *syn-* means "together" and the Greek root *agein* means "to lead," use the roots and context clues provided in the excerpt to determine the meaning of **synagogues.** Write your definition of *synagogues* and explain how you arrived at it.

# CLOSE READ

CA-CCSS: CA.RI.8.1, CA.RI.8.3, CA.RI.8.4, CA.RI.8.6, CA.W.8.3b, CA.W.8.4, CA.W.8.5, CA.W.8.6, CA.W.8.10

Reread the excerpt from *Parallel Journeys*. As you reread, complete the Focus Questions below. Then use your answers and annotations from the questions to help you complete the Writing Prompt.

 FOCUS QUESTIONS

1.  How does the author of *Parallel Journeys* make distinctions between Alfons's experience of *Kristallnacht* and Helen's experience? Highlight key details and descriptive language from the text to support your ideas. Make annotations to explain your choices.

2.  In Paragraph 16, Ayer discusses the idea that many Jews "simply refused to believe that things would get any worse." Helen echoes this opinion in the next paragraph, commenting that her father "was still stubbornly optimistic about the future." What do you think caused this disconnect between the brutal experience of the pogrom and the persistent optimism Ayer mentions? Support your inferences with textual evidence and make annotations to explain your choices.

3.  Think about the three perspectives shown in *Parallel Journeys*. How do Alfons, Helen, and the author communicate information on the same subject? What is the value of the different ways the text makes connections among the ideas, events, and individuals involved? Highlight evidence from the text to support your answer and annotate to explain your choices.

4.  Eleanor Ayer, the author of *Parallel Journeys,* chose to intertwine the stories of two people's lives, instead of focusing on only one. What does this choice tell you about her purpose? Highlight evidence from the text to support your explanation.

5.  In addition to presenting the narratives of Helen and Alfons, this excerpt from *Parallel Journeys* contains several examples of other people responding to conflict: Herschel Grynszpan, the SA and SS; Helen's father; the "helpful" neighbor in paragraph 14; and so on. Choose one or two groups or individuals and discuss what you learn from them about the conflict. Support your answer with evidence from the text, and annotate the text to show the evidence.

## WRITING PROMPT

What can you infer about Alfons and Helen, as adults, from their responses to the events described in *Parallel Journeys* by Eleanor Ayer? Use the informational text elements in this biographical account, including facts, opinions, historical details, and descriptive language to support your inferences. How can contributing to and reading historical accounts like this be useful for people today? Support your response with evidence from the text.

# DEAR MISS BREED

### NON-FICTION
Joanne Oppenheim
2006

## INTRODUCTION

S oon after the Japanese air attack on Pearl Harbor on December 7, 1941, the
United States government rounded up more than 110,000 people of
Japanese ancestry, most of them American citizens, and placed them in
hastily built internment camps. Despite the harsh conditions, dozens of young
Japanese Americans found inspiration in the form of a faithful correspondent,
advocate, and book supplier: Miss Clara Breed, the Children's Librarian at the San
Diego Public Library. In this excerpt from *Dear Miss Breed*, which compiles many of
the letters the librarian received from young people she helped, several children
have just arrived at the Poston Relocation Center in the blistering hot Arizona desert

# "P.S. There is no water on Sundays."

## FIRST READ

*Excerpt from Chapter Six: Greetings From Far-Off Poston*

1    Upon my arrival to the Poston Relocation Center, I stood bewildered, glaring at the hot dusty desert, wondering how we could survive. When my family and I were given our barrack number we spread our blankets and tried to put things in order. The first day here was so hot I should not know how I should express how I felt then. Whoever I met carried wet towels on his heads. Even in the mess hall people ate with wet towels on their heads. Small children had not eaten because of the heat. Even grownups lost their appetite.

2    That night, as I tumbled into bed, I kept thinking how we could ever survive in such a place and how the dusty soil could be made into fertile fields.

3    —Chiyoko Morita, ninth grade

4    After twenty hours on a train and another hour on a hot, dusty bus, the Nikkei arrived at the Poston Relocation Center. It seemed as if they had reached the ends of the earth. To get an idea of how removed from their former lives they must have felt: The nearest town, Parker, Arizona, was sixteen miles away and it had just one telephone! If one were driving toward California, the first service station would be eighty miles away.

5    It was so hot on the bus that they had opened the windows, only to be covered by powdery white dust the consistency of flour. When they stepped off the buses, friends didn't recognize one another. When they arrived in the **torrid** heat of summer, at **barracks** that were not complete, their hopes that Poston would be an improvement over Santa Anita were dashed. It was ten degrees hotter than the Libyan desert.

Please note that excerpts and passages in the StudySync® library and this workbook are intended as touchstones to generate interest in an author's work. The excerpts and passages do not substitute for the reading of entire texts, and StudySync® strongly recommends that students seek out and purchase the whole literary or informational work in order to experience it as the author intended. Links to online resellers are available in our digital library. In addition, complete works may be ordered through an authorized reseller by filling out and returning to StudySync® the order form enclosed in this workbook.

Reading & Writing Companion   **175**

6    The buildings had no window screens but plenty of bugs, there was a record-breaking temperature of more than 120 degrees, and windstorms coated everything with fine sand. Almost overnight, Poston became the third-largest community in Arizona. Where there had been nothing, a city of tar-papered barracks was hastily built to house more than eighteen thousand Nikkei. The camp was named for Charles D. Poston, the first congressman from the Territory of Arizona and first superintendent of Indian affairs in Arizona. In 1865, he had helped to establish the Colorado River Reservation.

7    Built on Indian land, Poston was the largest of all ten relocation centers. It was divided into three parts, officially known as Poston I, II, and III. Five thousand workers on a double work shift constructed the camps in record time. In fact, one builder boasted that they had erected sixteen barracks in twenty-two minutes! Due to a shortage of wood, barracks were built with green pine that shrank and left cracks between the boards, allowing sand and insects to seep and creep inside. The heat was so extreme that standard army barracks were redesigned with double roofs for insulation. But even double roofs did not block the oppressive heat. No guard towers were built at Poston since the location was "in the middle of nowhere" and towers were considered unnecessary.

8    As buses pulled in, a monitor climbed on board to explain how they were to line up for housing and registration. They arrived at odd hours, some in the middle of the night. People had endured a long, hot trip with poor food. They were weak from heat and dust. The shock of the whole experience was **overwhelming.** Still, a line had to be formed at the mess hall as the head of each family registered. Everyone over seventeen was fingerprinted and had to sign an agreement that he or she would live by the regulations of the center and work. Another line was formed in the recreation hall for housing assignments.

9    Even nine-year-old Jack Watanabe felt cut off from the world: "We are now in a strange place—Poston, Arizona. I doubt whether this is even on the map."

10   Afraid that there would not be enough housing to go around, the administration put four to eight people into a single room, twenty by twenty-five feet. In Poston III there were eighteen blocks. Each block had fourteen barracks with separate **latrines** and showers for men and women, a mess hall, a laundry and ironing room, and a recreation hall. Since there had to be a minimum of four people in an apartment, small families had to share a single room with another family. Almost all the San Diegans were sent to Poston III. Fusa and her mother had to live with another San Diego family until there were more barracks.

NOTES

11   Don Elberson, a sociologist who worked for the War Relocation Authority at Poston, could never erase his memory of the misery families encountered when they arrived:

12       It was brutal. Some days we had to process five hundred or more people. . . . But nothing **mitigated** the moment when I had to take them to their new homes. . . . You'd have to take these people into this dingy excuse for a room, twenty by twenty-five feet at best. These were people who'd left everything behind, sometimes fine houses. I learned after the first day not to enter with the family, but to stand outside. It was too terrible to witness the pain in people's faces, too shameful for them to be seen in this degrading situation.

13   Fourteen-year-old Babe Karasawa never forgot that moment. Here's how he described it to me sixty years later:

14       We opened the doors of our barrack and there were weeds growing between the spaces in the floorboards . . . they were three feet tall inside the barrack! I remember that because my two brothers and I, we just ripped those weeds out. We took buckets of water and washed all over the walls—we washed the dust and the grit. All the water goes right between the spaces—through the floorboards—the place is dry in thirty minutes because it was just so hot. This was the end of August in '42. The records show that in '42, in the middle of July, they had a record temperature of 144 degrees! I used to walk like this . . . my head tilted down and sideways so my face wouldn't go straight into the heat. When I drank water, it would just come right out of my arms. . . . Perspiration just poured right out. This was during the hottest time and I used to always have heat rash.

15   In her first letter from Poston, Louise tries hard to hold on to her rosy view of the world, but finding positive things to say about Poston was challenging. Now she not only missed San Diego; she missed Santa Anita! Still, sixteen-year-old Louise manages to see beauty in the bleakness.

16   *August 27, 1942*

17   *Dear Miss Breed,*

18   *Greetings from far-off Poston, Arizona! We arrived yesterday about 3:30 P.M. It was a very long train ride. . . . After leaving Barstow, we began to feel the heat. They say yesterday was a cool day but to us it was extremely hot.*

19   *We traveled through desert after desert. There were many houses which looked as if they were built many years ago. We seldom saw a*

NOTES

*human being except when passing through a small town. One of the most beautiful scenery was when crossing a bridge which was right above the Colorado River. It is, indeed, a beautiful river.*

20   *One common thing you see while coming here is—the beds and beddings are all placed outside the homes. It has been said that the heat is so hot that the people all sleep outside. It is very hot here. We traveled by bus through acres of cotton plants—so you can imagine the heat because cotton has to be grown in a hot climate.*

21   *After leaving the train, we had to travel by bus—about 20 miles. We are in Camp No. 3. It is not quite yet completed. It is so sandy here that everyone's hair looks gray. Sometimes the wind blows but when it does the sand comes with it. This camp is so far away from civilization that it makes me feel as if I was a convict who is not allowed to see anyone. I'd much rather sleep in the Santa Anita horse stables—this has made me realize how fortunate I was to be able to live in Santa Anita. The nearest town which is a very tiny one is about 20 miles away. This trip has made me realize the wonderful work of nature. Her delicate work in shaping the stone mountains, the beautiful coloring of the surroundings— it seemed as if I was looking at the picture or a painting of a genius.*

22   *This place differs greatly from . . . Santa Anita. In Santa Anita we were allowed to keep a bucket and a broom in our homes until the time came to leave but in Poston we are allowed to BORROW a bucket, broom or mop for 1/2 hrs. This makes it very inconvenient because often they run out of them and we have to wait until one is returned. Even in the dining rooms we have to take our own spoons and forks. They provide just the knife and cups + plates and, of course, food. Yesterday I ate rice, weenies, and cabbage with a knife. That was a new experience for me! You never realize how valuable a thing is until you experience it. The dining rooms are very small here because there is one to each block.*

23   *. . . We have to mop the house every day because of the dust but it does not do any good because before you know it it's dusty again.*

24   *My, this letter is getting too long and it's probably getting boring so I'll write again soon. If you have any questions, I'll be glad to answer them if I am able.*

25   *Most sincerely,*

26   *Louise Ogawa*

27   *P.S. There is no water on Sundays. The electricity is also turned off. Sunday morning everyone eats before 6:00 A.M. Water and electricity*

*turned off between 6:00 A.M. to 6:00 P.M. on Sundays. Very very inconvenient. Never realized how valuable water is. The place looked deserted all the time because of the sandiness every[one] stays inside and no one is outside—not even the children so it looks as if no one lives in the barracks.*

28  In spite of all the difficulties, Louise's positive and patriotic spirit rings true in these final words of her letter: "If American soldiers can endure hardships so can we!"

From DEAR MISS BREED by Joanne Oppenheim. Scholastic Inc./Nonfiction. Copyright © 2006 by Joanne Oppenheim. Reprinted by permission.

## THINK QUESTIONS   CA-CCSS: CA.RI.8.1, CA.RI.8.4, CA.L.8.4a, CA.L.8.4b

1.  Why were more than 110,000 people of Japanese ancestry in the United States relocated to places such as the Poston Relocation Center in Arizona? Include evidence from the Introduction and the text of this excerpt to explain your inferences.

2.  Describe the conditions at the Poston Relocation Center. What made living there so difficult? Use specific details from *Dear Miss Breed* in your answer.

3.  Don Elberson was a sociologist who worked for the War Relocation Authority. What was his job at the Poston Relocation Center, and why did he find it so difficult? Support your answer with textual evidence.

4.  Use context to determine the meaning of the word **barracks** as it is used in *Dear Miss Breed*. Write your definition of *barracks* and explain how you arrived at it.

5.  Remembering that the Latin root *mitis* means "to soften," use this knowledge as well as context clues in the passage to determine the meaning of **mitigated.** Write your definition of *mitigated* and explain how you arrived at it.

Please note that excerpts and passages in the StudySync® library and this workbook are intended as touchstones to generate interest in an author's work. The excerpts and passages do not substitute for the reading of entire texts, and StudySync® strongly recommends that students seek out and purchase the whole literary or informational work in order to experience it as the author intended. Links to online resellers are available in our digital library. In addition, complete works may be ordered through an authorized reseller by filling out and returning to StudySync® the order form enclosed in this workbook.

Reading & Writing Companion   179

# CLOSE READ
CA-CCSS: CA.RI.8.1, CA.RI.8.3, CA.RI.8.7, CA.RI.8.9, CA.W.8.1

Reread the excerpt from *Dear Miss Breed*. As you reread, complete the Focus Questions below. Then use your answers and annotations from the questions to help you complete the Writing Prompt.

## FOCUS QUESTIONS

1. *Dear Miss Breed* contains eyewitness accounts in two different media: Babe and Chiyoko's oral history interviews, in which they recall events from many years later, and Louise's letter to Miss Breed. Babe and Chiyoko both make very strong statements about the worst aspects of Poston: the unrelenting heat, the dust, and the poor quality of the housing provided. Contrast these two oral history interviews with Louise's letter. How does the letter differ from the interview statements in content and tone, and what conclusions can you draw by contrasting these two different media? Annotate the text and use specific details from the passages in your response.

2. Like Milton Eisenhower, Don Elberson worked for the War Relocation Authority. Compare and contrast Elberson's statement in *Dear Miss Breed* with Eisenhower's narration in the newsreel. How does each account enrich your understanding of the other? How do you explain the differences in the content of the two accounts? Use specific details from the passage and the newsreel to support your response.

3. The various interview statements, Louise's letter, and author Joanne Oppenheim's commentary contain many visual details that describe the Poston relocation center. The War Relocation Office newsreel gives you the opportunity to see film footage of the actual camp. How does the video compare to the mental images you formed while reading *Dear Miss Breed*? Use specific details from the text and newsreel in your response.

4. The Poston Relocation Center was named for Charles D. Poston, the first congressman from the Territory of Arizona and first superintendent of Indian affairs in Arizona. Why do you think the the government chose to name the relocation center after this man? What parallels can you find between the government's treatment of Japanese and Native Americans? Cite evidence from the text in your response.

5. With the attack on Pearl Harbor, a serious conflict arose between the U.S. government and the Japanese Americans living in California. Government officials felt they had to weigh the country's wartime security against the civil and constitutional rights of Japanese Americans in California. Louise's letter to Miss Breed shows her response to this conflict. What does Louise's response say about the kind of person she is? Use specific details from the text to support your response.

## WRITING PROMPT

Louise Ogawa, Babe Karasawa, Don Elberson, Chiyoko Morita, and Jack Watanabe all provide firsthand accounts of the relocation camp in Poston. What makes firsthand accounts of historical events more interesting and exciting than descriptions by people who weren't present at the scene? How do firsthand accounts help you visualize places and events in the past in a way that secondhand accounts do not? Support your writing with evidence from the text.

Please note that excerpts and passages in the StudySync® library and this workbook are intended as touchstones to generate interest in an author's work. The excerpts and passages do not substitute for the reading of entire texts, and StudySync® strongly recommends that students seek out and purchase the whole literary or informational work in order to experience it as the author intended. Links to online resellers are available in our digital library. In addition, complete works may be ordered through an authorized reseller by filling out and returning to StudySync® the order form enclosed in this workbook.

Reading & Writing Companion **181**

# NOBEL PRIZE ACCEPTANCE SPEECH

**NON-FICTION**
Elie Wiesel
1986

## INTRODUCTION

Elie Wiesel was a survivor of the Auschwitz and Buchenwald Nazi concentration camps, going on to write 57 books on the Holocaust and other subjects. The Nobel Committee called him a "messenger to mankind," stating that his struggle to come to terms with "his own personal experience of total humiliation and of the utter contempt for humanity shown in Hitler's death camps," as well as his "practical work in the cause of peace," delivered a powerful message "of peace, atonement, and human dignity" to humanity. The following is an excerpt from his acceptance speech.

# "...if we forget, we are guilty, we are accomplices."

## FIRST READ

NOTES

1   And it is with a profound sense of **humility** that I accept the honor—the highest there is—that you have chosen to bestow upon me. I know your choice transcends my person.

2   Do I have the right to represent the **multitudes** who have perished? Do I have the right to accept this great honor on their behalf? I do not. No one may speak for the dead, no one may interpret their mutilated dreams and visions. And yet, I sense their presence. I always do—and at this moment more than ever. The presence of my parents, that of my little sister. The presence of my teachers, my friends, my companions....

3   This honor belongs to all the survivors and their children and, through us to the Jewish people with whose destiny I have always identified.

4   I remember: it happened yesterday, or eternities ago. A young Jewish boy discovered the Kingdom of Night. I remember his bewilderment, I remember his anguish. It all happened so fast. The ghetto. The **deportation.** The sealed cattle car. The fiery altar upon which the history of our people and the future of mankind were meant to be sacrificed.

5   I remember he asked his father: "Can this be true? This is the twentieth century, not the Middle Ages. Who would allow such crimes to be committed? How could the world remain silent?"

6   And now the boy is turning to me. "Tell me," he asks, "what have you done with my future, what have you done with your life?"

7   And I tell him that I have tried. That I have tried to keep memory alive, that I have tried to fight those who would forget. Because if we forget, we are guilty, we are accomplices.

8   And then I explain to him how **naïve** we were, that the world did know and remained silent. And that is why I swore never to be silent whenever wherever human beings endure suffering and humiliation. We must take sides. Neutrality helps the oppressor, never the victim. Silence encourages the tormentor, never the tormented. Sometimes we must interfere. When human lives are endangered, when human dignity is in jeopardy, national borders and sensitivities become irrelevant. Wherever men and women are persecuted because of their race, religion, or political views, that place must—at that moment—become the center of the universe.

9   Human rights are being **violated** on every continent. More people are oppressed than free. How can one not be sensitive to their plight? Human suffering anywhere concerns men and women everywhere...

10   There is so much to be done, there is so much that can be done. One person—a Raoul Wallenberg, an Albert Schweitzer, Martin Luther King, Jr.—one person of integrity, can make a difference, a difference of life and death.

11   As long as one dissident is in prison, our freedom will not be true. As long as one child is hungry, our life will be filled with anguish and shame. What all these victims need above all is to know that they are not alone; that we are not forgetting them, that when their voices are stifled we shall lend them ours, that while their freedom depends on ours, the quality of our freedom depends on theirs.

12   This is what I say to the young Jewish boy wondering what I have done with his years. It is in his name that I speak to you and that I express to you my deepest gratitude as one who has emerged from the Kingdom of Night. We know that every moment is a moment of grace, every hour an offering; not to share them would mean to betray them.

13   Our lives no longer belong to us alone; they belong to all those who need us desperately.

## THINK QUESTIONS
CA-CCSS: CA.RI.8.1, CA.L.8.4a, CA.L.8.4b, CA.SL.8.1a, CA.SL.8.1c, CA.SL.8.1d

1. Who is the young boy who "discovered the Kingdom of Night" in paragraph 4? Use evidence from the text and your knowledge of Wiesel's history to support your answer.

2. What does Wiesel mean when he says in paragraph 7, "Because if we forget, we are guilty, we are accomplices"? Use evidence from the text to support your answer.

3. Write two or three sentences about what Wiesel is calling on his listeners to do. What responsibility does he give to those who listen? Support your answer with textual evidence.

4. Remembering that *multi* is a Latin root meaning "much or many," use this knowledge and context to determine the meaning of the word **multitudes** as it is used in the passage. Write your definition of *multitudes* and tell how you found it.

5. Use context to determine the meaning of the word **violated** as it is used in the passage. Write your synonyms of *violated* here and tell how you found them.

# CLOSE READ

CA-CCSS: CA.RI.8.1, CA.RI.8.2, CA.RI.8.3, CA.RI.8.7, CA.W.8.2b, CA.W.8.4, CA.W.8.5, CA.W.8.10

Reread the excerpt from Elie Wiesel's "Nobel Acceptance Speech." As you reread, complete the Focus Questions below. Then use your answers and annotations from the questions to help you complete the Writing Prompt.

## FOCUS QUESTIONS

1. How does the medium of video compare to reading a text version of Wiesel's "Nobel Acceptance Speech"? Focus on the first three paragraphs. Highlight examples from the text and annotate to <u>make comparisons to the video</u>, 3:04-4:59.

2. What does Wiesel mean by "the Kingdom of Night"? How does this image help reveal Wiesel's point of view in paragraphs 4–7? Highlight evidence from the text and annotate to explain the connections to his point of view.

3. What is the central idea of paragraph 8? What does Wiesel mean when he begins the paragraph, "And then I explain to him how naïve we were..."? Highlight examples from the text that illustrate this central idea. Then annotate to explain your answer.

4. What is Wiesel's purpose for delivering his speech? Highlight evidence from the last five paragraphs (9–13) of the text that will support your understanding. Annotate to explain how these details reveal the author's purpose.

5. According to Wiesel, what did the worldwide response to the Holocaust teach him about the world when he was still a young man? What does he feel the world's reaction should be when it faces future conflicts? Highlight evidence from the text and annotate to explain your ideas.

## WRITING PROMPT

How does the experience of reading the text of Elie Wiesel's "Nobel Prize Acceptance Speech" differ from the experience of watching the video of the speech? How do the visual and audio components of the video affect the message of the speech? Support your writing with evidence from both the video and the speech.

REMARKS
IN MEMORY OF
# THE VICTIMS OF THE HOLOCAUST

NON-FICTION
Ban Ki-Moon
2013

## INTRODUCTION

Ban Ki-moon is the eighth Secretary-General of the United Nations. He explained his call to serve the world's poorest and most vulnerable people as being rooted in his own experience: "I grew up in war and saw the United Nations help my country to recover and rebuild. That experience was a big part of what led me to pursue a career in public service." In the speech here, which was delivered at Park East Synagogue in New York City at a memorial for Holocaust victims, Ban famously asks, "Each time we hear 'never again', but can we truly say we have learned the lessons of these tragedies?"

# "The language of hatred is corrosive and contagious."

## FIRST READ

Rabbi Schneier,
President Hochberg,
Excellencies,
Ladies and gentlemen,

1   Shabat **Shalom.** Salaam. Peace to you all.

2   It is a great honour to be with you once again.

3   Thank you, Rabbi Schneier, for your gracious introduction. I hope every day to live up to your high praise and expectations.

4   On this day when we remember the victims of the Holocaust, let me pay special tribute to the survivors who have joined us.

5   Rabbi Schneier knows fully their pain and suffering, for he too is a survivor.

6   For most of us it is hard to imagine the anguish of knowing that you and your loved ones have been singled out to die because of your faith, your culture or your race.

7   Yet, this is the stark truth.

8   In the Second World War, Jews, Roma and Sinti, homosexuals, communists, the mentally ill—anyone who did not conform to Hitler's perverted ideology of Aryan perfection—were systematically persecuted, rounded up and transported to death camps.

9   Some were murdered immediately; others cruelly worked to death.

10  Such an operation takes extensive organization. It takes many people—from leaders to ordinary citizens—to participate, cooperate or simply turn a blind eye.

11   This is perhaps the greatest tragedy of **genocide**—and the reason why we must be ever vigilant.

12   The language of hatred is corrosive and contagious. Its moral corruption can eat into hearts and minds in even the most progressive or sophisticated societies.

13   The more often you hear that your neighbour is vile, subhuman, not worthy of the rights that you take for granted, the greater the chance of such beliefs taking root.

14   That is why I spoke so frankly and forcefully last year in Tehran about Holocaust denial.

15   It is why Rabbi Schneier and I and so many others are so committed to the United Nations Alliance of Civilizations.

16   Neither anti-Semitism nor Islamophobia nor other such forms of bias have a place in the 21st century world we are trying to build.

17   This is also why I worry about the continued stalemate in negotiations between Israel and the Palestinians.

18   We now have a whole generation of young people on both sides who risk growing up with a demonized, dehumanized—and utterly false—concept of their neighbours.

19   They need to be educated to co-exist peacefully with their neighbours.

20   The only way to build peace is to build bridges and break down walls.

21   Doing so will take courage, but it must be done.

22   This year, the United Nations has chosen "the courage to care" as the theme of the International Day of Commemoration in Memory of the Victims of the Holocaust.

23   We are honouring those who risked their lives and their families to save Jews and other victims of persecution from almost certain death.

24   Some, like Raoul Wallenberg, are household names.

25   But most are unsung heroes—brave men and women from all walks of life, and many nations. Teenagers and parents, parliamentarians and priests, journalists and diplomats—all had the courage to care.

26 Their example is as relevant today as ever—which is why the United Nations has produced an education kit for teachers to tell their story.

27 In a world where extremist acts of violence and hatred capture the headlines on an almost daily basis, we need to take inspiration from these ordinary people who took extraordinary steps to defend human dignity.

28 Ladies and gentlemen,

29 Last year I visited Srebrenica, the site of the worst act of genocide in Europe since the Holocaust.

30 I visited the graves and wept with the mothers of the slain.

31 It is not an easy place for a United Nations Secretary-General to visit.

32 The United Nations—the international community—failed to protect thousands of Bosnian Muslim men and boys from slaughter.

33 The shadow of Srebrenica has joined that of Rwanda, Cambodia, the Holocaust.

34 Each time we hear "never again."

35 But can we truly say we have learned the lessons of these tragedies?

36 As an international community, do we have the courage to care—and the resolve to act?

37 In 2005 the United Nations General Assembly—at the level of Heads of State and Governments—adopted the responsibility to protect.

38 It is a landmark concept. It puts the obligation firmly on States to protect their populations from genocide, crimes against humanity, war crimes or ethnic cleansing.

39 And in the face of these crimes and violations there is a corresponding duty of the international community to act.

40 The responsibility to protect applies everywhere and all the time. It has been implemented with success in a number of places, including in Libya and Côte d'Ivoire.

41 But today it faces a great test in Syria.

42 More than 60,000 people have now died in a conflict whose seeds lie in the peaceful demand of people for greater freedom.

43    We have seen a government brutally and mercilessly oppress dissent and fan the flames of a civil war that threatens to bring instability to a whole region.

44    I have repeatedly called for unity from the Security Council to decisively address this tragedy.

45    So too has the General Assembly—by an overwhelming majority.

46    Each day brings more suffering.

47    I met some of the refugees last month, in camps in Jordan and Turkey.

48    I talked to families who had fled with just what they could carry; children whose future has been thrown into uncertainty.

49    They told me that all they wanted was to go home and live in safety and security.

50    Today's theme challenges us: do we have the courage to care?

51    I am deeply concerned about the situation in Syria not simply because of the terrible suffering, but because of what may come next.

52    Each day's delay in resolving the crisis raises the spectre of the violence spreading along religious and ethnic lines.

53    Each day's delay sees new **atrocities** by both sides. It is essential that all perpetrators of international crimes understand that they will be held to account.

54    There will be no amnesties for those most responsible.

55    The old era of impunity is ending. In its place, slowly but surely, we are building a new age of accountability.

56    But the important thing is to end the violence in Syria—now—and begin the process of transition.

57    Too much blood has been shed. It is time for **reconciliation.**

58    There is a proverb that says: if you want revenge you should dig two graves.

59    Syria will need many men and women of courage who will reject revenge and embrace peace.

60    People like Rabbi Schneier.

Please note that excerpts and passages in the StudySync® library and this workbook are intended as touchstones to generate interest in an author's work. The excerpts and passages do not substitute for the reading of entire texts, and StudySync® strongly recommends that students seek out and purchase the whole literary or informational work in order to experience it as the author intended. Links to online resellers are available in our digital library. In addition, complete works may be ordered through an authorized reseller by filling out and returning to StudySync® the order form enclosed in this workbook.

Reading & Writing
Companion

**191**

61  He too visited Srebrenica last year.

62  He spoke in solidarity—as only someone who has shared indescribable suffering can.

63  And this is what he said:

64  "As a survivor I neither turned against man or God. Instead, in memory of my family and the many millions **exterminated** like them, I devoted my life to help build bridges between all of God's children in pursuit of peace and justice." End of quote.

65  Such forgiveness takes courage—the courage to see what is right and to do it.

66  Whatever one's faith, this is our duty—as individuals, as communities and as nations.

67  We have a responsibility to protect.

68  We must have the courage to care.

69  Thank you.

## THINK QUESTIONS   CA-CCSS: CA.RI.8.1, CA.RI.8.4, CA.L.8.4a, CA.L.8.4b

1. What does Ban Ki-moon mean when he uses the term "Aryan perfection" in his speech? Use evidence from the text to explain your inference.

2. Write two or three sentences explaining why the speaker believes hate speech, or the "language of hatred," causes problems. Support your answer with textual evidence.

3. Refer to one or more details from the text to support your understanding of why Ban Ki-moon wept on his visit to Srebrenica. In your evidence include ideas that are directly stated in the text as well as ideas that you have inferred from clues in the text.

4. Use context to determine the meaning of the word **atrocities** as it is used in "Remarks in Memory of the Victims of The Holocaust." Write your definition of *atrocities* and tell how you found it.

5. Use the context clues provided in the passage to determine the meaning of **shalom.** Write your definition of *shalom* and tell how you got it.

# CLOSE READ
CA-CCSS: CA.RI.8.1, CA.RI.8.2, CA.RI.8.3, CA.RI.8.4, CA.RI.8.5, CA.RI.8.6, CA.RI.8.8, CA.W.8.2

Reread the text "Remarks in Memory of the Victims of The Holocaust." As you reread, complete the Focus Questions below. Then use your answers and annotations from the questions to help you complete the Writing Prompt.

## FOCUS QUESTIONS

1. In about the middle of his speech, in the 34th paragraph, Ban Ki-moon recites two sentences: "Each time we hear 'never again.' But can we truly say we have learned the lessons of these tragedies?" Why does he place such a focus on what people say and how does he use these questions to reinforce the text structure of problem and solution?

2. Ban Ki-moon states that the Holocaust was an operation that demanded extensive organization and the participation of many people was needed to carry it out. In addition, too many people did nothing to try and stop it. What evidence does Ki-moon offer that this is still true today?

3. In discussing his visit to Srebrenica, Ban Ki-moon says he "wept with the mothers of the slain" and admits that Srebrenica is "not an easy place for a United Nations Secretary-General to visit." What is the effect of those statements on the tone of the speech? Highlight your textual evidence and make annotations to explain your choices.

4. At various points in the speech, Ban Ki-moon interjects himself into the events he is describing and the point he is making. How does he do this and what is his purpose in stressing his point of view?

5. What does Ban Ki-moon suggest the world do about genocide whenever it threatens to occur? What specific responses to dangerous conflicts does he suggest?

## WRITING PROMPT

What details does Ban Ki-moon include to support his purpose and point of view? Which details help create the tone of the speech? Use your understanding of informational text structure to determine how details in this speech support Ban Ki-moon's point of view. Include text evidence from the speech to support your response.

Please note that excerpts and passages in the StudySync® library and this workbook are intended as touchstones to generate interest in an author's work. The excerpts and passages do not substitute for the reading of entire texts, and StudySync® strongly recommends that students seek out and purchase the whole literary or informational work in order to experience it as the author intended. Links to online resellers are available in our digital library. In addition, complete works may be ordered through an authorized reseller by filling out and returning to StudySync® the order form enclosed in this workbook.

Reading & Writing Companion

**193**

# A LETTER FROM ROBERT

English Language
Development

**DRAMA**

## INTRODUCTION

This short play takes place in London after the Blitz, a period of intense bombing by the German Air Force during World War II. The Blitz, which lasted eight months from September 1940 to May 1941, destroyed or damaged over one million homes and killed more than 40,000 civilians. In the drama, a grieving mother returns to London after the bombing has ended, only to find that her home has been destroyed.

# "...I'll always wish to see him coming around the corner, but I never will."

## FIRST READ

1 [*A* **residential** *street in London. It is early morning on a day in July 1941. We see two tall buildings, damaged but standing. Rubble from a third building lies between them. MARGARET takes cautious steps toward the* **debris**. *When she reaches the spot that used to be her doorstep, she weeps. The front door of one of the buildings swings open, and HELEN steps out.*]

2 HELEN: I was starting to think I'd never see you again!

3 MARGARET *(jumping and wiping away tears)*: You **startled** me. I'm relieved to see you've survived. Attacking military bases during a war is one thing. But bombing innocent civilians? I had to go. I promised Robert I'd stay safe . . . You should have come to my sister's to wait out the attacks.

4 HELEN: It will take more than incendiary bombs to scare me. I was lucky. Broken windows and a hole in the wall. Nothing that can't be fixed. You have my sympathy about your house. You can stay with me until this **dreadful** war ends. No sense in starting construction now.

5 MARGARET *(sadly)*: I am not rebuilding. I am leaving London.

6 HELEN *(with surprise)*: You can't leave! Who will your son come home to after the war if you're not here?

7 MARGARET: My son won't be coming home. I received a telegram from the Royal Air Force. Robert was killed in combat.

8 HELEN: Stay with me. We will get through this together.

9 MARGARET: There are too many memories. Everywhere there's something that reminds me . . . I'll always wish to see him coming around the corner, but I never will. There is nothing left for me here.

10  HELEN: Some of your things survived the blast. [HELEN *pulls a letter out of her pocket.*]

11  MARGARET: It's Robert's letter. [*begins to read*] The twenty-second of May, nineteen forty. My dearest mother, two days ago our Prime Minister gave a radio address urging us to ready ourselves for **defense** during these terrible times. These past two days I have thought of little else.

12  [*As MARGARET reads, another voice joins hers, as if coming from a ghost. It is* ROBERT'S VOICE.]

13  MARGARET and ROBERT: I have thought about the German attacks in France, Denmark, Norway, Belgium, and the Netherlands. As much as it pains me to leave you, Mother, I know their pain is greater.

14  [*MARGARET'S VOICE dies out, and ROBERT'S VOICE continues alone.*]

15  ROBERT'S VOICE: It is my duty as a citizen of the world to rise up and fight against the forces of evil that are spreading across the continent. I will take my place among the brave men of the Royal Air Force. I will fight for Britain, for Europe, and, most of all, for you.

## USING LANGUAGE    CA-CCSS: ELD.PII.8.1.Ex

Complete the chart by sorting the items from the options below into those that are characters, those that are stage directions, and those that are dialogue.

| Options | | |
|---|---|---|
| Stay with me. We will get through this together. | [MARGARET *takes cautious steps toward the debris.*] | [MARGARET'S VOICE *dies out, and* ROBERT'S VOICE *continues alone.*] |
| I am leaving London. | ROBERT | Broken windows and a hole in the wall. Nothing that can't be fixed. |
| MARGARET | [HELEN *pulls a letter out of her pocket.*] | HELEN |

| Characters | Stage Directions | Dialogue |
|---|---|---|
| | | |
| | | |
| | | |

## MEANINGFUL INTERACTIONS    CA-CCSS: ELD.PI.8.1.Ex

Work with your group to discuss your first impressions of the text. First, take turns saying what you think about the characters, the setting, and Margaret's decision to leave London. Then, build on your peers' responses by asking questions and explaining why you agree or disagree with their ideas. Use the speaking frames to support your discussion. Last, use the self-assessment rubric to evaluate your participation in the discussion.

- In my opinion, Margaret / Helen / Robert is . . . because . . .

- In my opinion, London after the Blitz is . . . because . . .

- I think Margaret wants to leave London because . . .

- I think you said . . . Why do you think that?

- I agree / disagree because . . .

## SELF-ASSESSMENT RUBRIC    CA-CCSS: ELD.PI.8.1.Ex

|  | 4<br>I did this well. | 3<br>I did this pretty well. | 2<br>I did this a little bit. | 1<br>I did not do this. |
|---|---|---|---|---|
| I took an active part with others in doing the assigned task. |  |  |  |  |
| I contributed effectively to the group's discussion. |  |  |  |  |
| I waited my turn to speak. |  |  |  |  |
| I asked group members questions about their ideas. |  |  |  |  |
| I built on my group members' responses by explaining why I agreed or disagreed with their ideas. |  |  |  |  |

# REREAD

Reread paragraphs 1–8 of "A Letter from Robert." After you reread, complete the Using Language and Meaningful Interactions activities.

## ⚙ USING LANGUAGE   CA-CCSS: ELD.PI.8.6.c.Ex

Read each word, the root, and affix meanings in the first three columns. Complete each row by filling in the correct definition from the Definition Options box.

| Definition Options | |
|---|---|
| regular people; not members of the military | the process of building something |
| the feeling of support for someone else | relating to a weapon that sets fires |
| not deserving of harm | |

| Word | Root Meaning | Affix Meaning | Definition |
|---|---|---|---|
| innocent | *noc-* meaning "harm" | *in-* meaning "not" | |
| civilians | *civ-* meaning "citizen" | *-an* meaning "one that is" | |
| incendiary | *cend-* meaning "glowing" | *in-* meaning "on" *-ary* meaning "relating to" | |
| sympathy | *path-* meaning "feeling" | *sym-* meaning "with" | |
| construction | *struct-* meaning "build" | *con-* meaning "with" *-ion* meaning "act or process" | |

## MEANINGFUL INTERACTIONS CA-CCSS: ELD.PI.8.1.Ex

Based on what you have read in "A Letter from Robert," how do you think each character feels about London and the war? What textual evidence supports your ideas? Work in small groups to practice asking relevant questions and answering those questions using textual evidence. Use the speaking frames to support your discussion. Then, use the self-assessment rubric to evaluate your participation in the discussion.

- In my opinion, Margaret / Helen / Robert feels . . . about the war because . . .

- In my opinion, Margaret / Helen feels . . . about London because . . .

- The characters' perspectives are alike / different because . . .

- What text evidence do you base your ideas on? Is it . . . ?

- You said . . . , but did you consider . . . ?

- What else does the text say about . . . ?

## SELF-ASSESSMENT RUBRIC CA-CCSS: ELD.PI.8.1.Ex

|  | 4 I did this well. | 3 I did this pretty well. | 2 I did this a little bit. | 1 I did not do this. |
|---|---|---|---|---|
| I expressed my ideas clearly. |  |  |  |  |
| I used textual evidence to support my ideas. |  |  |  |  |
| I asked relevant questions during the discussion. |  |  |  |  |
| I answered questions using textual evidence. |  |  |  |  |

# REREAD

Reread paragraphs 9–15 of "A Letter from Robert." After you reread, complete the Using Language and Meaningful Interactions activities.

## USING LANGUAGE  CA-CCSS: ELD.PII.8.5.Ex

Fill in the blanks to complete the sentences about the characters in the play.

1.  Find the sentence in paragraph 9 that tells what Margaret wishes.

    I'll _____ wish to see him coming _____ .

2.  Find the sentence in paragraph 10 that tells where Helen gets the letter.

    HELEN pulls a letter _____ .

3.  Find the sentence in paragraph 11 that tells how people ready themselves for war.

    … our Prime Minister gave a radio address urging us to ready ourselves _____

    _____ .

4.  Find the sentence in paragraph 15 that shows what Robert thinks his duty is.

    It is my duty _____ to rise up and fight _____

    _____ that are spreading _____ .

5.  Find the sentence in paragraph 15 that shows what Robert will fight for.

    I will fight _____ , _____ , and, most of all, _____ .

## MEANINGFUL INTERACTIONS  CA-CCSS: ELD.PI.8.11.a.Ex

In "A Letter from Robert," Robert decides to join the Royal Air Force, Helen decides to stay in London during the Blitz, and Margaret decides to leave London after she loses her son and her home. Choose one character and tell whether or not you agree with his or her decision. What evidence from the text supports your opinion? Work in small groups to practice sharing and discussing your opinions, using the speaking frames.

*   I agree / disagree with Robert's / Helen's / Margaret's decision to … because …

*   My opinion is based on …

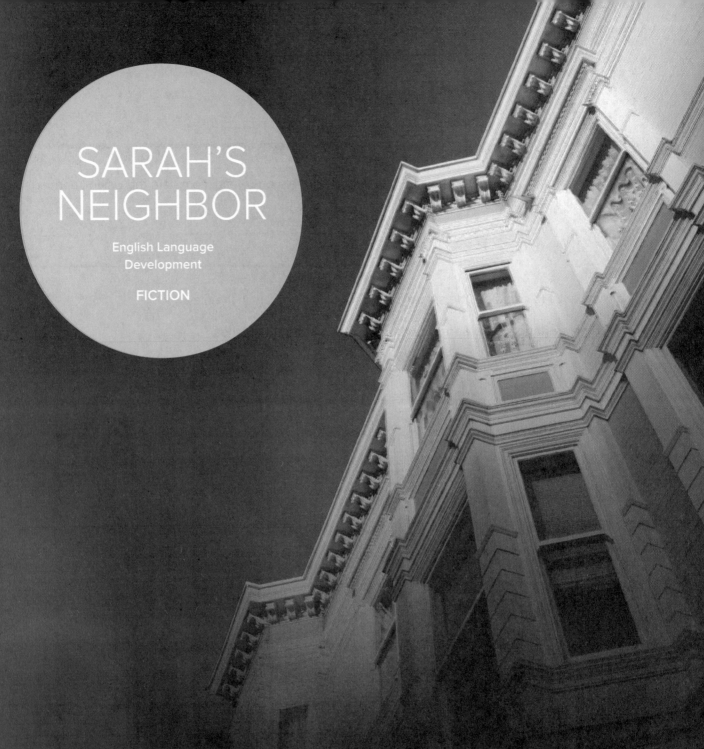

# SARAH'S NEIGHBOR

English Language
Development

**FICTION**

## INTRODUCTION

Set in San Francisco shortly after the bombing of Pearl Harbor during World War II, this short story focuses on a preteen girl's struggle to accept her parents' changing attitudes toward their Japanese neighbors, including her best friend, Ayako. As twelve year-old Sarah watches Ayako through the window, she longs to rekindle their friendship—but she is too scared of her father to disobey his orders.

# "'That girl and her family are the enemy,' he'd said."

## FIRST READ

1   Sarah looked through the kitchen window as she helped her mother do the dishes. Ayako, her neighbor and former best friend, sat on the swing set outside. She looked as lonely as a ghost. Nothing would have delighted Sarah more than dropping the silverware and **erupting** through the door to join Ayako, but she knew she couldn't. Her mind flashed to the conversation she had with her parents a few weeks ago, after the Japanese attacked Pearl Harbor.

2   Her father had just come home from an arduous shift at the San Francisco police department. People were angry about the bombing, he'd explained. There had been fighting in the streets. They couldn't trust the Japanese anymore—not even Ayako. He pulled out his sergeant's **badge** and started polishing it as a way of **accentuating** his **authority**. "That girl and her family are the enemy," he'd said.

3   Later, Sarah asked her mother to explain why she couldn't be friends with Ayako. It didn't make any sense. The bombing of Pearl Harbor was a serious attack. But Ayako hadn't been a part of it. Her mother **clasped** Sarah's hand. "Ayako didn't do anything bad. But she's a **symbol** of the people who did. The sergeant has given you your orders. It's best you follow them."

4   Sarah grabbed a plate to wash and focused on the circular movement of her own hands. She glued her eyes to the plate to take her mind off Ayako. There would be a harsh penalty for disobeying the sergeant's orders. She ached to ask her father for permission to go outside, but trepidation kept her mouth closed.

Please note that excerpts and passages in the StudySync® library and this workbook are intended as touchstones to generate interest in an author's work. The excerpts and passages do not substitute for the reading of entire texts, and StudySync® strongly recommends that students seek out and purchase the whole literary or informational work in order to experience it as the author intended. Links to online resellers are available in our digital library. In addition, complete works may be ordered through an authorized reseller by filling out and returning to StudySync® the order form enclosed in this workbook.

Reading & Writing Companion   **203**

5 The next morning, Sarah and her mother made a list of guests for her thirteenth birthday party. Her mother recited the names of each child from Sarah's class, and Sarah wrote them down. Then she had an idea. Tightening her grip on the pencil, she urgently sneaked another name into the middle of the list: Ayako's.

6 Without saying a word, she handed the list to her mother. At that moment, her father came in and began to scan the list over his wife's shoulder. When he got to Ayako's name, he practically **vibrated** with rage.

7 He faced Sarah and growled. "How many times have I told you that this girl cannot be your friend? I will not have my daughter spending time with someone like her! You will never see this girl again, or I will never see you again. Understand?"

8 Sarah opened her mouth. She wanted to stand up for herself. She wanted to tell her father that he was wrong, that Ayako is a good person. But all that came out was silence.

USING LANGUAGE CA-CCSS: ELD.PI.8.6.c.Ex, ELD.PI.8.12.b.Ex

Read each word. Complete each row by filling in the correct root or affix meaning in the second column and definition in the third column.

| Root/Affix Meaning Options | | Definition Options |
|---|---|---|
| *ardu-* meaning "difficult" <br> *-ous* meaning "full of" | *circ-* meaning "circle" <br> *-ar* meaning "relating to" | relating to circles <br><br> the state of feeling intense fear |
| *sil-* meaning "quiet" <br> *-ence* meaning "the state of" | *trepid-* meaning "tremble" <br> *-ation* meaning "the state of" | full of difficulty <br><br> the state of being quiet |
| | *pen-* meaning "punish" | a punishment |

| Word | Root/Affix Meaning | Definition |
|---|---|---|
| arduous | | |
| circular | | |
| penalty | | |
| trepidation | | |
| silence | | |

Please note that excerpts and passages in the StudySync® library and this workbook are intended as touchstones to generate interest in an author's work. The excerpts and passages do not substitute for the reading of entire texts, and StudySync® strongly recommends that students seek out and purchase the whole literary or informational work in order to experience it as the author intended. Links to online resellers are available in our digital library. In addition, complete works may be ordered through an authorized reseller by filling out and returning to StudySync® the order form enclosed in this workbook.

Reading & Writing Companion **205**

## MEANINGFUL INTERACTIONS  CA-CCSS: ELD.PI.8.1.Ex

Work with your group to discuss your first impressions of the text. Take turns saying what you think about the characters and their situation. How would you describe the characters? How do the events in the story make you feel? Why do you think Sarah does not say anything to her father at the end of the story? Be sure to listen to your group members' ideas and wait your turn before speaking. Use the speaking frames to support your discussion. Last, use the self-assessment rubric to evaluate your participation in the discussion.

- In my opinion, Sarah / Sarah's mother / Sarah's father is . . . because . . .

- The events of the story make me feel . . . because . . .

- In my opinion, Sarah cannot speak because . . .

- I think you said . . . Why do you think that?

- I heard you say . . . , but . . . said . . .

- I agree with . . . because . . .

## SELF-ASSESSMENT RUBRIC  CA-CCSS: ELD.PI.8.1.Ex

| | 4<br>I did this well. | 3<br>I did this pretty well. | 2<br>I did this a little bit. | 1<br>I did not do this. |
|---|---|---|---|---|
| I took an active part with others in doing the assigned task. | | | | |
| I contributed effectively to the group's discussion. | | | | |
| I waited my turn to speak. | | | | |
| I listened carefully to my group members' ideas. | | | | |

# REREAD

Reread paragraphs 1–3 of "Sarah's Neighbor." After you reread, complete the Using Language and Meaningful Interactions activities.

## USING LANGUAGE   CA-CCSS: ELD.PI.8.8.Ex

Read each quotation and note the word or phrase in bold. Then compare it to its synonym. Complete the chart by filling in the effect the bold word or phrase has on the sentence.

| The bold word or phrase emphasizes... Options | | |
|---|---|---|
| the sergeant's power over Sarah. | how isolated Ayako must feel. | the impact of the war. |
| the way the sergeant treats his family. | how restricted Sarah feels. | |

| Quotation | Synonym | The bold word or phrase emphasizes.... |
|---|---|---|
| [Ayako] looked **as lonely as a ghost**. | alone | |
| Nothing would have delighted Sarah more than dropping the silverware and **erupting** through the door to join Ayako, but she knew she couldn't. | running | |
| He pulled out his sergeant's badge and started polishing it as a way of accentuating his **authority**. | job | |
| "That girl and her family are the **enemy**," he'd said. | opponent | |
| "The sergeant has given you your **orders**." | instructions | |

## MEANINGFUL INTERACTIONS CA-CCSS: ELD.PI.8.1.Ex

Based on what you have read in "Sarah's Neighbor," what do you think about Sarah's relationship with each of her parents? What do you think about the characters' actions? Use the speaking frames below to ask and answer questions in small groups. Then, use the self-assessment rubric to evaluate your participation in the discussion.

- In my opinion, Sarah's relationship with her parents is . . . because . . .

- I think Sarah's relationship with her mother is . . . than her relationship with her father because . . .

- I think Sarah's choice to add Ayako's name to the list is . . . because . . .

- What should Sarah do when her father growls at her?

- I think Sarah should . . . because . . .

- Do you think Sarah should . . .

- I think this action is . . . because . . .

- I think you said . . . Why do you think that?

## SELF-ASSESSMENT RUBRIC CA-CCSS: ELD.PI.8.1.Ex

| | 4<br>I did this well. | 3<br>I did this pretty well. | 2<br>I did this a little bit. | 1<br>I did not do this. |
|---|---|---|---|---|
| I took an active part with others in doing the assigned task. | | | | |
| I contributed effectively to the group's discussion. | | | | |
| I asked relevant questions. | | | | |
| I answered questions clearly. | | | | |

# REREAD

Reread paragraphs 4–8 of "Sarah's Neighbor." After you reread, complete the Using Language and Meaningful Interactions activities.

 ## USING LANGUAGE CA-CCSS: ELD.PII.8.2.a.Ex

Read each sentence. Choose the noun each bold referring word or words refer to.

1.  Sarah grabbed a plate to wash and focused on the circular movement of her own hands. **She** glued her eyes to the plate to take her mind off Ayako.

    ○ Sarah          ○ Ayako

2.  There would be a harsh penalty for disobeying **the sergeant's** orders. She ached to ask her father for permission to go outside.

    ○ Sarah's father          ○ Sarah's mother

3.  The next morning, Sarah and her mother made a list of guests for **her** thirteenth birthday party.

    ○ Sarah's mother          ○ Sarah

4.  At that moment, her father came in and began to scan the list over **his wife's** shoulder.

    ○ Sarah          ○ Sarah's mother

5.  He faced Sarah and growled. "How many times have I told you that **this girl** cannot be your friend?"

    ○ Ayako          ○ Sarah

6.  **She** wanted to tell her father that he was wrong, that Ayako is a good person.

    ○ Sarah          ○ Ayako

 ## MEANINGFUL INTERACTIONS CA-CCSS: ELD.PI.8.1.Ex

What do you think the theme of "Sarah's Neighbor" is? What key ideas from the text support that theme? Use the speaking frames to practice determining the theme and paraphrasing key ideas with a partner.

- In my opinion, the theme of the text is . . .

- One key idea from the text that supports this theme is . . .

- Another key idea that supports this theme is . . .

- These key ideas help me determine the theme because . . .

- I think you said the theme is . . . I agree / disagree because . . .

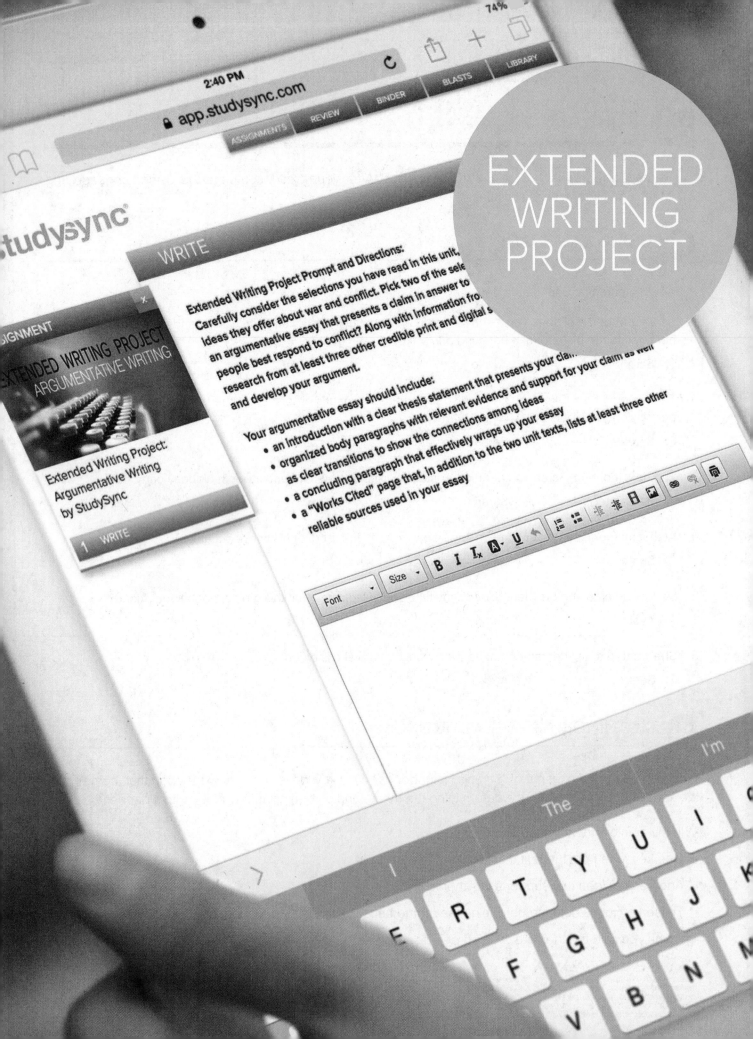

EXTENDED WRITING PROJECT

EXTENDED WRITING PROJECT
ARGUMENTATIVE WRITING

# ARGUMENTATIVE WRITING

## WRITING PROMPT

Carefully consider the selections you have read in this unit, including their themes and the ideas they offer about war and conflict. Pick two of the selections from the unit and write an argumentative essay that presents a claim in answer to the following question: how can people best respond to conflict? Along with information from the selections, include research from at least three other credible print and digital sources to support your claim and develop your argument.

Your argumentative essay should include:

- An introduction with a clear thesis statement that presents your claim
- Organized body paragraphs with relevant evidence and support for your claim as well as clear transitions to show the connections among ideas
- A concluding paragraph that effectively wraps up your essay
- A Works Cited page that, in addition to the two unit texts, lists at least three other reliable sources used in your essay

Argumentative writing introduces a claim, or proposition, and supports it with clear evidence from a variety of relevant and reliable sources. It ends with a conclusion that sums up the arguments and evidence that supports the claim and restates the main idea. In this regard, writing an argument has much in common with other types of nonfiction writing. For example, it has a main idea, it presents supporting details related to the main idea, and it has the same physical structure with an introduction, body, and conclusion. The main difference between argumentative writing and other kinds of writing is its purpose. Argumentative writing is used to convince the audience that a claim is correct or valid. It can also be used to persuade readers that the author's

Copyright © BookheadEd Learning, LLC

main idea is more valid than the ideas of others. This form of writing can be found in essays that offer opinions, such as editorials, letters to the editor in newspapers, debates, and similar texts. Features of argumentative writing include:

- Introduction with a clear claim or proposition, which can be thought of as a thesis statement
- A clear and logical organizational structure that includes an introduction, a body, and a conclusion
- Supporting details drawn from a combination of reliable, relevant sources
- Transitions that clearly show the relationships between ideas
- A formal style, achieved by precise language and domain-specific vocabulary
- Citations of sources and textual evidence to support claims
- A concluding paragraph that summarizes the proof that supports the thesis statement

As you continue with this extended writing project, you will receive additional instructions and practice to help you craft each of the elements of strong argumentative writing in your own essay.

##  STUDENT MODEL

Before you begin writing your own argumentative essay, read this essay that one student wrote in response to the writing prompt. As you read this Student Model, make note of the features of argumentative writing listed above by highlighting and annotating the points and structures that the student used in his text.

### Attitude: *One Secret to Survival*

For centuries, human beings have demonstrated countless ways to be cruel to other groups of people, especially during times of war. Entire ethnic groups have been targeted for the simple reason that they were born into the "wrong" culture or family. Enslavement, imprisonment, and even wholesale slaughter of people who were thought to be "different" have put black marks on the histories of many countries. This mistreatment by people in authority can damage its victims, even if they survive physically. Yet there are individuals who manage to come through their ordeal and heal. There are also people who, even though they did not survive, continue to inspire us to this day with stories of their courage.

One well-known example of such inspiration comes from *Anne Frank, in Anne Frank: The Diary of a Young Girl*. This young girl has inspired millions with her firsthand account of life for her and her Jewish family as they hid from the Nazis in Amsterdam. Other inspiring stories come from the real-life letters of children in the United States' internment camps for Japanese Americans during World War II. Some of these letters were collected in the book *Dear Miss Breed: True Stories of the Japanese American Incarceration During World War II and a Librarian Who Made a Difference* by Joanne Oppenheim. This book, along with *Anne Frank: The Diary of a Young Girl,* explain the situations these families underwent, but they also show one path to graceful endurance: a positive attitude. Coping with impossible situations, such as living in hiding from the Nazis or enduring the Japanese internment camps, took a certain kind of strength, along with a positive attitude. As these works show, positive thinking is one of the best ways to respond to conflict, as well as an effective path to healing for those who survive physical abuse or hardship at the hands of others.

The impact of a positive attitude is shown in the thoughts and words of real people. In *Anne Frank: The Diary of a Young Girl,* Anne's accounts reveal a positive attitude that later served as inspiration for millions of people. For example, in her diary entry dated Saturday, July 11, 1942, even while living in crowded, difficult conditions while hiding from the Nazis—worried that the entire family might be discovered at any time—Anne notes that "Thanks to Father—who brought my entire postcard and movie-star collection here beforehand—and to a brush and a pot of glue, I was able to plaster the wall with pictures. It looks much more cheerful" (Frank 20). She also writes of the everyday details of her life, such as the chiming of the clock near their hidden location. A similar example from a different situation comes from a Japanese internment camp in the United States from the same period. In *Dear Miss Breed: True Stories of the Japanese American Incarceration During World War II and a Librarian Who Made a Difference,* Louise Ogawa writes to Miss Breed about the beauty of the Colorado River they had crossed on their way to the incarceration camp. Louise showed that she was trying to find positive things to think about when she wrote, "Yesterday, I ate rice, weenies, and cabbage with a knife. That was a new experience for me!" (Oppenheim 114). These two individuals show that they were trying to keep a positive attitude in extremely difficult circumstances. Although some may argue that a positive attitude didn't really help Anne Frank, who ended up dying in the Bergen-Belsen concentration camp, her strength and spirit while enduring tremendously difficult circumstances have inspired countless individuals across the decades. The diary has been translated into 70 languages, and over 28 million people have visited her home since it opened as a museum in 1960 (The Anne Frank House). Her positive attitude therefore has had a profound impact beyond her own life and cannot be discounted.

More evidence about the effects of a positive attitude can be found in the writings of certain scholars. Some of them have studied how people react to hardships that are created by other human beings. An article from the Florida Center for Instructional Technology talks about different types of music that was created during the Holocaust as the Jewish people struggled to survive. So many resistance songs were written at the time, according to the article, that composers simply couldn't create enough tunes. This forced people to recycle existing music with the new words that expressed the things they were feeling (The Florida Center for Instructional Technology 1). One line from a play of the time has a child in a Warsaw ghetto orphanage crying, "I cannot sing . . . I'm so hungry." A caretaker replies, "We all are! That is why we must sing" (The Florida Center for Instructional Technology 1). Caroline Schaumann of Emory University argues that "Remaining mentally engaged in the world, whether the greater one beyond the physical barriers imposed by the Nazis or the lesser one inside the camps, was another significant aid to survival" (Schaumann 9). Obviously, attitude plays a key role in surviving such situations.

Psychologists also agree that the mental attitude of individuals in these horrible situations is very important. Karen Lawson, MD, states that ". . . positive emotions literally reverse the physical effects of negativity and build up psychological resources that contribute to a flourishing life" (Lawson 2). In one study cited by Lawson, people who focused on gratitude felt happier, slept better, and had fewer physical problems than those who did not. She also notes that strong people have the ability to maintain positive feelings while enduring extremely negative circumstances, allowing them to overcome some of the negative impacts of their situations (Lawson 2). She concludes that people who focus on the positive routinely become stronger in the face of crisis (Lawson 3). This shows that positive attitudes must have helped some people face these dire situations with such courage that we remember them today.

Attitude, then, is not only important in our day-to-day lives. It is also necessary for survival in situations where life has been turned upside down by outside forces, and even in circumstances when safety is threatened. Positive attitude contributes to the psychological strength that helps victims of even horrible situations like the Holocaust and the internment camps continue to survive under extremely harsh conditions. These thought patterns continue to serve victims of trauma after they are returned to safety. It can contribute to their healing. The stories told in *Anne Frank: The Diary of a Young Girl* and in *Dear Miss Breed: True Stories of the Japanese American Incarceration During World War II and a Librarian Who Made a Difference* show the importance of such an attitude and the inspiration that people such as Anne Frank and Louise Ogawa provide. Positive attitudes contribute to the mental and emotional strength that is necessary to survive physical abuse or hardship at the hands of others.

## Works Cited

Frank, Anne. *Anne Frank: The Diary of a Young Girl.* New York: Doubleday, 1952.

Lawson, Karen, M.D. "How Do Thoughts & Emotions Impact Health?" *Taking Charge of Your Health and Well-Being.* University of Minnesota. Web. 12 Dec. 2014. http://www.takingcharge.csh.umn.edu/enhance-your-wellbeing/health/thoughts-emotions/how-do-thoughts-emotions-impact-health

"Music of the Ghettos and Camps." *A Teacher's Guide to the Holocaust.* The Florida Center for Instructional Technology, College of Education, University of South Florida. C. 1997–2013. Web. 12 Dec. 2014. http://fcit.coedu.usf.edu/holocaust/arts/musVicti.htm

Oppenheim, Joanne. *Dear Miss Breed: True Stories of the Japanese American Incarceration During World War II and a Librarian Who Made a Difference.* New York: Scholastic, Inc., 2006.

Schaumann, Caroline. "Factors Influencing Survival During the Holocaust." *History in Dispute, Vol. 11: The Holocaust, 1933–1945.* Benjamin Frankel, ed. St. James Press, 1999. Web. 12 December 2014. 1999. Web. 12 December 2014. http://www.google.com/url?sa=t&rct=j&q=&esrc=s&source=web&cd=1&ved=0CCMQFjAA&url=http%3A%2F%2Ffacweb.northseattle.edu%2Fcadler%2FGlobal_Dialogues%2FReadings%2FMaus_Readings%2FFactors%2520Influencing%2520Survival%2520during%2520the%2520Holocaust.

doc&ei=YT-LVKu0KYq0yQSCpoCoDQ&usg=AFQjCNEoEdrB6D18vVuQyPy96
REwrVu1mQ&sig2=Ui_cnN68CkQxmdGvtLNPWA&bvm=bv.81828268,d.aWw&
cad=rja

Virtual Museum of The Anne Frank House. Anne Frank Stichting. 28 April 2010.
Web. 27 March 2015. http://www.annefrank.org/en/subsites/timeline/postwar-
period-1945—present-day/the-diary-is-published/1950/the-diary-of-anne-
frank-is-published-in-germany-in-an-edition-of-4500-copies-a-very-
successful-paperback-edition-follows-in-1955/#!/en/subsites/timeline/
postwar-period-1945—present-day/the-diary-is-published/1950/the-diary-
of-anne-frank-is-published-in-germany-in-an-edition-of-4500-copies-a-very-
successful-paperback-edition-follows-in-1955/

http://www.annefrank.org/en/News/Press/Visitor-numbers/

## THINK QUESTIONS

1. What is the claim in this essay, and where does it appear?

2. What support does the writer provide to convince her audience that her claim is valid?

3. How does the writer give proper credit to her sources?

4. As you consider the writing prompt, which selections or other resources do you plan to use to write your own argumentative essay? What are some ideas that you may want to develop in your own piece?

5. Based on what you have read, listened to, or researched, how would you respond to the question: *What does our response to conflict say about us?*

## PREWRITE

**CA-CCSS:** CA.RI.8.1, CA.RI.8.2, CA.RI.8.3, CA.W.8.1a, CA.W.8.5, CA.W.8.6, CA.W.8.9b, CA.SL.8.1a

### WRITING PROMPT

Carefully consider the selections you have read in this unit, including their themes and the ideas they offer about war and conflict. Pick two of the selections from the unit and write an argumentative essay that presents a claim in answer to the following question: how can people best respond to conflict? Along with information from the selections, include research from at least three other credible print and digital sources to support your claim and develop your argument.

Your argumentative essay should include:

- An introduction with a clear thesis statement that presents your claim
- Organized body paragraphs with relevant evidence and support for your claim as well as clear transitions to show the connections among ideas
- A concluding paragraph that effectively wraps up your essay
- A Works Cited page that, in addition to the two unit texts, lists at least three other reliable sources used in your essay

In addition to studying techniques authors use to present information, you have been reading and learning about stories that feature firsthand accounts of people who lived through times of conflict. In this Extended Writing Project, you will use argumentative writing techniques to compose your own argumentative essay about how people can best respond to conflict.

Since the topic of your argumentative essay will have to do with how people can best respond to conflicts, you will want to think about how the people you've read about handled the situations in which they found themselves. Consider the following questions:

Please note that excerpts and passages in the StudySync® library and this workbook are intended as touchstones to generate interest in an author's work. The excerpts and passages do not substitute for the reading of entire texts, and StudySync® strongly recommends that students seek out and purchase the whole literary or informational work in order to experience it as the author intended. Links to online resellers are available in our digital library. In addition, complete works may be ordered through an authorized reseller by filling out and returning to StudySync® the order form enclosed in this workbook.

Reading & Writing Companion    **217**

- What harsh situation or conflict did the people in the text face?
- How did this situation affect their daily lives?
- What specific behaviors and attitudes characterized their response to the situation?
- What impact did their response to the situation have on them?
- What ideas does the text suggest about how people can best respond to conflict?

Make a list of the answers to these questions and any others you think of for at least two different texts from this unit. As you note your ideas, do you see any patterns or commonalities? Are there ideas that are repeated? Remember that you will be designing a claim and then supporting it with evidence from the texts you've read in this unit and from your own research. Looking for patterns and thoughts that can be thoroughly supported will help you solidify the ideas that you want to address in your essay. Use this model to get started with your own prewriting:

**Text:** *Anne Frank: The Diary of a Young Girl* by Anne Frank

**Conflict:** Anne and her family were in danger from the Nazis during World War II. The Franks were Jewish, and the Nazis were sending Jewish people to concentration camps, where they were either killed upon arrival or worked to death.

**What Happened:** Anne and her family went into hiding in the home of a friend. They were uprooted from their own house, had little contact with others, and lived in cramped, crowded rooms. Anne's diary is a record of the many things she did to make the best of a bad situation, such as pasting cheerful postcards on the wall and attempting to view the experience as a kind of "vacation." These details reveal her positive attitude, which likely made the ordeal easier for her to bear.

## SKILL:
## RESEARCH AND
## NOTE-TAKING

## DEFINE

Several types of writing require authors to conduct research in order to find evidence to support their thesis or claim. **Research** is the process of asking questions about a topic and finding answers from multiple sources in print or online. Consider your topic and claim. Then ask yourself at least two or three questions whose answers will help you prove your point. Examine other articles, websites, books, speeches, or other related information to gather answers to your research questions. If you find too much information, and you're overwhelmed, you should consider narrowing your questions and making them more specific. If, on the other hand, you have difficulty finding enough sources to examine, you may need to broaden your research questions. In other words, your questions should guide your research, and your research results will lead you to refine your questions.

As you research to find support for your claim, you will need to consult multiple sources. **Sources** are the articles, documents, websites, books, or other information that an author uses to gather information about his or her topic. It is important to use only reliable sources. **Reliable sources** are those that provide accurate, trustworthy, and unbiased information about the topic. Examples of reliable sources include websites from the government or from academic institutions. Articles or books written by experts in the field, or firsthand accounts of events written by people who were present at the time (primary sources) are also reliable sources. Some types of sources are noted for being unreliable, and should not be used for academic writing. These include personal websites, blogs, advertisements, commercial literature (.com websites), and social media posts. These are not considered reliable because they contain personal opinions. The authors are also likely to have an agenda that may not include an honest or balanced presentation of facts.

As you explore the sources of information for your research, you will need to write down some of the information that you find. **Note-taking** is writing down the answers to your research questions as well as any other information that seems important about your topic or claim. It is also important when taking notes that you write down the details that identify the source. This includes the names of the authors, the title, and the publisher. If you copy words, phrases, or sentences directly, be sure to note where they came from within the document so you can give proper credit in your essay. If you do not write down direct quotations, be sure you have accurately paraphrased the author's ideas so you do not accidentally plagiarize the work of others. When you paraphrase, you express the meaning of something written or spoken using different words. But be careful. You do not want to misrepresent an author's ideas by paraphrasing them too broadly. At the same time, you need to change more than a word or two when you paraphrase.

## IDENTIFICATION AND APPLICATION

- Writers begin research by framing one, two, or more questions related to their topic and claim. These will guide research by providing a focus that the writer can search for.

- Research is a cycle in which you create a few questions, look for sources of related information, and then refine the questions and search again. There are several reasons to refine search questions:

  › Finding too much information means that the questions are too broad. Writers should make the questions more specific or eliminate some questions if too much information in too many sources is found.

  › Finding too little information or too few sources means that questions may be too narrowly focused. Change the questions to be more general or add more questions to the search.

  › Writers should keep in mind that more specific search terms will narrow their search results. For example, "Women in the Civil War" will likely lead to fewer but more specific results than "the Civil War."

  › Writers have several tools available for searching. In addition to search engines, other resources include scholarly databases, libraries, interviews with experts, museum collections, and so forth.

- Just as writers should use multiple tools for searching, they should also plan to consult a wide variety of sources as they research.

  › These can include (but are not limited to) print sources; audio-visual sources such as documentaries, podcasts, photographs, or films; and electronic sources such as websites, articles, speeches and interviews.

- Primary sources come directly from people who experienced an event. This can include letters, photographs, diaries or journals, official documents, autobiographies, and interviews. These sources can often provide very convincing evidence.

- Secondary sources generally include written interpretation and analysis of primary source materials. Secondary sources include articles from encyclopedias, textbooks or histories, news analyses, or documentaries about the topic. These sources can also provide useful information.

- It is important for writers of argumentative essays to use reliable sources only. The sources should be accurate and unbiased. Reliable sources include information from experts respected in the field, researchers, academic programs, or the government.

  › Writers should evaluate online sources based on the ending of the URL or web address. URLs that contain ".gov" are typically maintained by government agencies. Those that contain ".edu" are run by academic institutions such as universities or schools. Those that contain ".org" addresses are typically operated by museums or other non-profit agencies. All of these are likely to supply accurate information to support claims.

  › Other sources of reliable information include online news agencies or respected print publishers.

- The writer should think about and evaluate each source. Make sure it is accurate, related to the topic, and appropriate for your audience.

- Writers need to take many notes while doing research. It is important to keep these notes well-organized. The following strategies help writers take notes. They will be useful when writing an argumentative essay:

  › Put information about references on cards: Whether a writer chooses to use paper note cards or a computer system that serves the same purpose, note cards are very important. Writers must write down all of the information about the source that will later be needed for citations and a bibliography, which is an organized list of sources. This includes the author's name, title of the work, publisher, city and state of publication, date of publication, and the page numbers referenced. Note the date of access if the source is electronic.

  › Use a separate card for each fact, idea, observation, quotation, or other information found while you research. Code the cards with a letter or number that matches the source card where the information came from. Clearly mark quotations and note who to credit. If an item is not a direct quotation, be sure you have paraphrased accurately and avoided plagiarism, or copying another person's work.

 MODEL

The writer of the Student Model essay "Attitude: One Secret to Survival" supported her claim by finding textual evidence in two texts located during

Please note that excerpts and passages in the StudySync® library and this workbook are intended as touchstones to generate interest in an author's work. The excerpts and passages do not substitute for the reading of entire texts, and StudySync® strongly recommends that students seek out and purchase the whole literary or informational work in order to experience it as the author intended. Links to online resellers are available in our digital library. In addition, complete works may be ordered through an authorized reseller by filling out and returning to StudySync® the order form enclosed in this workbook.

Reading & Writing Companion    **221**

the research process. Her research note cards from the two texts are reproduced below:

**Bibliography Card: Source 1**

Article: "Music of the Ghettos and Camps"

Publication: *A Teacher's Guide to the Holocaust*

Publication date: 1952

Publisher: The Florida Center for Technology, College of Education, University of South Florida

Date: 1997–2013

Media: Web

Accessed: 12 Dec. 2014

**Bibliography Card: Source 2**

Article: "How Do Thoughts & Emotions Impact Health?"

Publication: *Taking Charge of Your Health and Well-Being*

Author: Karen Lawson, M.D.

Publication date: 18 August 2013

Publisher: University of Minnesota

Media: Web

Accessed: 12 Dec. 2014

**Holocaust: Songs**

Source 1

Songs showed will to survive

**Attitude and Health:**

Source 2

"Resilient people are able to experience tough emotions like pain, sorrow, frustration, and grief without falling apart—in fact, some people are able to look at challenging times with optimism and hope, knowing that their hardships will lead to personal growth and an expanded outlook on life."

**Holocaust: Positive Attitude**

Source 1

"Laughter became a necessity..."

**Attitude and Health:**

Source 2

"Positive emotions have a scientific purpose—to help the body recover from the ill effects of negative emotions."

NOTES

### Holocaust: Songs

#### Source 1

"A majority of ghetto street songs were sung to pre-existing melodies, a technique known as 'contra fact.' Contra fact became necessary because composers couldn't generate new music fast enough for all 'f the lyrics being written."

### Attitude and Health:

#### Source 2

"These positive emotions literally reverse the physical effects of negativity and build up psychological resources that contribute to a flourishing life."

### Holocaust: Other Arts

#### Source 1

"A majority of ghetto street songs were sung to pre-existing melodies, a technique known as contra fact. Contra fact became necessary because composers couldn't generate new music fast enough for all of the lyrics being written."

### Attitude and Health:

#### Source 2

Benefits of gratitude include good sleep, happier outlook, and fewer physical problems.

The author used two types of cards in her research: bibliography cards and note cards. The bibliography cards record all of the information necessary for the Works Cited page that should be placed at the end of the essay. The note cards each contain separate ideas from the sources that are clearly marked. They show where the ideas or information come from. Information that was taken directly from the source is recorded in quotes. If the sources had been print, each card would also have included a page number where the information was found. Organizing the note cards in this way saved the author a lot of time and energy when writing. The information for citations and the Works Cited page was readily available, so she did not have to retrace her research steps when she decided to use a piece of information that needed to be credited, and she was positive as to which bits of information were direct quotes and which were paraphrases.

By putting a subject on top, a code to connect the card with the matching source, and one fact, quote, idea, example, or definition on each card, the author made it much easier to organize her notes later when she was writing. Using this identification system, she could shuffle the note cards into any order and still connect the idea with the proper source.

Now, let's look at how this writer used some of her research notes to write the following excerpt from "Attitude: One Secret to Survival":

> Psychologists also agree that the mental attitude of individuals in these situations is important. **Karen Lawson, MD, states that "... positive emotions literally reverse the physical effects of negativity and build up psychological resources that contribute to a flourishing life"** (Lawson 2). In one study cited by Lawson, people who focused themselves on gratitude felt happier, slept better, and had fewer physical problems than those who did not. She also notes that resilient people have the ability to experience very negative circumstances while retaining positive feelings, allowing them to overcome some of the negative impacts of their situation (Lawson 2).

Examine the bold print in the paragraph. The writer used the information from "How Do Thoughts & Emotions Impact Health?" in *Taking Charge of Your Health and Well-Being* to begin to build a case for her claim that positive attitude contributes to survival. The pieces of information that she included begin to build a case for the idea that people try to stay positive in such circumstances. Let's look at the note card where this quotation came from again.

**Attitude and Health:**

Source 2

"These positive emotions literally reverse the physical effects of negativity and build up psychological resources that contribute to a flourishing life."

We can see that this direct quote came from Source 2.

 PRACTICE

Now it's your turn. Review the information you noted during the Prewrite lesson. Get some note cards or set up a digital note-card system on a computer, and complete the following tasks:

- Find at least three other reliable, relevant sources suitable for your topic.
- Create bibliography cards for these additional sources and label or code them so you can connect note cards to them.
- Make at least six note cards that contain pieces of evidence about your topic. These can be quotations, ideas, facts, statistics, or other pieces of

information. Make sure they are connected to what you plan to write in response to the prompt. Be sure to label each note card with the code for the matching bibliography card.

After you have found at least three additional sources and created at least six note cards, trade information with a peer for some feedback. Give your peer the prewriting information as well as at least two bibliography cards and at least six note cards with one piece of information on each. Review your peer's work while yours is being reviewed. Consider the following questions:

- Why are these additional sources considered to be reliable? How are they connected to the topic?

- How do these research card notes relate to the information from the prewriting exercise? In what way is the information from all the sources connected?

- If you were to read the paper written from these research notes, what questions would you still have about this topic?

- What suggestions can you make to your peer to improve his or her research?

Remember that suggestions will be most helpful if they are positive and specific. Be kind and polite as you review your peer's work.

**NOTES**

## SKILL: THESIS STATEMENT

### DEFINE

In argumentative writing, the thesis statement is the claim that the author makes in the introduction and then proves in the body of the essay with reasons and evidence. It is the most important sentence in the entire essay because it is the focal point. It expresses the author's main idea and tells the reader what position the author is taking on a debatable topic. The claim, or thesis statement, appears in the introductory paragraph and is often the last sentence in the paragraph. The body of the essay provides reasons in support of the author's claim and offers details such as facts, examples, quotations, or other evidence that the claim is correct.

### IDENTIFICATION AND APPLICATION

A thesis statement (or claim)

- takes a clear stand on an issue.
- lets the reader know what the author supports.
- responds fully and completely to an essay prompt.
- is presented in the introduction paragraph.

### MODEL

Reread the introduction paragraph from the Student Model essay, "Attitude: One Secret to Survival":

> For centuries, human beings have demonstrated countless ways to be cruel to other groups of people, especially during times of war. Entire ethnic groups have been targeted for the simple reason that they were born into the "wrong" culture or family. Enslavement, imprisonment, and even wholesale

NOTES

slaughter of people who were thought to be "different" have put black marks on the histories of many countries. This mistreatment by people in authority can damage its victims, even if they survive physically. Yet there are individuals who manage to come through their ordeal and heal. There are also people who, even though they did not survive, continue to inspire us to this day with stories of their courage. One well-known example of such inspiration comes from Anne Frank, in *Anne Frank: The Diary of a Young Girl*. This young girl has inspired millions with her firsthand account of life for her and her Jewish family as they hid from the Nazis in Amsterdam. Other inspiring stories come from the real-life letters of children in the United States' internment camps for Japanese Americans during World War II. Some of these letters were collected in the book, *Dear Miss Breed: True Stories of the Japanese American Incarceration During World War II and a Librarian Who Made a Difference* by Joanne Oppenheim. This book, along with *Anne Frank: The Diary of a Young Girl,* explain the situations these families underwent, but they also show one path to graceful endurance: a positive attitude. Coping with impossible situations, such as living in hiding from the Nazis or enduring the Japanese internment camps, took a certain kind of strength, along with a positive attitude. **As these works show, positive thinking is one of the best ways to respond to conflict, as well as an effective path to healing for those who survive physical abuse or hardship at the hands of others.**

The bold-faced sentence is the thesis statement, or claim. This student's thesis statement responds to the prompt by presenting a claim about how people can respond effectively to conflict. It reminds readers that the author believes a positive attitude is critical to survival in extreme and abusive circumstances.

 PRACTICE

Now it's your turn. Craft a thesis statement, or claim, for your argumentative essay that clearly answers the question: "How can people best respond to conflict?" Your thesis should clearly articulate your central idea as well as your opinion about it. When you have written your thesis statement, exchange with a partner and critique one another's work. How clear is the author's central idea? How does the thesis statement relate to the prompt? Does the author take a clear stand or express a clear opinion? Offer suggestions to one another, and remember to be kind and constructive when you discuss each other's work.

# SKILL: ORGANIZE ARGUMENTATIVE WRITING

 **DEFINE**

The purpose of argumentative writing is to convince readers to adopt a particular point of view on an issue, to take action, or to choose a side. To do this, writers must **organize** and present the case to support their **thesis,** or claim. They must give reasons the reader should agree with their view and then support those reasons with **evidence.** Evidence consists of ideas, facts, details, definitions, examples, and other information from other sources. This information is presented in a logical manner so that one idea naturally leads to the next. The purpose of writing an argument is to inform and persuade readers.

Writers of argumentative essays use an **organizational structure** that is appropriate, or correct, for their topic and its support. The essay is structured with an introduction that contains the thesis statement, **body paragraphs** that identify and explain the reasons and evidence that support the claim, and a conclusion that often includes a summary of the evidence and perhaps a call to action. Writers usually use a graphic organizer, **outline,** or other method for arranging their material. This helps them organize their ideas to express them effectively.

 **IDENTIFICATION AND APPLICATION**

- The introduction, or first paragraph of an argumentative essay, uses a "hook" to grab the reader's attention. A "hook" is an opening statement that will make it almost impossible for a reader to put down your essay. It may contain a fascinating fact or statistic. A good quotation is also an excellent way to attract your reader, as it connects the essay to a point in history. The first paragraph then introduces the issue and the main sources of information. It ends with a clear claim about the issue or thesis statement.

- The body paragraphs of the argumentative essay are built around the author's claims and the reasons that will convince the reader that the claim is correct. Each paragraph should focus on one claim, the reason for it, and its supporting evidence. Writers might consider:

> The reasons they wish to use to show the claim is correct. These should be presented in a logical order, such as least important to most important, most general to most specific, or less common to more common.

> The evidence from the sources that supports the claim. Each piece of evidence should clearly relate to the reason that is the topic of the paragraph. Each should add support that leads the reader to conclude that the claim is correct.

- The argumentative essay ends with a conclusion that summarizes the most important points. It clearly shows the logical path between the issue and proof that the claim is correct.

- Effective transitions create connections and make clear the relationships you find between reasons and the evidence in different sources. One idea should lead naturally to the next. The reader should be able to take small, logical steps through the essay and end up concluding that the writer's claim is correct. Some transitions to consider include:

> Sequential order: *first, next, then, finally, last, initially, ultimately*
> Cause and effect: *because, accordingly, as a result, effect, so*
> Compare and contrast: *like, unlike, also, both, similarly* or *similar, although, while, but, however*
> Problem and solution: *so, as a result, consequently, therefore*

##  MODEL

Writing a good argumentative essay is much like building a house. A builder needs to start with a good, solid foundation just like a writer needs a good, solid thesis statement. A builder needs to use strong wooden boards to build the walls and the roof, just like a writer must use solid reasons in the right places to build the body of the essay. A builder puts the strong boards together with nails, and a writer nails the reasons together with evidence.

The writer of the Student Model argumentative essay focused on answering the following question in the prompt: How can people best respond to conflict? She chose two example texts about people who lived through horrible abuse in the concentration camps and in the internment camps and found a commonality: the people who survived and those who are considered to be inspirational worked to keep a positive attitude in terrible situations. The sources that the author found in her research confirm this claim.

Please note that excerpts and passages in the StudySync® library and this workbook are intended as touchstones to generate interest in an author's work. The excerpts and passages do not substitute for the reading of entire texts, and StudySync® strongly recommends that students seek out and purchase the whole literary or informational work in order to experience it as the author intended. Links to online resellers are available in our digital library. In addition, complete works may be ordered through an authorized reseller by filling out and returning to StudySync® the order form enclosed in this workbook.

Reading & Writing Companion **229**

NOTES

The writer of the Student Model essay developed three reasons to prove that a positive attitude is one of the best ways to respond to conflict. The second paragraph, which has the topic sentence **"The impact of a positive attitude is shown in the thoughts and words of real people,"** allowed her to pull examples from primary sources to prove her point. The third body paragraph, which has the topic sentence of **"More evidence about the effects of a positive attitude can be found in the writings of certain scholars,"** enabled the writer to provide additional evidence from scholarly sources of the importance of a positive attitude. The fourth body paragraph, which has the topic sentence **"Psychologists also agree that the mental attitude of individuals in these horrible situations is very important,"** allowed the writer to introduce the opinions of medical experts to prove the claim. So the writer built her claim by moving from accounts in literature to commentary from scholars and teachers to expert testimony about the matter.

The writer of the Student Model argumentative essay, "Attitude: One Secret to Survival," knew that she had to give the proof for her claim in a logical fashion, and so she used a graphic organizer to sort through the ideas and put them in order. Remember that all notes should come from specific sources.

| **Claim:** Positive thinking is one of the best ways to respond to conflict, as well as an effective path to healing for those who survive physical abuse or hardship at the hands of others. | | |
|---|---|---|
| **The impact of a positive attitude is shown in the thoughts and words of real people.** | More evidence about the effects of a positive attitude can be found in the writings of certain scholars. | Psychologists also agree that the mental attitude of individuals in these horrible situations is very important. |

| | | |
|---|---|---|
| Firsthand accounts from those who experienced conflict demonstrate the benefits of positive thinking.<br><br>Firsthand Observation: Anne Frank had cheerful pictures on her wall. (*Anne Frank: The Diary of a Young Girl*)<br><br>Firsthand Observation: Anne Frank noticed the chiming of the clock. (*Anne Frank: The Diary of a Young Girl*)<br><br>Firsthand Observation: Louise Ogawa enjoyed learning how to eat weenies and cabbage with a knife. (*Dear Miss Breed*)<br><br>Firsthand Observation: Louise Ogawa noticed the beautiful scenery of the Colorado River. (*Dear Miss Breed*) | Scholar's Observation: So many song lyrics were written during the Holocaust that composers couldn't write enough music for them. (FCIT, online article)<br><br>Scholar's Observation: Line from a play: "So hungry I cannot sing / That is why we must sing" (FCIT, online article)<br><br>Scholar's Observation: Mental engagement impacted victims' survival. (Schaumann, online article) | Psychologist's conclusion: Positive attitude increased strength, and strength increased positive attitude. (Lawson, online article)<br><br>Psychologist's conclusion: Gratitude improved sleep and health. (Lawson, online article)<br><br>Psychologist's conclusion: Positive attitude reversed some physical problems. (Lawson, online article) |

Please note that excerpts and passages in the StudySync® library and this workbook are intended as touchstones to generate interest in an author's work. The excerpts and passages do not substitute for the reading of entire texts, and StudySync® strongly recommends that students seek out and purchase the whole literary or informational work in order to experience it as the author intended. Links to online resellers are available in our digital library. In addition, complete works may be ordered through an authorized reseller by filling out and returning to StudySync® the order form enclosed in this workbook.

Reading & Writing Companion **231**

## PRACTICE

Complete the StudySync *Organize Argumentative Writing Three-Column Chart* graphic organizer by filling in the information you gathered in the Prewrite and Research and Note-Taking stages of writing your essay, as well as any additional information you have gathered since then. You may choose to organize the chart according to three reasons in support of your claim, three types of support for your claim, or some other system of your choosing. Please include specific sources of information. When you are finished, trade with a partner and offer each other feedback. How well has the writer organized his or her ideas? Has the writer noted any differences between specific ideas? Does the organization of ideas make sense? Can you offer any suggestions for improvement? Remember to be considerate and respectful as you offer constructive suggestions to one another.

# SKILL:
# SUPPORTING
# DETAILS

 **DEFINE**

Writers of argumentative essays support their claim (or thesis) with relevant evidence called supporting details. These are pieces of information that help the reader understand the topic. The information comes from credible, or trustworthy sources. The author uses logical reasoning to connect these pieces of information. In this way, the author builds a solid case for the claim made in the introduction. The purpose is to persuade the reader to share the same view and perhaps take action related to the issue.

 **IDENTIFICATION AND APPLICATION**

The supporting details, or **evidence,** form the most important part of the argument and should include some of the following:

- Facts important to understanding the topic

- Examples that highlight the topic

- Research related to the main idea or thesis

- Quotations from experts, eyewitnesses, or other source material

- Conclusions of scientific findings and studies

- Definitions from reference material

As the writer does research to find supporting details, he or she should evaluate each detail to make sure it truly supports the claim. It can also lead to a new understanding of a topic or help the reader make logical connections between the evidence and the claim. Evidence, or supporting details, can come from many sources, including encyclopedias, online sources, research papers, newspaper articles, graphs and charts, critical reviews, documentaries, firsthand accounts, biographies, and more.

## MODEL

Let's examine the Counterpoint essay, "The Dangers of Fictionalizing History," in *Teaching History Through Fiction*. The Counterpoint writer begins his essay by stating his claim: "Teaching history through the use of fiction, including stories, novels, and films, is often misleading and can be dangerous, and John Boyne's *The Boy in the Striped Pajamas* shows why." In the first body paragraph of the essay, the Counterpoint writer quotes the same passage from children's book author Valerie Tripp that was used to support the claim in the Point essay: "Fiction can make history matter—make it irresistible—to young readers." But he then offers additional insight to show why Tripp's thoughts on the issue are actually more supportive of his own:

> No one would consider Valerie Tripp an opponent of using fiction to teach history. **On the teachinghistory.org website, Tripp notes that "fiction can make history matter—make it irresistible—to young readers" (Tripp, "Vitamins in Chocolate Cake"). Yet Tripp, an author of youth fiction herself, also knows the dangers.** She offers this warning to teachers: "When choosing historical fiction to use in the classroom as a way to interest students in history, I'd say: First, do no harm. That is, before it is used in a history classroom, historical fiction should be checked for bias, for anachronistic voice and views, and for shying away from honest presentation of the period. What is not said is as misleading as what is said!" (Tripp, "Neither Spinach Nor Potato Chip").

> **Judged according to Tripp's criteria, teachers should use *The Boy in the Striped Pajamas* with caution. Boyne's bias rests not in his personal beliefs about the Holocaust, but in his view of storytelling.**

Boyne's view of storytelling, which the Counterpoint writer illustrates by including a quote from Boyne's website, is that "'a fable' is a piece of fiction that contains a moral." The Point writer of the opposing essay had previously argued that by labeling *The Boy in the Striped Pajamas* a fable, Boyne acknowledged that it was not intended to be a realistic historical account but rather a piece of fiction with a valuable moral lesson. As we will see, however, the Counterpoint writer uses the same information presented by the Point writer to refute the validity of both Boyne's and the Point writer's reasoning and to support his own claim:

> Personally, I don't like fables. But that aside, **the problem with Boyne's premise is that writing a fable does not release him from an author's obligation not to distort history. This is particularly true when dealing with an event as serious as the Holocaust.** The danger of "serving the story" over serving the facts is that young readers will not know enough Holocaust history to understand what has been changed. As critic David

Copyright © BookheadEd Learning, LLC

Cesarani notes, "Except for a few peculiar cases there were no Jewish children in the extermination camps: they were gassed on arrival" (Cesarani). Thus the very premise of the story is, in Cesarani's words, "utterly implausible." **In his scathing review of the book, Cesarani explains why the implausibility matters:** "Should this matter if the book is a 'fable' which is presumably intended by its author to warn against the evils of prejudice? Yes. Because there are people at large who contest whether the systematic mass murder of the Jews occurred" (Cesarani). **This is a serious charge, especially given that, according to Boyne's website, the book has sold more than 6 million copies worldwide and has been made into a movie (Boyne).**

Although the paragraph begins with a personal opinion that is not relevant to the argument and should not be included ("Personally, I don't like fables"), it presents strong reasoning and evidence for the writer's claim and effectively distinguishes the writer's claim from the opposition. The evidence comes mainly from quotations from respected critic David Cesarani, who argues that the premise of the *The Boy in the Striped Pajamas* is "utterly implausible" and that this implausibility matters because there are still people who deny the reality of the Holocaust. The Counterpoint writer then cites statistical evidence also cited by the Point writer to show why it supports his claim more than hers: the fact that the book has sold over six million copies and been made into a movie is less evidence of its merit than proof of its threat.

Then, to counter the Point writer's evidence about critical praise for the book, the Counterpoint writer provides evidence of critical condemnation:

> **The critics of the book and the 2008 movie are many. One of their complaints is Boyne's use of clever word devices to avoid addressing the real facts of the Holocaust.** Young Bruno mishears "Auschwitz" as "Out-With" and "the Führer" as "the Fury." **As Cesarani points out, "Any normal German nine-year-old would have been able to pronounce Führer and Auschwitz correctly."** While not anachronistic in the sense of being from the wrong time, Bruno's word choices are culturally misplaced. **As reviewer A. O. Scott notes, "There is something illogical about them, since Bruno's native language is presumably German, in which the portentous puns would make no sense, not English, in which they do" (Scott).**

The writer supports the main idea or reason in this paragraph—that Boyne's word devices enable him to avoid addressing real facts about the Holocaust— with evidence in the form of direct quotations from two critics that point out an inherent lack of logic in Boyne's method.

PRACTICE

In the last lesson, you created a chart to help you organize your writing. Use that information for this exercise. You will also need highlighting markers in three different colors. Follow these steps:

- On your chart, categorize the details according to their type (facts, examples, research, quotations, conclusions, definitions). You can mark these in different ways if you have fewer than three colors for highlighting. For example, you could highlight the quotations in yellow and underline the definitions in yellow. Categorize each piece of information.

- Look at your highlights. How colorful is your organizer? Ideally, the colors should be somewhat balanced, with no one color dominating the paper. This means that you have a variety of supporting details that will grab your readers' attention and hold their interest.

- Next, evaluate your details for relevance and value. Rate each one on a scale of 1 to 3. Details with a rating of 1 should be the most relevant and the most valuable. Those with a rating of 2 should be somewhat relevant and somewhat valuable. Put a rating of 3 on any details that no longer seem relevant or valuable. Hopefully, you were able to rate most of your details at level 1. A few level 2 details can be used in your paper if you need to, but all of the level 3 details should be excluded. You may find that you need to return to the research step to find more information if you had a number of details that had a rating of 2 or 3.

- When you feel that most of your details are rated 1 and that you have a wide variety of information as reflected by the highlighting, exchange your work with a peer and give each other some feedback. Check your peer's work for a balance of supporting details. Make sure most of the details are rated a 1, meaning they are relevant and valuable. Be sure to keep your feedback constructive, positive, and polite.

NOTES

## PLAN

CA-CCSS: CA.W.8.1a, CA.W.8.1b, CA.W.8.5, CA.W.8.6, CA.W.8.9b, CA.SL.8.1a, CA.SL.8.1c, CA.SL.8.1d

### WRITING PROMPT

Carefully consider the selections you have read in this unit, including their themes and the ideas they offer about war and conflict. Pick two of the selections from the unit and write an argumentative essay that presents a claim in answer to the following question: how can people best respond to conflict? Along with information from the selections, include research from at least three other credible print and digital sources to support your claim and develop your argument.

Your argumentative essay should include:

- An introduction with a clear thesis statement that presents your claim

- Organized body paragraphs with relevant evidence and support for your claim as well as clear transitions to show the connections among ideas

- A concluding paragraph that effectively wraps up your essay

- A Works Cited page that, in addition to the two unit texts, lists at least three other reliable sources used in your essay

You have already created an *Organize Argumentative Writing Three-Column Chart* graphic organizer. You will use the information you recorded there to plan your argumentative essay. This three-column chart contains your claim, reasons that reinforce your claim or types of support you plan to use to reinforce your claim, and examples of evidence from each source that will convince the reader to adopt your point of view on the issue. This chart, along with your thesis statement, will help you create a "road map" that will, in turn, help you write your essay.

Please note that excerpts and passages in the StudySync® library and this workbook are intended as touchstones to generate interest in an author's work. The excerpts and passages do not substitute for the reading of entire texts, and StudySync® strongly recommends that students seek out and purchase the whole literary or informational work in order to experience it as the author intended. Links to online resellers are available in our digital library. In addition, complete works may be ordered through an authorized reseller by filling out and returning to StudySync® the order form enclosed in this workbook.

Reading & Writing Companion  **237**

Think about the following questions as you develop reasons and organize evidence to support your thesis statement in your road map. The answers to the questions will help you to plan the content for each body paragraph of your argumentative essay:

- In what order should you present your claims and supporting details? How do they naturally build on one another?
- What reason forms the next step in your argument?
- What pieces of evidence drawn from research will convince your reader to agree to your claim?
- How can you organize the evidence so that each piece forms a foundation for the next?
- What will make your argument more convincing?
- How can you acknowledge alternate or opposing claims and distinguish your own position from these?
- Through what logical steps can you guide the reader to agree that your main thesis and supporting claims are correct?

The author of the Student Model, "Attitude: One Secret to Survival," created this road map before she wrote her essay. Use this model as an example to get started with your own road map:

**Argumentative Essay Road Map**

Introductory paragraph: Present the topic with the hook of the history of cruelty between humans. Provide examples of the Nazi concentration camps and Japanese internment camps. Thesis statement (claim): Positive thinking is one of the best ways to respond to conflict, as well as an effective path to healing for those who survive physical abuse or hardship at the hands of others.

Body Paragraph 1 Topic: Examples from primary sources, including diaries and letters, of the impact of a positive attitude on survival in harsh circumstances

Supporting Detail #1: Anne Frank, quote about decorating walls, detail about chiming clock, shows engagement and positive attitude

Supporting Detail #2: Louise Ogawa, beauty of river, novelty of eating weenies with knife, shows engagement and positive attitude

Supporting Details #3 and #4: To address an alternate or opposing claim about the ultimate significance of Anne Frank's positive attitude: Statistics about the number of languages into which her diary has been translated and the number of people who have visited her home since it opened as a museum in Amsterdam in 1960

Body Paragraph 2 Topic: Scholars' analysis of the relationship between attitude and survival

> Supporting Detail #1: FCIT: music and Holocaust, too many lyrics for existing tunes, "so hungry I can't sing . . . that's why you must" quotation
> Supporting Detail #2: Schaumann quote about the connection between attitude and survival
> Body Paragraph 3 Topic: Experts' opinions about the relationship between attitude and survival
> Supporting Detail #1: Lawson quotes: positive emotions reverse negative effects and gratitude improves physical well-being
> Supporting Detail #2: Lawson conclusion: focus on positive leads to resilience

Concluding paragraph: Summarize—attitude is necessary to healthy living and survival, and it creates resilience. Anne Frank and Louise Ogawa are examples that inspire. Positive attitudes contribute to the emotional resilience necessary for survival in harsh conditions.

Please note that excerpts and passages in the StudySync® library and this workbook are intended as touchstones to generate interest in an author's work. The excerpts and passages do not substitute for the reading of entire texts, and StudySync® strongly recommends that students seek out and purchase the whole literary or informational work in order to experience it as the author intended. Links to online resellers are available in our digital library. In addition, complete works may be ordered through an authorized reseller by filling out and returning to StudySync® the order form enclosed in this workbook.

Reading & Writing Companion  **239**

Copyright © BookheadEd Learning, LLC

NOTES

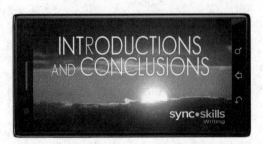

SKILL:
INTRODUCTIONS
AND
CONCLUSIONS

 DEFINE

The **introduction** is the opening paragraph or section of a nonfiction text. In an argumentative text, the introduction sets the stage for reading by **introducing the topic** or issue, **introducing the main sources** of information, and stating the **thesis or claim** in which the author takes a clear position on an issue. A strong introduction grabs the reader's attention with a **hook.** This can be a question, a startling fact or statistic, an engaging example, or a controversial statement.

The **conclusion** is the ending paragraph or section of an essay. In an argumentative text, the conclusion reviews the thesis or claim and **the most important evidence** that the writer has presented to support the claim. A good conclusion wraps up the case for the claim, showing why the reader should agree with the writer. The author restates the thesis in the conclusion and ends with a strong **call to action** or other statement that will leave a **lasting impression** on the reader.

 IDENTIFICATION AND APPLICATION

- The introduction of an argumentative paper begins with a **hook** that will immediately grab the reader's attention. There are a number of strategies for doing this, including:
  › Asking a question
  › Presenting a startling fact or statistic
  › Making a controversial statement
  › Relating an anecdote or example

- The introduction clearly tells the reader what the **topic** of the essay will be.

NOTES

- The introduction can sometimes be used to introduce the main **sources** of information that the writer will use later for **supporting evidence.**

  › The title and author should be included in the **reference.** Sources can also be people or examples the author plans to discuss.

- The introduction includes the author's **claim** or **thesis** near the end. This is the main idea of the essay, which the author plans to **prove** to be true. The claim statement should express a clear **point of view** on the issue discussed in the essay. This statement is very important because it controls the direction of the entire essay.

- Every argumentative essay ends with a **conclusion** that summarizes the evidence the author has offered to support the claim.

- The conclusion effectively brings the argument to a close and leaves no room for doubt that the author has proved the point in the claim. It should restate the thesis and review the strongest evidence that supports the main idea.

## MODEL

Look at the introduction from the Point essay "The Value of Teaching History Through Fiction" in *Teaching History Through Fiction.*

> **Every history teacher knows that making students believe that history is relevant to their lives is Challenge Number 1. The question is, how can this difficult feat be accomplished?** One answer lies in a source we might least expect: fiction. As Valerie Tripp points out in her blog entry on the teachinghistory.org website, "Fiction can make history matter—make it irresistible—to young readers" (Tripp). This effect is achieved by John Boyne's *The Boy in the Striped Pajamas.* By approaching the Holocaust through the eyes of two nine-year-old boys, the book provides a unique perspective on this dark and horrible chapter in history. **Fiction, including stories, novels, and films, is a great way to teach people about history, and John Boyne's *The Boy in the Striped Pajamas* is an excellent example.**

The first two sentences of the Point essay provide a hook for readers. The first sentence identifies the main problem every history teacher faces: making history relevant for students. This is a relevant concern for her academic audience. The second sentence asks how this problem can be solved, which provokes curiosity and leads both teachers and students to read on to find the answer.

Please note that excerpts and passages in the StudySync® library and this workbook are intended as touchstones to generate interest in an author's work. The excerpts and passages do not substitute for the reading of entire texts, and StudySync® strongly recommends that students seek out and purchase the whole literary or informational work in order to experience it as the author intended. Links to online resellers are available in our digital library. In addition, complete works may be ordered through an authorized reseller by filling out and returning to StudySync® the order form enclosed in this workbook.

Reading & Writing Companion    **241**

In the next sentence, the Point writer gives the answer: fiction. She provides support for this perhaps surprising idea in the form of a quote. To illustrate the point made in the quote, she then provides a specific example—namely, that John Boyne's *The Boy in the Striped Pajamas* offers a unique perspective on the Holocaust.

The final sentence is the Point writer's thesis statement. She clearly states her position on the controversial issue of whether fiction is an effective vehicle for teaching history and identifies the text she will analyze to demonstrate the validity of her claim: that fiction is a great way to teach people about history, and that *The Boy in the Striped Pajamas* is an excellent example.

Now read the conclusion from the same essay:

> *The goal of good fiction should be to move people. It should move them to laugh, to cry, to care, to think—or else why should they bother reading it? History too should move people—or else how will they learn from it? By exploring the moral issues of the Holocaust through the eyes of two innocent young boys, The Boy in the Striped Pajamas accomplishes what should be important aims of both fiction and history: it moves people to care and to think. Thus, the story is an excellent example of how to teach history through fiction.*

The first four sentences of the conclusion offer readers additional insight in the form of interesting though certainly debatable points: that both fiction and history should move people to care and to think, and that *The Boy in the Striped Pajamas* thus accomplishes what should be important aims of both fiction and history. The third sentence summarizes the author's main point about the book: that it explores moral issues related to the Holocaust. The last sentence then restates the author's thesis. In a brief space, therefore, the author summarizes her main reason, restates her central claim, and leaves readers with a lasting impression.

##  PRACTICE

Write an introduction for your argumentative essay that begins with a hook. Then introduce the issue, your main sources, and end with a clear thesis statement. When you have finished, write a conclusion for your essay. Summarize the strongest evidence supporting your claim. Restate the thesis statement, and leave the reader with a convincing argument to share your opinion on the issue. When you are finished, trade with a partner and offer each other feedback. Does the hook capture the reader's attention effectively? Are the topic and main sources clearly introduced? Does the thesis statement make a clear claim about the issue? Does the concluding paragraph follow from and support the claim introduced in the introduction? Offer constructive suggestions to your partner and remember to phrase everything in kind and helpful ways.

DRAFT

**CA-CCSS:** CA.W.8.1a, CA.W.8.1b, CA.W.8.1c, CA.W.8.1d, CA.W.8.1e, CA.W.8.4, CA.W.8.5, CA.W.8.6, CA.W.8.7, CA.W.8.8, CA.W.8.9b, CA.W.8.10, CA.L.8.2a

## WRITING PROMPT

Carefully consider the selections you have read in this unit, including their themes and the ideas they offer about war and conflict. Pick two of the selections from the unit and write an argumentative essay that presents a claim in answer to the following question: how can people best respond to conflict? Along with information from the selections, include research from at least three other credible print and digital sources to support your claim and develop your argument.

Your argumentative essay should include:

- An introduction with a clear thesis statement that presents your claim
- Organized body paragraphs with relevant evidence and support for your claim as well as clear transitions to show the connections among ideas
- A concluding paragraph that effectively wraps up your essay
- A Works Cited page that, in addition to the two unit texts, lists at least three other reliable sources used in your essay

You have already started writing your own argumentative essay. You have considered your purpose, your audience, and your topic. You have examined the texts featured in the unit and developed your claim. You have also located at least three outside reliable sources and have taken notes about the ideas they contain that support your claim. You know what you want to say about this topic and the stand you are prepared to take. You have already developed a plan for organization and gathered supporting details. You've drafted several paragraphs, including the introduction and conclusion. You have considered how to achieve a formal style and to use transitions appropriately. Now it is time to write a complete draft of your essay.

Use your outline, your notes, graphic organizers, and any other pre-writing materials that you have developed to help you write this draft. Remember that argumentative writing begins with an introduction that presents a claim about the topic in a sound thesis statement. Body paragraphs add substance to the claim by adding information drawn from research, including expert opinions, examples, details, and quotations. In your essay, these paragraphs will also contain information from the selections in the unit that will help support your claim. Include carefully chosen transitions to help build your case and convince the reader that your position is the correct one. Transitions will help clarify the relationship between your ideas and the evidence you've chosen to support them. Finally, a concluding paragraph should restate or reinforce your thesis statement or claim. Your reader should be left with a clear understanding of your position and how strongly it is supported. An effective conclusion will complete the job of convincing your reader that your claim is valid.

When drafting, ask yourself these questions:

- How can I make my hook in the introduction exciting or interesting in order to capture the reader's attention?

- What can I do to explain and clarify my thesis statement or claim?

- What textual evidence—including relevant facts, strong details, and interesting quotations in each body paragraph—supports my thesis statement or claim and thus helps achieve my purpose? Be sure to include information drawn from at least three reliable sources obtained during research, clearly and accurately citing the ideas from those authors in order to avoid plagiarism.

- How logical and effective is my organizational structure?

- Have I used transitions to connect the ideas and information in my essay?

- In what ways do I distinguish my claim from alternate or opposing claims?

- Can I make the text more interesting, exciting, or vivid by using more specific language or different details?

- In what ways can I improve my style to make it more formal and appropriate for an argumentative essay?

- Have I used dashes appropriately?

- How well did I relate the stories I have chosen for this essay? Did I explain how people responded to conflict or survived their situations?

- What final thought do I want to leave with my readers?

Before you submit your draft, read it over carefully. Be sure you have responded to all parts of the prompt.

Please note that excerpts and passages in the StudySync® library and this workbook are intended as touchstones to generate interest in an author's work. The excerpts and passages do not substitute for the reading of entire texts, and StudySync® strongly recommends that students seek out and purchase the whole literary or informational work in order to experience it as the author intended. Links to online resellers are available in our digital library. In addition, complete works may be ordered through an authorized reseller by filling out and returning to StudySync® the order form enclosed in this workbook.

Reading & Writing Companion    **245**

SKILL:
SOURCES AND
CITATIONS

 **DEFINE**

**Sources** are the documents and information that an author locates through research. They add authority and support to argumentative writing. They also provide the proof that an author's claim is correct. A **primary source** is an actual record of something that has survived from the past, such as a document or objects such as photographs or clothing. **Secondary sources** are accounts of the past created by people writing about events sometime after they took place.

Whether they use primary or secondary sources, authors must clearly identify where their information comes from. They do this by providing **citations,** or notes about the author or speaker and the publication or place where the information originated. Citations give credit for quotations or any ideas that did not come from the essay writer. In the body of the paper, the author often uses **in-line citations.** These give the name of the source and, if possible, the page number where the information can be found. In-line citations are placed in parentheses at the end of a sentence containing a quotation or an idea from another person. At the end of the paper, the **Works Cited** section forms a bibliography that gives complete information about each source. It allows readers to locate the source for further review.

 **IDENTIFICATION AND APPLICATION**

- Primary sources are the most convincing and respected sources in an argument. Primary sources are actual records of something that have survived from the past. They can include:

  › Letters
  › Diaries or journals
  › Photographs
  › Official documents
  › Artifacts
  › Memoirs

> › Autobiographies
> › Firsthand accounts and interviews
> › Audio recordings, video recordings, or media broadcasts
> › Works of art

- Secondary sources, interpretation and analysis of primary sources, are usually text. They provide expert opinions about the ideas, events, or accounts in primary sources. Some examples of secondary sources include:

> › Encyclopedia articles
> › Textbooks
> › Commentary or criticisms
> › Histories
> › Documentary films
> › News analyses

- All sources must be credible, or trustworthy, and accurate. Writers of argumentative text use primary source information whenever possible, as well as discussion and analysis from experts. Return to the Skills lesson on Research and Note-Taking to review guidelines for credible sources.

- Direct quotations from other people always need to be cited. The words must appear within quotation marks to show that the phrase, sentence, or selection came from another person. The words should be reproduced exactly as the source stated them, and the author should include an in-line citation to show the source of the text.

- Argumentative essay writers must also give credit for ideas that come from other sources, even if they are not quoted exactly. The essay author must cite paraphrased ideas.

 ## MODEL

The writer of the Student Model has used quotations in this excerpt. She has also paraphrased some information, and placed citations in parentheses to show where the information came from.

> *The impact of a positive attitude is shown in the thoughts and words of real people depicted in literature. In* Anne Frank: The Diary of a Young Girl, *Anne's accounts reveal a positive attitude that later served as inspiration for millions of people.* **For example, in her diary entry dated Saturday, July 11, 1942, even while living in crowded, difficult conditions while hiding from the Nazis—worried that the entire family might be discovered at any time—Anne notes that "Thanks to Father – who brought my entire postcard and**

movie-star collection here beforehand — and to a brush and a pot of glue, I was able to plaster the wall with pictures. It looks much more cheerful" (Frank 20). She also writes of the everyday details of her life, such as the chiming of the clock near their hidden location. **A similar example from a different situation comes from a Japanese internment camp in the United States from the same period. In** *Dear Miss Breed: True Stories of the Japanese American Incarceration During World War II and a Librarian Who Made a Difference,* **Louise Ogawa writes to Miss Breed about the beauty of the Colorado River they had crossed on their way to the incarceration camp. Louise showed that she was trying to find positive things to think about when she wrote, "Yesterday, I ate rice, weenies, and cabbage with a knife. That was a new experience for me!" (Oppenheim 114).** These two individuals show that they were trying to keep a positive attitude in extremely difficult circumstances. Although some may argue that a positive attitude didn't really help Anne Frank, who ended up dying in the Bergen-Belsen concentration camp, her strength and spirit while enduring tremendously difficult circumstances have inspired countless individuals across the decades. **The diary has been translated into 70 languages, and over 28 million people have visited her home since it opened as a museum in 1960 (The Anne Frank House).** Her positive attitude therefore has had a profound impact beyond her own life and cannot be discounted.

Before each sentence that includes a quotation, the student writer's own words introduce the source. The text appearing in quotation marks is exactly the same as the text of the source from which it was taken. The student writer did not change any words or punctuation. The student author also cited the source author's name and a page number in parentheses after each quote. In addition, the student writer gave credit to statistical information she paraphrased from a credible website through another parenthetical citation.

In the "Works Cited" list at the end of the essay, the writer has provided all the essential information about works she used in the research and preparation of her essay.

Works Cited

Frank, Anne. Anne Frank: The Diary of a Young Girl. New York: Doubleday, 1952.

Lawson, Karen, M.D. "How Do Thoughts & Emotions Impact Health?" *Taking Charge of Your Health and Well-Being.* University of Minnesota. Web. 12 Dec. 2014. http://www.takingcharge.csh.umn.edu/enhance-your-wellbeing/health/thoughts-emotions/how-do-thoughts-emotions-impact-health

"Music of the Ghettos and Camps." *A Teacher's Guide to the Holocaust.* The Florida Center for Instructional Technology, College of Education, University of South Florida. C. 1997–2013. Web. 12 Dec. 2014. http://fcit.coedu.usf.edu/holocaust/arts/musVicti.htm

Oppenheim, Joanne. *Dear Miss Breed: True Stories of the Japanese American Incarceration During World War II and a Librarian Who Made a Difference.* New York: Scholastic, Inc., 2006.

Schaumann, Caroline. "Factors Influencing Survival during the Holocaust." *History in Dispute, Vol. 11: The Holocaust, 1933–1945.* Benjamin Frankel, ed. St. James Press, 1999. Web. 12 December 2014. http://www.google.com/url?sa=t&rct=j&q=&esrc=s&source=web&cd=1&ved=0CCMQFjAA&url=http%3A%2F%2Ffacweb.northseattle.edu%2Fcadler%2FGlobal_Dialogues%2FReadings%2FMaus_Readings%2FFactors%2520Influencing%2520Survival%2520during%2520the%2520Holocaust.doc&ei=YT-LVKuOKYqOyQSCpoCoDQ&usg=AFQjCNEoEdrB6D18vVuQyPy96REwrVu1mQ&sig2=Ui_cnN68CkQxmdGvtLNPWA&bvm=bv.81828268,d.aWw&cad=rja

Virtual Museum of The Anne Frank House. Anne Frank Stichting. 28 April 2010. Web. 27 March 2015. http://www.annefrank.org/en/subsites/timeline/postwar-period-1945—present-day/the-diary-is-published/1950/the-diary-of-anne-frank-is-published-in-germany-in-an-edition-of-4500-copies-a-very-successful-paperback-edition-follows-in-1955/#!/en/subsites/timeline/postwar-period-1945--present-day/the-diary-is-published/1950/the-diary-of-anne-frank-is-published-in-germany-in-an-edition-of-4500-copies-a-very-successful-paperback-edition-follows-in-1955/

http://www.annefrank.org/en/News/Press/Visitor-numbers/

Notice that all the works referenced in the essay are listed here. For each work cited, complete bibliographic information is presented including the author's name, the title of the work, the place of publication, the publisher, and the date of publication.

It is common practice to present the titles of full-length works such as books, plays, and movies in italics. Shorter works, such as titles of articles, chapters, short stories, poems, and songs are presented within quotation marks.

If you scan the items in the Works Cited list, you will see that most types of sources follow the same general sequence: author, title of the work, publication information. Commas are used to set off elements within each of these general groupings, but each grouping ends with a period. Notice how, when a source is electronic, an element of the citation indicates that the item is from the "Web." In the event that a source has no named author, the citation begins with the title of the work or the website from which information was obtained.

The style for the material presented in this Works Cited list is based on standards established by the Modern Language Association (MLA). However, there are many other acceptable forms of citation. When completing academic writing, it is important to determine if any other particular style of citation is required by your teacher.

 PRACTICE

Check over the draft copy of your argumentative essay that you created in the previous lesson. Look for proper citations of all quotations, ideas, and information that came from other sources. Then make sure your Works Cited page contains correct and complete bibliographical information matching all of the sources you used in your paper. When you feel your citations are complete and correct, exchange your draft with a partner to give and receive feedback.

Review one draft from a peer. Check your peer's work to see if all ideas, quotations, and other information that came from outside sources is cited correctly. Check the Works Cited page to make sure each source is listed and that each listing contains correct and complete information so that a reader could locate the source or understand where the information came from. Remember to keep your comments kind, helpful, and constructive.

NOTES

REVISE

CA-CCSS: CA.W.8.1a, CA.W.8.1b, CA.W.8.1c, CA.W.8.1d, CA.W.8.1e, CA.W.8.4, CA.W.8.5, CA.W.8.6, CA.W.8.7, CA.W.8.8, CA.W.8.9b, CA.W.8.10, CA.SL.8.1a, CA.L.8.1b, CA.L.8.1d, CA.L.8.3a

## WRITING PROMPT

Carefully consider the selections you have read in this unit, including their themes and the ideas they offer about war and conflict. Pick two of the selections from the unit and write an argumentative essay that presents a claim in answer to the following question: how can people best respond to conflict? Along with information from the selections, include research from at least three other credible print and digital sources to support your claim and develop your argument.

Your argumentative essay should include:

- An introduction with a clear thesis statement that presents your claim

- Organized body paragraphs with relevant evidence and support for your claim as well as clear transitions to show the connections among ideas

- A concluding paragraph that effectively wraps up your essay

- A Works Cited page that, in addition to the two unit texts, lists at least three other reliable sources used in your essay

You have written a draft of your argumentative text. You have also received input from your peers about how to improve it and learned more information about how to properly cite your sources. Now you are going to revise your draft.

Here are some recommendations to help you revise.

- Think about the suggestions you received from the peer reviews. Which ones would you like to include as you revise?

- Consider what other changes you could make to improve your essay's evidence, analysis, or organization.

> Reread your introduction and your conclusion. Is your claim clear in both of these paragraphs? How can you improve these paragraphs?
> Reread the body paragraphs. Is your claim supported by evidence drawn from the unit texts and credible sources obtained from research? What new or additional textual evidence could you add to strengthen support for your claim? What details could you add to capture the readers' interest? For example, did you supply personal stories to serve as examples of how people cope with abusive situations in a positive manner? Could you relate an anecdote about a positive attitude in a time of war with students' lives today?
> Have you acknowledged an alternate or opposing claim and distinguished it from your own? How so?
> How effective is your organizational structure? Are ideas presented logically? Do transition words and phrases connect your paragraphs? Do the transitions that you have chosen clearly show the relationships among claims, counterclaims, reasons, and evidence? How could you strengthen your essay's flow by improving your use of transitions?
> Check for plagiarism. Did you use paraphrase and use direct quotations from your sources and give them credit in the proper format? Quotations will enliven your essay and make it more interesting for readers. Be sure to cite your sources when you use quotations.
> Is your Works Cited page correct, complete, and accurate?
> Examine your word choice and vocabulary. Can you improve your essay by choosing a more precise or vivid word instead of a less precise one?
> Have you formed and used verbs in the active and passive voice correctly to achieve particular effects?

- When you feel that your argumentative essay is complete in terms of content, examine your draft to make sure you have maintained a formal style. A formal style shows your audience the seriousness of your ideas.
  > As you revise, remove any slang terms, contractions, or other informal language.
  > Do not use any first-person pronouns such as *I, me,* or *my.* Do not address your readers as *you.* These terms are more suitable for informal writing, such as for letters to friends, informal descriptions, and so forth. Make sure that you have used all of the pronouns in your essay correctly.
  > Look for personal opinions that do not have supporting evidence. These do not belong in formal writing based on research. Make sure your essay is clear and direct, and that all of your points are supported by facts and logical reasoning.

# EDIT, PROOFREAD, AND PUBLISH

CA-CCSS: CA.W.8.1a, CA.W.8.1b, CA.W.8.1c, CA.W.8.1d, CA.W.8.1e, CA.W.8.4, CA.W.8.5, CA.W.8.6, CA.W.8.7, CA.W.8.8, CA.W.8.9b, CA.W.8.10, CA.SL.8.1a, CA.SL.8.3, CA.SL.8.4, CA.SL.8.4a, CA.L.8.1b, CA.L.8.1c, CA.L.8.1d, CA.L.8.2a, CA.L.8.3a

## WRITING PROMPT

Carefully consider the selections you have read in this unit, including their themes and the ideas they offer about war and conflict. Pick two of the selections from the unit and write an argumentative essay that presents a claim in answer to the following question: how can people best respond to conflict? Along with information from the selections, include research from at least three other credible print and digital sources to support your claim and develop your argument.

Your argumentative essay should include:

- An introduction with a clear thesis statement that presents your claim
- Organized body paragraphs with relevant evidence and support for your claim as well as clear transitions to show the connections among ideas
- A concluding paragraph that effectively wraps up your essay
- A Works Cited page that, in addition to the two unit texts, lists at least three other reliable sources used in your essay

You have revised your argumentative essay and submitted it to your peers for review. They gave you suggestions and feedback, so you are ready to edit your essay and proofread it so it is ready to be published. Read through your essay one more time and make sure you have considered and incorporated the valuable input from the peer reviews. Reread your claim, presented in the introduction, supported in the body paragraphs, and restated in the conclusion. Did you fully develop your claim and use strong evidence drawn from sources to support your stance? Did you adequately distinguish your claim from alternate or opposing ones? Did you cite your sources accurately? Is there any way to improve the organization or transitions? Have you

maintained a consistently formal style throughout the essay? What other aspects of this essay can still be improved?

After you have thoughtfully reviewed your essay and made adjustments to strengthen it, it is time to proofread for errors. As you proofread, think about your punctuation (especially punctuation of quotations and citations and to set off nonrestrictive or parenthetical elements). Have you used dashes correctly? Did you correctly form and use verbs in the active and passive voice, and in the indicative, imperative, interrogative, conditional, and subjunctive mood to achieve particular effects, avoiding inappropriate shifts in voice or mood? Look for misspelled words, as well.

Once you have made all necessary corrections, it is time to submit and publish your work. Who might be interested in reading this piece? You may distribute your finished essay to family and friends, post it on a bulletin board, or publish it on your blog. If you do publish online, remember to create links to your online sources and citations. This will help your readers have easy access to more information about the topic.

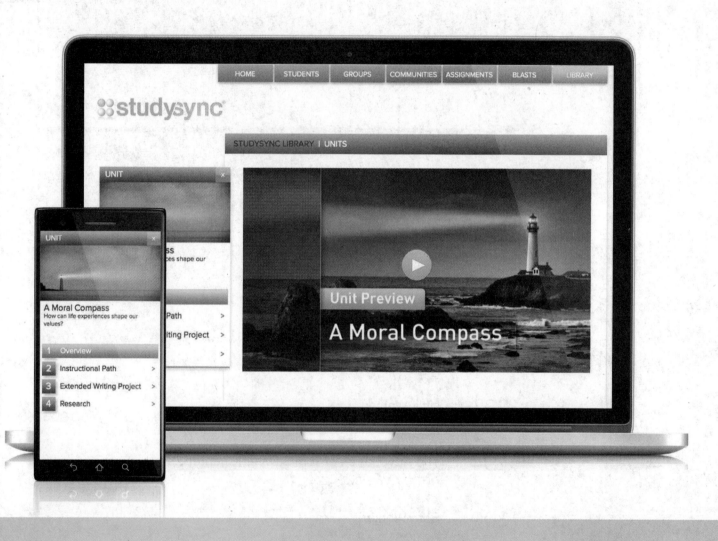

# :::studysync®

## Reading & Writing Companion

How can life experiences shape our values?

# A Moral Compass

UNIT 3    How can life experiences shape our values?

# A Moral Compass

## TEXTS

## ENGLISH LANGUAGE DEVELOPMENT TEXTS

## EXTENDED WRITING PROJECT

501

Text Fulfillment through StudySync

# ABUELA INVENTS THE ZERO

FICTION

Judith Ortiz Cofer

1996

## INTRODUCTION

Judith Ortiz Cofer's writing reflects the differences between her two childhood homes; one on the island of Puerto Rico and one in a *barrio* (neighborhood) on the mainland. In this short story, Constancia is a teenager whose *abuela* (grandmother) comes to visit her in New Jersey. Caught between her American and Puerto Rican identities, Constancia feels embarrassed by the "bizarre" behavior of her *abuela* at church, and hides her face in shame. Later, she is left to contemplate the meaning of "zero."

# "I realize to my horror that my grandmother is lost."

 **FIRST READ**

1   "You made me feel like a zero, like a nothing," she says in Spanish, *un cero, nada.* She is trembling, an angry little old woman lost in a heavy winter coat that belongs to my mother. And I end up being sent to my room, like I was a child, to think about my grandmother's idea of math.

2   It all began with Abuela coming up from the Island for a visit—her first time in the United States. My mother and father paid her way here so that she wouldn't die without seeing snow, though if you asked me, and nobody has, the dirty slush in this city is not worth the price of a ticket. But I guess she deserves some kind of award for having had ten kids and survived to tell about it. My mother is the youngest of the bunch. Right up to the time when we're supposed to pick up the old lady at the airport, my mother is telling me stories about how hard times were for *la familia* on *la isla,* and how *la abuela* worked night and day to support them after their father died of a heart attack. I'd die of a heart attack too if I had a troop like that to support. Anyway, I had seen her only three or four times in my entire life, whenever we would go for somebody's funeral. I was born here and I have lived in this building all my life. But when Mami says, "Connie, please be nice to Abuela. She doesn't have too many years left. Do you promise me, Constancia?"—when she uses my full name, I know she means business. So I say, "Sure." Why wouldn't I be nice? I'm not a monster, after all.

3   So we go to Kennedy to get *la abuela,* and she is the last to come out of the airplane, on the arm of the cabin attendant, all wrapped up in a black shawl. He hands her over to my parents like she was a package sent airmail. It is January, two feet of snow on the ground, and she's wearing a shawl over a thick black dress. That's just the start.

4   Once home, she refuses to let my mother buy her a coat because it's a waste of money for the two weeks she'll be in *el Polo Norte,* as she calls New

Jersey, the North Pole. So since she's only four feet eleven inches tall, she walks around in my mother's big black coat looking ridiculous. I try to walk far behind them in public so that no one will think we're together. I plan to stay very busy the whole time she's with us so that I won't be asked to take her anywhere, but my plan is ruined when my mother comes down with the flu and Abuela absolutely *has* to attend Sunday mass or her soul will be eternally damned. She's more Catholic than the Pope. My father decides that he should stay home with my mother and that I should escort *la abuela* to church. He tells me this on Saturday night as I'm getting ready to go out to the mall with my friends.

5   "No way," I say.

6   I go for the car keys on the kitchen table: he usually leaves them there for me
7   on Friday and Saturday nights. He beats me to them."No way," he says, pocketing them and grinning at me.

8   Needless to say, we come to a **compromise** very quickly. I do have a responsibility to Sandra and Anita, who don't drive yet. There is a Harley-Davidson fashion show at Brookline Square that we *cannot* miss.

9   "The mass in Spanish is at ten sharp tomorrow morning, entiendes?" My father is dangling the car keys in front of my nose and pulling them back when I try to reach for them. He's really enjoying himself.

10  "I understand. Ten o'clock. I'm out of here." I pry his fingers off the key ring. He knows that I'm late, so he makes it just a little difficult. Then he laughs. I run out of our apartment before he changes his mind. I have no idea what I'm getting myself into.

11  Sunday morning I have to walk two blocks on dirty snow to retrieve the car. I warm it up for Abuela as instructed by my parents, and drive it to the front of our building. My father walks her by the hand in baby steps on the slippery snow. The sight of her little head with a bun on top of it sticking out of that huge coat makes me want to run back into my room and get under the covers. I just hope that nobody I know sees us together. I'm dreaming, of course. The mass is packed with people from our block. It's a holy day of **obligation** and everyone I ever met is there.

12  I have to help her climb the steps, and she stops to take a deep breath after each one, then I lead her down the aisle so that everybody can see me with my bizarre grandmother. If I were a good Catholic, I'm sure I'd get some **purgatory** time taken off for my sacrifice. She is walking as slow as Captain Cousteau exploring the bottom of the sea, looking around, taking her sweet time. Finally she chooses a pew, but she wants to sit in the other end. It's like she had a spot picked out for some unknown reason, and although it's the

most inconvenient seat in the house, that's where she has to sit. So we squeeze by all the people already sitting there, saying, "Excuse me, please, *con permiso,* pardon me," getting annoyed looks the whole way. By the time we settle in, I'm drenched in sweat. I keep my head down like I'm praying so as not to see or be seen. She is praying loud, in Spanish, and singing hymns at the top of her creaky voice.

13   I ignore her when she gets up with a hundred other people to go take communion. I'm actually praying hard now—that this will all be over soon. But the next time I look up, I see a black coat dragging around and around the church, stopping here and there so a little gray head can peek out like a **periscope** on a submarine. There are giggles in the church, and even the priest has frozen in the middle of a blessing, his hands above his head like he is about to lead the congregation in a set of jumping jacks.

14   I realize to my horror that my grandmother is lost. She can't find her way back to the pew. I am so embarrassed that even though the woman next to me is shooting daggers at me with her eyes, I just can't move to go get her. I put my hands over my face like I'm praying, but it's really to hide my burning cheeks. I would like for her to disappear. I just know that on Monday my friends, and my enemies, in the barrio will have a lot of **senile**-grandmother jokes to tell in front of me. I am frozen to my seat. So the same woman who wants me dead on the spot does it for me. She makes a big deal out of getting up and hurrying to get Abuela.

15   The rest of the mass is a blur. All I know is that my grandmother kneels the whole time with her hands over *her* face. She doesn't speak to me on the way home, and she doesn't let me help her walk, even though she almost falls a couple of times.

16   When we get to the apartment, my parents are at the kitchen table, where my mother is trying to eat some soup. They can see right away that something is wrong. Then Abuela points her finger at me like a judge passing a sentence on a criminal. She says in Spanish, "You made me feel like a zero, like a nothing." Then she goes to her room.

17   I try to explain what happened. "I don't understand why she's so upset. She just got lost and wandered around for a while," I tell them. But it sounds lame, even to my own ears. My mother gives me a look that makes me cringe and goes in to Abuela's room to get her version of the story. She comes out with tears in her eyes.

18   "Your grandmother says to tell you that of all the hurtful things you can do to a person, the worst is to make them feel as if they are worth nothing."

19 I can feel myself shrinking right there in front of her. But I can't bring myself to tell my mother that I think I understand how I made Abuela feel. I might be sent into the old lady's room to apologize, and it's not easy to admit you've been a jerk—at least, not right away with everybody watching. So I just sit there not saying anything.

20 My mother looks at me for a long time, like she feels sorry for me. Then she says, "You should know, Constancia, that if it wasn't for the old woman whose existence you don't seem to value, you and I would not be here."

21 That's when *I'm* sent to *my* room to consider a number I hadn't thought much about—until today.

"Abuela Invents the Zero" from *An Island Like You: Stories of the Barrio* by Judith Ortiz Cofer and published by Scholastic, Inc. Copyright (c) 1995 by Judith Ortiz Cofer. Reprinted with permission. All rights reserved.

## THINK QUESTIONS   CA-CCSS: CA.RL.8.1, CA.L.8.4a, CA.L.8.4b

1. Describe Constancia's relationship with Abuela prior to her grandmother's visit to New Jersey. Cite details from the text to support your response.

2. Refer to details from the text to explain why Constancia considers her grandmother to be, in her eyes, "ridiculous" and "bizarre."

3. How does Constancia respond when Abuela becomes lost in the church? Describe her reaction, and support your answer with textual evidence.

4. Use context to determine the meaning of the word **obligation** as it is used in paragraph 11 of "Abuela Invents the Zero." Write your definition of *obligation* and explain how you found it.

5. Remembering that the Greek prefix peri- means "around," use your understanding of the Greek prefix as well as context clues in "Abuela Invents the Zero" to determine the meaning of **periscope** in paragraph 13. Write your definition of *periscope*.

# CLOSE READ

CA-CCSS: CA.RL.8.1, CA.RL.8.2, CA.RL.8.3, CA.W.8.4, CA.W.8.5, CA.W.8.6, CA.W.8.10

Reread the short story "Abuela Invents the Zero." As you reread, complete the Focus Questions below. Then use your answers and annotations from the questions to help you complete the Writing Prompt.

 FOCUS QUESTIONS

1. Before Abuela's arrival, which lines of dialogue in the story reveal that Constancia is unaware of the consequences her actions can have, and that Constancia's mother knows her daughter well and is trying to prevent any tension from occurring? Highlight evidence in the text and make annotations to support your answer.

2. Analyzing particular incidents in a story or drama can provide readers with details that point to the theme. Reread paragraphs 14 and 15 and highlight specific evidence that suggests how the incident at the church is a turning point in the relationship between Constancia and Abuela, and what it reveals about the theme.

3. Reread the last five paragraphs of the story. What information does the author include that suggests

Constancia still doesn't fully realize how much her behavior has hurt her grandmother? Highlight evidence in the text that supports your answer.

4. Throughout the story, how does the author reveal the importance Constancia places on clothes and appearance, and how does this character trait serve to create a distance between grandmother and granddaughter? Highlight evidence in the text that supports your answer.

5. Compare and contrast Abuela with her granddaughter. What values do each of them have at the beginning of the story? How have their life experiences helped to shape their values? Highlight evidence in the text that supports your answer.

## WRITING PROMPT

How does the theme of "Abuela Invents the Zero" help you understand a larger lesson about how life experiences can shape our values? Use the details you have compiled from examining the conflict between the characters, as well as the characters' thoughts, dialogue, feelings, and actions, to:

- identify the theme of the story
- analyze how it is developed over the course of the text

Remember to support your writing with evidence and inferences from the text.

Please note that excerpts and passages in the StudySync® library and this workbook are intended as touchstones to generate interest in an author's work. The excerpts and passages do not substitute for the reading of entire texts, and StudySync® strongly recommends that students seek out and purchase the whole literary or informational work in order to experience it as the author intended. Links to online resellers are available in our digital library. In addition, complete works may be ordered through an authorized reseller by filling out and returning to StudySync® the order form enclosed in this workbook.

Reading & Writing Companion    **263**

# HOME

**FICTION**
Anton Chekhov
1887

## INTRODUCTION

Anton Chekhov is one of Russia's most prized short story writers. He is known for his authentic and objective depictions of characters and situations and his humorous style. In this excerpt from Anton Chekhov's short story *Home*, a prosecutor discovers that his young son has been smoking, and uses the occasion to both teach the boy a lesson and muse on the nature of morality.

# "I tell you, my boy, I don't love you, and you are no son of mine..."

## FIRST READ

1 "SOMEONE came from the Grigoryevs' to fetch a book, but I said you were not at home. The postman brought the newspaper and two letters. By the way, Yevgeny Petrovitch, I should like to ask you to speak to Seryozha. To-day, and the day before yesterday, I have noticed that he is smoking. When I began to expostulate with him, he put his fingers in his ears as usual, and sang loudly to drown my voice."

2 Yevgeny Petrovitch Bykovsky, the prosecutor of the circuit court, who had just come back from a session and was taking off his gloves in his study, looked at the governess as she made her report, and laughed.

3 "Seryozha smoking . . ." he said, shrugging his shoulders. "I can picture the little cherub with a cigarette in his mouth! Why, how old is he?"

4 "Seven. You think it is not important, but at his age smoking is a bad and pernicious habit, and bad habits ought to be eradicated in the beginning."

5 "Perfectly true. And where does he get the tobacco?"

6 "He takes it from the drawer in your table."

7 "Yes? In that case, send him to me."

8 When the governess had gone out, Bykovsky sat down in an arm-chair before his writing-table, shut his eyes, and fell to thinking. He pictured his Seryozha with a huge cigar, a yard long, in the midst of clouds of tobacco smoke, and this caricature made him smile; at the same time, the grave, troubled face of the governess called up memories of the long past, half-forgotten time when smoking aroused in his teachers and parents a strange, not quite intelligible horror. It really was horror. Children were mercilessly flogged and expelled

from school, and their lives were made a misery on account of smoking, though not a single teacher or father knew exactly what was the harm or sinfulness of smoking. Even very intelligent people did not **scruple** to wage war on a vice which they did not understand. Yevgeny Petrovitch remembered the head-master of the high school, a very cultured and good-natured old man, who was so appalled when he found a high-school boy with a cigarette in his mouth that he turned pale, immediately summoned an emergency committee of the teachers, and sentenced the sinner to expulsion. This was probably a law of social life: the less an evil was understood, the more fiercely and coarsely it was attacked.

9  "The prosecutor remembered two or three boys who had been expelled and their subsequent life, and could not help thinking that very often the punishment did a great deal more harm than the crime itself. The living organism has the power of rapidly adapting itself, growing accustomed and **inured** to any atmosphere whatever, otherwise man would be bound to feel at every moment what an irrational basis there often is underlying his rational activity, and how little of established truth and certainty there is even in work so responsible and so terrible in its effects as that of the teacher, of the lawyer, of the writer. . . .

10  And such light and **discursive** thoughts as visit the brain only when it is weary and resting began straying through Yevgeny Petrovitch's head; there is no telling whence and why they come, they do not remain long in the mind, but seem to glide over its surface without sinking deeply into it. For people who are forced for whole hours, and even days, to think by routine in one direction, such free private thinking affords a kind of comfort, an agreeable solace.

11  It was between eight and nine o'clock in the evening. Overhead, on the second storey, someone was walking up and down, and on the floor above that four hands were playing scales. The pacing of the man overhead who, to judge from his nervous step, was thinking of something harassing, or was suffering from toothache, and the monotonous scales gave the stillness of the evening a drowsiness that disposed to lazy reveries. In the nursery, two rooms away, the governess and Seryozha were talking.

12  "Pa-pa has come!" carolled the child. "Papa has co-ome. Pa! Pa! Pa!"

13  *"Votre père vous appelle, allez vite!"* cried the governess, shrill as a frightened bird. "I am speaking to you!"

14  "What am I to say to him, though?" Yevgeny Petrovitch wondered.

15  But before he had time to think of anything whatever his son Seryozha, a boy of seven, walked into the study.

16 He was a child whose sex could only have been guessed from his dress: weakly, white-faced, and fragile. He was limp like a hot-house plant, and everything about him seemed extraordinarily soft and tender: his movements, his curly hair, the look in his eyes, his velvet jacket.

17 "Good evening, papa!" he said, in a soft voice, clambering on to his father's knee and giving him a rapid kiss on his neck. "Did you send for me?"

18 "Excuse me, Sergey Yevgenitch," answered the prosecutor, removing him from his knee. "Before kissing we must have a talk, and a serious talk . . . I am angry with you, and don't love you any more. I tell you, my boy, I don't love you, and you are no son of mine. . . ."

19 Seryozha looked intently at his father, then shifted his eyes to the table, and shrugged his shoulders.

20 "What have I done to you?" he asked in perplexity, blinking. "I haven't been in your study all day, and I haven't touched anything."

21 "Natalya Semyonovna has just been complaining to me that you have been smoking. . . . Is it true? Have you been smoking?"

22 "Yes, I did smoke once. . . . That's true. . . ."

23 "Now you see you are lying as well," said the prosecutor, frowning to disguise a smile. "Natalya Semyonovna has seen you smoking twice. So you see you have been detected in three misdeeds: smoking, taking someone else's tobacco, and lying. Three faults."

24 "Oh yes," Seryozha recollected, and his eyes smiled. "That's true, that's true; I smoked twice: to-day and before."

25 "So you see it was not once, but twice. . . . I am very, very much displeased with you! You used to be a good boy, but now I see you are spoilt and have become a bad one."

26 Yevgeny Petrovitch smoothed down Seryozha's collar and thought:

27 "What more am I to say to him!"

28 "Yes, it's not right," he continued. "I did not expect it of you. In the first place, you ought not to take tobacco that does not belong to you. Every person has only the right to make use of his own property; if he takes anyone else's . . . he is a bad man!" ("I am not saying the right thing!" thought Yevgeny Petrovitch.) "For instance, Natalya Semyonovna has a box with her clothes in it. That's her box, and we—that is, you and I—dare not touch it, as it is not ours. That's right,

isn't it? You've got toy horses and pictures. . . . I don't take them, do I? Perhaps I might like to take them, but . . . they are not mine, but yours!"

29  "Take them if you like!" said Seryozha, raising his eyebrows. "Please don't hesitate, papa, take them! That yellow dog on your table is mine, but I don't mind. . . . Let it stay."

30  "You don't understand me," said Bykovsky. "You have given me the dog, it is mine now and I can do what I like with it; but I didn't give you the tobacco! The tobacco is mine." ("I am not explaining properly!" thought the prosecutor. "It's wrong! Quite wrong!") "If I want to smoke someone else's tobacco, I must first of all ask his permission. . . ."

31  Languidly linking one phrase on to another and imitating the language of the nursery, Bykovsky tried to explain to his son the meaning of property. Seryozha gazed at his chest and listened attentively (he liked talking to his father in the evening), then he leaned his elbow on the edge of the table and began screwing up his short-sighted eyes at the papers and the inkstand. His eyes strayed over the table and rested on the gum-bottle.

32  "Papa, what is gum made of?" he asked suddenly, putting the bottle to his eyes.

33  Bykovsky took the bottle out of his hands and set it in its place and went on:

34  "Secondly, you smoke. . . . That's very bad. Though I smoke it does not follow that you may. I smoke and know that it is stupid, I blame myself and don't like myself for it." ("A clever teacher, I am!" he thought.) "Tobacco is very bad for the health, and anyone who smokes dies earlier than he should. It's particularly bad for boys like you to smoke. Your chest is weak, you haven't reached your full strength yet, and smoking leads to **consumption** and other illness in weak people. Uncle Ignat died of consumption, you know. If he hadn't smoked, perhaps he would have lived till now."

35  Seryozha looked pensively at the lamp, touched the lamp-shade with his finger, and heaved a sigh.

36  "Uncle Ignat played the violin splendidly!" he said. "His violin is at the Grigoryevs' now."

37  Seryozha leaned his elbows on the edge of the table again, and sank into thought. His white face wore a fixed expression, as though he were listening or following a train of thought of his own; distress and something like fear came into his big staring eyes. He was most likely thinking now of death, which had so lately carried off his mother and Uncle Ignat. Death carries mothers and uncles off to the other world, while their children and violins

remain upon the earth. The dead live somewhere in the sky beside the stars, and look down from there upon the earth. Can they endure the parting?

38 "What am I to say to him?" thought Yevgeny Petrovitch. "He's not listening to me. Obviously he does not regard either his misdoings or my arguments as serious. How am I to drive it home?"

39 The prosecutor got up and walked about the study.

40 "Formerly, in my time, these questions were very simply settled," he reflected. "Every urchin who was caught smoking was thrashed. The cowardly and faint-hearted did actually give up smoking, any who were somewhat more **plucky** and intelligent, after the thrashing took to carrying tobacco in the legs of their boots, and smoking in the barn. When they were caught in the barn and thrashed again, they would go away to smoke by the river . . . and so on, till the boy grew up. My mother used to give me money and sweets not to smoke. Now that method is looked upon as worthless and immoral. The modern teacher, taking his stand on logic, tries to make the child form good principles, not from fear, nor from desire for distinction or reward, but consciously."

41 While he was walking about, thinking, Seryozha climbed up with his legs on a chair sideways to the table, and began drawing. That he might not spoil official paper nor touch the ink, a heap of half-sheets, cut on purpose for him, lay on the table together with a blue pencil.

42 "Cook was chopping up cabbage to-day and she cut her finger," he said, drawing a little house and moving his eyebrows. "She gave such a scream that we were all frightened and ran into the kitchen. Stupid thing! Natalya Semyonovna told her to dip her finger in cold water, but she sucked it . . . And how could she put a dirty finger in her mouth! That's not proper, you know, papa!"

43 Then he went on to describe how, while they were having dinner, a man with a hurdy-gurdy had come into the yard with a little girl, who had danced and sung to the music.

44 "He has his own train of thought!" thought the prosecutor. "He has a little world of his own in his head, and he has his own ideas of what is important and unimportant. To gain possession of his attention, it's not enough to imitate his language, one must also be able to think in the way he does. He would understand me perfectly if I really were sorry for the loss of the tobacco, if I felt injured and cried. . . . That's why no one can take the place of a mother in bringing up a child, because she can feel, cry, and laugh together with the child. One can do nothing by logic and morality. What more shall I say to him? What?"

NOTES

45   And it struck Yevgeny Petrovitch as strange and absurd that he, an experienced advocate, who spent half his life in the practice of reducing people to silence, forestalling what they had to say, and punishing them, was completely at a loss and did not know what to say to the boy.

46   "I say, give me your word of honour that you won't smoke again," he said.

47   "Word of hon-nour!" carolled Seryozha, pressing hard on the pencil and bending over the drawing. "Word of hon-nour!"

48   "Does he know what is meant by word of honour?" Bykovsky asked himself. "No, I am a poor teacher of morality! If some schoolmaster or one of our legal fellows could peep into my brain at this moment he would call me a poor stick, and would very likely suspect me of unnecessary subtlety. . . . But in school and in court, of course, all these wretched questions are far more simply settled than at home; here one has to do with people whom one loves beyond everything, and love is exacting and complicates the question. If this boy were not my son, but my pupil, or a prisoner on his trial, I should not be so cowardly, and my thoughts would not be racing all over the place!"

49   Yevgeny Petrovitch sat down to the table and pulled one of Seryozha's drawings to him. In it there was a house with a crooked roof, and smoke which came out of the chimney like a flash of lightning in zigzags up to the very edge of the paper; beside the house stood a soldier with dots for eyes and a bayonet that looked like the figure 4.

50   "A man can't be taller than a house," said the prosecutor.

51   Seryozha got on his knee, and moved about for some time to get comfortably settled there.

52   "No, papa!" he said, looking at his drawing. "If you were to draw the soldier small you would not see his eyes."

53   Ought he to argue with him? From daily observation of his son the prosecutor had become convinced that children, like savages, have their own artistic standpoints and requirements peculiar to them, beyond the grasp of grown-up people. Had he been attentively observed, Seryozha might have struck a grown-up person as abnormal. He thought it possible and reasonable to draw men taller than houses, and to represent in pencil, not only objects, but even his sensations. Thus he would depict the sounds of an orchestra in the form of smoke like spherical blurs, a whistle in the form of a spiral thread. . . . To his mind sound was closely connected with form and colour, so that when he painted letters he invariably painted the letter L yellow, M red, A black, and so on.

54  Abandoning his drawing, Seryozha shifted about once more, got into a comfortable attitude, and busied himself with his father's beard. First he carefully smoothed it, then he parted it and began combing it into the shape of whiskers.

55  "Now you are like Ivan Stepanovitch," he said, "and in a minute you will be like our porter. Papa, why is it porters stand by doors? Is it to prevent thieves getting in?"

56  The prosecutor felt the child's breathing on his face, he was continually touching his hair with his cheek, and there was a warm soft feeling in his soul, as soft as though not only his hands but his whole soul were lying on the velvet of Seryozha's jacket.

57  He looked at the boy's big dark eyes, and it seemed to him as though from those wide pupils there looked out at him his mother and his wife and everything that he had ever loved.

58  "To think of thrashing him . . ." he mused. "A nice task to devise a punishment for him! How can we undertake to bring up the young? In old days people were simpler and thought less, and so settled problems boldly. But we think too much, we are eaten up by logic . . . . The more developed a man is, the more he reflects and gives himself up to subtleties, the more undecided and scrupulous he becomes, and the more timidity he shows in taking action. How much courage and self-confidence it needs, when one comes to look into it closely, to undertake to teach, to judge, to write a thick book. . . ."

59  It struck ten.

60  "Come, boy, it's bedtime," said the prosecutor. "Say good-night and go."

61  "No, papa," said Seryozha, "I will stay a little longer. Tell me something! Tell me a story. . . ."

62  "Very well, only after the story you must go to bed at once."

63  Yevgeny Petrovitch on his free evenings was in the habit of telling Seryozha stories. Like most people engaged in practical affairs, he did not know a single poem by heart, and could not remember a single fairy tale, so he had to improvise. As a rule he began with the stereotyped: "In a certain country, in a certain kingdom," then he heaped up all kinds of innocent nonsense and had no notion as he told the beginning how the story would go on, and how it would end. Scenes, characters, and situations were taken at random, impromptu, and the plot and the moral came of itself as it were, with no plan on the part of the story-teller. Seryozha was very fond of this improvisation,

and the prosecutor noticed that the simpler and the less ingenious the plot, the stronger the impression it made on the child.

64 "Listen," he said, raising his eyes to the ceiling. "Once upon a time, in a certain country, in a certain kingdom, there lived an old, very old emperor with a long grey beard, and . . . and with great grey moustaches like this. Well, he lived in a glass palace which sparkled and glittered in the sun, like a great piece of clear ice. The palace, my boy, stood in a huge garden, in which there grew oranges, you know . . . bergamots, cherries . . . tulips, roses, and lilies-of-the-valley were in flower in it, and birds of different colours sang there. . . . Yes. . . . On the trees there hung little glass bells, and, when the wind blew, they rang so sweetly that one was never tired of hearing them. Glass gives a softer, tenderer note than metals. . . . Well, what next? There were fountains in the garden. . . . Do you remember you saw a fountain at Auntie Sonya's summer villa? Well, there were fountains just like that in the emperor's garden, only ever so much bigger, and the jets of water reached to the top of the highest poplar."

65 Yevgeny Petrovitch thought a moment, and went on:

66 "The old emperor had an only son and heir of his kingdom—a boy as little as you. He was a good boy. He was never naughty, he went to bed early, he never touched anything on the table, and altogether he was a sensible boy. He had only one fault, he used to smoke. . . ."

67 Seryozha listened attentively, and looked into his father's eyes without blinking. The prosecutor went on, thinking: "What next?" He spun out a long rigmarole, and ended like this:

68 "The emperor's son fell ill with consumption through smoking, and died when he was twenty. His infirm and sick old father was left without anyone to help him. There was no one to govern the kingdom and defend the palace. Enemies came, killed the old man, and destroyed the palace, and now there are neither cherries, nor birds, nor little bells in the garden. . . . That's what happened."

69 This ending struck Yevgeny Petrovitch as absurd and naïve, but the whole story made an intense impression on Seryozha. Again his eyes were clouded by mournfulness and something like fear; for a minute he looked pensively at the dark window, shuddered, and said, in a sinking voice:

70 "I am not going to smoke any more. . . ."

71 When he had said good-night and gone away his father walked up and down the room and smiled to himself.

72  "They would tell me it was the influence of beauty, artistic form," he meditated. "It may be so, but that's no comfort. It's not the right way, all the same. . . . Why must morality and truth never be offered in their crude form, but only with embellishments, sweetened and gilded like pills? It's not normal. . . . It's falsification . . . deception . . . tricks . . . ."

73  He thought of the jurymen to whom it was absolutely necessary to make a "speech," of the general public who absorb history only from legends and historical novels, and of himself and how he had gathered an understanding of life not from sermons and laws, but from fables, novels, poems.

74  "Medicine should be sweet, truth beautiful, and man has had this foolish habit since the days of Adam . . . though, indeed, perhaps it is all natural, and ought to be so. . . . There are many deceptions and delusions in nature that serve a purpose."

75  He set to work, but lazy, intimate thoughts still strayed through his mind for a good while. Overhead the scales could no longer be heard, but the inhabitant of the second storey was still pacing from one end of the room to another.

 **THINK QUESTIONS**  CA-CCSS: CA.RL.8.1, CA.RL.8.3, CA.RL.8.4, CA.L.8.4a, CA.L.8.4d

1.  What problem does Yevgeny have at the beginning of the story, and why does he find it so difficult to solve? Cite textual evidence to support your answer.

2.  What line of reasoning does Yevgeny first use with his son about taking his tobacco, and why does it not get through to Seryozha? Cite textual evidence to support your answer.

3.  How does Yevgeny finally get through to Seryozha, getting a promise from his son that he will no longer smoke? Support your answer with textual evidence.

4.  Use context to determine the meaning of the word **discursive** as it is used in "Home." Write your definition of *discursive* and tell how you found it.

5.  Use the synonyms and antonyms provided in the passage to determine the meaning of **plucky** as it is used in "Home." Write your definition of *plucky* and tell how you got it.

Please note that excerpts and passages in the StudySync® library and this workbook are intended as touchstones to generate interest in an author's work. The excerpts and passages do not substitute for the reading of entire texts, and StudySync® strongly recommends that students seek out and purchase the whole literary or informational work in order to experience it as the author intended. Links to online resellers are available in our digital library. In addition, complete works may be ordered through an authorized reseller by filling out and returning to StudySync® the order form enclosed in this workbook.

Reading & Writing Companion  **273**

# CLOSE READ

CA-CCSS: CA.RL.8.1, CA.RL.8.3, CA.RL.8.4, CA.W.8.2

Reread the short story "Home." As you reread, complete the Focus Questions below. Then use your answers and annotations from the questions to help you complete the Writing Prompt

 FOCUS QUESTIONS

1. Reread the eighth and ninth paragraphs of the story. Why does Yevgeny have conflicting feelings about the idea of punishing someone for smoking? Highlight textual evidence from the story to support your answer.

2. How does Chekhov use interior monologue to show the changes Yevgeny goes through as he tries to think of ways to discipline his son? Highlight textual evidence from the story to explain your answer.

3. Why does Yevgeny become frustrated after attempting to reason logically with his son? Highlight evidence from the text and make annotations to support your explanation.

4. In the eleventh paragraph, Chekhov mentions the pacing of a man overhead who, to judge from his nervous step, was "thinking of something harassing." At the end of the story, after Yevgeny has sent Seryozha to bed, the author mentions that "the inhabitant of the second storey was still pacing from one end of the room to another." In what way do the actions of this unnamed, secondary character reflect Yevgeny's state of mind in the story? Highlight evidence from the text to support your answer.

5. Think about the title Chekhov has given this short story. In light of Yevgeny's profession, what takes place in the story, and what Yevgeny learns about how to get through to his son, why is the title "Home" so appropriate? Support your answer with textual evidence

## WRITING PROMPT

Yevgeny Petrovitch Bykovsky states that he achieves an understanding of life from sermons and laws, not from fables, novels, and poems. How does he change throughout the story? Write an essay of least 300 words explaining how he moves from logic to the use of stories and fairy tales as he attempts to reason with his son. Use textual evidence from the story to support your ideas.

# A CELEBRATION OF GRANDFATHERS

**NON-FICTION**
Rudolfo Anaya
1983

## INTRODUCTION

studysync®

As a young man, Rudolfo Anaya loved to read, but he could not find books that reflected his own Mexican American history and culture. Today, Anaya is a well-known writer who has published novels, short stories, plays, poems, and children's books that have contributed to the growing body of Chicano literature. In this essay, Anaya reflects on the life lessons he learned from his grandfather.

# "They learned that to survive one had to share in the process of life."

## FIRST READ

1   "Buenos Dias le de Dios, abuelo." God give you a good day, grandfather. This is how I was taught as a child to greet my grandfather, or any grown person. It was a greeting of respect, a cultural value to be passed on from generation to generation, this respect for the old ones.

2   The old people I remember from my childhood were strong in their beliefs, and as we lived daily with them we learned a wise path of life to follow. They had something important to share with the young, and when they spoke the young listened. These old abuelos and abuelitas had worked the earth all their lives, and so they knew the value of nurturing, they knew the sensitivity of the earth. The daily struggle called for cooperation, and so every person contributed to the social fabric, and each person was respected for his contribution.

3   The old ones had looked deep into the web that connects all animate and **inanimate** forms of life, and they recognized the great design of creation.

4   These ancianos from the cultures of the Rio Grande, lived side by side, sharing, growing together, they knew the rhythms and cycles of time, from the preparation of the earth in the spring to the digging of the acequias that bought the water to the dance of harvest in the fall. They shared good times and hard times. They helped each other through epidemics and the personal tragedies, they shared what little they had when the winds burned the land and no rain came. They learned that to survive one had to share in the process of life.

5   Hard workers all, they tilled the earth and farmed, ran the herds and spun wool, and carved their saints and their kachinas from cottonwood late in the winter nights. All worked with a deep faith which perplexes the modern mind.

6    Their faith shone in their eyes; it was in the strength of their grip, in the creases time wove into their faces. When they spoke, they spoke plainly and with few words, and they meant what they said. When they prayed, they went straight to the source of life. When there were good times, they knew how to dance in celebrations and how to prepare the foods of the fiestas. All this they passed on to the young, so that a new generation would know what they had known, so the string of life would not be broken.

7    Today we would say that the old abuelitos lived **authentic** lives.

8    Newcomers to New Mexico often say that time seems to move slowly here. I think they mean that they have come in contact with the inner strength of the people, a strength so solid it causes time itself to pause. Think of it. Think of the high northern New Mexico villages, or the lonely ranches on the open llano. Think of the Indian **pueblo** which lies as solid as rock in the face of time. Remember the old people whose eyes seem like windows that peer into the distant past that makes absurdity of our contemporary world. That is what one feels when one encounters the old ones and their land, a pausing of time.

9    We have all felt time stand still. We have all been in the presence of power, the knowledge of the old ones, the majestic peace of a mountain stream or an aspen grove or red buttes rising into blue sky. We have all felt the light of dusk permeate the earth and cause time to pause in its flow.

10   I felt this when I first touched the spirit of Ultima, the old curandera who appears in my first novel, Bless Me, Ultima. This is how the young Antonio describes what he feels:

11   When she came the beauty of the llano unfolded before my eyes, and the gurgling waters of the river sang to the hum of the turning earth. The magical time of childhood stood still, and the pulse of the living earth pressed its mystery into my living blood. She took my hand, and the silent, magical powers she possessed made beauty from the raw, sun-baked llano, the green river valley, and the blue bowl which was the white sun's home. My bare feet felt the throbbing earth, and my body trembled with excitement. Time stood still...

12   At other times, in other places, when I have been privileged to be with the old ones, to learn, I have felt this inner reserve of strength from which they draw. I have been held motionless and speechless by the power of curanderas. I have felt the same power when I hunted with Cruz, high on the Taos Mountain, where it was more than the incredible beauty of the mountain bathed in morning light, more that the shining of the quivering aspen, but a connection with life, as if a shining strand of light connected the particular and the cosmic. That feeling is an epiphany of time, a standing still of time.

13  But not all of our old ones are curanderos or hunters on the mountain. My grandfather was a plain man, a fan from the valley called Puerto de Luna on Pecos River. He was probably a descendant of those people who spilled over the mountain from Taos, following the Pecos River in search of farmland. There in that river valley he settled and raised a large family.

14  Bearded and walrus-mustached, he stood five feet tall, but to me as a child he was a giant. I remember him most for his silence. In the summers my parents sent me to live with him on his farm, for I was to learn the ways of a farmer. My uncles also lived in that valley, there where only the flow of the river and the whispering of the wind marked time. For me it was a magical place.

15  I remember once, while out in the fields, I came upon an anthill, and before I knew it I was badly bitten. After he had covered my welts with the cool mud from the irrigation ditch, my grandfather calmly said: "Know where you stand." That is the way he spoke, in short phrases, to the point.

16  One very dry summer, the river dried to a trickle, there was no water for the fields. The young plants withered and died. In my sadness and with the impulse of youth I said, "I wish it would rain!" My grandfather touched me, looked up into the sky and whispered, "Pray for rain." In his language there was a difference. He felt connected to the cycles that brought the rain or kept it from us. His prayer was a meaningful action, because he was a participant with the forces that filled our world, he was not a **bystander**.

17  A young man died at the village one summer. A very tragic death. He was dragged by his horse. When he was found I cried, for the boy was my friend. I did not understand why death had come to one so young. My grandfather took me aside and said: "Think of the death of the trees and the fields in the fall. The leaves fall, and everything rests, as if dead. But they bloom again in the spring. Death is only this small transformation in life."

18  These are the things I remember, these fleeting images, few words.

19  I remember him driving his horse-drawn wagon into Santa Rosa in the fall when he brought his harvest produce to sell in the town. What a tower of strength seemed to come in that small man huddled on the seat of the giant wagon. One click of his tongue and the horses obeyed, stopped or turned as he wished. He never raised his whip. How unlike today when so much teaching is done with loud words and threatening hands.

20  I would run to greet the wagon, and the wagon would stop. "Buenos Dias le de Dios, abuelo," I would say. "Buenos Dias te de Dios, mi hijo," he would answer and smile, and then I could jump up on the wagon and sit at his side. Then I, too, became a king as I rode next to the old man who smelled of earth

and sweat and the other deep aromas from the orchards and fields of Puerto de Luna.

21  We were all sons and daughters to him. But today the sons and daughters are breaking with the past, putting aside los abuelitos.' The old values are threatened, and threatened most where it comes to these relationships with the old people. If we don't take the time to watch and feel the years of their final transformation, a part of our humanity will be lessened.

22  I grew up speaking Spanish, and oh! how difficult it was to learn English. Sometimes I give up and cry out that I couldn't learn. Then he would say, "Ten paciencia." Have patience. Paciencia, a word with the strength of centuries, a word that said that someday we would overcome. Paciencia, how soothing a word coming from this old man who could still sling hundred-pound bags over his shoulder, chop wood for hundreds of hours on end, and hitch up his own horses and ride to town and back in one day.

23  "You have to learn the language of the Americanos," he said. "Me, I will live my last days in my valley. You will live in a new time, the time of the gringos."

24  A new time did come, a new time is here. How will we form it so it is fruitful? We need to know where we stand. We need to speak softly and respect others, and to share what we have. We need to pray not for material gain, but for rain for the fields, for the sun to nurture growth, for nights in which we can sleep in peace, and for a harvest in which everyone can share. Simple lessons from a simple man. These lessons he learned from his past, which was as deep and strong as the currents of the river of life, a life which could be stronger than death.

25  He was a man; he died. Not in his valley, but nevertheless cared for by his sons and daughters and flocks of grandchildren. At the end, I would enter his room, which carried the smell of medications and Vicks. Gone were the aromas of the fields, the strength of his young manhood. Gone also was his patience in the face of crippling old age. Small things bothered him; he shouted or turned sour when his expectations were not met. It was because he could not care for himself, because he was returning to that state of childhood, and all those wishes and desires were now wrapped in a crumbling old body.

26  "Ten paciencia," I once said to him, and he smiled. "I didn't know I would grow this old," he said.

27  I would sit and look at him and remember what was said of him when he was a young man. He could mount a wild horse and break it, and he could ride as far as any man. He could dance all night at a dance, then work the acequia

Please note that excerpts and passages in the StudySync® library and this workbook are intended as touchstones to generate interest in an author's work. The excerpts and passages do not substitute for the reading of entire texts, and StudySync® strongly recommends that students seek out and purchase the whole literary or informational work in order to experience it as the author intended. Links to online resellers are available in our digital library. In addition, complete works may be ordered through an authorized reseller by filling out and returning to StudySync® the order form enclosed in this workbook.

Reading & Writing Companion     **279**

the following day. He helped the neighbors, they helped him. He married, raised children. Small legends, the kind that make up every man's life.

28   He was ninety-four when he died. Family, neighbors, and friends gathered; they all agreed he had led a rich life. I remembered the last years, the years he spent in bed. And as I remember now, I am reminded that it is too easy to romanticize old age. Sometimes we forget the pain of the transformation into old age, we forget the natural breaking down of the body. Not all go gentle into the last years, some go crying and cursing, forgetting the names of those they love the most, withdrawing into an internal anguish few of us can know. May we be granted the patience and care to deal with our ancianos.

29   For some time we haven't looked at these changes and needs of the old ones. The American image created by the mass media is an image of youth, not of old age. It is the beautiful and the young who are praised in this society. If analyzed carefully, we see that same damaging thought has crept into the way society views the old. In response to the old, the mass media have just created old people who act like the young. It is only the healthy, pink-cheeked, outgoing, older persons we are shown in the media. And they are always selling something, as if an entire generation of old people were salesmen in their lives. Commercials show very lively old men, who must always be in excellent health according to the new myth, selling insurance policies or real estate as they are out golfing; older women selling coffee or toilet paper to those just married. That image does not illustrate the real life of old ones.

30   Real life takes into account the natural cycle of growth and change. My grandfather pointed to the leaves falling from the tree. So time brings with its transformation the often painful, wearing-down process. Vision blurs, health wanes even the act of walking carries with it the painful reminder of the autumn of life. But this process is something to be faced, not something to be hidden away by false images. Yes, the old can be young at heart, but in their own way, with their own dignity. They do not have to copy the always-young image of the Hollywood star.

31   My grandfather wanted to return to his valley to die. But by then the families of the valley had left in search of a better future. It is only now that there seems to be a return to the valley, a revival. The new generation seeks its roots, that value of love for the land moves us to return to the place where our ancianos formed the culture.

32   I returned to Puerto de Luna last summer, to join the community in a celebration of the founding of the church. I drove by my grandfather's home, my uncles' ranches, the neglected **adobe** washing down into the earth from whence it came. And I wondered, how might the values of my grandfather's generation live in our own? What can we retain to see us through these hard times? I was

NOTES

to become a farmer, and I became a writer. As I plow and plant my words, do I nurture as my grandfather did in his fields and orchards? The answers are not simple.

33 "They don't make men like that anymore," is a phrase we hear when one does honor to a man. I am glad I knew my grandfather. I am glad there are still times when I can see him in my dreams, hear him in my reverie. Sometimes I think I catch a whiff of that earthy aroma that was his smell. Then I smile. How strong these people were to leave such a lasting impression.

34 So, as I would greet my abuelo long ago, it would help us all to greet the old ones we know with this kind and respectful greeting: "Buenos Dias le de Dios."

From "A Celebration of Grandfathers." Copyright © 1983 by Rudolfo Anaya. First published in NEW MEXICO MAGAZINE, March 1983. By permission of Susan Bergholz Literary Services, New York, NY and Lamy, NM. All rights reserved.

 **THINK QUESTIONS**  CA-CCSS: CA.RI.8.1, CA.L.8.4a, CA.L.8.4b

1. Who are the *ancianos?* Write two or three sentences describing the different ways the author remembers them. Use textual evidence to explain your answer.

2. What does the author say about the importance of "sharing" among the old ones? Use textual evidence to explain your answer.

3. What is Anaya's memory of his grandfather's size? Why is this important? Provide textual evidence to describe how the grandfather looked and acted, as the author remembers him.

4. The Spanish word *pueblo* comes from the Latin root *populus,* meaning "people." Use this information as well as context clues to determine the meaning of **pueblo** as it is used in "A Celebration of Grandfathers." Write your definition of *pueblo* and tell how you found it.

5. The Spanish word adobe often appears in English. Use context clues to determine the meaning of **adobe**. Write your definition of *adobe* and tell how you got it.

## CLOSE READ
CA-CCSS: CA.RI.8.1, CA.RI.8.2, CA.RI.8.6, CA.W.8.4, CA.W.8.5, CA.W.8.6, CA.W.8.10

Reread the essay "A Celebration of Grandfathers." As you reread, complete the Focus Questions below. Then use your answers and annotations from the questions to help you complete the Writing Prompt.

## FOCUS QUESTIONS

1. In paragraph 4, the author says that the old people "shared good times and hard times." How is the concept of *sharing* key to understanding the central idea of this essay? Highlight evidence from the text and make annotations to explain your choices. In your annotations, explain how *sharing* relates both to the old people Anaya discusses and to readers today.

2. In paragraph 8, Anaya talks about the concept of time. How does Anaya describe time, and how does this relate to other ideas in the essay? Highlight textual evidence and make annotations to support your explanation.

3. Review paragraph 22, which begins, "I grew up speaking Spanish....". The author emphasizes his grandfather's physical abilities, but he also discusses his mental abilities. What is the main idea of this paragraph, and how do the details support it? Highlight textual evidence and make annotations to explain your choices.

4. Review paragraph 32, which begins, "I returned to Puerto de Luna...". Here, the author offers a summary of what he has been discussing. What does this summary help emphasize about the essay? Finally, what is the essay's central or main idea? Highlight evidence from the text and make annotations to support your explanation.

5. How do you think the author would answer the Essential Question of this unit: "How can life experiences shape our values?" Keep in mind what the author has stressed as the central or main idea, as well as the details he has used to support it. Highlight evidence from the text and make annotations to support your explanation.

## WRITING PROMPT

How does the central or main idea that the author has advanced in "A Celebration of Grandfathers" help you understand the author's purpose for writing this essay? How does his use of personal memories help to make his purpose clear? Use your understanding of supporting details and ideas to explain how the author builds up a central or main idea in the essay. Support your writing with evidence from the text.

# MOTHER TO SON

**POETRY**
Langston Hughes
1922

## INTRODUCTION

African-American poet Langston Hughes is a one of the best-known poets of the Harlem Renaissance, a cultural and intellectual movement that began in the 1920s and resulted in the production of African-American literature, art, and music that challenged racism and promoted progressive politics, such as racial and social integration. In Hughes' poem "Mother to Son," the speaker is a mother who draws on her own experiences to teach her son about perseverance.

# "Life for me ain't been no crystal stair."

## FIRST READ

1   Well, son, I'll tell you:
2   Life for me ain't been no **crystal** stair.
3   It's had tacks in it,
4   And **splinters,**
5   And boards torn up,
6   And places with no carpet on the floor—
7   Bare.
8   But all the time.
9   I'se been a-climbin' on,
10  And reachin' **landin's,**
11  And turnin' corners,
12  And sometimes goin' in the dark
13  Where there ain't been no light.
14  So, boy, don't you turn back.
15  Don't you set down on the steps
16  'Cause you finds it's kinder hard.
17  Don't you fall now—
18  For I'se still goin', honey,
19  I'se still climbin',
20  And life for me ain't been no crystal stair.

"Mother to Son" from THE COLLECTED POEMS OF LANGSTON HUGHES by Langston Hughes, edited by Arnold Rampersad with David Roessel, Associate Editor, copyright © 1994 by the Estate of Langston Hughes. Used by permission of Alfred A. Knopf, an imprint of the Knopf Doubleday Publishing Group, a division of Random House LLC. All rights reserved.

THINK QUESTIONS CA-CCSS: CA.RL.8.1, CA.L.8.4a, CA.L.8.5a

1. What does the poem's speaker mean when she says that her life "ain't been no crystal stair"? Which details in lines 1–7 of the poem explain her meaning, as well as who she is?

2. How does the poet continue using the image of the staircase in lines 8–13? What do you think the mother means by these images? Use textual evidence to support your answer.

3. Refer to lines 15–20 to summarize the mother's advice to her son. Support your answer with textual evidence.

4. Use context clues to determine the meaning of the figure of speech **crystal stair** as it is used in "Mother to Son." Write your definition of *crystal stair* and tell how you got it.

5. Use context clues in the poem to determine the meaning of **splinters**. Write your definition of *splinters* and tell how you got it.

Please note that excerpts and passages in the StudySync® library and this workbook are intended as touchstones to generate interest in an author's work. The excerpts and passages do not substitute for the reading of entire texts, and StudySync® strongly recommends that students seek out and purchase the whole literary or informational work in order to experience it as the author intended. Links to online resellers are available in our digital library. In addition, complete works may be ordered through an authorized reseller by filling out and returning to StudySync® the order form enclosed in this workbook.

Reading & Writing Companion 285

# CLOSE READ
CA-CCSS: CA.RL.8.1, CA.RL.8.2, CA.RL.8.3, CA.RL.8.4, CA.W.8.2

Reread the poem "Mother to Son." As you reread, complete the Focus Questions below. Then use your answers and annotations from the questions to help you complete the Writing Prompt.

 FOCUS QUESTIONS

1. The mother begins by saying, "Well, son, I'll tell you: / Life for me ain't been no crystal stair." What kind of a life might be described as a "crystal stair"? How is this kind of stair different from the mother's "stair"? Highlight your textual evidence and make annotations to explain your inferences, noting how the descriptions affect the poem's tone.

2. Lines 3–7 describe the wooden staircase that is the metaphor or image for the mother's life. What might the "tacks," "splinters," and "boards torn up" in the staircase represent? What could the "Bare" places stand for? Finally, what do these details reveal about the poem's speaker? Highlight these details in the poem. Use them as textual evidence for the annotations that you make to explain what each of these represents.

3. Why is the mother so proud of "a-climbin' on," "reachin' landin's," and "turnin' corners"? What might this figurative language refer to? Highlight

these details in the poem. Use them as textual evidence for the annotations that you make to explain what each of these phrases might represent.

4. What actions in life might the mother be referring to when she tells her son, "Don't you turn back. / Don't you set down on the steps / 'Cause you finds it's kinder hard. / Don't you fall now—"? What might have caused the mother to give this advice to her son? Highlight the advice she gives. Then make annotations to explain your inferences about the son's life.

5. Think about the poem as a whole. How does the mother's figurative language help readers understand the poem's tone, or the author's attitude toward the woman and her values? Highlight textual evidence and make annotations to explain your answer. Finally, state the poem's theme or meaning.

## WRITING PROMPT

Write an objective summary of the poem "Mother to Son," including its theme or message. Explain how the author creates a specific tone using figurative language and dialect to convey this message. Then compare and contrast the poem with the structure and theme of another text you have read in this unit, such as "Home" or "Abuela Invents the Zero." Analyze how the differing structure of each text contributes to its meaning and style. Support your writing with evidence from both texts.

# LITTLE WOMEN

FICTION
Louisa May Alcott
1869

## INTRODUCTION

Louisa May Alcott (1832–1888) is one of America's most beloved and popular authors. Originally published in two volumes, *Little Women* follows the lives of the four March sisters—Meg, Jo, Beth, and Amy—as they grow up lacking money but not love in Civil War-era New England. In this excerpt, the girls prepare to surprise their mother at Christmas and, in the process, learn something about the spirit of giving.

# "That was a very happy breakfast, though they didn't get any of it."

## FIRST READS

*From Chapter 1: "Playing Pilgrims"*

1   The clock struck six and, having swept up the **hearth**, Beth put a pair of slippers down to warm. Somehow the sight of the old shoes had a good effect upon the girls, for Mother was coming, and everyone brightened to welcome her. Meg stopped lecturing, and lighted the lamp, Amy got out of the easy chair without being asked, and Jo forgot how tired she was as she sat up to hold the slippers nearer to the blaze.

2   "They are quite worn out. Marmee must have a new pair."

3   "I thought I'd get her some with my dollar," said Beth.

4   "No, I shall!" cried Amy.

5   "I'm the oldest," began Meg, but Jo cut in with a decided, "I'm the man of the family now Papa is away, and I shall provide the slippers, for he told me to take special care of Mother while he was gone."

6   "I'll tell you what we'll do," said Beth, "let's each get her something for Christmas, and not get anything for ourselves."

7   "That's like you, dear! What will we get?" exclaimed Jo.

8   Everyone thought soberly for a minute, then Meg announced, as if the idea was suggested by the sight of her own pretty hands, "I shall give her a nice pair of gloves."

9   "Army shoes, best to be had," cried Jo.

10  "Some handkerchiefs, all hemmed," said Beth.

NOTES

11   "I'll get a little bottle of cologne. She likes it, and it won't cost much, so I'll have some left to buy my pencils," added Amy.

12   "How will we give the things?" asked Meg.

13   "Put them on the table, and bring her in and see her open the bundles. Don't you remember how we used to do on our birthdays?" answered Jo.

14   "I used to be so frightened when it was my turn to sit in the chair with the crown on, and see you all come marching round to give the presents, with a kiss. I liked the things and the kisses, but it was dreadful to have you sit looking at me while I opened the bundles," said Beth, who was toasting her face and the bread for tea at the same time.

15   "Let Marmee think we are getting things for ourselves, and then surprise her. We must go shopping tomorrow afternoon, Meg. There is so much to do about the play for Christmas night," said Jo, marching up and down, with her hands behind her back, and her nose in the air.

• • •

*From Chapter 2: "A Merry Christmas"*

16   "Where is Mother?" asked Meg, as she and Jo ran down to thank her for their gifts, half an hour later.

17   "Goodness only knows. Some poor creeter came a-beggin', and your ma went straight off to see what was needed. There never was such a woman for givin' away vittlesand drink, clothes and firin'," replied Hannah, who had lived with the family since Meg was born, and was considered by them all more as a friend than a servant.

18   "She will be back soon, I think, so fry your cakes, and have everything ready," said Meg, looking over the presents which were collected in a basket and kept under the sofa, ready to be produced at the proper time. "Why, where is Amy's bottle of cologne?" she added, as the little flask did not appear.

19   "She took it out a minute ago, and went off with it to put a ribbon on it, or some such notion," replied Jo, dancing about the room to take the first stiffness off the new army slippers.

20   "How nice my handkerchiefs look, don't they? Hannah washed and ironed them for me, and I marked them all myself," said Beth, looking proudly at the somewhat uneven letters which had cost her such labor.

Copyright © BookheadEd Learning, LLC

21 "Bless the child! She's gone and put 'Mother' on them instead of 'M. March'. How funny!" cried Jo, taking one up.

22 "Isn't that right? I thought it was better to do it so, because Meg's initials are M.M., and I don't want anyone to use these but Marmee," said Beth, looking troubled.

23 "It's all right, dear, and a very pretty idea, quite sensible too, for no one can ever mistake now. It will please her very much, I know," said Meg, with a frown for Jo and a smile for Beth.

24 "There's Mother. Hide the basket, quick!" cried Jo, as a door slammed and steps sounded in the hall.

25 Amy came in hastily, and looked rather **abashed** when she saw her sisters all waiting for her.

26 "Where have you been, and what are you hiding behind you?" asked Meg, surprised to see, by her hood and cloak, that lazy Amy had been out so early.

27 "Don't laugh at me, Jo! I didn't mean anyone should know till the time came. I only meant to change the little bottle for a big one, and I gave all my money to get it, and I'm truly trying not to be selfish any more."

28 As she spoke, Amy showed the handsome flask which replaced the cheap one, and looked so earnest and humble in her little effort to forget herself that Meg hugged her on the spot, and Jo pronounced her 'a trump', while Beth ran to the window, and picked her finest rose to ornament the **stately** bottle.

29 "You see I felt ashamed of my present, after reading and talking about being good this morning, so I ran round the corner and changed it the minute I was up, and I'm so glad, for mine is the handsomest now."

30 Another bang of the street door sent the basket under the sofa, and the girls to the table, eager for breakfast.

31 "Merry Christmas, Marmee! Many of them! Thank you for our books. We read some, and mean to every day," they all cried in chorus.

32 "Merry Christmas, little daughters! I'm glad you began at once, and hope you will keep on. But I want to say one word before we sit down. Not far away from here lies a poor woman with a little newborn baby. Six children are huddled into one bed to keep from freezing, for they have no fire. There is nothing to eat over there, and the oldest boy came to tell me they were suffering hunger and cold. My girls, will you give them your breakfast as a Christmas present?"

33 They were all unusually hungry, having waited nearly an hour, and for a minute no one spoke, only a minute, for Jo exclaimed impetuously, "I'm so glad you came before we began!"

34 "May I go and help carry the things to the poor little children?" asked Beth eagerly.

35 "I shall take the cream and the muffins," added Amy, heroically giving up the article she most liked.

36 Meg was already covering the buckwheats, and piling the bread into one big plate.

37 "I thought you'd do it," said Mrs. March, smiling as if satisfied. "You shall all go and help me, and when we come back we will have bread and milk for breakfast, and make it up at dinnertime."

38 They were soon ready, and the procession set out. Fortunately it was early, and they went through back streets, so few people saw them, and no one laughed at the queer party.

39 A poor, bare, miserable room it was, with broken windows, no fire, ragged bedclothes, a sick mother, wailing baby, and a group of pale, hungry children cuddled under one old quilt, trying to keep warm.

40 How the big eyes stared and the blue lips smiled as the girls went in.

41 "Ach, mein Gott! It is good angels come to us!" said the poor woman, crying for joy.

42 "Funny angels in hoods and mittens," said Jo, and set them to laughing.

43 In a few minutes it really did seem as if kind spirits had been at work there. Hannah, who had carried wood, made a fire, and stopped up the broken panes with old hats and her own cloak. Mrs. March gave the mother tea and **gruel**, and comforted her with promises of help, while she dressed the little baby as tenderly as if it had been her own. The girls meantime spread the table, set the children round the fire, and fed them like so many hungry birds, laughing, talking, and trying to understand the funny broken English.

44 "Das ist gut!" "Die Engel-kinder!" cried the poor things as they ate and warmed their purple hands at the comfortable blaze. The girls had never been called angel children before, and thought it very agreeable, especially Jo, who had been considered a 'Sancho' ever since she was born. That was a very happy breakfast, though they didn't get any of it. And when they went away, leaving comfort behind, I think there were not in all the city four merrier people than

the hungry little girls who gave away their breakfasts and contented themselves with bread and milk on Christmas morning.

45 "That's loving our neighbor better than ourselves, and I like it," said Meg, as they set out their presents while their mother was upstairs collecting clothes for the poor Hummels.

## THINK QUESTIONS  CA-CCSS: CA.RL.8.1, CA.RL.8.4, CA.L.8.4a, CA.L.8.4c, CA.L.8.4d, CA.SL.8.1a, CA.SL.8.1c, CA.SL.8.1d, CA.SL.8.4

1. Which of the four March sisters seems to be the most "in charge," or confident? Which of them seems to be more hesitant, and unsure of herself? Use textual evidence from Chapter 1 to support your answer.

2. What kind of relationship do the four March daughters seem to have with their mother? Support your answer with evidence from the text.

3. What textual clues does the author provide to indicate that the people in need on Christmas morning are an immigrant family?

4. Use context to determine the meaning of the word **abashed** as it is used in Chapter 2. Write your definition of the word, and tell how you figured it out.

5. Use context to determine the meaning of the word vittles as it is used in Chapter 2 of *Little Women*. Write your definition of **vittles** and explain how you found it. Consult a dictionary or other resource to check the pronunciation as well as the word's etymology, or origin. In addition, verify the meaning you determined using context.

# CLOSE READ
CA-CCSS: CA.RL.8.1, CA.RL.8.2, CA.RL.8.3, CA.W.8.4, CA.W.8.5, CA.W.8.6, CA.W.8.10

Reread the excerpt from *Little Women*. As you reread, complete the Focus Questions below. Then use your answers and annotations from the questions to help you complete the Writing Prompt.

## FOCUS QUESTIONS

1. How does Louisa May Alcott use dialogue rather than description to reveal aspects, or character traits, of each of the March sisters? Highlight evidence in the text and make annotations to support your answer.

2. What does Amy's sudden decision to exchange the original gift she bought for Marmee reveal about her character? Highlight and label evidence in Chapter 2 to support your answer.

3. How does Marmee provoke a decision from her daughters by asking them if they will help a needy family, instead of simply telling them to do so? Highlight evidence to support your answer.

4. How is the theme of sacrifice for the greater good developed over the course of these two chapters in *Little Women*? Highlight evidence from the text to support your answer.

5. How does an experience with a needy immigrant family help shape the values of the March sisters? Highlight and annotate evidence to support your answer.

## WRITING PROMPT

In this excerpt from *Little Women,* how do the similarities and differences of the four March sisters help propel the plot? Explain the similarities and differences between each of these characters, and then explain how they affect the events of the plot. Use dialogue and other details from the text to support your statements about both the characters and the plot events.

Please note that excerpts and passages in the StudySync® library and this workbook are intended as touchstones to generate interest in an author's work. The excerpts and passages do not substitute for the reading of entire texts, and StudySync® strongly recommends that students seek out and purchase the whole literary or informational work in order to experience it as the author intended. Links to online resellers are available in our digital library. In addition, complete works may be ordered through an authorized reseller by filling out and returning to StudySync® the order form enclosed in this workbook.

Reading & Writing Companion **293**

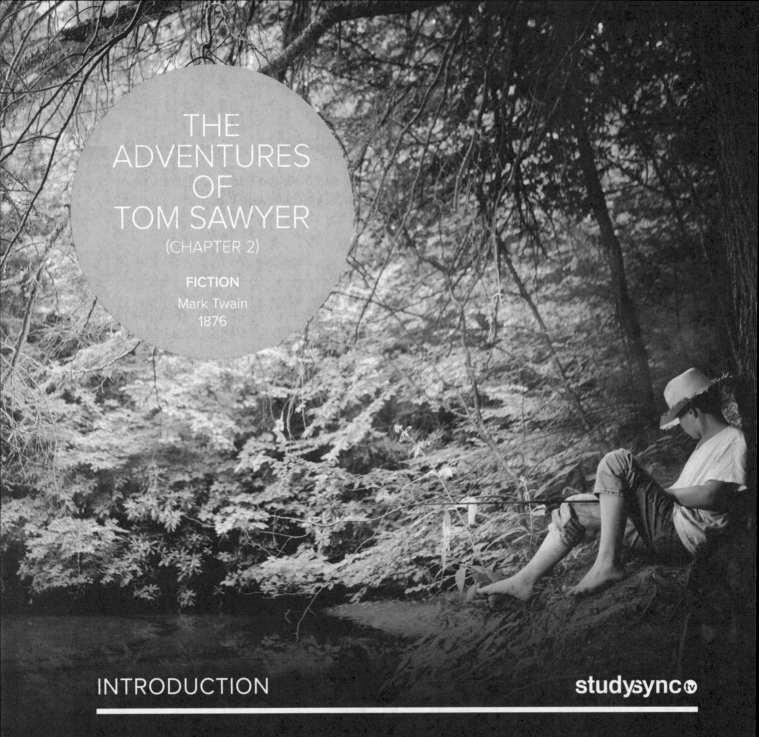

# THE ADVENTURES OF TOM SAWYER
(CHAPTER 2)

**FICTION**
Mark Twain
1876

## INTRODUCTION

**studysync**

Humorously written by Mark Twain in the colorful vernacular found in the mid-19th Century along the Mississippi, *The Adventures of Tom Sawyer* is the coming of age story of one of America's great fictional characters. On a beautiful Saturday morning when he'd rather be down by the river with his friends, Tom Sawyer's Aunt Polly has given him a dreary task: whitewashing the front fence, thirty yards long and nine feet high. The charismatic Tom must use his sharp wit to try to get someone to do his work for him. But how? In this excerpt, Mark Twain's endearing character returns to the whitewashing determined to leverage all he knows about human nature to free himself of his chore.

# "At this dark and hopeless moment an inspiration burst upon him!"

## FIRST READ

NOTES

1   He began to think of the fun he had planned for this day, and his sorrows multiplied. Soon the free boys would come tripping along on all sorts of delicious expeditions, and they would make a world of fun of him for having to work—the very thought of it burnt him like fire. He got out his worldly wealth and examined it—bits of toys, marbles, and trash; enough to buy an exchange of WORK, maybe, but not half enough to buy so much as half an hour of pure freedom. So he returned his straitened means to his pocket, and gave up the idea of trying to buy the boys. At this dark and hopeless moment an inspiration burst upon him! Nothing less than a great, magnificent inspiration.

2   He took up his brush and went tranquilly to work. Ben Rogers hove in sight presently—the very boy, of all boys, whose ridicule he had been dreading. Ben's gait was the hop-skip-and-jump—proof enough that his heart was light and his anticipations high. He was eating an apple, and giving a long, melodious whoop, at intervals, followed by a deep-toned ding-dong-dong, ding-dong-dong, for he was personating a steamboat. As he drew near, he slackened speed, took the middle of the street, leaned far over to **starboard** and rounded to ponderously and with laborious pomp and circumstance—for he was personating the Big Missouri, and considered himself to be drawing nine feet of water. He was boat and captain and engine-bells combined, so he had to imagine himself standing on his own hurricane-deck giving the orders and executing them:

3   "Stop her, sir! Ting-a-ling-ling!" The headway ran almost out, and he drew up slowly toward the sidewalk.

4   "Ship up to back! Ting-a-ling-ling!" His arms straightened and stiffened down his sides.

NOTES

5  "Set her back on the stabboard! Ting-a-ling-ling! Chow! ch-chow-wow! Chow!" His right hand, mean-time, describing stately circles—for it was representing a forty-foot wheel....

6  Tom went on whitewashing—paid no attention to the steamboat. Ben stared a moment and then said: "Hi-YI! YOU'RE up a stump, ain't you!"

7  No answer. Tom surveyed his last touch with the eye of an artist, then he gave his brush another gentle sweep and surveyed the result, as before. Ben ranged up alongside of him. Tom's mouth watered for the apple, but he stuck to his work. Ben said:

8  "Hello, old chap, you got to work, hey?"

9  Tom wheeled suddenly and said:

10  "Why, it's you, Ben! I warn't noticing."

11  "Say—I'm going in a-swimming, I am. Don't you wish you could? But of course you'd druther WORK—wouldn't you? Course you would!"

12  Tom contemplated the boy a bit, and said:

13  "What do you call work?"

14  "Why, ain't THAT work?"

15  Tom resumed his whitewashing, and answered carelessly:

16  "Well, maybe it is, and maybe it ain't. All I know, is, it suits Tom Sawyer."

17  "Oh come, now, you don't mean to let on that you LIKE it?"

18  The brush continued to move.

19  "Like it? Well, I don't see why I oughtn't to like it. Does a boy get a chance to whitewash a fence every day?"

20  That put the thing in a new light. Ben stopped nibbling his apple. Tom swept his brush daintily back and forth—stepped back to note the effect—added a touch here and there—criticised the effect again—Ben watching every move and getting more and more interested, more and more absorbed. Presently he said:

21  "Say, Tom, let ME whitewash a little."

22  Tom considered, was about to consent; but he altered his mind:

23  "No—no—I reckon it wouldn't hardly do, Ben. You see, Aunt Polly's awful particular about this fence—right here on the street, you know—but if it was the back fence I wouldn't mind and SHE wouldn't. Yes, she's awful particular about this fence; it's got to be done very careful; I reckon there ain't one boy in a thousand, maybe two thousand, that can do it the way it's got to be done."

24  "No—is that so? Oh come, now—lemme just try. Only just a little—I'd let YOU, if you was me, Tom."

25  "Ben, I'd like to, honest injun; but Aunt Polly—well, Jim wanted to do it, but she wouldn't let him; Sid wanted to do it, and she wouldn't let Sid. Now don't you see how I'm fixed? If you was to tackle this fence and anything was to happen to it—"

26  "Oh, shucks, I'll be just as careful. Now lemme try. Say—I'll give you the core of my apple."

27  "Well, here—No, Ben, now don't. I'm afeard—"

28  "I'll give you ALL of it!"

29  Tom gave up the brush with reluctance in his face, but **alacrity** in his heart. And while the late steamer Big Missouri worked and sweated in the sun, the retired artist sat on a barrel in the shade close by, dangled his legs, munched his apple, and planned the slaughter of more innocents. There was no lack of material; boys happened along every little while; they came to jeer, but remained to whitewash. By the time Ben was fagged out, Tom had traded the next chance to Billy Fisher for a kite, in good repair; and when he played out, Johnny Miller bought in for a dead rat and a string to swing it with—and so on, and so on, hour after hour. And when the middle of the afternoon came, from being a poor poverty-stricken boy in the morning, Tom was literally rolling in wealth. He had besides the things before mentioned, twelve marbles, part of a jews-harp, a piece of blue bottle-glass to look through, a spool cannon, a key that wouldn't unlock anything, a fragment of chalk, a glass stopper of a **decanter**, a tin soldier, a couple of tadpoles, six fire-crackers, a kitten with only one eye, a brass door-knob, a dog-collar—but no dog—the handle of a knife, four pieces of orange-peel, and a **dilapidated** old window sash.

30  He had had a nice, good, idle time all the while—plenty of company—and the fence had three coats of whitewash on it! If he hadn't run out of whitewash he would have bankrupted every boy in the village.

31  Tom said to himself that it was not such a hollow world, after all. He had discovered a great law of human action, without knowing it—namely, that in order to make a man or a boy covet a thing, it is only necessary to make the

NOTES

thing difficult to attain. If he had been a great and wise philosopher, like the writer of this book, he would now have comprehended that Work consists of whatever a body is OBLIGED to do, and that Play consists of whatever a body is not obliged to do. And this would help him to understand why constructing artificial flowers or performing on a tread-mill is work, while rolling ten-pins or climbing Mont Blanc is only amusement. There are wealthy gentlemen in England who drive four-horse passenger-coaches twenty or thirty miles on a daily line, in the summer, because the privilege costs them considerable money; but if they were offered wages for the service, that would turn it into work and then they would resign.

32      The boy mused awhile over the substantial change which had taken place in his worldly circumstances, and then **wended** toward headquarters to report.

## THINK QUESTIONS   CA-CCSS: CA.RL.8.1, CA.L.8.4a, CA.SL.8.1c, CA.SL.8.1d

1.  What kind of inspiration bursts upon Tom Sawyer as he returns his "straitened means" to his pocket at the beginning of the excerpt? Refer to evidence in the text to explain your answer.

2.  After Ben first asks Tom to let him whitewash, why does Tom keep stalling, seeming about to consent and then suddenly changing his mind more than once? Refer to evidence in the text to explain your answer.

3.  What does Tom learn about the difference between work and play at the end of the excerpt? Cite evidence from the text to support your answer.

4.  Use context to determine the meaning of the word **dilapidated** as it is used in *The Adventures of Tom Sawyer*. Write your definition of *dilapidated* and tell how you found it.

5.  Determine the meaning of the word **alacrity** as it is used in *The Adventures of Tom Sawyer* using context clues in the text. Write your definition of *alacrity* and tell how you found it.

# CLOSE READ

CA-CCSS: CA.RL.8.1, CA.RL.8.3, CA.RL.8.6, CA.RL.8.7, CA.W.8.4, CA.W.8.5, CA.W.8.6, CA.W.8.10

Reread the excerpt from *The Adventures of Tom Sawyer*. As you reread, complete the Focus Questions below. Then use your answers and annotations from the questions to help you complete the Writing Prompt.

## FOCUS QUESTIONS

1. How do the first two paragraphs of *The Adventures of Tom Sawyer* indicate that the narrator is using a third-person omniscient point of view? Highlight evidence from the text and make annotations to support your explanation.

2. After Ben starts whitewashing, Twain writes that Tom "planned the slaughter of more innocents," and then continues: "There was no lack of material; boys happened along every little while; they came to jeer, but remained to whitewash. By the time Ben was fagged out, Tom had traded the next chance to Billy Fisher for a kite, in good repair; and when he played out, Johnny Miller bought in for a dead rat and a string to swing it with—and so on, and so on, hour after hour. And when the middle of the afternoon came, from being a poor poverty-stricken boy in the morning, Tom was literally rolling in wealth." How does the film take these plot events and condense, or reduce them, into a single, brief shot lasting only a few seconds? Cite evidence from the film to support your answer.

3. At the end of the excerpt, how does using third-person omniscient point of view allow the author, Mark Twain, to reveal not only what Tom Sawyer has learned from his experience, but also a general rule about human behavior? Highlight textual evidence to support your ideas and write annotations to explain your choices.

4. Mark Twain utilizes the omniscient narrator in *The Adventures of Tom Sawyer* to create humor. How does he accomplish this? Cite textual evidence and evidence from the film to support your ideas.

5. How does Tom's life experience shape his values? Cite evidence from the text to support your answer.

## WRITING PROMPT

Dramatic irony occurs when the words and actions of the characters in a work of literature have a different meaning for the reader than they do for the characters. This happens when readers have more knowledge about what its taking place than the characters themselves. How does Mark Twain use dramatic irony to create humor in *The Adventures of Tom Sawyer*? Use evidence from the story to support your response.

Please note that excerpts and passages in the StudySync® library and this workbook are intended as touchstones to generate interest in an author's work. The excerpts and passages do not substitute for the reading of entire texts, and StudySync® strongly recommends that students seek out and purchase the whole literary or informational work in order to experience it as the author intended. Links to online resellers are available in our digital library. In addition, complete works may be ordered through an authorized reseller by filling out and returning to StudySync® the order form enclosed in this workbook.

Reading & Writing Companion **299**

# BORN WORKER

**FICTION**
Gary Soto
1998

## INTRODUCTION

Mexican-American author Gary Soto grew up in California's Central Valley and worked as a field laborer before becoming a distinguished writer and professor. Soto draws inspiration from Latino poets to write about his experiences as farm worker and to describe the daily lives of his characters. In this short story, Soto explores the Mexican-American experience through two teenaged cousins and business partners, José and Arnie. Despite coming from the same family, differences in lifestyle and values emerge when José reluctantly agrees to work with his cousin and an emergency occurs at the work site.

# "...his palms were already rough by the time he was three..."

## FIRST READ

1   They said that José was born with a ring of dirt around his neck, with grime under his fingernails, and skin calloused from the grainy twist of a shovel. They said his palms were already rough by the time he was three, and soon after he learned his primary color, his squint was the squint of an aged laborer. They said he was a born worker. By seven he was drinking coffee slowly, his mouth pursed the way his mother sipped. He wore jeans, a shirt with sleeves rolled to his elbows. His eye could measure a length of board, and his knees **genuflected** over flower beds and leafy gutters.

2   They said lots of things about José, but almost nothing of his parents. His mother stitched at a machine all day, and his father, with a steady job at the telephone company, climbed splintered, sun-sucked poles, fixed wires and looked around the city at tree level.

3   "What do you see up there?" José once asked his father.

4   "Work," he answered. "I see years of work, *mi'jo.*"

5   José took this as a truth, and though he did well in school, he felt destined to labor. His arms would pump, his legs would bend, his arms would carry a world of earth. He believed in hard work, believed that his strength was as ancient as a rock's.

6   "Life is hard," his father repeated from the time José could first make out the meaning of words until he was stroking his fingers against the grain of his sandpaper beard.

7   His mother was an example to José. She would raise her hands, showing her fingers pierced from the sewing machines. She bled on her machine, bled because there was money to make, a child to raise, and a roof to stay under.

8 One day when José returned home from junior high, his cousin Arnie was sitting on the lawn sucking on a stalk of grass. José knew that grass didn't come from his lawn. His was cut and pampered, clean.

9 "José!" Arnie shouted as he took off the earphones of his CD Walkman.

10 "Hi, Arnie," José said without much enthusiasm. He didn't like his cousin. He thought he was lazy and, worse, spoiled by the trappings of being middle class. His parent had good jobs in offices and showered him with clothes, shoes, CDs, vacations, almost anything he wanted. Arnie's family had never climbed a telephone pole to size up the future.

11 Arnie rose to his feet, and José saw that his cousin was wearing a new pair of high-tops. He didn't say anything.

12 "Got an idea," Arnie said cheerfully. "Something that'll make us money."

13 José looked at his cousin, not a muscle of curiosity twitching in his face.

14 Still, Arnie explained that since he himself was so clever with words, and his best cousin in the whole world was good at working with his hands, that maybe they might start a company.

15 "What would you do?" José asked.

16 "Me?" he said brightly. "Shoot, I'll round up all kinds of jobs for you. You won't have to do anything." He stopped, then started again. "Except—you know—do the work."

17 "Get out of here," José said.

18 "Don't be that way," Arnie begged. "Let me tell you how it works."

19 The boys went inside the house, and while José stripped off his school clothes and put on his jeans and a T-shirt, Arnie told him that they could be rich.

20 "You ever hear of this guy named Bechtel?" Arnie asked.

21 José shook his head.

22 "Man, he started just like us," Arnie said. "He started digging ditches and stuff, and the next thing you knew, he was sitting by his own swimming pool. You want to sit by your own pool, don't you?" Arnie smiled, waiting for José to speak up.

23 "Never heard of this guy Bechtel," José said after he rolled on two huge socks, worn at the heels. He opened up his chest of drawers and brought out a packet of Kleenex.

24 Arnie looked at the Kleenex.

25 "How come you don't use your sleeve?" Arnie joked.

26 José thought for a moment and said, "I'm not like you." He smiled at his retort.

27 "Listen, I'll find the work, and then we can split it fifty-fifty."

28 José knew fifty-fifty was a bad deal.

29 "How about sixty-forty?" Arnie suggested when he could see that José wasn't going for it. "I know a lot of people from my dad's job. They're waiting for us."

30 José sat on the edge of his bed and started to lace up his boots. He knew that there were agencies that would find you work, agencies that took a portion of your pay. They're cheats, he thought, people who sit in air-conditioned offices while others work.

31 "You really know a lot of people?" José asked.

32 "Boatloads," Arnie said. "My dad works with this millionaire—honest—who cooks a steak for his dog every day."

33 He's a liar, José thought. No matter how he tried, he couldn't picture a dog grubbing on steak. The world was too poor for that kind of silliness.

34 "Listen, I'll go eighty-twenty." José said.

35 "Aw, man," Arnie whined. "That ain't fair."

36 José laughed.

37 "I mean, half the work is finding the jobs," Arnie explained, his palms up as he begged José to be reasonable.

38 José knew this was true. He had had to go door-to-door, and he disliked asking for work. He assumed that it should automatically be his since he was a good worker, honest, and always on time.

39 "Where did you get this idea, anyhow?" José asked.

40 "I got a business mind," Arnie said proudly.

41 "Just like that Bechtel guy," José retorted.

42 "That's right."

43 José agreed to a seventy-thirty split, with the condition that Arnie had to help out. Arnie hollered, arguing that some people were meant to work and others to come up with brilliant ideas. He was one of the latter. Still, he agreed after José said it was that or nothing.

44 In the next two weeks, Arnie found an array of jobs. José peeled off shingles from a rickety garage roof, carried rocks down a path to where a pond would go, and spray-painted lawn furniture. And while Arnie accompanied him, most of the time he did nothing. He did help occasionally. He did shake the cans of spray paint and kick aside debris so that José didn't trip while going down the path carrying the rocks. He did stack the piles of shingles, but almost cried when a nail bit his thumb. But mostly he told José what he had missed or where the work could be improved. José was bothered because he and his work had never been criticized before.

45 But soon José learned to ignore his cousin, ignore his comments about his spray painting, or about the way he lugged rocks, two in each arm. He didn't say anything, either, when they got paid and Arnie rubbed his hands like a fly, muttering, "It's payday."

46 Then Arnie found a job scrubbing a drained swimming pool. The two boys met early at José's house. Arnie brought his bike. José's own bike had a flat that grinned like a clown's face.

47 "I'll pedal," José suggested when Arnie said that he didn't have much leg strength.

48 With Arnie on the handlebars, José tore off, his pedaling so strong that tears of fear formed in Arnie's eyes.

49 "Slow down!" Arnie cried.

50 José ignored him and within minutes they were riding the bike up a gravel driveway. Arnie hopped off at first chance.

51 "You're scary," Arnie said, picking a gnat from his eye.

52 José chuckled.

53 When Arnie knocked on the door, an old man still in pajamas appeared in the window. He motioned for the boys to come around to the back.

54 "Let me do the talking," Arnie suggested to his cousin. "He knows my dad real good. They're like this." He pressed two fingers together.

55 José didn't bother to say OK. He walked the bike into the backyard, which was lush with plants—roses in their last bloom, geraniums, hydrangeas, pansies with their skirts of bright colors. José could make out the splash of a fountain. Then he heard the hysterical yapping of a poodle. From all his noise, a person might have thought the dog was on fire.

56 "Hi, Mr. Clemens," Arnie said, extending his hand. "I'm Arnie Sanchez. It's nice to see you again."

57 José had never seen a kid actually greet someone like this. Mr. Clemens said, hiking up his pajama bottoms, "I only wanted one kid to work."

58 "Oh," Arnie stuttered. "Actually, my cousin José really does the work and I kind of, you know, supervise."

59 Mr. Clemens pinched up his wrinkled face. He seemed not to understand. He took out a pea-sized hearing aid, fiddled with its tiny dial, and fit it into his ear, which was surrounded with wiry gray hair.

60 "I'm only paying for one boy," Mr. Clemens shouted. His poodle click-clicked and stood behind his legs. The dog bared its small crooked teeth.

61 "That's right," Arnie said, smiling a strained smile. "we know that you're going to **compensate** only one of us."

62 Mr. Clemens muttered under his breath. He combed his hair with his fingers. He showed José the pool, which was shaped as round as an elephant. It was filthy with grime. Near the bottom some grayish water shimmered and leaves floated as limp as cornflakes.

63 "It's got to be real clean," Mr. Clemens said, "or it's not worth it."

64 "Oh, José's a great worker," Arnie said. He patted his cousin's shoulders and said that he could lift a mule.

65 Mr. Clemens sized up José and squeezed his shoulders, too.

66 "How do I know you, anyhow?" Mr. Clemens asked Arnie, who was aiming a smile at the poodle.

67 "You know my dad," Arnie answered, raising his smile to the old man. "He works at Interstate Insurance. You and he had some business deals."

Please note that excerpts and passages in the StudySync® library and this workbook are intended as touchstones to generate interest in an author's work. The excerpts and passages do not substitute for the reading of entire texts, and StudySync® strongly recommends that students seek out and purchase the whole literary or informational work in order to experience it as the author intended. Links to online resellers are available in our digital library. In addition, complete works may be ordered through an authorized reseller by filling out and returning to StudySync® the order form enclosed in this workbook.

Reading & Writing Companion    **305**

68 Mr. Clemens thought for a moment, a hand on his mouth, head shaking. He could have been thinking about the meaning of life, his face was so dark.

69 "Mexican fella?" he inquired.

70 "That's him," Arnie said happily.

71 José felt like hitting his cousin for his cheerful attitude. Instead, he walked over and picked up the white plastic bottle of bleach. Next to it was a wire brush, a **pumice** stone, and some rags. He set down the bottle and, like a surgeon, put on a pair of rubber gloves.

72 "You know what you're doing, boy?" Mr. Clemens asked.

73 José nodded as he walked into the pool. If it had been filled with water, his chest would have been wet. The new hair on his chest would have been floating like the legs of a jellyfish.

74 "Oh, yeah," Arnie chimed, speaking for his cousin. "José was born to work."

75 José would have drowned his cousin if there had been more water. Instead, he poured a bleach solution into a rag and swirled it over an area. He took the wire brush and scrubbed. The black algae came up like a foamy monster.

76 "We're a team," Arnie said to Mr. Clemens.

77 Arnie descended into the pool and took the bleach bottle from José. He held it for José and smiled up at Mr. Clemens, who, hands on hips, watched for a while, the poodle at his side. He cupped his ear, as if to pick up the sounds of José's scrubbing.

78 "Nice day, huh?" Arnie sang.

79 "What?" Mr. Clemens said.

80 "Nice day," Arnie repeated, this time louder. "So which ear can't you hear in?" Grinning, Arnie wiggled his ear to make sure that Mr. Clemens knew what he was asking.

81 Mr. Clemens ignored Arnie. He watched José, whose arms worked back and forth like he was sawing logs.

82 "We're not only a team," Arnie shouted, "but we're also cousins."

83 Mr. Clemens shook his head at Arnie. When he left, the poodle leading the way, Arnie immediately climbed out of the pool and sat on the edge, legs dangling.

84  "It's going to be blazing," Arnie complained. He shaded his eyes with his hand and looked east, where the sun was rising over a sycamore, its leaves hanging like bats.

85  José scrubbed. He worked the wire brush over the black and green stains, the grime dripping like tears. He finished a large area. He hopped out of the pool and returned hauling a garden hose with an attached nozzle. He gave the cleaned area a blast. When the spray got too close, his cousin screamed, got up, and, searching for something to do, picked a **loquat** from a tree.

86  "What's your favorite fruit?" Arnie asked.

87  José ignored him.

88  Arnie stuffed a bunch of loquats into his mouth, then cursed himself for splattering juice on his new high-tops. He returned to the pool, his cheeks fat with the seeds, and once again sat at the edge. He started to tell José how he had first learned to swim. "We were on vacation in Mazatlán. You been there, ain't you?"

89  José shook his head. He dabbed the bleach solution onto the sides of the pool with a rag and scrubbed a new area.

90  "Anyhow, my dad was on the beach and saw this drowned dead guy," Arnie continued. "And right there, my dad got scared and realized I couldn't swim."

91  Arnie rattled on about how his father had taught him in the hotel pool and later showed him where the drowned man's body had been.

92  "Be quiet," José said.

93  "What?"

94  "I can't concentrate," José said, stepping back to look at the cleaned area.

95  Arnie shut his mouth but opened it to lick loquat juice from his fingers. He kicked his legs against the swimming pool, bored. He looked around the backyard and spotted a lounge chair. He got up, dusting off the back of his pants, and threw himself into the cushions. He raised and lowered the back of the lounge. Sighing, he snuggled in. He stayed quiet for three minutes, during which time José scrubbed. His arms hurt but he kept working with long strokes. José knew that in an hour the sun would drench the pool with light. He hurried to get the job done.

96  Arnie then asked, "You ever peel before?"

97    José looked at his cousin. His nose burned from the bleach. He scrunched up his face.

98    "You know, like when you get sunburned."

99    "I'm too dark to peel," José said, his words echoing because he had advanced to the deep end. "Why don't you be quiet and let me work?"

100    Arnie babbled on that he had peeled when on vacation in Hawaii. He explained that he was really more French than Mexican, and that's why his skin was sensitive. He said that when he lived in France, people thought that he could be Portuguese or maybe Armenian, never Mexican.

101    José felt like soaking his rag with bleach and pressing it over Arnie's mouth to make him be quiet.

102    Then Mr. Clemens appeared. He was dressed in white pants and flowery shirt. His thin hair was combed so that his scalp, as pink as a crab, showed.

103    "I'm just taking a little rest," Arnie said.

104    Arnie leaped back into the pool. He took the bleach bottle and held it. He smiled at Mr. Clemens, who came to inspect their progress.

105    "José's doing a good job," Arnie said, then whistled a song.

106    Mr. Clemens peered into the pool, hands on knees, admiring the progress.

107    "Pretty good, huh?" Arnie asked.

108    Mr. Clemens nodded. Then his hearing aid fell out, and José turned in time to see it roll like a bottle cap toward the bottom of the pool. It leaped into the stagnant water with a plop. A single bubble went up, and it was gone.

109    "Dang," Mr. Clemens swore. He took shuffling steps toward the deep end. He steadied his gaze on where the hearing aid had sunk. He leaned over and suddenly, arms waving, one leg kicking out, he tumbled into the pool. He landed standing up, then his legs buckled, and he crumbled, his head striking against the bottom. He rolled once, and half of his body settled in the water.

110    "Did you see that!" Arnie shouted, big-eyed.

111    José had already dropped his brushes on the side of the pool and hurried to the old man, who moaned, eyes closed, his false teeth jutting from his mouth. A ribbon of blood immediately began to flow from his scalp.

112    "We better get out of here!" Arnie suggested. "They're going to blame us!"

NOTES

113  José knelt on both knees at the old man's side. He took the man's teeth from his mouth and placed them in his shirt pocket. The old man groaned and opened his eyes, which were shiny wet. He appeared startled, like a newborn.

114  "Sir, you'll be all right," José cooed, then snapped at his cousin. "Arnie, get over here and help me!"

115  "I'm going home," Arnie whined.

116  "You punk!" José yelled. "Go inside and call 911."

117  Arnie said that they should leave him there.

118  "Why should we get involved?" he cried as he started for his bike. "It's his own fault."

119  José laid the man's head down and with giant steps leaped out of the pool, shoving his cousin as he passed. He went into the kitchen and punched in 911 on a telephone. He explained to the operator what had happened. When asked the address, José dropped the phone and went onto the front porch to look for it.

120  "It's 940 East Brown," José breathed. He hung up and looked wildly about the kitchen. He opened up the refrigerator and brought out a plastic tray of ice, which he twisted so that a few of the cubes popped out and slid across the floor. He wrapped some cubes in a dish towel. When he raced outside, Arnie was gone, the yapping poodle was doing laps around the edge of the pool, and Mr. Clemens was trying to stand up.

121  "No, sir," José said as he jumped into the pool, his own knees almost buckling. "Please, sit down."

122  Mr. Clemens staggered and collapsed. José caught him before he hit his head again. The towel of ice cubes dropped from his hands. With his legs spread to absorb the weight, José raised the man up in his arms, this fragile man. He picked him up and carefully stepped toward the shallow end, one slow elephant step at a time.

123  "You'll be all right," José said, more to himself than to Mr. Clemens, who moaned and struggled to be let free.

124  The sirens wailed in the distance. The poodle yapped, which started a dog barking in the neighbor's yard.

125  "You'll be OK," José repeated, and in the shallow end of the pool, he edged up the steps. He lay the old man in the lounge chair and raced back inside for more ice and another towel. He returned outside and placed the bundle of cubes on the man's head, where the blood flowed. Mr. Clemens was awake,

NOTES

looking about. When the old man felt his mouth, José reached into his shirt pocket and pulled out his false teeth. He fit the teeth into Mr. Clemens's mouth and a smile appeared, something bright at a difficult time.

126 "I hit my head," Mr. Clemens said after smacking his teeth so that the fit was right.

127 José looked up and his gaze floated to a telephone pole, one his father might have climbed. If he had been there, his father would have seen that José was more than just a good worker. He would have seen a good man. He held the towel to the old man's head. The poodle, now quiet, joined them on the lounge chair.

128 A fire truck pulled into the driveway and soon they were surrounded by firemen, one of whom brought out a first-aid kit. A fireman led José away and asked what happened. He was starting to explain when his cousin reappeared, yapping like a poodle.

129 "I was scrubbing the pool," Arnie shouted, "and I said, 'Mr. Clemens, you shouldn't stand so close to the edge.' But did he listen? No, he leaned over and . . . Well, you can just imagine my horror."

130 José walked away from Arnie's **jabbering**. He walked away, and realized that there were people like his cousin, the liar, and people like himself, someone he was getting to know. He walked away and in the midmorning heat boosted himself up a telephone pole. He climbed up and saw for himself what his father saw—miles and miles of trees and houses, and a future lost in the layers of yellowish haze.

"Born Worker" from Petty Crimes: Stories by Gary Soto. Copyright (c) 1998 by Gary Soto. Reprinted by permission of Houghton Mifflin Harcourt Publishing Company. All rights reserved.

 THINK QUESTIONS CA-CCSS: CA.RL.8.1, CA.RL.8.4, CA.L.8.4a, CA.L.8.4c, CA.L.8.4d

1. Why do you think José feels he is "destined to labor"? Support your answer with textual evidence.

2. José doesn't like his cousin Arnie, so why does he decide to go into business with him? Support your answer with textual evidence.

3. Use details from the text to cite some of the major differences between Arnie and José.

4. Use context to determine the meaning of the word **genuflected** as it is used in "Born Worker." Write your definition of *genuflected* and explain how you found it.

5. Use context to determine the meaning of the word **jabbering** as it is used in "Born Worker." Write your definition of *jabbering* and show how you found it. Check your answer against the dictionary definition.

## CLOSE READ  CA-CCSS: CA.RL.8.1, CA.RL.8.2, CA.RL.8.3, CA.RL.8.4, CA.RL.8.5, CA.RL.8.9, CA.W.8.4, CA.W.8.5, CA.W.8.6, CA.W.8.10

Reread the short story "Born Worker." As you reread, complete the Focus Questions below. Then use your answers and annotations from the questions to help you complete the Writing Prompt.

## FOCUS QUESTIONS

1. As trickster archetypes, how do Arnie (in this story) and Tom Sawyer (in *The Adventures of Tom Sawyer)* both use lies and deception to get what they want? Use textual evidence from both texts to support your answer.

2. José doesn't like his cousin because he feels Arnie is "lazy and, worse, spoiled by the trappings of being middle class." What details does the author include in the story that reveal how Arnie really feels about José? Does he see José as his equal? Support your answer with textual evidence.

3. Highlight the paragraph that presents the climax of the story. What do the characters' responses to this event reveal about both José and Arnie, and how are their responses linked to the theme of the story? Cite textual evidence to support your answer.

4. José's father works for the telephone company, and throughout the story, Gary Soto refers to telephone poles. What is the significance of the telephone pole as the author uses it in the story? How does it relate to the theme? Cite textual evidence to support your answer.

5. How does José's experience with Mr. Clemens shape, and ultimately change, his values? How does it compare to what Tom Sawyer realizes after his whitewashing experience? Highlight evidence from both texts and make annotations to support your answer.

## WRITING PROMPT

Read the excerpt from *The Adventures of Tom Sawyer.* Think about how both Tom Sawyer and Arnie Sanchez represent the trickster, a deceptive character who acts in a way that opposes conventional behavior. Write a short essay in which you compare and contrast Tom and Arnie. Who is more likeable, Tom or Arnie? Cite evidence from both texts to support your response.

Please note that excerpts and passages in the StudySync® library and this workbook are intended as touchstones to generate interest in an author's work. The excerpts and passages do not substitute for the reading of entire texts, and StudySync® strongly recommends that students seek out and purchase the whole literary or informational work in order to experience it as the author intended. Links to online resellers are available in our digital library. In addition, complete works may be ordered through an authorized reseller by filling out and returning to StudySync® the order form enclosed in this workbook.

Reading & Writing Companion  **311**

# ODE TO THANKS

POETRY
Pablo Neruda
1995

## INTRODUCTION

Chilean-born Pablo Neruda is an internationally recognized poet who was awarded the Nobel Prize in Literature in 1971. His poetry provides descriptions of everyday objects and events as well as reflections about grand ideas. In his poem "Ode to Thanks," Neruda pays tribute to the word *thanks*.

# "Your light brightens the altar of harshness."

 FIRST READ

1  Thanks to the word
2  that says *thanks!*
3  Thanks to *thanks,*
4  word
5  that melts
6  iron and snow!

7  The world is a threatening place
8  until
9  *thanks*
10  makes the rounds
11  from one pair of lips to another,
12  soft as a bright
13  feather
14  and sweet as a petal of sugar,
15  filling the mouth with its sound
16  or else a **mumbled**
17  whisper.
18  Life becomes human again:
19  it's no longer an open window.
20  A bit of brightness
21  strikes into the forest,
22  and we can sing again beneath the leaves.
23  *Thanks,* you're the medicine we take
24  to save us from
25  the bite of **scorn.**
26  Your light brightens the **altar** of harshness.

27  Or maybe
28  a **tapestry**

29 known
30 to far distant peoples.
31 Travelers
32 fan out
33 into the wilds,
34 and in the jungle
35 of strangers,
36 *merci*
37 rings out
38 while the hustling train
39 changes countries,
40 sweeping away borders,
41 then *spasibo*
42 **clinging** to pointy
43 volcanoes, to fire and freezing cold,
44 or *danke,* yes! and *gracias,* and
45 the world turns into a table:
46 a single word has wiped it clean,
47 plates and glasses gleam,
48 silverware tinkles,
49 and the tablecloth is as broad as a plain.

50 Thank you, *thanks,*
51 for going out and returning,
52 for rising up
53 and settling down.
54 We know, *thanks,*
55 that you don't fill every space-
56 you're only a word-
57 but
58 where your little petal
59 appears
60 the daggers of pride take cover,
61 and there's a penny's worth of smiles.

---

From *Ode to Opposites* by Pablo Neruda, translated by Ken Krabbenhoft . Odes (Spanish) copyright © 1995 by Pablo Neruda and Fundación Pablo Neruda; Odes (English translation) copyright © 1995 by Ken Krabbenhoft; Illustrations and compilation copyright © 1995 by Ferris Cook. Used by permission of Bullfinch/Hachette Book Group USA.

Pablo Neruda, "Oda a las gracias", NAVEGACIONES Y REGRESOS @ Fundación Pablo Neruda

# THINK QUESTIONS  CA-CCSS: CA.RL.8.1, CA.L.8.4a, CA.L.8.4c

1. How does the word *thanks* make the speaker of the poem feel, and why? Cite textual evidence to support your answer.

2. Why does the poet use the word *thanks* in different languages? Cite textual evidence to support your reason.

3. At the end of the poem, to what does the poet compare the word *thanks,* and why? Use textual evidence to support your answer.

4. Use context to determine the meaning of the word **scorn** as it is used in "Ode to Thanks." Write your definition of *scorn* and tell how you got it.

5. The speaker says that *thanks* is "a tapestry known to far distant peoples." What does the context tell you about the meaning of the word **tapestry?** Use textual evidence to explain. Then look up *tapestry* in a dictionary and compare what you learned about the word with the one in the dictionary. How does the dictionary definition help you understand the meaning of the line?

Please note that excerpts and passages in the StudySync® library and this workbook are intended as touchstones to generate interest in an author's work. The excerpts and passages do not substitute for the reading of entire texts, and StudySync® strongly recommends that students seek out and purchase the whole literary or informational work in order to experience it as the author intended. Links to online resellers are available in our digital library. In addition, complete works may be ordered through an authorized reseller by filling out and returning to StudySync® the order form enclosed in this workbook.

Reading & Writing Companion  **315**

# CLOSE READ    CA-CCSS: CA.RL.8.1, CA.RL.8.2, CA.RL.8.4, CA.RL.8.5

Reread the poem "Ode to Thanks." As you reread, complete the Focus Questions below. Then use your answers and annotations from the questions to help you complete the Writing Prompt.

## FOCUS QUESTIONS

1. In the second stanza, or section, of "Ode to Thanks," what does the speaker mean when he says, "Life becomes human again"? How is this a result of expressing thanks? How does the structure of this stanza develop this idea? Highlight evidence from the poem to support your response and make annotations to explain your choices.

2. In the third stanza of "Ode to Thanks," what is the impact of describing *thanks* in so many different languages? How do images such as the "hustling train" and "clinging to pointy volcanoes, to fire and freezing cold" add to the impact? Highlight textual evidence to support your answer. Make annotations to explain how these images and their part in the poetic structure of the stanza help Neruda further his idea of praising *thanks*.

3. In the fourth stanza of "Ode to Thanks," what does the speaker mean when he says "Thank you, *thanks,* / for going out and returning, / for rising up / and settling down"? What images come to mind, and how does the structuring of

the images affect the meaning of the poem? Highlight textual evidence to support your answer. Make annotations to explain your ideas.

4. Think about the poet's message or theme in "Ode to Thanks." How might the simple act of saying the word *thanks* help to shape people's values? How does each stanza of the poem help to develop this theme? Highlight textual evidence and make annotations to explain your ideas.

5. Just as Pablo Neruda, in his poem "Ode to Thanks" gives thanks to the concept of giving thanks, author Rudolfo Anaya celebrates something important by giving thanks, too, in his essay "A Celebration of Grandfathers." Why do you think Neruda uses the form of a poem to celebrate his subject, while Anaya uses the form of an essay? Compare and contrast the structures of the two texts to explain how the differing structures contribute to each author's meaning and style. Highlight textual evidence and make annotations to explain your ideas.

## WRITING PROMPT

In "Ode to Thanks," how does poet Pablo Neruda invite readers to appreciate the concept of gratitude? In an essay of at least 300 words, explain how the poetic structure, as well as the poet's use of connotative word meanings and figurative language, help you understand the poem's message. If you were to write your own ode in the style of Pablo Neruda, what would you praise, and why?

# THE LITTLE BOY LOST/ THE LITTLE BOY FOUND

**POETRY**
William Blake
1789

# INTRODUCTION

Villiam Blake was an 18th century British artist and poet known in part for his richly illustrated poetry collections *Songs of Innocence* and *Songs of Experience*. As the two titles suggest, Blake viewed the world in contrasts. The poems in *Songs of Innocence* focus on the naivety and simplicity of youth, while the poems from the later *Experience* volume explore the darker, corrupted side of human nature. "The Little Boy Lost" and "The Little Boy Found" are from *Songs of Innocence*.

# "The night was dark, no father was there..."

## FIRST READ

"The Little Boy Lost"

1   "Father, father, where are you going?
2   O do not walk so fast!
3   Speak, father, speak to your little boy,
4   Or else I shall be lost."

5   The night was dark, no father was there;
6   The child was wet with dew;
7   The mire was deep, & the child did weep,
8   And away the vapour flew.

"The Little Boy Found"

9   The little boy lost in the lonely **fen**,
10  Led by the wand'ring light,
11  Began to cry, but God, ever **nigh**,
12  Appeared like his father, in white.

13  He kissed the child, & by the hand led
14  And to his mother brought,
15  Who in sorrow pale, thro' the lonely **dale;**
16  Her little boy weeping sought.

THINK QUESTIONS  CA-CCSS: CA.RL.8.1, CA.L.8.4a, CA.SL.8.1a, CA.SL.8.1b, CA.SL.8.1d

1. Summarize what the speaker in the first stanza, or section, is saying in the poem "The Little Boy Lost." What do you think is happening in the poem? Support your understanding both from ideas that are directly stated and ideas that you have inferred from clues in the text.

2. Summarize what the speaker is saying in the first stanza of "The Little Boy Found." Use details from the poem to write two or three sentences explaining what has happened to the little boy in the second stanza. Support your understanding both from ideas that are directly stated and ideas that you have inferred from clues in the text.

3. Who do you think the "father" is in these two poems? Write two or three sentences exploring the idea of the "father" in the two poems. Support your answer with textual evidence from both poems.

4. Use context to determine the meaning of the word **mire** as it is used in "The Little Boy Lost." Write your definition of *mire* and explain how you figured it out. Also explain its effect in the poem.

5. Use context to determine the meaning of the word **nigh** as it is used in "The Little Boy Found." Write your definition of *nigh* and state the clue(s) from the text you used to determine your answer.

# CLOSE READ

CA-CCSS: CA.RL.8.1, CA.RL.8.2, CA.RL.8.4, CA.L.8.5c, CA.W.8.4, CA.W.8.5, CA.W.8.6, CA.W.8.10

Reread the poems "The Little Boy Lost/The Little Boy Found." As you reread, complete the Focus Questions below. Then use your answers and annotations from the questions to help you complete the Writing Prompt.

## FOCUS QUESTIONS

1. The first stanza of "The Little Boy Lost" is not really descriptive, but it still creates a vivid image in the reader's mind. Explain how you visualized what is happening in the stanza and what parts of the text helped create your visualization. Support your answer with textual evidence and make annotations to explain your choices.

2. Explain how the poet creates a tone of unease and eeriness in "The Little Boy Lost," through the use of figurative language, connotative word meanings, and other word choices. Highlight evidence from the text and make annotations to explain your answer.

3. What is the tone of the first lines of "The Little Boy Found"? What figurative language, connotative word meanings, and word choices help to create the tone? Highlight evidence from the text and make annotations to explain your answer.

4. How does the tone change over the two stanzas of "The Little Boy Found"? What words and phrases help create the new tone? Highlight your textual evidence and make annotations to explain your answer.

5. What important life experiences does the boy have as Blake depicts them in "The Little Boy Lost" and "The Little Boy Found"? How might these experiences affect the boy and shape his values? Make annotations stating your inferences about the poems and their deeper meanings. Highlight textual evidence and make annotations to explain your ideas.

## WRITING PROMPT

The poems "The Little Boy Lost" and "The Little Boy Found" by William Blake are, on the surface, about a child's responses to being left behind by his father and returned to his mother, with God's help. Think about what the poet might be saying about earthly life and spiritual life through these events. How do the words "lost" and "found" help develop the poems' themes? Use your understanding of figurative language and connotative meanings, as well as other textual evidence, to support your analysis.

# A POISON TREE

**POETRY**
William Blake
1794

## INTRODUCTION

William Blake was an 18th century British artist and poet known in part for his richly illustrated poetry collections *Songs of Innocence* and *Songs of Experience*. As the two titles suggest, Blake viewed the world in contrasts. The poems in *Songs of Innocence* focus on the naivety and simplicity of youth, while the poems from the later *Experience* volume explore the darker, corrupted side of human nature. "A Poison Tree" is from *Songs of Experience*

# "I water'd it in fears, Night & morning with my tears..."

 FIRST READ

1 I was angry with my friend:
2 I told my **wrath,** my wrath did end.
3 I was angry with my foe:
4 I told it not, my wrath did grow.

5 And I water'd it in fears,
6 Night & morning with my tears;
7 And I sunned it with smiles,
8 And with soft **deceitful wiles.**

9 And it grew both day and night,
10 Till it bore an apple bright;
11 And my foe **beheld** it shine,
12 And he knew that it was mine,

13 And into my garden stole
14 When the night had **veil'd** the pole;
15 In the morning glad I see
16 My foe outstretch'd beneath the tree.

THINK QUESTIONS    CA-CCSS: CA.RL.8.1, CA.RL.8.4, CA.L.8.4a

1. What emotion does the speaker discuss over the course of the poem? What accounts for the differences in the way he expresses it or deals with it? Support your answer with textual evidence.

2. How does the speaker of the poem behave toward others when he is angry with them? Support your inference with textual evidence.

3. What does the poem reveal about the foe? What does the poem **not** reveal about the foe? Support your answer with textual evidence.

4. Use context to determine the meaning of the word **wrath** as it is used in "A Poison Tree." Write your definition of *wrath* and tell how you found it.

5. Use the context clues provided in the passage to determine the meaning of **beheld.** You may also use your knowledge of word forms. Write your definition of *beheld* and tell how you got it.

# CLOSE READ CA-CCSS: CA.RL.8.1, CA.RL.8.2, CA.RL.8.4, CA.RL.8.9, CA.L.8.5b, CA.W.8.4, CA.W.8.5, CA.W.8.6, CA.W.8.9a, CA.W.8.10

Reread the poem "A Poison Tree." As you reread, complete the Focus Questions below. Then use your answers and annotations from the questions to help you complete the Writing Prompt.

 **FOCUS QUESTIONS**

1. What is the relationship between the words "night" and "morning" in the second stanza, and "day and night" and the third stanza? Explain what these word pairs suggest about the speaker and how they add to the poem's meaning. Highlight textual evidence and annotate to explain your answer.

2. Write two or three sentences describing how allusion adds to the meaning of the third and fourth stanzas of "A Poison Tree." How is this allusion tied to the theme or message of the poem? Highlight textual evidence and write annotations to explain your answer.

3. In the last line of the poem, the foe is found "outstretch'd beneath the tree." What connotations does Blake's choice of the word "outstretch'd" (or outstretched), instead of a related word such as "lying" or "dead" or

"motionless," add to the poem? Highlight relevant textual details and annotate to explain your ideas.

4. Think about the poem's title. How are the tree and the speaker's "wrath" related? State how the two things can be compared, including the type of figurative language the poet is using. Explain how this comparison contributes to the poem's meaning. Highlight textual evidence and write annotations to explain your analysis.

5. Based on the poem, what does the speaker value most and what guides his choices? What can you infer about the quality of the speaker's life based on his values? Finally, how do the poet's use of biblical allusions contribute to your understanding of the speaker? Highlight details in the poem and annotate to explain your inferences.

## WRITING PROMPT

William Blake wrote "The Poison Tree" as part of a collection called *Songs of Experience*. What theme is most strongly present in "A Poison Tree"? Why is this poem a "song of experience"? Use textual evidence to explain your reasons and to support your claim. Include the poem's word relationships and figurative language, as well as your understanding of allusion, in your evidence.

# MANDATORY VOLUNTEER WORK FOR TEENAGERS

NON-FICTION
2014

## INTRODUCTION

In these two articles, the writer make cases for and against making volunteer work a mandatory part of school curriculum. While volunteering can be a valuable experience that enriches the lives of both the volunteers and the people they help, some are concerned that forcing teens to volunteer may do more harm than good. Each article presents strong arguments and supports its claims with evidence. Which argument do you feel is more convincing?

# "Everyone knows that volunteers make the United States a better place."

## FIRST READ

NOTES

**Volunteer Work: Should We Make It a Requirement for Teens?**

**Point: Give Teens Some Work to Do! It's Good for Them and Everyone Else**

1   Teenagers today live in a confusing world. The media sends many mixed messages about what it means to be a helpful person in society. One of the best ways to help teens find their way is to make volunteer work a **mandatory** part of their school curriculum. Some people would immediately argue that this is an unnecessary action—many teens already volunteer without it being a requirement. It's true: teens have a **propensity** to volunteer more than adults. However, as a society we should make sure that not just some, but all, teens volunteer. Many of the teens that volunteer do so as part of a religious group or a youth leadership organization. In fact, 46 percent of teens who volunteer are working with a religious group or a youth leadership organization while only 18 percent of teens who volunteer are working with school-based groups. This shows that clearly the best way to include all teens in the benefits of volunteering is to add mandatory volunteer work to the school curriculum.

2   There are many benefits to volunteering. One obvious benefit is that volunteering helps the community—volunteers help the elderly, the disabled, and children. Furthermore, many people are able to receive food and medical assistance that they would not receive otherwise thanks to the hard work of volunteers. And let's not forget the environment! Volunteers make our world a cleaner place by doing things like picking up trash and teaching others about recycling. However, volunteering brings advantages that many people don't think of right away: benefits to the volunteers themselves! According to the United Way, volunteering helps people make important networking contacts, develop new skills, gain work experience, and enhance their resume. All of these benefits are crucial to teens who will soon be entering the workforce. The United Way also says that volunteering gives people the

opportunity to teach their skills to others and build self-esteem and confidence. These two benefits are helpful to teens who are developing their social skills. Finally, the United Way says that volunteering improves people's health and helps to make a difference in someone's life, benefits that are wonderful for volunteers at any age! The numerous advantages that come from volunteering definitely warrant making volunteering a compulsory part of school curriculum.

3   One very specific reason to tie volunteer work to education is that teen volunteers are more likely to succeed academically than teens who don't volunteer. Back in 2005, a collaborative study conducted by the Corporation for National and Community Service and the U.S. Census Bureau revealed that students who do better in school are more likely to be volunteers. There are numerous possible reasons for this trend. It may be because teenagers who volunteer learn new skills, or because the work helps teenagers build confidence, or because volunteering provides a sense of purpose. Whatever the reason, the abundantly clear link between students who volunteer and academic success is too important to be ignored.

4   What happens to teenagers who volunteer as they grow into adults? They continue to volunteer, of course! According to the United Way, volunteering as a youth will increase the chances that a person will volunteer as an adult, which makes sense given the many benefits of volunteering. Unfortunately, however, adults who were never encouraged to volunteer as youths may never start because they are oblivious of the benefits. A simple solution to this would be to make volunteer work a mandatory part of the school curriculum so that everyone will be provided the opportunity to be exposed to the helpful benefits of volunteering. Aside from the benefits to the individual volunteer, think about the benefit to society as a whole. Community service programs across the country will have a fresh new crop of enthusiastic, lifelong volunteers to count on. Everyone knows that volunteers make the United States a better place. The more volunteers, young and old, the better!

5   The evidence is clear: Volunteering is beneficial to both the community and the volunteers themselves. Because the advantages of volunteering so heavily outweigh the disadvantages, it makes sense to start people on a path of volunteerism early by making volunteering a mandatory part of the school curriculum.

## Counterpoint: Mandatory Volunteer Work Does More Harm Than Good

6   Most people agree that teenagers today live in a difficult world. There are more pressures facing the modern teen than we can count: school, work, family, sports, and other extracurricular activities, just to name a few. However, some people think that we should add to that load of pressures by making volunteer work a mandatory part of the school curriculum. One of the greatest

NOTES

arguments for this action is that mandatory volunteer work will prepare students for the future by giving them work experience, but the flaw in this logic is that many teens already gain work experience through paying jobs. In fact, many of the teens working paying jobs are doing so out of necessity— to pay for gas to get back and forth to school, or to help their families with extra money. Those teens without paying jobs still have plenty of prospects for gaining work experience in other ways such as an internship, or working at a school paper. Another argument for making volunteer work a mandatory part of school curriculum is that this work will help teens gain self-esteem and self-confidence. However, having time to socialize and develop hobbies and other interests is more important for self-esteem and self-confidence than volunteering.

7　The most compelling argument *against* making volunteer work a mandatory part of school curriculum is time. Teens today are just too busy to add another stressor to their lives. Let's take a look at twenty-four hours in the life of a typical teen. Allocate eight hours per day for sleep, eight hours for school (including getting ready and travel time), three hours for homework, two hours for activities such as sports or a part-time job, two hours for dinner and family time, and one hour for socializing. These activities take up all twenty-four hours leaving scarcely any time for volunteer work. Should students have to sacrifice their one hour of socializing per day, or sacrifice an hour of precious family time? These options just don't make sense as making more demands on teens' packed schedules can have serious side effects. Teens who are too busy feel tired, anxious, or depressed. Studies show they often have headaches or stomachaches due to stress, missed meals, or lack of sleep and they may fall behind in school, causing their grades to suffer. These drawbacks clearly outweigh the benefits of volunteering.

8　Another problem with making volunteer work a mandatory part of curriculum is that it defeats the purpose of volunteering in the first place. People volunteer because they have extra time and energy to give, and they genuinely want to help. Students that are forced to volunteer may resent the demand on their time, and therefore perform the work grudgingly. This will not help to make students feel useful or helpful, which would be counterproductive. Furthermore, students will not be able to experience the positive social benefits of volunteering because they see it as a requirement rather than a positive experience. Because of forced volunteer work, students may hesitate to explore volunteering as an adult. This is a huge drawback because there are genuine benefits to volunteering when someone actually has the time and means to do so.

9　Finally, there is great evidence that the teens that do have the time to volunteer already do! This eliminates the need to make volunteer work mandatory. In 2005, a collaborative study on the volunteering habits of teenagers conducted by the Corporation for National and Community Service and the U.S. Census Bureau revealed that an estimated 15.5 million teens between the ages of 12 and 18 do volunteer work. This is about 55 percent of youth, a number all the more astounding when compared to the meager 29 percent of adults who do volunteer work. They also found that young people complete more than 1.3 billion hours of volunteer work each year. These findings demonstrate that a significant number of teenagers are already participating in service to their communities when they are able. Since volunteer work is clearly popular among teenagers, it is safe to assume that the minority of teenagers who do not volunteer are only choosing not to participate because they do not have the time.

10    Making volunteer work a mandatory part of school curriculum may seem like a good idea at first glance. Volunteering is good for the community and offers many benefits for the person volunteering as well. However, upon further examination it becomes clear that this is not a good plan. Adding another time stressor into the lives of teenagers just isn't worth it.

 **THINK QUESTIONS**   CA-CCSS: CA.RI.8.1, CA.RI.8.4, CA.L.8.4a

1.  How do the first paragraphs of both essays serve as summaries for the entire essays? Cite words and phrases that show how each of the first paragraphs outlines the entire essays.

2.  One way to draw inferences about writers' points of view is to make a list of the points they emphasize in a text. What points does the writer emphasize in each of the essays? Highlight these places in the text. What inferences can you draw from this evidence?

3.  What kinds of evidence do the authors offer as support for their points? Do you think their support is effective? Highlight places in the text where evidence is introduced, and explain why you think it is effective or not effective.

4.  Use context to determine the meaning of the word **grudgingly** as it is used in the third paragraph of "Counterpoint: Mandatory Volunteer Work Does More Harm Than Good." Write your definition of *grudgingly* and tell how you found it.

5.  Use context to determine the meaning of the word **allocate** as it is used in the second paragraph of "Counterpoint: Mandatory Volunteer Work Does More Harm Than Good." Write your definition of *allocate* and tell how you found it.

# CLOSE READ
CA-CCSS: CA.RI.8.1, CA.RI.8.4, CA.RI.8.6, CA.RI.8.8, CA.RI.8.9, CA.W.8.4, CA.W.8.5, CA.W.8.6, CA.W.8.10, CA.SL.8.3

Reread the essays arguing for and against mandatory volunteer work for teenagers. As you reread, complete the Focus Questions below. Then use your answers and annotations from the questions to help you complete the Writing Prompt.

## FOCUS QUESTIONS

1. Explain how the authors' points of view are shown in both the Point and the Counterpoint essay. Where do they exhibit conflicting evidence or viewpoints? Support your answer with textual evidence and make annotations to explain your answer choices.

2. Select one paragraph from the body of both the Point and the Counterpoint essays and compare and contrast how each author uses evidence to support his or her reasons. Which essay do you think does a better job of using evidence to support their reasons? Support your answer with textual evidence and make annotations to explain your answer choices.

3. Contrast the connotations, or emotional qualities, of language used in both of the essays. Use this information to describe the tone of each essay.

Highlight your textual evidence and make annotations to explain your descriptions.

4. Do you think that both Point and Counterpoint supporters might agree on any issues or ideas brought up in these essays? Explain and highlight your textual evidence and make annotations to explain your thoughts.

5. How do our own life experiences and preferences help us to determine what is work and what is play? According to the Counterpoint essay, mandating volunteer work could result in adults who are too resentful to volunteer. Do you agree with this warning? Why or why not? Highlight evidence, including the way the argument is structured, to support your ideas. Write annotations to explain your opinion.

## WRITING PROMPT

Mark Twain's narrator in *The Adventures of Tom Sawyer* shares many ideas on the idea of working and volunteering. In the two essays that make up *Mandatory Volunteer Work for Teenagers,* what is each writer's point of view on teen volunteerism? What can you infer about the writers' values from the reasons and evidence presented in the Point and the Counterpoint? Compare and contrast the way reasons and evidence are presented in the two essays. Which essay do you think makes the most convincing arguments? Use textual evidence to support your opinion.

# MOM'S FIRST DAY

English Language
Development

FICTION

## INTRODUCTION

Sometimes life takes you by surprise and challenges you without warning. When this happens, you rely on your values to pull you through. In "Mom's First Day," Yvette is startled when her mother addresses her in a familiar way in front of her classmates. In a flash, this innocent, awkward encounter swells into a moment of truth.

# "I look up. There she is, in her favorite church outfit, standing in front of the class."

## FIRST READ

NOTES

1   "Be nice to Mom today," my dad tells me, setting my sack lunch on the counter. It's not even 7:30 am on Monday and already I'm wishing the week were over. How will I possibly survive a week with my mother as my substitute teacher? "Make her feel welcome," my dad continues. "Remember what school felt like on *your* first day?"

2   Just then my mother enters the kitchen. As she **flutters** between the coffee pot and the refrigerator, she looks as nervous as the hummingbird that **hovers** outside the window. To my horror, she is dressed in one of her church outfits: a green silk dress with beige pumps. I am about to tell her she is *way* too **dressy** for school, when I remember my father's words.

3   None of this would be happening if Pepe hadn't been born. For years, Mom had a job teaching science at a private school in town, but she quit toward the end of her pregnancy. She's pretty much been home with Pepe ever since. If I were her, I'd want to get out of the house, too. Don't get me wrong, Pepe is cute and everything, but he cries a lot, and it's a safe bet there's something wet on his body at all times.

4   Lucky for me, my best friend Katie and I have science class together. We get there early and sit in the back. As the class fills up around us, I **slump** low in my seat and doodle in my notebook, keeping my head down. As the minutes tick by, my worries increase. What if people laugh at her? What if they laugh at me because she's my mom? Suddenly, everybody gets quiet.

5   I look up. There she is, in her favorite church outfit, standing in front of the class. For a moment, I think she is going to single me out, but she just gives me a little, knowing smile and starts her lesson.

6   To my surprise, Mom does a good job. She even makes the class laugh a few times. But still I keep my eyes on the clock, praying for the hands to move faster.

7   Finally the bell rings. Katie and I jump up. We are almost out the door when I hear her.

8   "Yvette," she says. She's holding my sack lunch. "You forgot your lunch."

9   "Thanks," I mumble. I take it from her without meeting her eyes.

10  "Love you," says Mom, just like she often does, only this time it's in front of my classmates. Everybody freezes. I feel my cheeks start to burn. I'm so **humiliated**, all I can do is turn and bury my face in Katie's shoulder. To my relief, the kids around me start to laugh, and so I laugh, too. But then, almost by accident, I see the sad expression on my mother's face. Her disappointment hits like a **tidal wave**. I don't know what to call this new feeling, but I know I'll be left thinking about it for a long time.

Please note that excerpts and passages in the StudySync® library and this workbook are intended as touchstones to generate interest in an author's work. The excerpts and passages do not substitute for the reading of entire texts, and StudySync® strongly recommends that students seek out and purchase the whole literary or informational work in order to experience it as the author intended. Links to online resellers are available in our digital library. In addition, complete works may be ordered through an authorized reseller by filling out and returning to StudySync® the order form enclosed in this workbook.

Reading & Writing
Companion

333

USING LANGUAGE  CA-CCSS: ELD.PI.8.6.c.Ex, ELD.PI.8.12.b.Ex

Read each word. Complete each row by filling in the correct root or affix meaning in the second column and definition in the third column.

| Root/Affix Meaning Options | | Definition Options |
|---|---|---|
| *priv-* meaning "separate" | *qui-* meaning "rest" | separate from others; being alone |
| *super-* meaning "above, over" | *sci-* meaning "know" | resting one's lips; not talking |
| *viv-* meaning "live" | *-ence* meaning "the state of having" | to live through or overcome something |
| | | knowledge about the natural world |

| Word | Root/Affix Meaning | Definition |
|---|---|---|
| survive | | |
| private | | |
| science | | |
| quiet | | |

Reading & Writing Companion

MEANINGFUL INTERACTIONS  CA-CCSS: ELD.PI.8.1.Ex

Work with your group to discuss your first impressions of the text. First, take turns saying what you think about Yvette, Mom, and their relationship. Then, build on your peers' responses by asking questions and explaining why you agree or disagree with their ideas. Use the speaking frames to support your discussion. Last, use the self-assessment rubric to evaluate your participation in the discussion.

- I think Yvette is . . . because . . .

- In my opinion, Mom is . . . because . . .

- I would describe Yvette's relationship with Mom as . . . because . . .

- I think their relationship changes / does not change because . . .

- I think you said . . . Why do you think that?

- I agree / disagree because . . .

 SELF-ASSESSMENT RUBRIC  CA-CCSS: ELD.PI.8.1.Ex

| | 4<br>I did this well. | 3<br>I did this pretty well. | 2<br>I did this a little bit. | 1<br>I did not do this. |
|---|---|---|---|---|
| I took an active part with others in doing the assigned task. | | | | |
| I contributed effectively to the group's discussion. | | | | |
| I waited my turn to speak. | | | | |
| I asked group members questions about their ideas. | | | | |
| I built on my group members' responses by explaining why I agreed or disagreed with their ideas. | | | | |

# REREAD

Reread paragraphs 1–3 of "Mom's First Day." After you reread, complete the Using Language and Meaningful Interactions activities.

## USING LANGUAGE   CA-CCSS: ELD.PII.8.1.Ex

Complete the chart by arranging the events from the story into chronological order, starting with what happens first and ending with what happens last.

| Event Options | |
|---|---|
| Mom quits her job. | Mom stays home with Pepe. |
| Mom becomes a substitute teacher at Yvette's school. | Mom teaches at a private school. |

| First | Next | Then | Last |
|---|---|---|---|
| | | | |

## MEANINGFUL INTERACTIONS   CA-CCSS: ELD.PI.8.1.Ex

Based on what you have read in "Mom's First Day," describe the conflict between Yvette and her mother. What happened? How do the characters feel about it? Whose fault is it? In small groups, identify and paraphrase details from the text about the events and feelings that led to the conflict. Use the writing frames to support your discussion. Then, use the self-assessment rubric to evaluate your participation in the discussion.

- In the story, the main conflict is _____.

- In the text, Yvette says "_____" about her mother substitute teaching at her school.

  In other words, Yvette feels _____ because _____
  _____.

- At the end of Yvette's science class, Yvette's mother says "_____."

  The text says Yvette's reaction is "_____."

  In other words, Yvette feels _____ because her mother _____
  _____.

- Then the text says Yvette's mother feels "_____" because Yvette "_____
  _____."

  In other words, Yvette's mother feels _____ because _____
  _____.

- I think the conflict is _____'s fault because _____
  _____.

## SELF-ASSESSMENT RUBRIC   CA-CCSS: ELD.PI.8.1.Ex

|  | 4<br>I did this well. | 3<br>I did this pretty well. | 2<br>I did this a little bit. | 1<br>I did not do this. |
|---|---|---|---|---|
| I identified details in the text that told about the conflict. | | | | |
| I identified details in the text that told about how the characters feel about the conflict. | | | | |
| I used my own words to paraphrase details from the text. | | | | |
| I used details from the text to support my ideas about who is to blame for the conflict. | | | | |

Please note that excerpts and passages in the StudySync® library and this workbook are intended as touchstones to generate interest in an author's work. The excerpts and passages do not substitute for the reading of entire texts, and StudySync® strongly recommends that students seek out and purchase the whole literary or informational work in order to experience it as the author intended. Links to online resellers are available in our digital library. In addition, complete works may be ordered through an authorized reseller by filling out and returning to StudySync® the order form enclosed in this workbook.

Reading & Writing Companion   **337**

# REREAD

Reread paragraphs 4–10 of "Mom's First Day." After you reread, complete the Using Language and Meaningful Interactions activities.

## USING LANGUAGE   CA-CCSS: ELD.PI.8.8.Ex

Read each sentence from "Mom's First Day," and note the figurative language in bold. Then choose the meaning of the figurative language in each sentence.

1. Everybody **freezes**.
   - ○ Everyone stands still.
   - ○ Everyone is covered in ice.

2. I'm so humiliated, all I can do is **bury my face** in Katie's shoulder.
   - ○ Yvette puts her face in a hole.
   - ○ Yvette hides her face.

3. Her disappointment hits **like a tidal wave**.
   - ○ Mom has very strong feelings.
   - ○ Mom was hit by a large wave.

## MEANINGFUL INTERACTIONS   CA-CCSS: ELD.PI.8.1.Ex

What has Yvette done to make her mother feel unwelcome? What should she have done to make her feel welcome? Work with a partner to practice sharing and discussing your opinion. Use the speaking frames to add relevant information and evidence from the text to support your opinion.

- Yvette made her mother feel unwelcome by . . .

- I think this makes her mother feel unwelcome because . . .

- My opinion is that Yvette should have . . .

- Evidence supporting my opinion is . . .

- Do you think that Yvette should have . . . ?

- I think you said . . .

- I agree / don't agree because . . .

# IT'S NOT FAIR

English Language
Development

FICTION

## INTRODUCTION

" I t's Not Fair" is a retelling of the memorable episode from Mark Twain's *The Adventures of Tom Sawyer* in which Tom uses charm and ingenuity to trick others into doing chores for him. In this retelling, a girl named Cassie must plant her aunt's flower garden on the same day as the annual county fair. Cassie relies on her own cleverness—and a scheme learned from reading classic American literature—to trick her friends into doing the work.

# "A satisfied smile crept across Cassie's face."

NOTES

## FIRST READ

1   Cassie imagined the taste of caramel apples and the feel of the wind in her hair at the top of the Ferris wheel. She could practically smell the freshly made popcorn and hear the sounds of children's laughter. Her despair deepened. It was bad enough that she got roped into planting her aunt's garden. Now she had to do it on the same day as the county fair. It wasn't fair. The path leading to the fairgrounds ran along her aunt's property. Cassie's friends would skip along this path on their way to a world of wonders she could only dream about, and she was certain they'd stop to ridicule her about how she had to work while they had the time of their lives at the fair. The mere thought of it was enough to make her wish she could bury her head in the dirt instead of the flower bulbs she was supposed to plant.

2   Cassie took up the **trowel** and started to dig. Bella Stevenson, the most popular girl in class and the person Cassie was dreading the most, **ambled** down the path. She was dragging a red wagon behind her, which was carrying an apple pie.

3   Cassie kept digging. A plan was forming in her brain. She remembered reading how Tom Sawyer convinced his friends to whitewash a fence for him. If she played the role perfectly, she could accomplish the same task.

4   "It's too bad you're stuck here while the rest of us get to have fun at the fair!" Bella called out.

5   "Fun? This is more fun than that silly fair. The same food and rides every year! Planting bulbs under the sweet spring sunshine? That's a **novelty**!"

6   "If it's that much fun, it's not fair that you keep it all to yourself."

7   A satisfied smile crept across Cassie's face. Her plan had worked.

8   "I don't know. Aunt Lucy entrusted this job to me. I can't let just anyone do it. Tell you what. I'll trade you a few **bulbs** for some of that pie you made."

9   Bella was planning on entering the pie in the contest at the fair, but she didn't want to miss this chance. She accepted, handing Cassie a slice of pie and taking the trowel in exchange.

10   When Bella had grown tired, Penelope Winters strolled by. Cassie pulled the trick on her—this time trading the trowel for Penelope's sunglasses. By the end of the afternoon, Cassie had Bella's pie, Penelope's sunglasses, Randy's harmonica, Betty's kite, and Clark's bag of marbles.

11   Cassie was amazed at her classmates' **gullibility** and her own good fortune. "Tom Sawyer was right," she thought, "All you have to do to make somebody want something is make it seem hard to get."

## ⚙ USING LANGUAGE   CA-CCSS: ELD.PI.8.6.c.Ex

Read each quotation and think about the meaning of the word in bold. Then choose the context clue that helped you determine the meaning of the word.

1.   . . . the mere thought of it was enough to make her wish she could bury her head in the dirt instead of the flower **bulbs** she was supposed to plant.

   ○ flower
   ○ wish

2.   Cassie took up the **trowel** and started to dig.

   ○ took up
   ○ to dig

3.   Bella Stevenson, the most popular girl in class and the person Cassie was dreading the most, **ambled** down the path.

   ○ popular girl
   ○ down the path

4.   Cassie pulled the trick on her — this time trading the trowel for Penelope's sunglasses. . . . Cassie was amazed at her classmates' **gullibility** and her own good fortune.

   ○ good fortune
   ○ pulled the trick

## MEANINGFUL INTERACTIONS  CA-CCSS: ELD.PI.8.1.Ex

Before you start your discussion, set turn-taking rules for the group.

1. _____

2. _____

3. _____

4. _____

5. _____

Use these questions to discuss your first impressions of "It's Not Fair":

- What is Cassie's problem?

- How does she solve her problem?

- Do you think Cassie's solution is clever or unfair? Why?

Work in small groups to practice taking turns speaking and listening during a discussion. Use the speaking frames to support your discussion. Then, use the self-assessment rubric to evaluate your participation in the discussion.

- Cassie's problem is . . .

- Cassie solves her problem by . . .

- In my opinion, Cassie's solution is . . . because . . .

- What evidence do you base your opinion on? Is it . . . ?

- I think you said . . . I agree / disagree because . . .

## SELF-ASSESSMENT RUBRIC  CA-CCSS: ELD.PI.8.1.Ex

|  | 4<br>I did this well. | 3<br>I did this pretty well. | 2<br>I did this a little bit. | 1<br>I did not do this. |
|---|---|---|---|---|
| I expressed my opinion clearly. |  |  |  |  |
| I listened carefully to others' opinions. |  |  |  |  |
| I waited my turn before speaking. |  |  |  |  |
| I responded thoughtfully to my group members' ideas. |  |  |  |  |

# REREAD

Reread paragraphs 1–3 of "It's Not Fair." After you reread, complete the Using Language and Meaningful Interactions activities.

## USING LANGUAGE   CA-CCSS: ELD.PI.8.8.Ex

Read the first draft of each sentence from the text and note the bold word or phrase. Then read the final draft of the text and consider the change the author made in bold. Then complete the chart by choosing the correct option for how the author's word choice helps readers understand.

| Helps readers understand... Options | | |
|---|---|---|
| how Cassie feels about Bella<br>how great the fair is | how much fun Cassie's friends had<br>how carefree the other children are | how strongly Cassie feels |

| First Draft | Final Draft | Helps readers understand... |
|---|---|---|
| Her **sadness** deepened. | Her **despair** deepened. | |
| Cassie's friends would **walk** along this path on their way to the fair... | Cassie's friends would **skip** along this path on their way to a world of wonders she could only dream about... | |
| Cassie's friends would travel along this path on their way to **the fair**... | Cassie's friends would skip along this path on their way to **a world of wonders she could only dream about**... | |
| ... she was certain they'd stop to ridicule her about how she had to work while they had **fun** at the fair... | ...she was certain they'd stop to ridicule her about how she had to work while they had **the time of their lives** at the fair... | |
| Bella Stevenson, **a girl from Cassie's class**, ambled down the path. | Bella Stevenson, **the most popular girl in class and the person Cassie was dreading the most**, ambled down the path. | |

## MEANINGFUL INTERACTIONS  CA-CCSS: ELD.PI.8.1.Ex

Based on what you have read in "It's Not Fair," what do you think the conflict suggests about human nature? Would you try to resolve the conflict in the same way as Cassie? Why or why not? Work in small groups to practice sharing and discussing your opinions, using the speaking frames. Then, use the self-assessment rubric to evaluate your participation in the discussion.

- I would / would not resolve the conflict in the same way as Cassie because . . .

- In my opinion, the conflict shows that humans are . . . because . . .

- I think . . . said that . . .

- I agree / don't agree with . . . that . . .

## SELF-ASSESSMENT RUBRIC  CA-CCSS: ELD.PI.8.1.Ex

|  | 4 I did this well. | 3 I did this pretty well. | 2 I did this a little bit. | 1 I did not do this. |
|---|---|---|---|---|
| I expressed my opinion clearly. |  |  |  |  |
| I listened carefully to others' opinions. |  |  |  |  |
| I spoke respectfully when disagreeing with others. |  |  |  |  |
| I was courteous when persuading others to share my view. |  |  |  |  |

# REREAD

Reread paragraphs 4–11 of "It's Not Fair." After you reread, complete the Using Language and Meaningful Interactions activities.

 **USING LANGUAGE**  CA-CCSS: ELD.PII.8.4.Ex

Complete the sentences by filling in the blanks.

1.  Find the sentence in paragraph 5 that shows a comparison Cassie makes.

    This is more fun than that _____.

2.  Find the sentence in paragraph 5 that shows what Cassie pretends to think about the fair.

    The _____ and _____ every year!

3.  Find the sentence in paragraph 7 that shows how Cassie reacts when Bella falls for her trick.

    A _____ crept across Cassie's face.

4.  Find the sentence in paragraph 8 that shows what Cassie wants to trade.

    I'll trade you a _____ for some of _____ you made.

5.  Find the sentence in paragraph 10 that shows what Cassie is doing to her friends.

    Cassie pulled _____ on her—this time trading the trowel for Penelope's sunglasses.

6.  Find the sentence in paragraph 11 that shows what Cassie thinks about her classmates and the results of her plan.

    Cassie was amazed at her _____ and her own _____.

MEANINGFUL INTERACTIONS  CA-CCSS: ELD.PI.8.1.Ex

What do you think of Cassie and the way she treats her classmates? What evidence from the text supports your opinion? Work with a partner to practice sharing and discussing your opinions, using the writing and speaking frames.

- My opinion is that the way Cassie treats her classmates is _____

  because _____

  _____.

- The evidence I used to form my opinion is _____

  _____.

- I think you said that . . . ,  but the text says . . .

- Why do you think that . . . ?

- I agree / disagree with your opinion because . . .

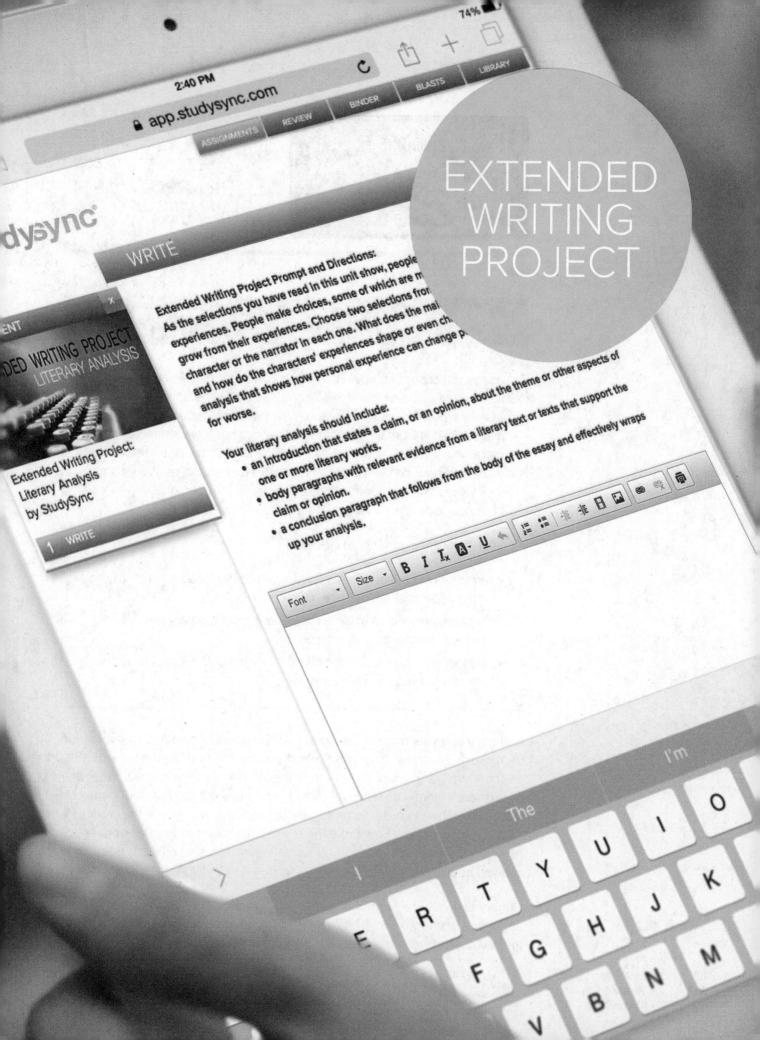

**EXTENDED WRITING PROJECT**

WRITE

**Extended Writing Project Prompt and Directions:**

As the selections you have read in this unit show, people
experiences. People make choices, some of which are m
grow from their experiences. Choose two selections fron
character or the narrator in each one. What does the mai
and how do the characters' experiences shape or even ch
analysis that shows how personal experience can change p
for worse.

Your literary analysis should include:

- an introduction that states a claim, or an opinion, about the theme or other aspects of
  one or more literary works.
- body paragraphs with relevant evidence from a literary text or texts that support the
  claim or opinion.
- a conclusion paragraph that follows from the body of the essay and effectively wraps
  up your analysis.

Extended Writing Project:
Literary Analysis
by StudySync

# LITERARY ANALYSIS

## WRITING PROMPT

As the selections you have read in this unit show, people are shaped by their individual life experiences. People make choices, some of which are mistakes, but they often learn and grow from their experiences. Choose two selections from this unit and think about the main character or the narrator in each one. What does the main character or narrator value most, and how do the characters' experiences shape or even change their values? Write a literary analysis that shows how personal experience can change people for better or sometimes for worse.

Your literary analysis should include:

- an introduction that states a claim, or an opinion, about the theme or other aspects of one or more literary works.
- body paragraphs with relevant evidence from a literary text or texts that support the claim or opinion.
- a conclusion paragraph that follows from the body of the essay and effectively wraps up your analysis.

A **literary analysis** presents a writer's personal understanding or evaluation of a work of literature and then provides textual evidence—details, descriptions, and quotations—to support the evaluation. As with any evaluation, a literary analysis requires a writer to examine different parts of a work of literature in order to better understand and appreciate the work as a whole. It may discuss how the various elements of an individual work—such as setting, characters, and plot events—relate to each other. It might also analyze how two separate literary works handle similar themes and ideas.

Literary analysis is a form of argumentative writing. The writer makes a claim about one or more works of literature, and then provides evidence to support the claim. A strong literary analysis begins with a sound thesis statement that clearly expresses the writer's opinion or claim about some part of the work. After introducing the claim, the writer develops his or her ideas in the body of the text. Like all good essays, a literary analysis develops and supports the thesis with text evidence, and connects the ideas together with clear and specific transitions. These help readers to understand the logic behind the argument, and identify how well it is supported. The piece ends with a conclusion that clearly restates the main idea and shows that the analysis is sound and well-supported. The features of a literary analysis include:

- a clear thesis statement expressing the author's claim, or opinion, about the work

- an organizational structure with clear transitions that logically moves the reader through each step of the argument

- text evidence that supports the argument, in the form of quotations and other details from the text or texts

- precise language

- a conclusion that summarizes the author's position

You will receive more instructions and practice to help you create each of the elements that make up a literary analysis as you continue with this Extended Writing Project.

 ## STUDENT MODEL

Before you begin your own literary analysis, start by reading this essay. This is one student's response to the writing prompt. Be sure to highlight and annotate the features of a literary analysis that the student included as you read the essay.

### Personal Experiences: The Pathway to Values

*How do you define your own personal values? Are they the ideas that you feel are most important in life, the foundation for your every action and belief? Many people believe personal values form the core of a person's being, shaping our individual personalities as well as our decisions about what is right and wrong. But where do values come from? Many works of literature reveal how personal experiences can shape or even change a character's values. Mark Twain shows how this can occur in The Adventures of Tom Sawyer. Judith Ortiz Cofer also illustrates this process in her short story, "Abuela Invents the Zero." Even though their main characters exist many years apart, and have very different lives, both*

Twain and Ortiz Cofer show how personal experiences can shape a person's values for a lifetime.

Both Twain and Cofer Ortiz put characters into situations that reveal their personal values. In an excerpt from *The Adventures of Tom Sawyer,* readers find the main character painting a fence. The narrator relates how unhappy Tom is with the job. In the first paragraph of the excerpt, Tom "began to think of the fun he had planned for this day, and his sorrows multiplied" (Twain). This shows that Tom values fun more than the hard work of painting the fence. In Ortiz Cofer's short story, the author makes Constancia's values very clear. This teen-aged girl values her identity and standing in her American neighborhood far more than she values her family's Puerto Rican heritage and her grandmother's feelings. One illustration of this is when Constancia describes her embarrassment at being with her grandmother in public: "I try to walk far behind them in public so that no one will think we are together" (Ortiz Cofer).

Like every other human being, Tom Sawyer's and Constancia's values have been shaped by their personal experiences. Twain's Tom Sawyer has had experiences that lead him to value fun more than work as well as to value the opinions of his friends. This is shown when the narrator describes his thoughts: ". . . and they would make a world of fun of him for having to work—the very thought burnt him like fire" (Twain). The narrator even describes how Tom thinks about bribing his friends to do his work for him. He rejects the idea because he does not have enough valuables to trade for his freedom. Like Tom Sawyer, Ortiz Cofer's character's values are also shaped by her experiences. Constancia, the main character, is a teen-aged girl whose family has come to the United States from Puerto Rico. Her mother recalls the difficulty of her early life in Puerto Rico. She tells Constancia about how her grandmother "worked night and day to support them after their father died of a heart attack" (Ortiz Cofer). Constancia's mother values her mother's efforts and wants to make sure that Abuela's visit is fun for her. However, Constancia has not had the same experiences with Abuela. She has only met her a few times and does not feel close to her. She does not value Abuela in the same way her mother does. This is demonstrated by her behavior in the story. For example, when Constancia is forced to take her grandmother to church, she describes going into the building: ". . . Then I lead her down the aisle so that everybody can see me with my bizarre grandmother" (Ortiz Cofer).

Twain and Ortiz Cofer describe brief moments in their characters' lives, but even these small events influence the characters' values. In the case of Tom Sawyer, his values are confirmed and supported. He comes up with a scheme to get the other boys to do the painting for him. He does this by convincing them that the chore of painting the fence is not actually work at all, but rather great fun. The other boys happily part with their treasures in return for a turn with the paintbrush, and Tom learns that he can manipulate others to get the things he values, namely, free time and fun. Twain's narrator notes, "Tom said to himself that it was not such a hollow world, after all. He had discovered a great law of human action, without knowing it—namely, that in order to make a man or a boy covet a thing, it is only necessary to make the thing difficult to attain" (Twain). Constancia, on the other hand, suffers through her embarrassing moments with her grandmother only to discover that her feelings are not the only ones that mattered. Her grandmother was made to feel "like a zero, like a nothing" (Ortiz Cofer). Constancia's mother reminded her that the grandmother deserved more respect, because "if it wasn't for the old woman whose existence you don't seem to value, you and I would not be here" (Ortiz Cofer). As a result, Constancia's values begin to change. As she describes her thoughts, she notes "I think I understand how I made Abuela feel" and ". . . it's not easy to admit you've been a jerk" (Ortiz Cofer). These revelations show that Constancia's values were changing because of her experiences.

In both selections, the authors show how personal experiences shaped the values of the main characters. The importance Tom Sawyer placed on fun is only reinforced by the events in the story. He may have turned work into fun for others, but that was not his aim. Conversely, Constancia's personal values, and how she felt about her heritage and her grandmother, were shaken and perhaps changed now that she understands how her grandmother feels. Tom Sawyer's values arguably changed for the worse, but Constancia's values improved as she learned more about her *Abuela*. In these excerpts, both authors show how personal experiences and the responses of other people shape and mold everyone's values every day.

Please note that excerpts and passages in the StudySync® library and this workbook are intended as touchstones to generate interest in an author's work. The excerpts and passages do not substitute for the reading of entire texts, and StudySync® strongly recommends that students seek out and purchase the whole literary or informational work in order to experience it as the author intended. Links to online resellers are available in our digital library. In addition, complete works may be ordered through an authorized reseller by filling out and returning to StudySync® the order form enclosed in this workbook.

Reading & Writing Companion    **351**

THINK QUESTIONS

1. What is the claim or central idea of this essay?

2. How does the author of the Student Model support the claim or central idea?

3. How does the author show a connection between the character development in the selections and the development of values in real life? Support your answer with textual evidence from the essay.

4. Consider the prompt that will guide your writing project. Which selections or other resources could you use to write your own literary analysis? What ideas will you include in your piece?

5. Based on what you have read, listened to, or researched, how would you answer the following questions: *How can personal experiences impact values? How do values change based on experiences?* Provide some details that helped inform your answers.

# PREWRITE

CA-CCSS: CA.RI.8.1, CA.W.8.5, CA.W.8.6, CA.W.8.9a

## WRITING PROMPT

As the selections you have read in this unit show, people are shaped by their individual life experiences. People make choices, some of which are mistakes, but they often learn and grow from their experiences. Choose two selections from this unit and think about the main character or the narrator in each one. What does the main character or narrator value most, and how do the characters' experiences shape or even change their values? Write a literary analysis that shows how personal experience can change people for better or sometimes for worse.

Your literary analysis should include:

- an introduction that states a claim, or an opinion, about the theme or other aspects of one or more literary works.
- body paragraphs with relevant evidence from a literary text or texts that support the claim or opinion.
- a conclusion paragraph that follows from the body of the essay and effectively wraps up your analysis.

You have been reading and learning from selections that feature a cross-section of characters learning more about themselves and others through personal experiences. Now you will analyze these selections and use the information to write your own essay about how personal experiences can shape the values of individuals.

As you prepare to write your literary analysis in response to the Extended Writing Prompt above, consider the following questions for each of the selections you will use as the basis for your literary analysis:

- Which selections from the unit are you choosing to write about?

- What do the characters experience in these selections? Summarize the important life experience or experiences of the main character in each selection you choose.
- Are the experiences short, specific and limited, or will they have an impact that will last a lifetime?
- How does the author show what kind of impact the experience had on the character's values?
- Does the experience change the character for better or for worse?
- What predictions can you make about the future behavior of the character, based on the information given in the selection?
- How do you think this character's values will be challenged or reinforced as his or her life experiences continue?

Make a list of the answers to these questions for the characters in the selections you have chosen as the basis for your literary analysis. Do you see any patterns? Do you find any ideas that surface again and again? Looking for patterns and similarities that may emerge in more than one selection can help you solidify the ideas you want to discuss in your essay. Use this model to help you get started with your own prewriting:

**Text:** *The Adventures of Tom Sawyer* by Mark Twain

**Character Experience:** Tom Sawyer wished that he didn't have to work at whitewashing his aunt's fence, and he was envious of the "free" boys who passed by, all of whom were planning "delicious expeditions." By pretending that his work was more enjoyable and engaging than any game or adventure— and that only he was skilled enough to do it correctly—Tom convinced the boys to give him their treasures for a chance to join him and experience the "fun" of whitewashing.

**How It Shaped the Character's Values:** Tom learned that people will work hard if they don't feel that they are obliged to do it, and that "in order to make a man or boy covet a thing, it is only necessary to make the thing difficult to attain." The great value Tom once placed on "freedom" was lessened by his new understanding of the "great law of human action" he discovered through experience.

# SKILL:
# THESIS
# STATEMENT

## DEFINE

Literary analysis is a form of argumentative writing, and the focal point of argumentative writing is the thesis statement. This is a single sentence that summarizes the central or main idea of an essay by introducing the writer's claim about the essay topic. This is the claim that the writer will develop in the body of the essay and support with organized facts, details, quotations, definitions and other pieces of textual evidence. The thesis statement most often appears as the last sentence in the introductory paragraph of an essay.

## IDENTIFICATION AND APPLICATION

- To identify the thesis statement in a passage:
  › Look at the last sentence of the introductory paragraph.
  › Find a sentence that makes a claim about the selection or selections.
  › Find a sentence that connects literary elements (like plot, style, imagery, structure, theme, or symbolism). It may also connect a literary element with real life.

- To evaluate the thesis statement in a passage:
  › Determine the author's claim.
  › Look for strong verbs (action verbs instead of verbs of being).
  › Look for clear and specific transitions that clearly show the relationship between ideas.
  › Determine if each of the passage's main ideas support the thesis in a logical manner.

## MODEL

The following paragraph is the introduction from the student model literary analysis "Personal Experiences: The Pathway to Values":

Please note that excerpts and passages in the StudySync® library and this workbook are intended as touchstones to generate interest in an author's work. The excerpts and passages do not substitute for the reading of entire texts, and StudySync® strongly recommends that students seek out and purchase the whole literary or informational work in order to experience it as the author intended. Links to online resellers are available in our digital library. In addition, complete works may be ordered through an authorized reseller by filling out and returning to StudySync® the order form enclosed in this workbook.

Reading & Writing  Companion

**355**

NOTES

How do you define your own personal values? Are they the ideas that you feel are most important in life, the foundation for your every action and belief? Many people believe personal values form the core of a person's being, shaping our individual personalities as well as our decisions about what is right and wrong. But where do values come from? Many works of literature reveal how personal experiences can shape or even change a character's values. Mark Twain shows how this can occur in *The Adventures of Tom Sawyer*. Judith Ortiz Cofer also illustrates this process in her short story, "Abuela Invents the Zero." **Even though their main characters exist many years apart, and have very different lives, both Twain and Ortiz Cofer show how personal experiences can shape a person's values for a lifetime.**

Notice the boldfaced claim at the end of the paragraph. This student's claim responds to the prompt, by addressing how two authors, Mark Twain and Julia Cofer Ortiz, show how personal experiences can shape a person's values for a lifetime. It also expresses the writer's opinion: even though the main characters live in two totally different time periods, the power of personal experience transcends, or goes beyond, these differences.

 PRACTICE

Write a thesis statement for your literary analysis that clearly states the central claim or idea that you will address in your essay. When you are finished, trade with a partner and give feedback to one another. Consider these questions: Does this statement express a clear claim? Does this statement make the focus of the essay obvious? Does this statement specifically address the prompt for this assignment? Give suggestions to your partner that will help him or her strengthen the thesis statement, and remember to keep your suggestions kind and constructive.

SKILL:
ORGANIZE
ARGUMENTATIVE
WRITING

## DEFINE

A literary analysis is a type of argumentative essay. It is intended to convince readers of an author's position or point of view on a subject that is related to one or more pieces of literature. Authors state their claim, or argument, in a thesis statement. Then they support that claim with valid reasoning and logical, relevant evidence from reliable sources. To do so, the author must organize and present the reasons and relevant evidence—the details and quotations from the text or texts—in a logical and convincing way. The writer must select an organizational structure that best suits the argument.

The writer of a literary analysis can choose from a number of organizational structures, including compare and contrast, sequential order, problem and solution, cause and effect, and chronological order.

## IDENTIFICATION AND APPLICATION

- When selecting an organizational structure for a piece of writing, writers consider the connections between most of the information they are writing about. They ask themselves these questions:

  › To support my idea, will I compare and contrast ideas or details in the text?

  › Will I raise a question or identify a problem in my argument? Do I have supporting evidence that suggests a solution or an answer?

  › Does most of my supporting evidence suggest a cause and effect relationship?

  › To support my claim, does it make sense to retell the events from the text or texts in sequential order?

- Writers often use specific cue words and phrases to help readers recognize the organizational structure of their writing:

  › Compare and contrast: *like, unlike, and, both, similar to, different from, while, but, conversely, although, also*

> › Order of importance: *most, most important, least, least important, first, finally, mainly, to begin with*
> › Problem and solution: *consequently, so,* and *as a result* can signal a solution
> › Cause-effect: *because, as a consequence of, as a result, cause, effect, so*
> › Sequential order: *first, next, then, second, finally*

- The writer develops an opinion or point of view on the topic and states a claim.
- The claim is stated in a thesis statement and is supported by logical reasoning.
- Text evidence is factual information from the text that supports the author's claim. In a literary analysis this would include examples and quotations from the texts that support the claim and do not include bias or personal opinions.
- A restatement of the claim is found in the concluding paragraph.

##  MODEL

Organization is a critical part of crafting a convincing literary analysis or other type of argumentative essay. The essay's organization leads the reader from the claim made in the introductory paragraph, through a series of main ideas with supporting details that are designed to build a body of evidence that will persuade the reader. The concluding paragraph should restate the thesis and make all of the connections clear. Read through these paragraphs from the Student Model once again, and pay special attention to the organizational structure used by the author.

### Personal Experiences: The Pathway to Values

How do you define your own personal values? Are they the ideas that you feel are most important in life, the foundation for your every action and belief? Many people believe personal values form the core of a person's being, shaping our individual personalities as well as our decisions about what is right and wrong. But where do values come from? Many works of literature reveal how personal experiences can shape or even change a character's values. Mark Twain shows how this can occur in *The Adventures of Tom Sawyer*. Judith Ortiz Cofer also illustrates this process in her short story, "Abuela Invents the Zero." **Even though their main characters exist** many years apart, and have very different lives, both Twain and Ortiz Cofer show how personal experiences can shape a person's values for a lifetime.

**Both Twain and Ortiz Cofer put characters into situations that reveal their personal values.** In an excerpt from *The Adventures of Tom Sawyer*, readers find the main character painting a fence. The narrator relates how unhappy Tom is with the job. In the first paragraph of the excerpt, Tom "began to think of the fun he had planned for this day, and his sorrows multiplied" (Twain). This shows that Tom values fun more than the hard work of painting the fence. In Ortiz Cofer's short story, the author makes Constancia's values very clear. This teen-aged girl values her identity and standing in her American neighborhood far more than she values her family's Puerto Rican heritage and her grandmother's feelings. One illustration of this is when Constancia describes her embarrassment at being with her grandmother in public: "I try to walk far behind them in public so that no one will think we are together" (Ortiz Cofer).

The author used a chart to organize the information he had brainstormed in earlier lessons.

| Character | Initial Value(s) | Experiences | Ending Value(s) |
|---|---|---|---|
| Tom Sawyer | Values fun and freedom | • Had to paint fence<br>• Tried to get others to do his work<br>• Successfully convinced other boys to work by telling them it was fun | Values of fun and freedom strengthened; learned how to manipulate others |

Please note that excerpts and passages in the StudySync® library and this workbook are intended as touchstones to generate interest in an author's work. The excerpts and passages do not substitute for the reading of entire texts, and StudySync® strongly recommends that students seek out and purchase the whole literary or informational work in order to experience it as the author intended. Links to online resellers are available in our digital library. In addition, complete works may be ordered through an authorized reseller by filling out and returning to StudySync® the order form enclosed in this workbook.

Reading & Writing Companion **359**

| Character | Initial Value(s) | Experiences | Ending Value(s) |
|---|---|---|---|
| Constancia | Values social standing, being like her peers, and her own feelings | • Had to escort grandmother<br>• Was embarrassed by grandmother's clothing<br>• Was embarrassed by grandmother getting lost<br>• Got into trouble with parents<br>• Made her grandmother feel bad | Reconsiders values of family and respect for elders, changes from valuing self, peers and social standing alone to including family, tradition, and elders |

The introductory paragraph contains the following thesis statement: "Even though their main characters exist many years apart, and have very different lives, both Twain and Ortiz Cofer show how personal experiences can shape a person's values for a lifetime." This statement makes a clear claim that the two authors use their characters to show how personal experiences influence values. In the second paragraph, the author claims that "Both Twain and Ortiz Cofer put characters into situations that reveal their personal values." The author is using a compare and contrast organizational pattern here, with the clue word "both" indicating the similarities that exist between the characters created by Mark Twain and Julia Ortiz Cofer.

 PRACTICE

Using either the *Compare and Contrast Literary Analysis Graphic Organizer,* the *Cause and Effect Literary Analysis Graphic Organizer,* or another organizer of your choosing, gather information about the main characters in the texts you will be analyzing and use that information to determine an appropriate organizational structure for your literary analysis. As possible, you should include ideas that emerged during the prewriting exercise. Ask yourself: Based on the information I collected in the organizer, does the text structure I initially chose work well, or would some other structure be more effective? Exchange your chart with a partner and offer each other feedback.

SKILL:
SUPPORTING
DETAILS

## ⭐ DEFINE

In argumentative writing, writers develop their main idea with relevant evidence called **supporting details.** These details can include any fact, definition, concrete information, example, or quotation that helps to prove the author's claim and is closely related to the thesis statement, or main idea. Relevant supporting details are the key to the success of a writer's argument. It makes the argument more convincing and persuasive to the reader, helps develop the ideas the author presents, and clarifies the writer's understanding and interpretation of the text. Without reasons and relevant evidence, the writer would simply be stating his or her opinion about a theme or a central idea.

##  IDENTIFICATION AND APPLICATION

**Step 1:**

Review your thesis statement. To identify relevant supporting details, ask this question: What is the claim I am making about this topic? Here is the thesis statement from the student model, "Personal Experiences: The Pathway to Values":

> **Even though their main characters exist many years apart and have very different lives, both Mark Twain and Julia Ortiz Cofer show how personal experiences can shape one's values for a lifetime.**

What claim is the author making? The author is saying that both Mark Twain and Julia Ortiz Cofer demonstrate through their characters in *The Adventures of Tom Sawyer* and "Abuela Invents the Zero" that personal experiences influence a person's values.

**Step 2:**

Ask what a reader needs to know about the topic, or claim, in order to understand it. To understand the thesis statement of this analysis, a reader must first know what values the characters have at the beginning of their respective tales. The writer explains how Mark Twain reveals Tom's initial values in *The Adventures of Tom Sawyer*:

> In the first paragraph of the excerpt, Tom "began to think of the fun he had planned for this day, and his sorrows multiplied" (Twain). This shows that Tom values fun more than the hard work of painting the fence.

He then supplies additional details to show how Ortiz Cofer reveals Constancia's initial values:

> This teen-aged girl values her identity and standing in her American neighborhood far more than she values her family's Puerto Rican heritage and her grandmother's feelings. One illustration of this is when Constancia describes her embarrassment at being with her grandmother in public: "I try to walk far behind them in public so that no one will think we are together" (Ortiz Cofer).

**Step 3:**

Search for facts, quotations, research, and the conclusions of others to help strengthen and support your thesis statement. As you search for details, carefully evaluate their relevance to your main idea. Ask yourself:

- Is this information necessary to the reader's understanding of the topic?
- Does this information help to develop and support my claim?
- Does this information relate closely to my thesis? Is it taken directly from the texts I am analyzing?
- Can I find better evidence that will provide stronger support for my point?

 MODEL

Read the following excerpt from the student model essay, "Personal Experiences: The Pathway to Values":

> **Twain and Ortiz Cofer describe brief moments in their characters' lives, but even these small events influence the characters' values.** In the case of Tom Sawyer, his values are confirmed and supported. He comes up with a scheme to get the other boys to do the painting for him. He does this by convincing them that the chore of painting the fence is not actually work at all, but rather great fun. The other boys happily part with their treasures in return

NOTES

for a turn with the paintbrush, and Tom learns that he can manipulate others to get the things he values, namely, free time and fun. **Twain's narrator notes, "Tom said to himself that it was not such a hollow world, after all. He had discovered a great law of human action, without knowing it—namely, that in order to make a man or a boy covet a thing, it is only necessary to make the thing difficult to attain"** (Twain). Constancia, on the other hand, suffers through her embarrassing moments with her grandmother only to discover that her feelings are not the only ones that mattered. Her grandmother was made to feel "like a zero, like a nothing" (Ortiz Cofer). Constancia's mother reminded her that the grandmother deserved more respect, because "if it wasn't for the old woman whose existence you don't seem to value, you and I would not be here" (Cofer Ortiz). As a result, Constancia's values begin to change. **As she describes her thoughts, she notes "I think I understand how I made Abuela feel" and ". . . it's not easy to admit you've been a jerk"** (Ortiz Cofer). These revelations show that Constancia's values were changing because of her experiences.

Notice how the paragraph begins with the author's clear statement of a main idea that builds on the claim of the thesis: "Twain and Ortiz Cofer describe brief moments in their characters' lives, but even these small events influence the characters' values." Next, the author pulls supporting evidence from Twain's passage about Tom Sawyer, describing how Tom manipulates the other boys into doing his work. This evidence is quoted directly from the text. Then the author includes supporting evidence from Ortiz Cofer's story, citing the change in Constancia. These examples provide strong supporting evidence that the snippets of experience described in both texts affected the characters' values.

The author includes evidence about both characters in the paragraph, setting up a contrast between them that is in keeping with the essay's compare and contrast organizational structure. The supporting evidence includes quotations from both authors' works, adding strength to the analysis and reinforcing the writer's original claim that personal experiences influence values.

 PRACTICE

Write a paragraph for your literary analysis that supports a claim or main idea in that paragraph as well as your overall thesis by drawing relevant evidence from one or more of the unit texts. Be sure to include an explanation of how the evidence supports the claim you are trying to make. Exchange your paragraphs with a partner and provide each other feedback. Remember that you can use this paragraph or a revised version in later stages of the writing process.

Please note that excerpts and passages in the StudySync® library and this workbook are intended as touchstones to generate interest in an author's work. The excerpts and passages do not substitute for the reading of entire texts, and StudySync® strongly recommends that students seek out and purchase the whole literary or informational work in order to experience it as the author intended. Links to online resellers are available in our digital library. In addition, complete works may be ordered through an authorized reseller by filling out and returning to StudySync® the order form enclosed in this workbook.

Reading & Writing Companion **363**

PLAN

CA-CCSS: CA.W.8.1a, CA.W.8.1b, CA.W.8.4, CA.W.8.5, CA.W.8.6, CA.W.8.9a, CA.W.8.10, CA.SL.8.1a, CA.SL.8.1b, CA.SL.8.1c, CA.SL.8.1d

## WRITING PROMPT

As the selections you have read in this unit show, people are shaped by their individual life experiences. People make choices, some of which are mistakes, but they often learn and grow from their experiences. Choose two selections from this unit and think about the main character or the narrator in each one. What does the main character or narrator value most, and how do the characters' experiences shape or even change their values? Write a literary analysis that shows how personal experience can change people for better or sometimes for worse.

Your literary analysis should include:

- an introduction that states a claim, or an opinion, about the theme or other aspects of one or more literary works.
- body paragraphs with relevant evidence from a literary text or texts that support the claim or opinion.
- a conclusion paragraph that follows from the body of the essay and effectively wraps up your analysis.

You have been studying techniques that authors use to convey information, as well as examining selections that discuss the relationship between personal experiences and values. Now you will use these ideas to create your own literary analysis essay.

In previous lessons, you have created one or more graphic organizers containing information about different authors and how they have shown the connection between their characters' personal experiences and their personal values. You have created a thesis statement, considered audience and purpose, identified an organizational structure that would work best for

NOTES

your analysis, and drafted a body paragraph with a main idea supported by details drawn from one or more unit texts. Now it's time to create a roadmap that will help you put all of the pieces into place. It's time to plan your essay.

Consider and answer the following questions as you develop the roadmap to your essay:

- What can you tell about each character's values at the beginning of each selection?
- What personal experiences are related in each selection?
- What changes do you perceive in the characters' values at the conclusion of each selection?
- How did each of the characters' personal experiences impact his or her values?
- In what ways do you think these changes in values will impact the characters' future behavior or actions?
- What connection do you see between experiences and values in the lives of others and in your own life?

Now make a model to use in writing your own essay. You can follow this guide:

Literary Analysis Road Map

    Introductory Paragraph

        Interesting beginning or hook:

        Introduction of sources:

        Thesis Statement or Claim:

    Body Paragraph 1 Topic:

        Supporting Detail #1:

        Supporting Detail #2:

    Body Paragraph 2 Topic:

        Supporting Detail #1:

        Supporting Detail #2:

Body Paragraph 3 Topic:

Supporting Detail #1:

Supporting Detail #2:

Closing Paragraph:

Powerful closing argument:

# SKILL:
# INTRODUCTIONS

 **DEFINE**

The introduction is the opening paragraph or section of a literary analysis or other nonfiction text. The introduction of a literary analysis identifies the texts or the topic to be discussed, states the writer's claim or thesis statement, and previews the supporting evidence that will appear in the body of the text. The introduction is also the place where most writers include a "hook" that is intended to connect with and engage readers.

 **IDENTIFICATION AND APPLICATION**

- In a literary analysis, the introduction is where the writer identifies the texts and the topic to be discussed. Once readers have that information, they can concentrate on the writer's claim, which is expressed in the thesis statement.

- A literary analysis is a form of argument, so the writer's claim is an important part of the introduction. The claim is a direct statement that gives the writer's opinion or interpretation of some aspect of the texts under discussion. By stating the claim in the introduction, the writer lets readers know the ideas he or she will explore in the body of the analysis. Establishing a claim here also allows readers to form their own opinions, which they can then measure against the writer's as they read the literary analysis.

- Another use of the introduction is to provide a preview of the supporting evidence that will follow in the body of the text. By using the introduction to hint at key details, the writer can establish an effective argument, increasing the likelihood that readers will agree with his or her claim.

- Authors sometimes include counter arguments in a literary analysis or argumentative essay. A counter argument is an argument or set of reasons put forward to oppose an idea or theory developed in another argument. A counter argument can make an argument stronger. This is because it gives the writer the chance to respond to readers' possible

Please note that excerpts and passages in the StudySync® library and this workbook are intended as touchstones to generate interest in an author's work. The excerpts and passages do not substitute for the reading of entire texts, and StudySync® strongly recommends that students seek out and purchase the whole literary or informational work in order to experience it as the author intended. Links to online resellers are available in our digital library. In addition, complete works may be ordered through an authorized reseller by filling out and returning to StudySync® the order form enclosed in this workbook.

Reading & Writing
Companion

**367**

objections before they have finished reading. It also shows that the writer is a reasonable person who has considered both sides of the debate. Both of these can make an essay more persuasive.

- A "hook" in the opening of an essay is something that grabs a reader and draws him or her in. In other words, a good hook engages readers' interest and makes them want to keep reading. A hook might be an intriguing image, a surprising detail or opinion, a funny anecdote, or a startling statistic. The hook should appeal to the audience and help readers connect to the topic in a meaningful way so that they will take the writer's claim seriously.

##  MODEL

Read this introduction from "Point: Give Teens Some Work to Do! It's Good for Them and Everyone Else" from *Mandatory Volunteer Work for Teenagers.* Try to find all of the attributes of a strong introduction as you read.

> **Teenagers today live in a confusing world. The media sends many mixed messages about what it means to be a helpful person in society.** One of the best ways to help teens find their way is to **make volunteer work a mandatory part of their school curriculum.** Some people would immediately argue that this is an unnecessary action—many teens already volunteer without it being a requirement. It's true: teens have a propensity to volunteer more than adults. However, as a society we should make sure that not just some, but all, teens volunteer. Many of the teens that volunteer do so as part of a religious group or a youth leadership organization. In fact, 46 percent of teens who volunteer are working with a religious group or a youth leadership organization while only 18 percent of teens who volunteer are working with school-based groups. **This shows that clearly the best way to include all teens in the benefits of volunteering is to add mandatory volunteer work to the school curriculum.**

The author opens with the sentence, "Teenagers today live in a confusing world." What type of hook is used here? This author chose to capture readers' attention by stating a provocative opinion about the world of teens today. This opinion is engaging because most readers would agree with it. Teens themselves are likely to view their world as confusing and challenging, simply because, as they leave childhood behind, they find they have more responsibilities as well as decisions to make. Older readers may look at the increasing complexity of a world filled with gadgets, tests, and opportunities that weren't available to them at the same age, and so agree that today's world is confusing for teenagers. The author used that one sentence to grab the attention of a wide cross-section of readers.

The very next sentence, "The media sends many mixed messages about what it means to be a helpful person in society," shows that the topic is the center of a controversy. This is why readers might consider this information to be important, which provides the second characteristic of a strong introduction: giving readers a reason to read.

The writer then presents a counter argument: "Some people would immediately argue that this is an unnecessary action—many teens already volunteer without it being a requirement." While in agreement with the last part of this statement, the writer also presents statistics that show most teens do not volunteer as part of a school-based group, and mandatory volunteering in schools would make it possible for all teens to volunteer. The author, however, does not introduce sources for these statistics in this paragraph. The sources are listed at the end in a bibliography, but mentioning them here would strengthen and add credibility to the introduction.

The thesis statement for this essay is found in the last sentence of the paragraph, "This shows that clearly the best way to include all teens in the benefits of volunteering is to add mandatory volunteer work to the school curriculum." The author makes it very clear that the entire essay will be arguing in favor of adding mandatory volunteer requirements to students' coursework.

 PRACTICE

Write an introduction for your literary analysis that includes a hook to engage the reader's interest, some background information about your topic, an overview of your sources and a sound thesis statement that clearly states the central claim that you will prove in your essay. When you are finished, trade with a partner and give feedback to one another. Consider these questions: What hook did the author use to capture reader's interest? Was it effective? Why or why not? Does this introduction provide background information to orient the reader and give an overview of the sources? Is there a clear and strong thesis statement at the end of the paragraph? Give suggestions to your partner that will help him or her strengthen the introduction, and remember to keep your suggestions kind and constructive.

# SKILL: CONCLUSIONS

 **DEFINE**

The conclusion is the final paragraph or section of a nonfiction text. In a literary analysis, the conclusion brings the writer's argument to a close. It follows directly from the claim made in the introduction and the reasons and relevant evidence provided in the body of the text. A conclusion should restate the thesis statement and summarize the central idea (or ideas) covered. In some kinds of writing, a conclusion might also include a recommendation or solution, a call to action, or a statement of insight. Many conclusions try to connect with readers by encouraging them to apply what they have learned from the text to their own lives.

 **IDENTIFICATION AND APPLICATION**

- The conclusion of a literary analysis draws a clear line of reasoning between all of the author's supporting points back to the claim made in the thesis statement.

- A strong conclusion restates the thesis or author's claim and leaves no doubt in the reader's mind that the claim has been fully supported.

- The conclusion may also include some action for the reader to take, a recommendation, or some overall insight that the author wants to be sure the reader understands.

- The conclusion affects the reader's final impression of the essay, and so it must be strong in order to convince the reader that the claim has been completely proven.

 **MODEL**

In the opening paragraph of the student model, "Personal Experiences: The Pathway to Values," the writer states the claim he will attempt to prove in his literary analysis:

Copyright © BookheadEd Learning, LLC

**Even though their main characters exist many years apart and have very different lives, both Twain and Julia Ortiz Cofer show how personal experiences can shape one's values for a lifetime.**

Now, reread the conclusion from the student model. Look for the elements of a strong conclusion as you read.

In both selections, the authors show how personal experiences shaped the values of the main characters. The importance Tom Sawyer placed on fun is only reinforced by the events in the story. He may have turned work into fun for others, but that was not his aim. Conversely, Constancia's personal values, and how she felt about her heritage and her grandmother, were shaken and perhaps changed now that she understands how her grandmother feels. **Tom Sawyer's values arguably changed for the worse, but Constancia's values improved as she learned more about her *Abuela*. In these excerpts, both authors show how personal experiences and the responses of other people shape and mold everyone's values every day.**

First, notice how the author rephrased the claim from the thesis statement in the last sentence of the paragraph. Compare the closing sentence—"In these excerpts, both authors show how personal experiences and the responses of other people shape and mold everyone's values every day"— with the thesis statement shared earlier: "Even though their main characters exist many years apart and have very different lives, both Twain and Julia Ortiz Cofer show how personal experiences can shape one's values for a lifetime." The two sentences are not identical, but both include references to the authors and characters that were used as supporting details in the essay, and both include the claim that the author wanted to prove. The essay's conclusion connects back to the ideas in the introduction.

In the middle of the concluding paragraph, the author adds an additional insight for the reader to consider. The sentence, "Tom Sawyer's values arguably changed for the worse, but Constancia's values improved as she learned more about her *Abuela*," indicates that not only do experiences influence values, but also that values and the experiences that create them can be positive or negative.

Finally, the author of the student model devotes some effort in the conclusion to summarizing the main points of the essay. He reviews the experiences and their impact on the personal values of both characters, though this information was presented in greater detail earlier in the essay. This summary of the main points refreshes the reader's memory and highlights the important ideas that the author wanted to stress.

This conclusion is a strong one because it restates the thesis statement, it summarizes the main ideas, it provides an additional insight, and it offers closure to the reader. The author of the student essay seems confident that he has proven his original claim and that the reader now believes that personal experiences shape values.

## ⚡ PRACTICE

Write a conclusion for your literary analysis. When you have finished, trade with a partner and review each other's concluding paragraphs. Consider the following questions to help your partner improve his or her conclusion: "Did the author review the main supporting ideas of the argument for the essay's claim or thesis? Did the author offer any additional insight or a call to action? What is your overall impression of the conclusion? How could it be improved?" Remember to offer your suggestions in a positive, helpful manner.

DRAFT

**CA-CCSS:** CA.W.8.1a, CA.W.8.1b, CA.W.8.1c, CA.W.8.1e, CA.W.8.4, CA.W.8.5, CA.W.8.6, CA.W.8.9a, CA.W.8.10, CA.SL.8.1a, CA.SL.8.1c, CA.L.8.1a, CA.L.8.6

## WRITING PROMPT

As the selections you have read in this unit show, people are shaped by their individual life experiences. People make choices, some of which are mistakes, but they often learn and grow from their experiences. Choose two selections from this unit and think about the main character or the narrator in each one. What does the main character or narrator value most, and how do the characters' experiences shape or even change their values? Write a literary analysis that shows how personal experience can change people for better or sometimes for worse.

Your literary analysis should include:

- an introduction that states a claim, or an opinion, about the theme or other aspects of one or more literary works.
- body paragraphs with relevant evidence from a literary text or texts that support the claim or opinion.
- a conclusion paragraph that follows from the body of the essay and effectively wraps up your analysis.

You have generated many ideas for your literary analysis, chosen an organizational structure, created a thesis statement, gathered supporting information, and considered your audience and purpose. Look over all of the organizers and notes you have made from previous lessons. Think about the things you have learned about writing introductions and conclusions and including transitions. You can use these skills to mold all of the pieces into a strong essay.

Reread the writing prompt above. Do any new ideas come to mind? Incorporate these into the information you've already prepared. Use this opportunity to write the first draft of your essay.

NOTES

When drafting, use these questions as a guide:

- How can I make the hook in my introduction more effective?
- How can I clarify my thesis statement to make my claim stronger?
- Which facts, details, quotations and supporting details best support my claim?
- In what way can I improve the organizational structure of my essay to create a more logical flow of ideas?
- How can I improve my use of transitions to better show the connections between ideas?
- Where can I use more precise language, such as academic or domain-specific words and phrases, or more vivid details to make my point?
- Have I used verbals, including gerunds, participles, and infinitives, correctly?
- How can I draw all of these ideas together to show that I have proven my claim?

It's time to write the draft of your essay. Use the lists, notes, graphic organizers, roadmaps, and paragraphs that you have already created in previous lessons. Remember to pay special attention to finalizing your thesis statement because a strong thesis statement is the first step to a strong analysis essay. Build your introductory paragraph and your body paragraphs. Use your closing paragraph to review the details you have included to support your claim and leave your readers with a lasting impression. Draw everything together so the reader can have no doubt that you have proven your claim. Before you submit your draft, reread it carefully. Be sure that you have addressed all of the aspects of the prompt.

**SKILL:**
**STYLE**

 **DEFINE**

Style is how authors express their ideas and convey information through language. It is revealed through the author's choice of words and sentence construction. An author's style can be formal, suitable for academic or professional work, or informal, suitable for relaxed communication between family and friends. Before starting to write, an author must think about his or her purpose and audience and then tailor the language to suit both. Style also requires an awareness of the rules for writing standardized English. Tone is another element of style. In written composition, tone is the attitude a writer has toward a subject or an audience.

 **IDENTIFICATION AND APPLICATION**

- Style is the way the author uses words and constructs sentences. It also includes the tone, or the author's attitude toward the audience or the topic.

- Literary essays have a formal style. This means that the author uses third person, employs precise and/or specialized vocabulary suitable to the topic, varies the sentence structure, and avoids the use of slang.

- A formal style uses varied sentence structure. The writing does not sound choppy due to too many short, simple sentences. It also does not sound confusing because of too many long, complicated sentences.

- The tone of formal writing is respectful, thoughtful and serious.

- When using a formal style, a writer tries to choose words and phrases that mean exactly what he or she intends. The author avoids vague words and phrases such as "sometimes" or "in most cases" and instead substitutes specific words and figures, such as "in 75 percent of all cases" or "in each instance."

NOTES

- The author pays special attention to transitions, making them as clear and specific as possible. The transitions in formal writing should show the relationship between ideas, instead of simply stringing them together.

 MODEL

The reading selection *Mandatory Volunteer Work for Teenagers* includes two essays. Although the authors express opposing positions on the central question of mandatory teen volunteering, both essays maintain a formal style. Read the two introductions to examine the elements of formal style.

**Point: Give Teens Some Work to Do! It's Good for Them and Everyone Else**

**Teenagers today live in a confusing world.** The media sends many mixed messages about what it means to be a helpful person in society. One of the best ways to help teens find their way is to make volunteer work a mandatory part of their school curriculum. Some people would immediately argue that this is an unnecessary action—many teens already volunteer without it being a requirement. It's true: teens have a propensity to volunteer more than adults. **However, as a society we should make sure that not just some, but all, teens volunteer.** Many of the teens that volunteer do so as part of a religious group or a youth leadership organization. In fact, 46 percent of teens who volunteer are working with a religious group or a youth leadership organization while only 18 percent of teens who volunteer are working with school-based groups. This shows that clearly the best way to include all teens in the benefits of volunteering is to add mandatory volunteer work to the school curriculum.

**Counterpoint: Mandatory Volunteer Work Does More Harm Than Good**

Most people agree that **teenagers** today live in a difficult world. **There are more pressures facing the modern teen than we can count: school, work, family, sports, and other extracurricular activities, just to name a few.** However, some people think that we should add to that load of pressures by making volunteer work a mandatory part of the school curriculum. One of the greatest arguments for this action is that mandatory volunteer work will prepare students for the future by giving them work experience, but the flaw in this logic is that many teens already gain work experience through paying jobs. In fact, many of the teens working paying jobs are doing so out of necessity—to pay for gas

NOTES

to get back and forth to school, or to help their families with extra money. Those teens without paying jobs still have plenty of prospects for gaining work experience in other ways such as an internship, or working at a school paper. Another argument for making volunteer work a mandatory part of school curriculum is that this work will help teens gain self-esteem and self-confidence. However, having time to socialize and develop hobbies and other interests is more important for self-esteem and self-confidence than volunteering.

What did you notice about the two introductions that indicates the authors' use of formal style? Let's begin with the language that the authors chose. Notice that neither author used any slang or informal words or phrases. Instead of using a phrase such as "kids today live in a crazy, kooky, mixed-up world" in the first paragraph, the author writes "teenagers today live in a confusing world." Both authors also used precise vocabulary in their introductions. They refer to "teenagers" as opposed to "young people" or "kids." Both authors also use the word "mandatory," as well. This word has a more forceful connotation than its synonym, "required."

When you examine sentence structure, you will find that both authors varied the lengths of sentences. The author of "Give Teens Some Work To Do!" opens with a very simple sentence to grab the attention of readers right away: "Teenagers today live in a confusing world." Later in the same paragraph, you will find the sentence, "However, as a society we should make sure that not just some, but all, teens volunteer." This sentence is not only longer than "teenagers today live in a confusing world" but far more complex grammatically. The author of the second paragraph uses the same technique, and varies sentence structure to help achieve a formal tone. This author includes additional variations in sentence structure, such as this list in the following sentence: "There are more pressures facing the modern teen than we can count: school, work, family, sports, and other extracurricular activities just to name a few."

Both authors offer logical, reasoned explanations for their points of view, and they explain their ideas carefully. Each writer uses examples and other evidence to persuade the reader. Both authors pay close attention to style and tone. This strengthens the essays and helps make them more memorable and convincing.

 PRACTICE

Review the draft of your literary analysis essay. Circle any examples in which you use the first or second person or include slang. Underline any examples

in which you think varying the sentence structure might create a more formal style or in which you could substitute a more precise academic or domain-specific word to create a more formal tone. Provide corrections and revisions in the margins of your essay. Exchange your work with a partner and offer each other feedback.

# REVISE

**CA-CCSS:** CA.W.8.1a, CA.W.8.1b, CA.W.8.1c, CA.W.8.1d, CA.W.8.1e, CA.W.8.4, CA.W.8.5, CA.W.8.6, CA.W.8.9a, CA.W.8.10, CA.SL.8.1a, CA.SL.8.1c, CA.L.8.1c, CA.L.8.1d, CA.L.8.6

## WRITING PROMPT

As the selections you have read in this unit show, people are shaped by their individual life experiences. People make choices, some of which are mistakes, but they often learn and grow from their experiences. Choose two selections from this unit and think about the main character or the narrator in each one. What does the main character or narrator value most, and how do the characters' experiences shape or even change their values? Write a literary analysis that shows how personal experience can change people for better or sometimes for worse.

Your literary analysis should include:

- an introduction that states a claim, or an opinion, about the theme or other aspects of one or more literary works.
- body paragraphs with relevant evidence from a literary text or texts that support the claim or opinion.
- a conclusion paragraph that follows from the body of the essay and effectively wraps up your analysis.

You have written a draft of your literary analysis and also received some feedback from your peers about how to improve it. It is time to revise your draft.

Here are some suggestions to help you revise.

- Consider the feedback you received during the peer review process.
- Examine your style throughout the essay. Be sure you have maintained a formal style. This will add credibility to your analysis and it suits your audience, which includes teachers and students.
  › Remove any slang words or phrases.

Please note that excerpts and passages in the StudySync® library and this workbook are intended as touchstones to generate interest in an author's work. The excerpts and passages do not substitute for the reading of entire texts, and StudySync® strongly recommends that students seek out and purchase the whole literary or informational work in order to experience it as the author intended. Links to online resellers are available in our digital library. In addition, complete works may be ordered through an authorized reseller by filling out and returning to StudySync® the order form enclosed in this workbook.

Reading & Writing Companion **379**

> Locate and revise any places where you have used first or second person pronouns, such as "I," "me," "mine," "you," "your," or "yours." These pronouns are used in informal writing, giving the essay a personal and conversational style. Your literary analysis should be more formal.
> Read through the essay once more to find and remove your personal opinions. Your essay should be clear, logical, and unbiased.

- Once you are certain the essay maintains a formal style, examine the essay's content and organization. If the answer to any of the following questions is "no," revise accordingly.
  > Is your introduction effective, containing an interesting hook, clear thesis statement, and preview of your pain points?
  > Does your chosen organizational structure truly suit your claim and the information you are using to support it?
  > Consider the steps you are citing to support your claim. Does each point clearly and logically develop the claim? Does each piece of supporting information add evidence to your case?
  > Quotations can add credibility to your case. Did you add quotations from your sources to support your claim?
  > Examine your vocabulary choices. Are there any places where you could substitute a more precise or a more vivid word, such as an academic or domain-specific one, for a general or common one?
  > Take a close look at the transitions you have placed between main points and paragraphs, between sentences, and between ideas. Do they clearly show the relationships you intend?
  > Does your concluding paragraph effectively wrap up your essay by restating your thesis, summarizing your main points, and leaving readers with a lasting impression?

- Finally, read your essay with a focus on punctuation. It is very easy to change ideas or sentences while forgetting to update punctuation. Look for sentence fragments and run-ons. Pay particular attention to commas. Make sure that complex sentences are punctuated correctly.
- Check one last time for pronouns. Make sure the entire essay is in third-person to help maintain a formal style. Be sure pronouns agree with verbs in number, as well.
- Check to make sure that verb moods are consistent and make sense with the ideas you are expressing.

NOTES

SKILL:
SOURCES AND
CITATIONS

 **DEFINE**

Sources are the documents and information that authors use to research their writing. A primary source is direct evidence from a specific time and place. It includes any material that was produced by eyewitnesses to an event or who lived during an historical period. Secondary sources, in contrast, interpret and analyze primary sources. These sources are one or more steps removed from an event. Secondary sources may have pictures, quotes, or graphics from primary sources in them. Citations provide information within the text about the sources an author used to research and write a text or essay. Citations are required whenever authors quote someone else's words or refer to someone else's ideas in their writing. They let readers know who originally came up with these words and ideas. When writing a literary analysis, writers cannot simply make up information, or draw on their personal opinions or ideas. To make a convincing argument, writers must use solid research from reliable sources. If an author does not identify sources of information, the quality of the text will suffer and the writer may be accused of plagiarism.

 **IDENTIFICATION AND APPLICATION**

- Sources give authors the information they need to prove their claim in an argumentative essay such as a literary analysis.

- A source should provide examples or proof that support the claim the author has made in the thesis statement.

- Sources selected by the author should be reliable primary or secondary sources. Primary sources are first-hand accounts or original materials and can include the following:
  › diaries or personal journals
  › photographs or documentary film footage
  › autobiographies
  › letters and official records

> relics or artifacts such as pottery or clothing
> speeches

- Secondary sources interpret and analyze primary sources and can include the following:
  > online encyclopedia
  > textbooks or history books
  > magazine articles

- Authors of literary analyses should support the points they make throughout the essay by using quotations from the works they are analyzing.

- Authors should show direct quotations from a source by enclosing the exact words within quotation marks.

- A writer includes a citation to give credit to any source, whether primary or secondary, that is quoted word for word. There are several different ways to cite a source.

- One way is to put the author's last name in parenthesis at the end of the sentence in which the quote appears. This is what the writer of the Student Model essay does after every quotation. For print sources, the author's name should be followed by the page number on which the text of the quotation appears.

- Your citations can also appear as a list at the end of your essay. In the body of your essay, place a number after each reference to a primary or secondary source. At the back of your essay, list the numbers and identify the source that goes with each number.

- Citations are also necessary when a writer borrows ideas from another source, even if the writer paraphrases, or puts those ideas in his or her own words. Citations credit the source, but they also help readers discover where they can learn more.

 MODEL

The sources and citations used by the author lend credibility to a literary analysis and help prove the author's claim. Reread this section of the Student Model, "Personal Experiences: Pathways to Values," and pay particular attention to the citations used by the author.

> Both Twain and Ortiz Cofer put characters into situations that reveal their personal values. **In an excerpt from *The Adventures of Tom Sawyer*, readers find the main character painting a fence.** The narrator relates how unhappy Tom is with the job. **In the first paragraph of the excerpt, Tom "began to**

*think of the fun he had planned for this day, and his sorrows multiplied"* **(Twain).** *This shows that Tom values fun more than the hard work of painting the fence.* **In Ortiz Cofer's short story, the author makes Constancia's values very clear.** *This teen-aged girl values her identity and standing in her American neighborhood far more than she values her family's Puerto Rican heritage and her grandmother's feelings.* **One illustration of this is when Constancia describes her embarrassment at being with her grandmother in public:** *"I try to walk far behind them in public so that no one will think we are together"* **(Ortiz Cofer).**

Notice how the author of the student model refers to both of the sources he used in this paragraph. He mentions Twain's book and Ortiz Cofer's short story. He includes quotations that support the points he outlines. For example, the author used the quote "began to think of the fun he had planned for this day, and his sorrows multiplied" (Twain) to show that Tom was unhappy because of his situation. He included the quote "I try to walk far behind them in public so that no one will think we are together" (Ortiz Cofer) to provide an example from "Abuela Invents the Zero" that supports the same point.

The author of the student model had to become familiar enough with the sources to find quotations that related to the claim he is making in his analysis. Quotations need to be carefully selected so that they provide examples or other support for the claim or thesis statement.

Each of these quotations includes a reference in parentheses that indicates the source author's last name after the quote. This shows that the author of the student model does not want to take credit for the ideas or the words, but rather acknowledges that they came from other sources. This is very important, because plagiarism, or copying someone else's ideas or words and claiming them as your own, is a very serious problem and can affect the essay author's credibility and even his reputation.

The next step the writer of the Student Model must take to fully give credit for his sources is to provide complete bibliographic information for *The Adventures of Tom Sawyer* and "Abuela Invents the Zero" in a Works Cited page. This Works Cited page should appear at the end of the essay and include, for each work cited in the essay, the author's name, the title of the work, the place of publication, the publisher, and the date of publication. If the work is in a collection, sometimes the name of the editor will also be included. According to Modern Language Association (MLA) style, commas are used to set off elements within each of these general groupings, but each grouping ends with a period. If a source is electronic, the last element of the citation indicates that the item is from the "Web."

NOTES

It is common practice to present the titles of full-length works such as books, plays, and movies in italics. Shorter works, such as titles of articles, chapters, speeches, short stories, poems, and songs are presented within quotation marks. If a short story is part of a collection, both the title of the short story and the title of the collection should be included in the proper format. Consider the following example:

Ortiz Cofer, Julia. "Abuela Invents the Zero." *An Island Like You: Stories of the Barrio.* Gloucester: Peter Smith Publisher, Incorporated, 1998.

You will need to search online for each text you cite in your essay and gather its complete bibliographic information. Then use this information to create a Works Cited page to accompany your essay.

 PRACTICE

Write in-text citations for quoted information in your informative essay. When you are finished, trade with a partner and offer each other feedback. How successful was the writer in citing sources for the essay? Offer each other suggestions, and remember that they are most helpful when they are constructive.

NOTES

# EDIT, PROOFREAD, AND PUBLISH

**CA-CCSS:** CA.W.8.1a, CA.W.8.1b, CA.W.8.1c, CA.W.8.1d, CA.W.8.1e, CA.W.8.4, CA.W.8.5, CA.W.8.6, CA.W.8.7, CA.W.8.8, CA.W.8.9a, CA.W.8.10, CA.L.8.1a, CA.L.8.1c, CA.L.8.1d, CA.L.8.2a, CA.L.8.2b, CA.L.8.6, CA.SL.8.1a, CA.SL.8.1c

## WRITING PROMPT

As the selections you have read in this unit show, people are shaped by their individual life experiences. People make choices, some of which are mistakes, but they often learn and grow from their experiences. Choose two selections from this unit and think about the main character or the narrator in each one. What does the main character or narrator value most, and how do the characters' experiences shape or even change their values? Write a literary analysis that shows how personal experience can change people for better or sometimes for worse.

Your literary analysis should include:

- an introduction that states a claim, or an opinion, about the theme or other aspects of one or more literary works.
- body paragraphs with relevant evidence from a literary text or texts that support the claim or opinion.
- a conclusion paragraph that follows from the body of the essay and effectively wraps up your analysis.

The final steps to complete your literary analysis are to polish your piece by editing, proofreading, and publishing it. You should have the revised draft that you completed in a previous lesson. Think about all of the lessons in this sequence. As you reread your essay, be sure to apply what you have learned about audience and purpose, thesis statement, organization, supporting details, introductions and conclusions, transitions, style, and sources and citations. Review the suggestions that you received from the peer reviews during each step in the process and make sure you have applied them. Here are some suggestions to guide you through the process of finalizing your essay:

- Is my literary analysis essay organized effectively?

- Does my introduction grab the readers' attention in an interesting yet relevant way? Is my thesis statement part of my introduction as well as my conclusion? Does it respond to the prompt clearly and effectively and present a claim?

- Have I included strong main ideas, supporting details, and relevant evidence drawn from the texts to support my analysis and reinforce my claim?

- Have all of my sources been cited properly both within the body of my essay and in a Works Cited page at the end of my essay?

- Do I use appropriate and smooth transitions to connect ideas and details within paragraphs as well as between paragraphs?

- Have I presented my readers with a conclusion that coherently restates my thesis statement, summarizes my main ideas, and convinces readers that my argument has been fully supported?

- Have I established a formal style tone through the use of precise language and academic, domain-specific words and the elimination of slang and first or second person?

- Have I varied my sentence structure? If I read my essay out loud, does it have the right rhythm and pacing, or does it sound choppy or confusing?

- Have I incorporated all the valuable suggestions from my peers?

When you are satisfied with your work, move on to proofread it for errors. For example, check that you have used the correct punctuation for quotations and citations. Have you used ellipses to indicate where in direct quotations you have omitted material? Have you used verbals correctly? Is your use of verb moods appropriate and consistent? Are commas and dashes used appropriately? Be sure to correct any misspelled words.

Once your essay has been proofread and edited, it is time to publish your work. You can add it to your classroom's website or blog, post it on a bulletin board, or share it with family and friends. Be sure to include a list of the works you used for sources, and if you publish online, add links to those resources so that interested readers can gather more information.

Copyright © BookheadEd Learning, LLC

# studysync®

## Reading & Writing Companion

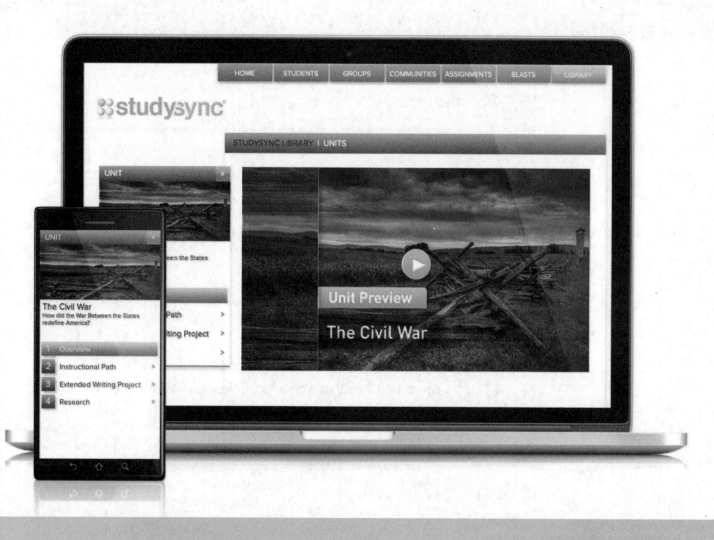

How did the War Between the States redefine America?

# The Civil War

# The Civil War

## TEXTS

## ENGLISH LANGUAGE DEVELOPMENT TEXTS

## EXTENDED WRITING PROJECT

Please note that excerpts and passages in the StudySync® library and this workbook are intended as touchstones to generate interest in an author's work. The excerpts and passages do not substitute for the reading of entire texts, and StudySync® strongly recommends that students seek out and purchase the whole literary or informational work in order to experience it as the author intended. Links to online resellers are available in our digital library. In addition, complete works may be ordered through an authorized reseller by filling out and returning to StudySync® the order form enclosed in this workbook.

Reading & Writing
Companion **389**

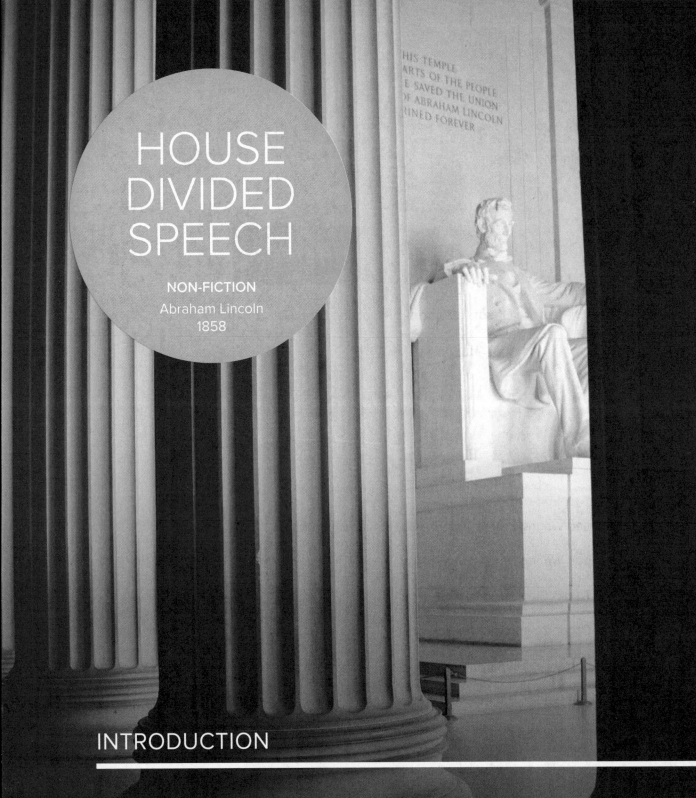

# HOUSE DIVIDED SPEECH

### NON-FICTION
Abraham Lincoln
1858

## INTRODUCTION

Abraham Lincoln delivered his famous speech, "House Divided," in 1858, when tensions were running high before the start of the Civil War. Lincoln explained the use of the "house divided" imagery in this way: "I want to use some universally known figure, expressed in simple language as universally known, that it may strike home to the minds of men in order to rouse them to the peril of the times." This excerpt reproduces the introduction, which contains the best-known passage, and the close of Lincoln's speech.

# "A house divided against itself cannot stand."

## FIRST READ

1 Mr. President and Gentlemen of the Convention.

2 If we could first know where we are, and **whither** we are tending, we could then better judge what to do, and how to do it.

3 We are now far into the fifth year, since a **policy** was initiated, with the avowed object, and confident promise, of putting an end to slavery **agitation**.

4 Under the operation of that policy, that agitation has not only, not ceased, but has constantly **augmented**.

5 In my opinion, it will not cease, until a crisis shall have been reached, and passed.

6 "A house divided against itself cannot stand."

7 I believe this government cannot endure, permanently half slave and half free.

8 I do not expect the Union to be dissolved—I do not expect the house to fall—but I do expect it will cease to be divided.

9 It will become all one thing or all the other.

10 Either the opponents of slavery, will arrest the further spread of it, and place it where the public mind shall rest in the belief that it is in the course of ultimate extinction; or its **advocates** will push it forward, till it shall become alike lawful in all the States, old as well as new—North as well as South.

11 . . .

NOTES

12  Our cause, then, must be intrusted to, and conducted by its own undoubted friends—those whose hands are free, whose hearts are in the work—who do care for the result.

13  Two years ago the Republicans of the nation mustered over thirteen hundred thousand strong.

14  We did this under the single impulse of resistance to a common danger, with every external circumstance against us.

15  Of strange, discordant, and even, hostile elements, we gathered from the four winds, and formed and fought the battle through, under the constant hot fire of a disciplined, proud, and pampered enemy.

16  Did we brave all then to falter now?—now—when that same enemy is wavering, dissevered and belligerent?

17  The result is not doubtful. We shall not fail—if we stand firm, we shall not fail.

18  Wise councils may accelerate or mistakes delay it, but, sooner or later the victory is sure to come.

## THINK QUESTIONS  CA-CCSS: CA.RI.8.1, CA.L.8.4a, CA.L.8.4b

1.  To whom is Abraham Lincoln speaking and why is he addressing them? Cite textual evidence to support your answer.

2.  According to Lincoln, which issue is dividing or splitting the nation, and why? Cite evidence from the text in your response.

3.  What does Lincoln predict will happen to the country if this issue is not rectified, or corrected? Include evidence from the text to support your response.

4.  Use the antonym of "opponents" to determine the meaning of the word **advocates** as it is used in the "House Divided" speech. Explain how you figured out the word's meaning and write your definition. List some other synonyms of *advocates*.

5.  Remembering that the Latin suffix *-tion* means "act" or "process," use the dictionary definition of the term **agitate** to determine the meaning of *agitation*, and write its definition.

# CLOSE READ

CA-CCSS: CA.RI.8.1, CA.RI.8.4, CA.RI.8.5, CA.RI.8.6, CA.W.8.4, CA.W.8.5, CA.W.8.6, CA.W.8.10

Reread the speech "House Divided." As you reread, complete the Focus Questions below. Then use your answers and annotations from the questions to help you complete the Writing Prompt.

## FOCUS QUESTIONS

1. As you reread the text of the "House Divided" speech, remember that Abraham Lincoln uses a particular text structure to present information. Analyze the structure of a few specific paragraphs. What is the effect of the structure on the speech? Highlight evidence in the text to show the structure and make annotations to explain how the structure affects the speech.

2. Formal language can contribute to the tone of a text. Highlight words or phrases from the first part of the excerpt that are examples of formal language. What is the effect of the language on the tone? Make annotations to explain your ideas.

3. Highlight words or phrases from the second excerpt that are examples of formal language. Then make annotations to explain how these word choices contribute to the tone of the text.

4. How does the tone of the speech and the use of allusion help readers understand Lincoln's point of view about slavery? Highlight textual evidence that supports your understanding. Write an annotation to explain how the author uses tone and allusion to convey his meaning.

5. Think about the structure, tone, and content of Lincoln's speech. How might Lincoln's speech of 1858 have helped redefine the United States? Write an annotation to explain your answer. Then highlight evidence from the text that helps support your ideas.

## WRITING PROMPT

In the "House Divided" speech, Abraham Lincoln wrote about an issue that he felt strongly about and that was very important to him. Write a short speech about a topic that is important to you, using specific word choice to convey tone. Choose an informational text structure that helps communicate and develop your ideas clearly in each paragraph. In your speech, include an allusion or image that you think conveys the situation in a powerful and memorable way. Make it your goal to persuade your audience to accept your point of view.

Please note that excerpts and passages in the StudySync® library and this workbook are intended as touchstones to generate interest in an author's work. The excerpts and passages do not substitute for the reading of entire texts, and StudySync® strongly recommends that students seek out and purchase the whole literary or informational work in order to experience it as the author intended. Links to online resellers are available in our digital library. In addition, complete works may be ordered through an authorized reseller by filling out and returning to StudySync® the order form enclosed in this workbook.

Reading & Writing Companion   **393**

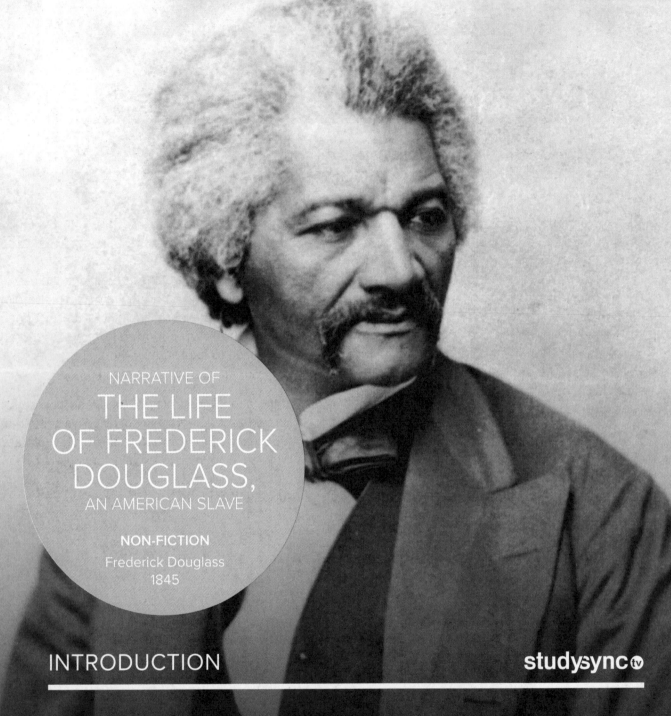

NARRATIVE OF
THE LIFE
OF FREDERICK
DOUGLASS,
AN AMERICAN SLAVE

**NON-FICTION**
Frederick Douglass
1845

# INTRODUCTION

Published in 1845, the autobiography, *Narrative of the Life of Frederick Douglass, An American Slave*, describes Douglass's journey from slavery to freedom. This great American orator provides a factual account of his struggle to educate and free himself and others from the oppression of his times. The memoir's vivid descriptions of life as a slave played a key role in fueling the abolitionist movement in the North prior to the Civil War. In the following excerpt from the middle of the text, Douglass overcomes the odds against him, procuring the assistance of others in teaching himself to read despite laws prohibiting slaves from learning such skills.

# "The more I read, the more I was led to abhor and detest my enslavers."

## FIRST READ

1 The plan which I adopted, and the one by which I was most successful, was that of making friends of all the little white boys whom I met in the street. As many of these as I could, I converted into teachers. With their kindly aid, obtained at different times and in different places, I finally succeeded in learning to read. When I was sent of errands, I always took my book with me, and by going one part of my errand quickly, I found time to get a lesson before my return. I used also to carry bread with me, enough of which was always in the house, and to which I was always welcome; for I was much better off in this regard than many of the poor white children in our neighborhood. This bread I used to bestow upon the hungry little urchins, who, in return, would give me that more valuable bread of knowledge. I am strongly tempted to give the names of two or three of those little boys, as a testimonial of the gratitude and affection I bear them; but **prudence** forbids;—not that it would injure me, but it might embarrass them; for it is almost an unpardonable offence to teach slaves to read in this Christian country. It is enough to say of the dear little fellows, that they lived on Philpot Street, very near Durgin and Bailey's ship-yard. I used to talk this matter of slavery over with them. I would sometimes say to them, I wished I could be as free as they would be when they got to be men. "You will be free as soon as you are twenty-one, but I am a slave for life! Have not I as good a right to be free as you have?" These words used to trouble them; they would express for me the liveliest sympathy, and console me with the hope that something would occur by which I might be free.

2 I was now about twelve years old, and the thought of being a slave for life began to bear heavily upon my heart. Just about this time, I got hold of a book entitled "The Columbian **Orator**." Every opportunity I got, I used to read this book. Among much of other interesting matter, I found in it a dialogue between a master and his slave. The slave was represented as having run away from his master three times. The dialogue represented the conversation which took place between them, when the slave was retaken the third time. In this

dialogue, the whole argument in behalf of slavery was brought forward by the master, all of which was disposed of by the slave. The slave was made to say some very smart as well as impressive things in reply to his master—things which had the desired though unexpected effect; for the conversation resulted in the voluntary emancipation of the slave on the part of the master.

3   In the same book, I met with one of Sheridan's mighty speeches on and in behalf of Catholic emancipation. These were choice documents to me. I read them over and over again with **unabated** interest. They gave tongue to interesting thoughts of my own soul, which had frequently flashed through my mind, and died away for want of utterance. The moral which I gained from the dialogue was the power of truth over the conscience of even a slaveholder. What I got from Sheridan was a bold **denunciation** of slavery, and a powerful **vindication** of human rights.

4   The reading of these documents enabled me to utter my thoughts, and to meet the arguments brought forward to sustain slavery; but while they relieved me of one difficulty, they brought on another even more painful than the one of which I was relieved. The more I read, the more I was led to abhor and detest my enslavers. I could regard them in no other light than a band of successful robbers, who had left their homes, and gone to Africa, and stolen us from our homes, and in a strange land reduced us to slavery. I loathed them as being the meanest as well as the most wicked of men. As I read and contemplated the subject, behold! that very discontentment which Master Hugh had predicted would follow my learning to read had already come, to torment and sting my soul to unutterable anguish. As I writhed under it, I would at times feel that learning to read had been a curse rather than a blessing. It had given me a view of my wretched condition, without the remedy. It opened my eyes to the horrible pit, but to no ladder upon which to get out. In moments of agony, I envied my fellow-slaves for their stupidity. I have often wished myself a beast. I preferred the condition of the meanest reptile to my own. Any thing, no matter what, to get rid of thinking! It was this everlasting thinking of my condition that tormented me. There was no getting rid of it. It was pressed upon me by every object within sight or hearing, animate or inanimate. The silver trump of freedom had roused my soul to eternal wakefulness. Freedom now appeared, to disappear no more forever. It was heard in every sound, and seen in everything. It was ever present to torment me with a sense of my wretched condition. I saw nothing without seeing it, I heard nothing without hearing it, and felt nothing without feeling it. It looked from every star, it smiled in every calm, breathed in every wind, and moved in every storm.

## THINK QUESTIONS   CA-CCSS: CA.RI.8.1, CA.RI.8.4, CA.L.8.4, CA.L.8.4b, CA.SL.8.1c, CA.SL.8.1d

1. Identify textual evidence from the excerpt that reveals why learning to read was so important to Frederick Douglass when he was a boy.

2. What parallels, or similarities, do you see between the books Douglass reads and his own life? Cite textual evidence from the excerpt to support the similarities you find.

3. What does Douglass learn about the history of slavery through the books that he reads that lead him to detest his master, even though in some ways, as a boy, Douglass felt he was "much better off" than some of the white boys in his neighborhood. Cite textual evidence to support your answer.

4. Use context to determine the meaning of the word **unabated** as it is used in *Narrative of the Life of Frederick Douglass, An American Slave*. Write your definition of *unabated* and tell how you arrived at it.

5. Remembering that the Latin root *nunci* means "to speak or carry a message" and the prefix *de-* means "from or against," use the context clues provided in the passage to determine the meaning of **denunciation** and write its definition.

## CLOSE READ   CA-CCSS: CA.RI.8.1, CA.RI.8.3, CA.RI.8.4, CA.W.8.4, CA.W.8.5, CA.W.8.6, CA.W.8.10

Reread the excerpt from *Narrative of the Life of Frederick Douglass, An American Slave*. As you reread, complete the Focus Questions below. Then use your answers and annotations from the questions to help you complete the Writing Prompt.

## FOCUS QUESTIONS

1. Explain the way Douglass infers, through word choice and description, how he regards himself as the equal of the "little white boys" he sees on the street. Highlight textual evidence that supports your answer and write a brief annotation to explain it.

2. Douglass does not begin to detest his slaveholder, and regard his enslavers as the "most wicked of men," until he reads "The Columbian Orator." What is it about this text and its content that really disturbs him, apart from the idea that he might not be able to escape slavery?

3. In the first paragraph, Douglass writes that he does not want to reveal the names of the white boys who taught him to read, because "it is an almost unpardonable offence." What personal comment does Douglass add to this statement? What does he later come to realize when he reads one of Sheridan's speeches in "The Columbian Orator," and what distinctions does he make between these ideas? Highlight textual evidence that supports your answer.

4. Informational texts blend facts and details about events, individuals, and ideas. Each of these details interact and combine in a text, often resulting in cause-and-effect relationships. Trace the cause-and-effect relationships in *Narrative of the Life of Frederick Douglass, An American Slave* and how they result in Douglass feeling tormented "with a sense of my wretched condition." Highlight textual evidence that supports your answer

5. Douglass frequently uses figurative language, and specifically certain figures of speech, to help readers understand his situation in vivid and dramatic ways. Identify the figure of speech Douglass uses in the third paragraph of the excerpt. What does it mean, and in what way does it indicate an important turning point in his life? Highlight textual evidence that supports your answer and write a brief annotation to explain it.

## WRITING PROMPT

In some informational texts, authors try to persuade readers to accept a specific point of view about a subject. In what way does Frederick Douglass use elements of figurative language to express the anger and torment that he feels, and help readers understand it? How does the use of these figures of speech strengthen his argument against slavery? Use your understanding of figurative language and informational text elements to determine how successfully Douglass uses them in his narrative. Support your writing with evidence from the text.

# ACROSS FIVE APRILS

FICTION
Irene Hunt
1964

## INTRODUCTION

With two brothers fighting in the Civil War, one for the North and one for the South, 9-year-old Jethro Creighton finds himself the only son remaining in a house as divided as the country. Following the war through newspaper articles, and weathering the conflicts at home on the family farm in Illinois, Jethro takes his first steps into manhood. In this excerpt, news of the war enters the Creighton's kitchen conversation.

# "There is an awakenin' inside us of human decency and responsibility."

NOTES

## FIRST READ

*From Chapter 2*

1    The two older brothers and Wilse Graham talked as they splashed in the cold water, and Jethro could sense the pleasure they felt in seeing one another again after the **lapse** of several years.

2    In the kitchen, Jenny and Nancy hurried about getting the "comp'ny supper" ready. A couple of chickens had been dressed hastily and thrown into the pot; sweet potatoes were set to bake in the hot ashes, and dried apples were cooked in a syrup of wild honey and then topped with thick cream from one of the crocks in the spring house. Nancy made a flat cake of white flour with a sprinkling of sugar on top, and Jenny pulled tender radishes and onions from her garden to give the taste of spring to their meal.

3    A coal-oil lamp was lighted and placed in the middle of the table when supper was at last ready; gold light filled the kitchen, pouring from the open fireplace and from the sparkling lamp chimney. Black shadows hung in the adjoining room where the bed had been spread with Ellen's newest quilt and the pillows dressed in fresh covers in honor of the guest. Jethro was sensitive to color and contrast; the memory of the golden kitchen and the velvet shadows of the room beyond was firmly stamped in his mind.

4    At the table, the talk for a while was of family affairs; there had been a death of someone in Kentucky who was only a name to Jethro, but a name that brought a shadow to his mother's face; there were reports of weddings and births, of tragedies, and now and then a happy note of good fortune. Then the conversation began to turn. Slowly and inevitably the troubles of the nation began to move into the crowded little kitchen.

5    "Will Kaintuck go secesh, Wilse?" Matthew Creighton asked finally, his eyes on his plate.

6   "Maybe, Uncle Matt, maybe it will. And how will southern Illinois feel about it in case that happens?"

7   No one answered. Wilse took a drink of water, and then setting the glass down, twirled it a few times between his thumb and fingers.

8   "It will come hard fer the river states if Missouri and Kaintuck join up with the Confederacy. Ol' Mississippi' won't be the safest place fer north shippin' down to the Gulf."

9   "That's true, Wilse. That's in the minds of a lot of us," Matthew said quietly. Bill's eyes were fixed on the yellow light around the lamp chimney; John was studying his cousin's face.

10  "As fer southern Illinois," Wilse continued, "you folks air closer by a lot to the folks in Missouri and Kaintuck than you are to the bigwigs up in Chicago and northern Illinois. You're southern folks down here."

11  "We're from Kaintuck as you well know, Wilse; our roots air in that state. I'd say that eighty per cent of the folks in this part of the country count Missouri or Kaintuck or Tennessee as somehow bein' their own. But this separation, Wilse, it won't do. We're a union; separate, we're jest two weakened, puny pieces, each needin' the other."

12  "We was a weak and puny country eighty odd years ago when the great-granddaddy of us young uns got mixed up in a rebel's fight. Since then we've growed like weeds in the spring, and what's happened? Well, I'll tell you: a hall of the country has growed rich, favored by Providence, but still jealous and fearful that the other half is apt to find good fortune too. Face it, Uncle Matt; the North has become arrogant toward the South. The high-**tariff** industrialists would sooner hev the South starve than give an inch that might cost them a penny."

13  Then Ellen's voice was heard, timid and a little **tremulous**; farm women didn't enter often into man-talk of politics or national affairs.

14  "But what about the downtrodden people, Wilse? Ain't slavery becomin' more of a festerin' hurt each year? Don't we *hevto* make a move against it?"

15  "Yore own Ol' Abe from this fair state of Illinois is talkin' out of both sides of his mouth—fer the time bein' anyway." Wilse brought his hand down sharply on the table. "What the South wants is the right to live as it sees fit to live without interference. And it kin live! Do you think England won't come breakin' her neck to help the South in case of war? She ain't goin' to see her looms

Reading & Writing Companion

starve fer cotton because the northern industrialists see fit to butt in on a way of life that the South has found good. Believe me, Uncle Matt; the South kin fight fer years if need be—till this boy here is a man growed with boys of his own."

16    Young Tom's face was red with anger, but a warning look from his mother kept him quiet. From the far end of the table, however, John's voice came, strained and a little unnatural.

17    "You hev hedged Ma's question, Cousin Wilse. What about the right and wrong of one man ownin' the body—and sometimes it looks as if the soul, too—of another man?"

18    Wilse hesitated a moment, his eyes on the plate of food, which he had barely touched during the last few minutes. "I'll say this to you, Cousin John," he said finally. "I own a few slaves, and if I stood before my Maker alongside one of em, I'd hev no way to justify the fact that I was master and he was slave. But leavin' that final **reckonin'** fer the time, let me ask you this: ain't there been slavery from the beginnin' of history? Didn't the men that we give honor to, the men that shaped up the Constitution of our country, didn't they recognize slavery? Did they see it as a festerin' hurt?"

19    "Some of em did, I reckon," John answered gravely. "I can't help but believe that some of em must not ha' been comftable with them words 'a peculiar institution.'"

20    "Well then, I'll ask you this: if tomorrow every slave in the South had his freedom and come up North, would yore **abolitionists** git the crocodile tears sloshed out of their eyes so they could take the black man by the hand? Would they say, 'We'll see that you git good-payin' work fitted to what you're able to do—we'll see that you're well housed and clothed—we want you to come to our churches and yore children to come to our schools, why, we danged near fergit the difference in the colors of our skins because we air so almighty full of brotherly love!' Would it be like that in yore northern cities, Cousin John?"

21    "It ain't like that fer the masses of white people in our northern cities—nor in the southern cities either. And yet, there ain't a white man, lean-bellied and hopeless as so many of them are, that would change lots with a slave belongin' to the kindest master in the South."

22    Then Bill spoke for the first time, his eyes still on the yellow light of the lamp.

23    "Slavery, I hate. But it is with us, and them that should suffer fer the evil they brought to our shores air long dead. What I want us to answer in this year of 1861 is this, John: does the trouble over slavery come because men's hearts

is purer above the Mason-Dixon line? Or does slavery throw a shadder over greed and keep that greed from showin' up quite so bare and ugly?"

24    Wilse Graham seemed to leap at Bill's question. "You're right, Cousin Bill. It's greed, not slavery, that's stirrin' up this trouble. And as fer human goodness—men's hearts is jest as black today as in the Roman times when they nailed slaves to crosses by the hunderd and left them there to point up a lesson.

25    Matt Creighton shook his head. "Human nature ain't any better one side of a political line than on the other—we all know that—but human nature, the all-over picture of it, *is* better than it was a thousand—five hundred—even a hundred years ago. There is an awakenin' inside us of human decency and responsibility. If I didn't believe that, I wouldn't grieve fer the children I've buried; I wouldn't look for'ard to the manhood of this youngest one."

Excerpted from *Across Five Aprils* by Irene Hunt, published by The Berkley Publishing Group.

 **THINK QUESTIONS**   CA-CCSS: CA.RL.8.1, CA.L.8.4a

1.   Why are members of the Creighton family so divided about the idea of secession from the Union? Cite textual evidence to support your answer.

2.   Use details from the text to write two or three sentences that describe the differing points of view the members of the Graham family have toward slavery.

3.   Write two or three sentences comparing Bill and Matthew's views on the possibility of a war between North and South. Cite textual evidence that reveals their views.

4.   Use context clues to determine the meaning of the word **tremulous** as it is used in *Across Five Aprils*. Write your definition of *tremulous* and explain how you arrived at it.

5.   Determine the meaning of the word **abolitionist** as it is used in *Across Five Aprils*, using context clues in the text. Write your definition of *abolitionist* and explain how you arrived at it.

## CLOSE READ
CA-CCSS: CA.RL.8.1, CA.RL.8.3, CA.RL.8.6, CA.W.8.3, CA.W.8.4, CA.W.8.5, CA.W.8.6, CA.W.8.10

Reread the excerpt from *Across Five Aprils*. As you reread, complete the Focus Questions below. Then use your answers and annotations from the questions to help you complete the Writing Prompt.

## FOCUS QUESTIONS

1. The bond between family members is apparent in this excerpt from *Across Five Aprils*. How does using third-person limited omniscient point of view help reveal this bond? Highlight textual evidence to support your ideas and write annotations to explain your choices.

2. Wilse Graham is reluctant to answer Ellen's question about slavery becoming more of a "festerin' hurt" each year, and whether or not "we hev to make a move against it." How does the author reveal that Wilse feels in his heart that slavery is wrong, even though he defends it as an economic necessity? Highlight evidence from the text that will help support your answer.

3. In the sixteenth paragraph, one of Ellen and Matthew's sons has a reaction to what his cousin Wilse says in the previous paragraph. What does this reaction reveal about the family and about how the character of Bill Creighton stands apart from what the rest of what his family believes? Highlight textual evidence to support your ideas, and make annotations to explain your choices.

4. An author creates characters through dialogue and their reactions to plot events. What situation has provoked Wilse and John to argue about slavery? What do their differing attitudes toward slavery reveal about each man's character? Highlight textual evidence to support your ideas and make annotations to explain your choices.

5. In the last paragraph of the excerpt, Matt Creighton makes his final statement on human decency and the evils of slavery. How does the author make use of dramatic irony in this statement, as a way of foreshadowing, or giving readers a hint, of the Civil War to come and of the many ways it will change the country? Highlight textual evidence and make annotations to support your explanation.

## WRITING PROMPT

Think about how the various characters in this excerpt from *Across Five Aprils* feel about the institution of slavery and the prospect of civil war. Imagine what might happen if, as war is declared, Jethro Creighton announces to his family that he intends to enlist in the Union army. Establish a context and point of view and organize a sequence of events that unfolds naturally and logically after Jethro's announcement, based on the traits of the characters you have read about. How might Matt feel about Jethro's decision? Use your understanding of point of view and character traits in your narrative, as well as techniques such as dialogue, pacing, description, and reflection to develop experiences, events and the characters in your story.

# PAUL REVERE'S RIDE

POETRY
Henry Wadsworth Longfellow
1861

## INTRODUCTION

studysync tv

enry Wadsworth Longfellow is considered the first professional American poet and, thanks to "Paul Revere's Ride", one of the most popular of his time. Just weeks after Longfellow finished the poem, Abraham Lincoln won the presidency. America was on the verge of the Civil War. An abolitionist, Longfellow published the work not only to commemorate the actions of Paul Revere on the eve of the Revolution, but to inspire Americans to fight for the Union and to abolish slavery. The poet took intentional liberties in his telling of the story, greatly enhancing the actual historical events and creating an American hero in the process. Notable for both its poetic form and its link between the two great wars fought on American soil, "Paul Revere's Ride" has inspired generations of readers with its vivid portrayal of an American hero's call to arms.

# "One, if by land, and two, if by sea..."

## FIRST READ

1  Listen, my children, and you shall hear
2  Of the midnight ride of Paul Revere,
3  On the eighteenth of April, in Seventy-Five;
4  Hardly a man is now alive
5  Who remembers that famous day and year.

6  He said to his friend, "If the British march
7  By land or sea from the town to-night,
8  Hang a lantern aloft in the belfry arch
9  Of the North Church tower, as a signal light, —
10  One, if by land, and two, if by sea;
11  And I on the opposite shore will be,
12  Ready to ride and spread the alarm
13  Through every Middlesex village and farm,
14  For the country-folk to be up and to arm."

15  Then he said "Good-night!" and with muffled oar
16  Silently rowed to the Charlestown shore,
17  Just as the moon rose over the bay,
18  Where swinging wide at her **moorings** lay
19  The Somerset, British man-of-war;
20  A phantom ship, with each mast and spar
21  Across the moon like a prison-bar,
22  And a huge black hulk, that was magnified
23  By its own reflection in the tide.

24  Meanwhile, his friend, through alley and street
25  Wanders and watches with eager ears,
26  Till in the silence around him he hears
27  The muster of men at the barrack door,

NOTES

28  The sound of arms, and the tramp of feet,
29  And the measured tread of the **grenadiers,**
30  Marching down to their boats on the shore.

31  Then he climbed the tower of the Old North Church,
32  By the wooden stairs, with stealthy tread,
33  To the belfry-chamber overhead,
34  And startled the pigeons from their perch
35  On the somber rafters, that round him made
36  Masses and moving shapes of shade, —
37  By the trembling ladder, steep and tall,
38  To the highest window in the wall,
39  Where he paused to listen and look down
40  A moment on the roofs of the town,
41  And the moonlight flowing over all.

42  Beneath, in the churchyard, lay the dead,
43  In their night-encampment on the hill,
44  Wrapped in silence so deep and still
45  That he could hear, like a sentinel's tread,
46  The watchful night-wind, as it went
47  Creeping along from tent to tent,
48  And seeming to whisper, "All is well!"
49  A moment only he feels the spell
50  Of the place and the hour, the secret dread
51  Of the lonely belfry and the dead;
52  For suddenly all his thoughts are bent
53  On a shadowy something far away,
54  Where the river widens to meet the bay, —
55  A line of black, that bends and floats
56  On the rising tide, like a bridge of boats.

57  Meanwhile, impatient to mount and ride,
58  Booted and spurred, with a heavy stride
59  On the opposite shore walked Paul Revere.
60  Now he patted his horse's side,
61  Now gazed on the landscape far and near,
62  Then, **impetuous,** stamped the earth,
63  And turned and tightened his saddle-girth;
64  But mostly he watched with eager search
65  The belfry-tower of the Old North Church,
66  As it rose above the graves on the hill,
67  Lonely and **spectral** and **somber** and still.
68  And lo! as he looks, on the belfry's height
69  A glimmer, and then a gleam of light!

70 He springs to the saddle, the bridle he turns,
71 But lingers and gazes, till full on his sight
72 A second lamp in the belfry burns!

73 A hurry of hoofs in a village street,
74 A shape in the moonlight, a bulk in the dark,
75 And beneath, from the pebbles, in passing, a spark
76 Struck out by a steed flying fearless and fleet:
77 That was all! And yet, through the gloom and the light,
78 The fate of a nation was riding that night;
79 And the spark struck out by that steed, in his flight,
80 Kindled the land into flame with its heat.

81 He has left the village and mounted the steep,
82 And beneath him, tranquil and broad and deep,
83 Is the Mystic, meeting the ocean tides;
84 And under the alders that skirt its edge,
85 Now soft on the sand, now loud on the ledge,
86 Is heard the tramp of his steed as he rides.

87 It was twelve by the village clock,
88 When he crossed the bridge into Medford town.
89 He heard the crowing of the cock,
90 And the barking of the farmer's dog,
91 And felt the damp of the river fog,
92 That rises after the sun goes down.

93 It was one by the village clock,
94 When he galloped into Lexington.
95 He saw the gilded weathercock
96 Swim in the moonlight as he passed,
97 And the meeting-house windows, blank and bare,
98 Gaze at him with a spectral glare,
99 As if they already stood aghast
100 At the bloody work they would look upon.

101 It was two by the village clock,
102 When he came to the bridge in Concord town.
103 He heard the bleating of the flock,
104 And the twitter of birds among the trees,
105 And felt the breath of the morning breeze
106 Blowing over the meadow brown.
107 And one was safe and asleep in his bed
108 Who at the bridge would be first to fall,
109 Who that day would be lying dead,
110 Pierced by a British musket-ball.

NOTES

111 You know the rest. In the books you have read,
112 How the British regulars fired and fled, —
113 How the farmers gave them ball for ball,
114 From behind each fence and farm-yard wall,
115 Chasing the red-coats down the lane,
116 Then crossing the fields to emerge again
117 Under the trees at the turn of the road,
118 And only pausing to fire and load.

119 So through the night rode Paul Revere;
120 And so through the night went his cry of alarm
121 To every Middlesex village and farm, —
122 A cry of defiance and not of fear,
123 A voice in the darkness, a knock at the door,
124 And a word that shall echo forevermore!
125 For, borne on the night-wind of the Past,
126 Through all our history, to the last,
127 In the hour of darkness and peril and need,
128 The people will waken and listen to hear
129 The hurrying hoof-beat of that steed,
130 And the midnight-message of Paul Revere.

 ## THINK QUESTIONS    CA-CCSS: CA.RL.8.1, CA.L.8.4a, CA.SL.8.1c, CA.SL.8.1d

1. What details does Longfellow include to explain the time and place in which the events of the poem take place? Support your answer with evidence from the text.

2. What does Longfellow mean when he writes that Revere's friend wanders and watches through alley and street "with eager ears"? What does he hear that causes him to climb the tower of the Old North Church? Support your answer with evidence from the text.

3. Use details from the poem to write two or three sentences that describe how Longfellow felt about Paul Revere.

4. Use context to determine the meaning of the word **moorings** as it is used in "Paul Revere's Ride." Write your definition of *moorings* and explain how you figured it out.

5. Determine the meaning of the word **impetuous** as it is used in this poem. Write your definition of *impetuous* and explain how you figured it out.

# CLOSE READ
CA-CCSS: CA.RL.8.1, CA.RL.8.4, CA.L.8.4a, CA.L.8.5b, CA.L.8.5c, CA.W.8.4, CA.W.8.5, CA.W.8.6, CA.W.8.10

Reread the poem "Paul Revere's Ride." As you reread, complete the Focus Questions below. Then use your answers and annotations from the questions to help you complete the Writing Prompt.

## FOCUS QUESTIONS

1. Longfellow uses many figures of speech in "Paul Revere's Ride," including similes and personification. Find an example of a simile in the third stanza and an example of personification in the eleventh stanza. What images do these two examples of figurative language create? How do they add to the meaning of the poem? Cite textual evidence and annotate to support your answer.

2. The denotation, or dictionary definition, of the word pierced is "to make a hole in; to bore into or through." The word pierced can have a positive connotation when referring, for example, to a light that pierced the darkness. Does Longfellow's use of pierced in line 110 of the twelfth stanza have a negative or a positive connotation? What does his word choice add to the poem? Use textual evidence to support your answer.

3. Longfellow substitutes the word steed for horse once Paul Revere begins his famous ride to warn the people of Middlesex and its surrounding villages that the British are coming. How does the substitution of this word affect the meaning and tone of the poem? Annotate your answer and use textual evidence to support it.

4. The word aghast can have multiple denotative meanings: to be stunned or astonished; to be horrified at something; to be amazed; to be startled. What meaning of the word aghast does Longfellow use in line 99 of the eleventh stanza? Does it have a positive or a negative connotation? Use evidence from the text to support your answer.

5. Longfellow uses the word tread twice in the poem. "Tread" has a number of denotative meanings, including "to walk; to crush; to step on or through; to step across something; to trample." Sometimes the relationship between words can help readers understand the word's denotative and connotative meanings. In the fifth stanza, how does the adjective *stealthy* help define the word *tread* in line 32, and what kind of connotative meaning does it give the word the way it is used in the poem? Support your answer with textual evidence.

6. "Paul Revere's Ride" was first published just as the Civil War was beginning. What words or phrases does Longfellow use in the poem to create a dramatic tone that would resonate with a nation on the brink of Civil War? Highlight your answers and annotate to show how his poem was also capturing the drama of a nation full of civil unrest.

## WRITING PROMPT

How does Henry Wadsworth Longfellow's use of language in "Paul Revere's Ride" set the tone for the events described in the poem? How does the poet use connotation and denotation to create visual images that add to the meaning of the poem? Use your understanding of figurative language as well as connotation and denotation to determine how the author's word choices impact meaning and tone. Support your writing with evidence from the text.

SPEECH TO
THE OHIO WOMEN'S
CONFERENCE:

# AIN'T
# I A WOMAN

**NON-FICTION**
Sojourner Truth
1851

## INTRODUCTION

Sojourner Truth (1797–1883) was an abolitionist and women's rights advocate who was born an enslaved woman but escaped to freedom in 1826. Twenty-two years later, the first women's rights convention in the United States was held in Seneca Falls, NY, in 1848. Many of the attendees signed a document arguing for equal rights for women, including the right to vote. The document, called the Declaration of Sentiments, summoned people from around the country to organize conventions that would urge lawmakers, clergy, and journalists to support the cause. Three years later, at one such assembly in Akron, Ohio, Truth gave a rousing and memorable speech. Two accounts of that speech are provided here. The most widely read account of this speech, the Frances Gage version, was published twelve years after Truth spoke and its accuracy remains questionable. Many contemporary historians agree that Marius Robinson's 1851 transcription, also presented here, offers a more faithful account of Truth's remarks.

# "I can't read, but I can hear."

  FIRST READ

**Account by Frances Dana Gage,** *Anti-Slavery Standard*, **1863**

1   Well, children, where there is so much racket there must be something out of kilter. I think that **'twixt** the negroes of the South and the women at the North, all talking about rights, the white men will be in a fix pretty soon. But what's all this here talking about?

2   That man over there says that women need to be helped into carriages, and lifted over ditches, and to have the best place everywhere. Nobody ever helps me into carriages, or over mud-puddles, or gives me any best place! And ain't I a woman? Look at me! Look at my arm! I have ploughed and planted, and gathered into barns, and no man could head me! And ain't I a woman? I could work as much and eat as much as a man - when I could get it - and bear the lash as well! And ain't I a woman? I have borne thirteen children, and seen most all sold off to slavery, and when I cried out with my mother's grief, none but Jesus heard me! And ain't I a woman?

3   Then they talk about this thing in the head; what's this they call it? [Member of audience whispers, "intellect."] That's it, honey. What's that got to do with women's rights or negroes' rights? If my cup won't hold but a pint, and yours holds a quart, wouldn't you be mean not to let me have my little half measure full?

4   Then that little man in black there, he says women can't have as much rights as men, 'cause Christ wasn't a woman! Where did your Christ come from? Where did your Christ come from? From God and a woman! Man had nothing to do with Him.

5   If the first woman God ever made was strong enough to turn the world upside down all alone, these women together ought to be able to turn it back, and get it right side up again! And now they is asking to do it, the men better let them.

6   **Obliged** to you for hearing me, and now old Sojourner ain't got nothing more to say.

**Account by Marius Robinson, *Anti-Slavery Bugle*, 1851:**

7   I want to say a few words about this matter. I am for a woman's rights. I have as much muscle as any man, and can do as much work as any man. I have plowed and reaped and husked and chopped and mowed, and can any man do more than that? I have heard much about the sexes being equal. I can carry as much as any man, and can eat as much too, if I can get it. I am as strong as any man that is now.

8   As for intellect, all I can say is, if a woman have a pint, and a man a quart—why can't she have her little pint full? You need not be afraid to give us our rights for fear we will take too much—for we can't take more than our pint'll hold.

9   The poor men seems to be all in confusion and don't know what to do. Why children, if you have woman's rights, give it to her and you will feel better. You will have your own rights, and they won't be so much trouble.

10  I can't read, but I can hear. I have heard the Bible and have learned that Eve caused man to sin. Well, if woman upset the world, do give her a chance to set it right side up again. The lady has spoken about Jesus, how he never **spurned** woman from him, and she was right. When Lazarus died, Mary and Martha came to him with faith and love and **besought** him to raise their brother. And Jesus wept and Lazarus came forth. And how came Jesus into the world? Through God who created him and the woman who bore him. Man, where was your part?

11  But the women are coming up, blessed be God, and a few of the men are coming up with them. But man is in a tight place, the poor slave is on him, woman is coming on him, he is surely between a hawk and a **buzzard.**

## THINK QUESTIONS   CA-CCSS: CA.RI.8.1, CA.L.8.4a, CA.L.8.5b, CA.SL.8.1a, CA.SL.8.1b, CA.SL.8.1c, CA.SL.8.1d

1.  Use details from the text to summarize Sojourner Truth's opinion about men thinking "women need to be helped into carriages, and lifted over ditches, and to have the best place everywhere."

2.  Why are there two versions of the speech?

3.  Refer to two or more details in the text to support the idea that, in some ways, Sojourner Truth thinks women are actually stronger than men.

4.  Use context to determine the meaning of the word **obliged** as it is used in Sojourner Truth's speech to the Ohio Women's Conference. Write your definition of *obliged* and explain how you arrived at it.

5.  Use context clues to determine the meaning of the word **intellect** as it is used in the third paragraph of Truth's speech. Write your definition of *intellect* and explain how you arrived at it.

# CLOSE READ   CA-CCSS: CA.RI.8.1, CA.RI.8.9, CA.W.8.4, CA.W.8.5, CA.W.8.6, CA.W.8.10

Reread the two accounts of Truth's speech. As you reread, complete the Focus Questions below. Then use your answers and annotations from the questions to help you complete the Writing Prompt.

 FOCUS QUESTIONS

1. Do you think the repetition of the words "Ain't I a Woman?" make the first account more effective to the reader or audience member than the second account? Cite textual evidence from both versions of Sojourner Truth's speech to support your answer.

2. How did Truth's faith help her make an argument for women's rights? What is the difference between both accounts of the speech? Use textual evidence from both accounts to support your answer.

3. Annotate each paragraph of the first account of Truth's speech to explain how each one supports her message about women's rights.

4. According to the text, what makes Sojourner Truth feel that she is equal to a man? Cite textual evidence from both accounts to support your answer, and explain how they differ.

5. Explain the following sentence from the second account: "As for intellect, all I can say is, if a woman have a pint and a man a quart—why can't she have her little pint full?" Highlight the text in the first account that expresses the same information.

6. How does the first paragraph of Gage's account foreshadow the changes that are coming, with the Civil War just around the corner? Highlight evidence and annotate to support your answer.

## WRITING PROMPT

Consider Sojourner Truth's statement in the first account: "If my cup won't hold but a pint, and yours holds a quart, wouldn't you be mean not to let me have my little half measure full?" What does she mean by "cup, pint, and quart?" How does Robinson present this idea in the second account, and how is the meaning of Sojourner Truth's statement changed slightly in Robinson's account? Write an explanation of the analogies that Truth makes and compare and contrast the two accounts of the speech and how they present these analogies. Then write an answer to the second question, comparing the two presentations. Use textual evidence to support your answer.

# SULLIVAN BALLOU LETTER

**NON-FICTION**
Sullivan Ballou
1861

## INTRODUCTION

---

Rhode Islander Sullivan Ballou was an officer in the Union Army during the Civil War. He is best remembered for an eloquent letter he wrote to his wife in July, 1861, in which Ballou describes the conflicting pulls of duty to country and love of his wife. A week after he wrote the letter, Ballou was killed at the first Battle of Bull Run.

# "Not my will, but thine, O God be done."

 FIRST READ

*July 14, 1861*

*Camp Clark, Washington*

1   My very dear Sarah:

2   The indications are very strong that we shall move in a few days—perhaps tomorrow. Lest I should not be able to write again, I feel **impelled** to write a few lines that may fall under your eye when I am no more. Our movements may be of a few days' duration and full of pleasure—and it may be of some conflict and death to me. "Not my will, but thine, O God be done." If it is necessary that I should fall on the battlefield for my Country, I am ready.

3   I have no **misgivings** about, or lack of confidence in the cause in which I am engaged, and my courage does not halt or falter. I know how strongly American Civilization now leans on the triumph of the Government and how great a debt we owe to those who went before us through the blood and suffering of the Revolution. And I am willing—perfectly willing—to lay down all my joys in this life, to help maintain this government, and to pay that debt.

4   Sarah my love for you is deathless, it seems to bind me with mighty cables that nothing but **Omnipotence** could break; and yet my love of Country comes over me like a strong wind and bears me unresistibly on with all these chains to the battlefield.

5   The memories of the blissful moments I have spent with you come creeping over me, and I feel most gratified to God and to you that I have enjoyed them for so long. And hard it is for me to give them up and burn to ashes the hopes of future years, when, God willing, we might still have lived and loved together, and seen our sons grown up to honorable manhood, around us. I have, I know, but few and small claims upon Divine Providence, but something

whispers to me—perhaps it is the **wafted** prayer of my little Edgar, that I shall return to my loved ones unharmed. If I do not my dear Sarah, never forget how much I love you, and when my last breath escapes me on the battlefield, it will whisper your name. Forgive my many faults and the many pains I have caused you. How thoughtless and foolish I have often times been! How gladly would I wash out with my tears every little spot upon your happiness and struggle with all the misfortunes of this world to shield you and your children from harm. But I cannot. I must watch you from the Spirit-land and hover near you, while you buffet the storm, with your precious little freight, and wait with sad patience till we meet to part no more.

6   But, O Sarah! If the dead can come back to this earth and **flit** unseen around those they loved, I shall always be near you; in the gladdest days and in the darkest nights. . . always, always, and if there be a soft breeze upon your cheek, it shall be my breath, as the cool air fans your throbbing temple, it shall be my spirit passing by. Sarah do not mourn me dead; think I am gone and wait for thee, for we shall meet again.

7   As for my little boys—they will grow up as I have done, and never know a father's love and care. Little Willie is too young to remember me long, and my blue-eyed Edgar will keep my frolics with him among the deep memories of childhood. Sarah, I have unlimited confidence in your maternal care and your development of their character, and feel that God will bless you in your holy work.

8   Tell my two Mothers I call God's blessing upon them. O! Sarah. I wait for you there; come to me and lead thither my children.

9   Sullivan

## THINK QUESTIONS   CA-CCSS: CA.RI.8.1, CA.RI.8.4, CA.L.8.5a

1.  What is the purpose behind Sullivan Ballou's letter to his wife? Cite textual evidence to support your answer.

2.  Cite textual evidence that explains why Ballou tells his wife that she should not mourn him when he is dead.

3.  Is Sullivan Ballou proud of his life and his family? Cite textual evidence to support your answer.

4.  In Paragraph 3, Ballou uses the word **Omnipotence** to refer to God. That is why it is capitalized even though it appears in the middle of a sentence. **Omnipotence** comes from a Latin word that means "all" and from the Latin root poten-, which means "powerful" and "capable." The same root is found in the words *potency* and *potential*. Write your definition of *omnipotence* and explain how you arrived at it.

5.  Use context in the selection to determine the meaning of the word **flit** as it is used in "Sullivan Ballou Letter." Write your definition and explain how you arrived at it, citing textual evidence.

Reading & Writing Companion   **417**

# CLOSE READ
**CA-CCSS:** CA.RI.8.1, CA.RI.8.2, CA.RI.8.3, CA.RI.8.4, CA.RI.8.7, CA.L.8.2a, CA.L.8.2b, CA.W.8.4, CA.W.8.5, CA.W.8.6, CA.W.8.10

Reread the letter from Sullivan Ballou. As you reread, complete the Focus Questions below. Then use your answers and annotations from the questions to help you complete the Writing Prompt.

## FOCUS QUESTIONS

1. Explain how Sullivan Ballou uses the first two paragraphs in his letter to indicate that he understands the seriousness of his situation, and yet is determined to follow through on the task he has set for himself. How does Sullivan provide a transition to the third paragraph where he changes the subject to his feelings for his wife Sarah? Highlight textual evidence to support your answer.

2. What kind of punctuation does Sullivan use to highlight and emphasize the depth of his feelings? Why would this kind of punctuation not appear very often in a tweet or text message, and how would its absence affect the emotion and feelings expressed in Sullivan's letter?

3. Although Sullivan wrote this letter to comfort his wife, in what way does the letter also reveal what the risks were, and why the war was so important for many fighting on the Union side? Why do you think it was important for Sullivan to mention these things to his wife? Use textual evidence to support your answer.

4. Sullivan's sons Edgar and Willie are important subjects in this letter, even though it is not addressed to them. Why are they important? Why might Sullivan leave out this information if this were a text message to his wife? Highlight textual evidence to support your answers.

5. Sullivan uses many kinds of figurative language in his letter. For example, he fears the hopes he has for many more years with his wife may be "burned to ashes," as if they were something physical that could actually be burned. What kind of analogy does Sullivan use in the sixth paragraph? Highlight textual evidence and make annotations to explain your ideas.

What does Ballou mean when he says that "American Civilization now leans on the triumph of the Government?" Why does he link the Civil War to the American Revolution as "a debt to America that must be repaid"?

## WRITING PROMPT

On the basis of the letter that Ballou wrote to his wife, do you think he feels that he led a good, fulfilling life? As you explain, use evidence from the text to support your response.

# CIVIL WAR JOURNAL

**NON-FICTION**
Louisa May Alcott
1861–1863

## INTRODUCTION

Louisa May Alcott is best known for her semi-autobiographical novel *Little Women*, but she also authored numerous other works and kept extensive journals about her life. Like many women who wanted to participate during the Civil War, Alcott volunteered as a nurse and served six weeks at a Union hospital in Washington, D.C. These excerpts from her personal journals document some of her experiences during the tumultuous period in American history

# "I've often longed to see a war, and now I have my wish."

## FIRST READ

1  *April.* [1861]—War declared with the South, and our Concord **company** went to Washington. A busy time getting them ready, and a sad day seeing them off, for in a little town like this we all seem like one family in times like these. At the station the scene was very dramatic, as the brave boys went away perhaps never to come back again.

2  I've often longed to see a war, and now I have my wish. I long to be a man, but as I can't fight, I will content myself with working for those who can. . . .

3  *September, October.* [1862]—. . . War news bad. Anxious faces, beating heart, and busy minds.

4  I like the stir in the air, and long for battle like a warhorse when he smells powder. The blood of the Mays is up!

5  *November.*—Thirty years old. Decided to go to Washington as a nurse if I could find a place. Help needed, and I love nursing, and *must* let out my pent-up energy in some new way. Winter is always a hard and a dull time, and if I am away there is one less to feed and warm and worry over.

6  I want new experiences, and am sure to get 'em if I go. So I've sent in my name, and bide my time writing tales, to leave all snug behind me, and mending up my old clothes,—for nurses don't need nice things, thank Heaven!

7  *December.*—On the 11th I received a note from Miss H. M. Stevenson telling me to start for Georgetown next day to fill a place in the Union Hotel Hospital. Mrs. Ropes of Boston was matron, and Miss Kendall of Plymouth was a nurse there, and though a hard place, help was needed. I was ready, and when my commander said "March!" I marched. Packed my trunk, and reported in B.[oston] that same evening.

NOTES

8　We had all been full of courage till the last moment came, then we all broke down. I realized that I had taken my life in my hand, and might never see them all again. I said, "Shall I stay, Mother?" as I hugged her close. "No, go! And the Lord be with you!" answered the **Spartan** woman, and till I turned the corner she bravely smiled and waved her wet handkerchief on the doorstep. Shall I ever see that dear old face again?

9　So I set forth in the December twilight, with May and Julian Hawthorne as an escort, feeling as if I was the son of the house going to war.

10　Friday, the 12th, was a very memorable day, spent in running all over Boston to get my pass, etc., calling for parcels, getting a tooth filled, and buying a veil,—my only purchase. A.C. gave me some old clothes, the dear Sewalls money for myself and boys, lots of love and help, and at 5 P.M., saying "goodby" to a group of tearful faces at the station, I started on my long journey, full of hope and sorrow, courage and plans.

11　A most interesting journey into a new world full of stirring sights and sounds, new adventures, and an ever growing sense of the great task I had undertaken.

12　I said my prayers as I went rushing through the country white with tents, all alive with patriotism, and already red with blood.

13　A solemn time, but I'm glad to live in it, and am sure it will do me good whether I come out alive or dead.

14　All went well, and I got to Georgetown one evening very tired. Was kindly welcomed, slept in my narrow bed with two other room-mates, and on the morrow began my new life by seeing a poor man die at dawn, and sitting all day between a boy with pneumonia and a man shot through the lungs. A strange day, but I did my best, and when I put mother's little black shawl round the boy while he sat up panting for breath, he smiled and said, "You are real motherly, ma'am." I felt as if I was getting on. The man only lay and stared with his big black eyes, and made me very nervous. But all were well behaved, and I sat looking at the twenty strong faces as they looked back at me,— hoping that I looked "motherly" to them, for my thirty years made me feel old, and the suffering round me made me long to comfort every one. . . .

15　*January.* [1863]—I never began the year in a stranger place than this, five hundred miles from home, alone among strangers, doing painful duties all day long, & leading a life of constant excitement in this greathouse surrounded by 3 or 4 hundred men in all stages of suffering, disease & death. Though often home sick, heart sick & worn out, I like it—find real pleasure in comforting tending & cheering these poor souls who seem to love me, to feel my sympathy though unspoken, & acknowledge my hearty good will in spite of the ignorance, awkwardness, & bashfulness which I cannot help showing in so new & trying a situation. The men are docile, respectful, & affectionate, with but few exceptions, truly lovable & manly many of them. John Suhre a Virginia blacksmith is the prince of patients, & though what we call a common man, in education & condition, to me is all that I could expect or ask from the first gentleman in the land. Under his plain speech & unpolished manner I seem to see a noble character, a heart as warm & tender as a woman's, a nature fresh & frank as any child's. He is about thirty, I think, tall & handsome, mortally wounded & dying royally, without **reproach**, repining, or remorse. Mrs. Ropes & myself love him & feel indignant that such a man should be so early lost, for though he might never distinguish himself before the world, his influence and example cannot be without effect, for real goodness is never wasted.

16   Mon 4th—I shall record the events of a day as a sample of the days I spend— Up at six, dress by gas light, run through my ward & fling up the windows though the men grumble & shiver; but the air is bad enough to breed a **pestilence** & as no notice is taken of our frequent appeals for better ventilation I must do what I can. Poke up the fire, add blankets, joke, coax, & command, but continue to open doors & windows as if life depended on it; mine does, & doubtless many another, for a more perfect pestilence-box than this house I never saw—cold, damp, dirty, full of vile odors from wounds, kitchens, wash rooms, & stables. No competent head, male or female, to right matters, & a jumble of good, bad, & indifferent nurses, surgeons & attendants to complicate the Chaos still more.

17   After this unwelcome progress through my **stifling** ward I go to breakfast with what appetite I may; find the inevitable fried beef, salt butter, husky bread & washy coffee; listen to the clack of eight women & a dozen men; the first silly, stupid or possessed of but one idea, the last absorbed in their breakfast & themselves to a degree that is both ludicrous and provoking, for all the dishes are ordered down the table *full* & returned *empty*; the conversation is entirely among themselves & each announces his opinion with an air of importance that frequently causes me to choke up in my cup or bolt my meals with undignified speed lest a laugh betray to these pompous beings that a "child's among them takin notes." Till noon I trot, trot, giving out rations, cutting up food for helpless "boys," washing faces, teaching my attendants how beds are made or floor swept, dressing wounds, taking Dr. Fitz Patrick's orders, (privately wishing all the time that he would be more gentle with my big babies,) dusting tables, sewing bandages, keeping my tray tidy, rushing up & down after pillows, bed linen, sponges, books & directions, till it seems as if I would joyfully pay down all I possess for fifteen minutes rest.

18   At twelve the big bell rings & up comes dinner for the boys who are always ready for it & never entirely satisfied. Soup, meat, potatoes, & bread is the bill of fare. Charley Thayer the attendant travels up & down the room serving out

NOTES

the rations, saving little for himself yet always thoughtful of his mates & patient as a woman with their helplessness. When dinner is over some sleep, many read, & others want letters written. This I like to do for they put in such odd things & express their ideas so comically I have great fun interiorally while as grave as possible exteriorly. A few of the men word their paragraphs well & make excellent letters. John's was the best of all I wrote. The answering of letters from friends after some one has died is the saddest & hardest duty a nurse has to do.

19  Supper at five sets every one to running that can run & when that flurry is over all settle down for the evening amusements which consist of newspapers, gossip, Drs last round, & for such as need them the final doses for the night. At nine the bell rings, gas is turned down & day nurses go to bed.

20  Night nurses go on duty, & sleep & death have the house all to themselves. . . .

21  My work is changed to night watching or half night & half day, from twelve to twelve. I like it as it leaves me time for a morning run which is what I need to keep well, for bad air, food, water, work & watching are getting to be too much for me. I trot up & down the streets in all directions, some times to the Heights, then half way to Washington, again to the hill over which the long trains of army wagons are constantly vanishing & ambulances appearing.

22  That way the fighting lies, & long to follow. . . .

 **THINK QUESTIONS**  CA-CCSS: CA.RI.8.1, CA.RI.8.4, CA.L.8.5

1.  Refer to one or more details in the text to support your understanding of why Louisa May Alcott was anxious to participate, in some way, in the Civil War—both from ideas that are explicitly stated and from ideas that you have inferred from clues in the text.

2.  In paragraphs 7–10, Alcott bids an emotional goodbye to her mother and then journeys to Boston to prepare for her trip. Why is leaving such a big decision for Louisa? What does her decision say about her character? Cite textual evidence to support your answer.

3.  As Louisa May Alcott begins her duties in Georgetown, she feels conflicting emotions. Cite evidence from the text that shows how she feels at the beginning of the new year, 1863.

4.  Use context to determine the meaning of the word **Spartan** as it is used in "Civil War Journal." Write your definition of *Spartan* and tell how you arrived at it.

5.  Alcott describes the ward she works in as a **pestilence**-box. Use context clues in the text to determine the meaning of *pestilence*, and explain how you found it.

# CLOSE READ
CA-CCSS: CA.RI.8.1, CA.RI.8.3, CA.RI.8.4, CA.RI.8.5, CA.RI.8.6, CA.W.8.4, CA.W.8.5, CA.W.8.6, CA.W.8.10

Reread the excerpt from *Civil War Journal*. As you reread, complete the Focus Questions below. Then use your answers and annotations from the questions to help you complete the Writing Prompt.

## FOCUS QUESTIONS

1. A journal is a daily record. If it is not kept for business reasons, it is often private and, like a diary, records the writer's personal feelings and reactions to events. Journals often feature informal language and may even contain run-on sentences and other grammatical errors. Find features of journal writing in Louisa May Alcott's "Civil War Journal" that give it an informal tone, and support your answers with textual evidence.

2. What does Alcott reveal in her January 4th entry about the difficulty of her days in the ward, and also the fact that she may want to take her journal entries and turn them into a book one day? Support your answer with textual evidence.

3. Highlight and annotate Alcott's descriptions of the soldiers she treats. How does she make distinctions between each of these individuals?

4. What does Louisa May Alcott's attitude toward her duties in the ward, as well as the last sentence in this excerpt, reveal about her character? Highlight textual evidence to support your answer.

5. Write an annotation to explain how the last sentence of the journal contributes to Alcott's overall text structure.

6. The Civil War changed the way many Americans felt about war and about themselves. At the beginning of her journal, what were Alcott's feelings about war and about her role in the war? How did the war and her time as a nurse for Union soldiers encourage Alcott to redefine herself? Highlight textual evidence to support your answer.

## WRITING PROMPT

Consider the events that take place in Alcott's *Civil War Journal*. How do these events and the way they are presented help to indicate the text structure she employs in her writing? Give specific examples to support your answer.

# THE RED BADGE OF COURAGE

FICTION
Stephen Crane
1895

## INTRODUCTION

studysync tv

Published in 1894, the Civil War novel *The Red Badge of Courage* was popularized through a serial release in hundreds of newspapers throughout the country. Although author Stephen Crane never witnessed a battle, his vivid descriptions of war and the psychology of its soldiers captured readers' imaginations and brought home the stark realities of America's bloody divide. The story follows young Private Henry Fleming as he experiences firsthand the horrors of battle and a personal crisis of will. In these excerpts we join Henry on his journey through both internal and external landscapes in pursuit of courage.

# "So he went far, seeking dark and intricate places."

## FIRST READ

*Excerpt from Chapter 1*

1　There was a youthful private who listened with eager ears to the words of the tall soldier and to the varied comments of his comrades. After receiving a fill of discussions concerning marches and attacks, he went to his hut and crawled through an intricate hole that served it as a door. He wished to be alone with some new thoughts that had lately come to him.

2　He lay down on a wide bunk that stretched across the end of the room. In the other end, cracker boxes were made to serve as furniture. They were grouped about the fireplace. A picture from an illustrated weekly was upon the log walls, and three rifles were paralleled on pegs. Equipments hung on handy projections, and some tin dishes lay upon a small pile of firewood. A folded tent was serving as a roof. The sunlight, without, beating upon it, made it glow a light yellow shade. A small window shot an oblique square of whiter light upon the cluttered floor. The smoke from the fire at times neglected the clay chimney and wreathed into the room, and this flimsy chimney of clay and sticks made endless threats to set ablaze the whole establishment.

3　The youth was in a little trance of astonishment. So they were at last going to fight. On the morrow, perhaps, there would be a battle, and he would be in it. For a time he was obliged to labor to make himself believe. He could not accept with assurance an omen that he was about to mingle in one of those great affairs of the earth.

4　He had, of course, dreamed of battles all his life—of vague and bloody conflicts that had thrilled him with their sweep and fire. In visions he had seen himself in many struggles. He had imagined peoples secure in the shadow of his eagle-eyed prowess. But awake he had regarded battles as crimson blotches on the pages of the past. He had put them as things of the bygone with his thought-images of heavy crowns and high castles. There was a portion of the world's history which he had regarded as the time of wars, but it, he thought, had been long gone over the horizon and had disappeared forever.

5   From his home his youthful eyes had looked upon the war in his own country with distrust. It must be some sort of a play affair. He had long despaired of witnessing a Greeklike struggle. Such would be no more, he had said. Men were better, or more timid. Secular and religious education had effaced the throat-grappling instinct, or else firm finance held in check the passions.

6   He had burned several times to enlist. Tales of great movements shook the land. They might not be distinctly Homeric, but there seemed to be much glory in them. He had read of marches, sieges, conflicts, and he had longed to see it all. His busy mind had drawn for him large pictures extravagant in color, **lurid** with breathless deeds.

7   But his mother had discouraged him. She had affected to look with some contempt upon the quality of his war **ardor** and patriotism. She could calmly seat herself and with no apparent difficulty give him many hundreds of reasons why he was of vastly more importance on the farm than on the field of battle. She had had certain ways of expression that told him that her statements on the subject came from a deep conviction. Moreover, on her side, was his belief that her ethical motive in the argument was **impregnable**.

8   At last, however, he had made firm rebellion against this yellow light thrown upon the color of his ambitions. The newspapers, the gossip of the village, his own picturings, had aroused him to an uncheckable degree. They were in truth fighting finely down there. Almost every day the newspaper printed accounts of a decisive victory.

*Excerpt from Chapter 7*

9   The youth cringed as if discovered in a crime. By heavens, they had won after all! The imbecile line had remained and become victors. He could hear cheering.

10  He lifted himself upon his toes and looked in the direction of the fight. A yellow fog lay wallowing on the treetops. From beneath it came the clatter of musketry. Hoarse cries told of an advance.

11  He turned away amazed and angry. He felt that he had been wronged.

12  He had fled, he told himself, because annihilation approached. He had done a good part in saving himself, who was a little piece of the army. He had considered the time, he said, to be one in which it was the duty of every little piece to rescue itself if possible. Later the officers could fit the little pieces together again, and make a battle front. If none of the little pieces were wise

enough to save themselves from the flurry of death at such a time, why, then, where would be the army? It was all plain that he had proceeded according to very correct and commendable rules. His actions had been **sagacious** things. They had been full of strategy. They were the work of a master's legs.

13 Thoughts of his comrades came to him. The brittle blue line had withstood the blows and won. He grew bitter over it. It seemed that the blind ignorance and stupidity of those little pieces had betrayed him. He had been overturned and crushed by their lack of sense in holding the position, when intelligent deliberation would have convinced them that it was impossible. He, the enlightened man who looks afar in the dark, had fled because of his superior perceptions and knowledge. He felt a great anger against his comrades. He knew it could be proved that they had been fools.

14 He wondered what they would remark when later he appeared in camp. His mind heard howls of derision. Their density would not enable them to understand his sharper point of view.

15 He began to pity himself acutely. He was ill used. He was trodden beneath the feet of an iron injustice. He had proceeded with wisdom and from the most righteous motives under heaven's blue only to be frustrated by hateful circumstances.

16 A dull, animal-like rebellion against his fellows, war in the abstract, and fate grew within him. He shambled along with bowed head, his brain in a tumult of agony and despair. When he looked loweringly up, quivering at each sound, his eyes had the expression of those of a criminal who thinks his guilt little and his punishment great, and knows that he can find no words.

17 He went from the fields into a thick woods, as if resolved to bury himself. He wished to get out of hearing of the crackling shots which were to him like voices.

18 The ground was cluttered with vines and bushes, and the trees grew close and spread out like bouquets. He was obliged to force his way with much noise. The creepers, catching against his legs, cried out harshly as their sprays were torn from the barks of trees. The swishing saplings tried to make known his presence to the world. He could not **conciliate** the forest. As he made his way, it was always calling out protestations. When he separated embraces of trees and vines the disturbed foliages waved their arms and turned their face leaves toward him. He dreaded lest these noisy motions and cries should bring men to look at him. So he went far, seeking dark and intricate places.

19 After a time the sound of musketry grew faint and the cannon boomed in the distance. The sun, suddenly apparent, blazed among the trees. The insects

were making rhythmical noises. They seemed to be grinding their teeth in unison. A woodpecker stuck his impudent head around the side of a tree. A bird flew on lighthearted wing.

20  Off was the rumble of death. It seemed now that Nature had no ears.

 THINK QUESTIONS  CA-CCSS: CA.RL.8.1, CA.L.8.4a, CA.L.8.4b, CA.SL.8.1a, CA.SL.8.1c, CA.SL.8.1d, CA.SL.8.3

1.  Refer to one or more details in Chapter 1 that describe the narrator's ideas about war, both before he joins the army and when he finds out he'll actually be going into battle. Cite textual evidence that is directly stated as well as inferences you have made from clues in the text.

2.  At first, the narrator looks on the Civil War with distrust, as if it were some "play affair." What happens to change his mind about the war and encourage him to enlist? Cite textual evidence to support your answer.

3.  Why does Henry consider his fellow soldiers "imbeciles," or "the imbecile line" after they manage to win the battle in which Henry was also fighting? Support your answer with textual evidence.

4.  Use context clues to determine the meaning of the word **ardor** as it is used in *The Red Badge of Courage*. Write your definition of **ardor** and tell how you arrived at it.

5.  Remembering that the Latin prefix *im-* means "not," use the context clues provided in the passage to determine the meaning of **impregnable.** Write your definition of impregnable and explain how you arrived at it.

# CLOSE READ

CA-CCSS: CA.RL.8.1, CA.RL.8.2, CA.RL.8.3, CA.RL.8.4, CA.W.8.4, CA.W.8.5, CA.W.8.6, CA.W.8.10, CA.L.8.2c, CA.L.8.5a

Reread the excerpt from *The Red Badge of Courage*. As you reread, complete the Focus Questions below. Then use your answers and annotations from the questions to help you complete the Writing Prompt.

## FOCUS QUESTIONS

1. As you reread Chapter 7 of *The Red Badge of Courage*, highlight the following sentences in paragraphs 9 and 11: *The youth cringed as if discovered in a crime. He turned away amazed and angry. He felt that he had been wronged.* How do these three sentences reveal how conflicted Henry feels after he runs away from the battle? In what way do they provide clues about the central theme? Cite textual evidence to support your answer.

2. In paragraph 12, Henry feels that his actions had been full of strategy. He thinks "they were the work of a master's legs." What does he mean by this figure of speech? How is Henry attempting to convince himself that his actions were praiseworthy? Support your answer with textual evidence.

3. What do Henry's conclusions about how the other soldiers will react when he returns to camp reveal about his character? Highlight textual evidence to explain your answer.

4. How does the author use personification to highlight the inner conflict Henry feels as he runs farther and farther away from the battle, and into the woods? Highlight textual evidence and make annotations to explain your answer.

5. What is the overarching theme of this excerpt from *The Red Badge of Courage*? Highlight specific evidence from the text to support your answer. Then make annotations to state the theme in one or two sentences.

6. The Civil War challenged and changed many Americans. How do the soldier's conflicts about war reflect the conflicts of many Americans during this time period? Highlight specific evidence from the text to support your answer.

## WRITING PROMPT

How does the point of view Stephen Crane uses in *The Red Badge of Courage* help you understand the thoughts, reactions, and feelings of Private Henry Fleming? How does the use of personification contribute to the text? Use your understanding of point of view and personification to determine the themes that emerge in this excerpt. Support your writing with evidence from the text.

# GETTYSBURG ADDRESS

**NON-FICTION**
Abraham Lincoln
1863

## INTRODUCTION

studysync tv

O n November 19, 1863, Abraham Lincoln gives perhaps the most famous speech in American history. Evoking the spirit of the nation's founding fathers, Lincoln stands beside the quiet Civil War battlefield of Gettysburg, Pennsylvania, and consecrates the hallowed ground to the sacrifice of the soldiers who fought and died there. Reasserting the commitment to preserve the Union and the pursuit of the principles for which it was founded, the elegant words of the Gettysburg Address stand as testament to the greatest challenge in American history.

# "[G]overnment of the people, by the people, for the people, shall not perish from the earth."

## FIRST READ

1   Four **score** and seven years ago our fathers brought forth on this continent, a new nation, conceived in liberty, and dedicated to the **proposition** that all men are created equal.

2   Now we are engaged in a great civil war, testing whether that nation, or any nation so conceived and so dedicated, can long endure. We are met on a great battlefield of that war. We have come to dedicate a portion of that field, as a final resting place for those who here gave their lives that that nation might live. It is altogether fitting and proper that we should do this.

3   But in a larger sense, we cannot dedicate—we cannot **consecrate**—we cannot **hallow**—this ground. The brave men, living and dead, who struggled here, have consecrated it, far above our poor power to add or detract. The world will little note, nor long remember what we say here, but it can never forget what they did here. It is for us, the living, rather to be dedicated here to the unfinished work which they who fought here have thus far so nobly advanced.

4   It is rather for us to be here dedicated to the great task remaining before us, that from these honored dead we take increased **devotion** to that cause for which they gave the last full measure of devotion; that we here highly resolve that these dead shall not have died in vain; that this nation, under God, shall have a new birth of freedom, and that government of the people, by the people, for the people, shall not perish from the earth.

## THINK QUESTIONS
CA-CCSS: CA.RI.8.1, CA.RI.8.4, CA.L.8.4a, CA.L.8.5b, CA.SL.8.1d, CA.SL.8.2, CA.SL.8.3

1. Write two or three sentences explaining why Lincoln was giving the Gettysburg address. Cite textual evidence to support your answer.

2. Using textual evidence, describe what Lincoln felt the nation should do to prevent the fallen soldiers from having "died in vain."

3. Lincoln said that "in a larger sense," he and the others gathered at Gettysburg "cannot" do something. What was it that they could not do, and why not, according to Lincoln? What did he say they should do instead? Cite textual evidence to support your answer.

4. Use the context of the use of the word **proposition** in the first sentence to determine its definition. Write its definition and indicate the context clues that helped you arrive at this meaning.

5. Based on the relationships among the words *dedicate, consecrate,* and *hallow* in the context of the third paragraph, what might be some synonyms for **consecrate?** How does using synonyms help you understand the word and check for meaning?

# CLOSE READ
CA-CCSS: CA.RI.8.1, CA.RI.8.2, CA.RI.8.8, CA.W.8.4, CA.W.8.5, CA.W.8.6, CA.W.8.9b, CA.W.8.10, CA.SL.8.3

Reread the text of the Gettysburg Address. As you reread, complete the Focus Questions below. Then use your answers and annotations from the questions to help you complete the Writing Prompt.

## FOCUS QUESTIONS

1. As you reread the text of the Gettysburg Address, remember that one of the main ideas is that the Civil War is being fought to preserve the Union. What are some aspects of the text that seem to fit this main idea? Highlight evidence to support your ideas and write annotations to explain your choices.

2. Highlight some key details in paragraph 3 of the text. Then use your details to write a one- or two-sentence summary of that paragraph.

3. Identify a different main idea than the one discussed in Question #1. Annotate each paragraph of the text to explain how each one supports this main idea.

4. Lincoln argues that the war must continue. Highlight evidence that he uses to support this argument. Annotate each piece of evidence to explain how it proves this claim.

5. How does Lincoln believe that the Civil War will redefine America? Highlight Lincoln's claim about how the nation will change after the war. In your annotation, summarize his argument in your own words.

## WRITING PROMPT

Choose one paragraph of the Gettysburg Address. What is the main idea of the paragraph? How does this main idea tie to a larger argument Lincoln is making throughout the entire speech? Focus specifically on the structure of the paragraph and how the sentences in the paragraph build on each other to convey the main idea. Respond in an argumentative essay of 300 words. Support your ideas with evidence from the text.

# CHASING LINCOLN'S KILLER

NON-FICTION
James L. Swanson
2009

## INTRODUCTION

James L. Swanson's fascination with the assassination of Abraham Lincoln traces back to his childhood and the birthday he shares with the famous president. In researching his book, the author pored through trial transcripts, interviews, photographs, and other archival materials to fully understand the circumstances surrounding the infamous events at Ford's Theatre. Here, he takes readers into the mind of Lincoln's killer.

# "Now, by God, I'll put him through."

## FIRST READ

*From the Prologue*

1   John Wilkes Booth was drinking with a friend at a saloon on Houston Street in New York City. Booth struck the bar table with his fist and regretted a lost opportunity. "What an excellent chance I had, if I wished, to kill the President on Inauguration day! I was on the stand, as close to him nearly as I am to you."

2   Crushed by the fall of Richmond, the former rebel capital, John Wilkes Booth left New York City on April 8 and returned to Washington. The news there was terrible for him. On April 9, Confederate General Robert E. Lee and the Army of Northern Virginia surrendered to Union General Grant at Appomattox. Booth wandered the streets in despair.

3   On April 10, Abraham Lincoln appeared at a second-floor window of the executive mansion, as the White House was known then, to greet a crowd of citizens celebrating General Lee's surrender. Lincoln did not have a prepared speech. He used humor to entertain the audience.

4   On the night of April 11, a torchlight parade of a few thousand people, with bands and banners, assembled on the semi-circular driveway in front of the Executive Mansion. This time Lincoln delivered a long speech, without gloating over the Union victory. He intended to prepare the people for the long task of rebuilding the South. When someone in the crowd shouted that he couldn't see the president Lincoln's son, Tad, volunteered to illuminate his father. When Lincoln dropped each page of his speech to the floor it was Tad who scooped them up.

5   Lincoln described recent events and gave credit to Union General Grant and his officers for the successful end to the war. He also discussed his desire that black people, especially those who had served in the Union army, be granted the right to vote. As Lincoln spoke, one observer, Mrs. Lincoln's

dressmaker, standing a few steps from the president, remarked that the lamplight made him "stand out boldly in the darkness." The perfect target. "What an easy matter would it be to kill the President as he stands there! He could be shot down from the crowd," she whispered," and no one would be able to tell who fired the shot."

6    In that crowd standing below Lincoln was John Wilkes Booth. He turned to his companion, David Herold, and objected to the idea that blacks and former slaves would become voting citizens. In the darkness Booth threatened to kill Lincoln: "Now, by God, I'll put him through."

7    And as Booth left the White House grounds he spoke to companion and co-conspirator, Lewis Powell: "that is the last speech he will ever give."

8    On the evening of April 13, Washington celebrated the end of the war with a grand illumination of the city. Public buildings and private homes glowed from candles, torches, gaslights, and fireworks. It was the most beautiful night in the history of the capital.

9    John Wilkes Booth saw all of this-the grand illumination, the crowds delirious with joy, the insults to the fallen Confederacy and her leaders. He returned to his room at the National Hotel after midnight. He could not sleep.

*From Chapter I*

10    John Wilkes Booth awoke depressed. It was Good Friday morning, April 14, 1865. The Confederacy was dead. His cause was lost and his dreams of glory over. He did not know that this day, after enduring more than a week of bad news, he would enjoy a stunning reversal of fortune. No, all he knew this morning when he crawled out of bed was that he could not stand another day of Union victory celebrations.

11    Booth assumed that the day would unfold as the latest in a blur of days that had begun on April 3 when the Confederate capital, Richmond, fell to the Union. The very next day, the **tyrant** Abraham Lincoln had visited his captive prize and had the nerve to sit behind the desk occupied by the first and last president of the Confederate States of America, Jefferson Davis. Then, on April 9, at Appomattox Court House, Virginia, General Robert E. Lee and his beloved Army of Northern Virginia surrendered. Two days later, Lincoln had made a speech proposing to give blacks the right to vote and last night, April 13, all of Washington had celebrated with a grand illumination of the city. These days had been the worst in Booth's young life.

12    Twenty-six years old, impossibly vain, an extremely talented actor, and a star member of a celebrated theatrical family, John Wilkes Booth was willing to throw away fame, wealth, and a promising future for the cause of the

Confederacy. He was the son of the legendary actor Junius Brutus Booth and brother to Edwin Booth, one of the finest actors of his generation. Handsome and appealing, he was instantly recognizable to thousands of fans in both the North and South. His physical beauty astonished all who saw him. A fellow actor described his eyes as being "like living jewels." Booth's passions included fine clothing, Southern honor, good manners, beautiful women, and the romance of lost causes.

13   On April 14, Booth's day began in the dining room of the National Hotel, where he ate breakfast. Around noon, he walked over to nearby Ford's Theatre, a block from Pennsylvania Avenue, to pick up his mail: Ford's **customarily** accepted personal mail as a **courtesy** to actors. There was a letter for Booth.

14   That same morning a letter arrived at the theater for someone else. There had been no time to mail it, so its sender, First Lady Mary Todd Lincoln, had used the president's messenger to hand-deliver it to the owners of Ford's Theater. The mere arrival of the White House messenger told them the president was coming to the theater tonight! Yes, the president and Mrs. Lincoln would attend this evening's performance of the popular if silly comedy *Our American Cousin*. But the big news was that General Ulysses S. Grant was coming with them.

15   The Lincolns had given the Fords enough advance notice for the **proprietors** to decorate and join together the two theater boxes — seven and eight — that, by removal of a partition, formed the president's box at the theater.

16   By the time Booth arrived at the Theater, the president's messenger had come and gone. Some time between noon and 12:30 P.M., as he sat on the top step in front of the entrance to Ford's reading his letter, Booth heard the big news: In just eight hours, the man who was the subject of all his hating and plotting would stand on the very stone steps where he now sat. Here. Of all places, Lincoln was coming here.

17   Booth knew the layout of Ford's **intimately**: the exact spot on Tenth Street where Lincoln would step out of his carriage, the box inside the theater where the president sat when he came to a performance, the route Lincoln could walk and the staircase he would climb to the box, the dark underground passageway beneath the stage. He knew the narrow hallway behind the stage where a back door opened to the alley and he knew how the president's box hung directly above the stage.

18   Though Booth had never acted in *Our American Cousin*, he knew it well — its length, its scenes, its players and, most important, the number of actors onstage at any given moment during the performance. It was perfect. He would not have to hunt Lincoln. The president was coming to him.

Excerpted from *Chasing Lincoln's Killer* by James Swanson, published by Scholastic Inc.

 THINK QUESTIONS    CA-CCSS: CA.RI.8.1, CA.L.8.4a, CA.L.8.4b

1.  What were some of the key events that outraged John Wilkes Booth and led him to decide to assassinate President Lincoln? Cite evidence from the text to support your answer.

2.  Why did Booth go to Ford's Theater on the morning of April 14, 1865? What unexpected news did he hear while at the theater? Cite evidence from the text to support your answers.

3.  Citing evidence from the text, explain why Ford's Theater was an ideal place for Booth to attempt to assassinate Lincoln.

4.  Use context clues in the passage to determine the meaning of the word **tyrant** as it is used in *Chasing Lincoln's Killer*. Write your definition of *tyrant* and explain how you arrived at the definition.

5.  Remembering that the Latin suffix *-or* means "a person who has," and also the meaning of the base word *property*, determine the meaning of **proprietor**. Write your definition of *proprietor* and explain how you arrived at it.

# CLOSE READ
CA-CCSS: CA.RI.8.1, CA.RI.8.3, CA.RI.8.4, CA.W.8.4, CA.W.8.5, CA.W.8.6, CA.W.8.9b, CA.W.8.10

Reread the excerpt from *Chasing Lincoln's Killer*. As you reread, complete the Focus Questions below. Then use your answers and annotations from the questions to help you complete the Writing Prompt.

## FOCUS QUESTIONS

1.  Explain how, throughout the text, the author presents the South's defeat in the Civil War as a deeply personal event for John Wilkes Booth. Highlight evidence from the text and make annotations to support your answer.

2.  How did John Wilkes Booth's profession help him with his plan to kill the president? Highlight your textual evidence and make annotations to explain your choices.

3.  What idea expressed by Lincoln in his speech at the Executive Mansion on the evening of April 11th angered Booth the most? Why did this particular idea anger Booth? Highlight textual evidence that supports your answer and write an annotation to explain it.

4.  What event occurred on April 4th that outraged Booth and, according to the author, made him think of Lincoln as a *tyrant*? Why might Lincoln's action on this day have affected Booth so negatively? Highlight evidence from the text and make annotations to explain your choices.

5.  What evidence does the author, James Swanson, include in the passage in support of the idea that John Wilkes Booth was a somewhat reckless person? Highlight details that support your answer and write an annotation to explain it.

## WRITING PROMPT

In this excerpt of *Chasing Lincoln's Killer*, how does the author's focus on John Wilkes Booth affect the way the events are developed? Why do you think the author takes this approach? In your analysis, include evidence that is explicitly stated, as well as inferences you draw from the text. Include textual evidence to support your inferences.

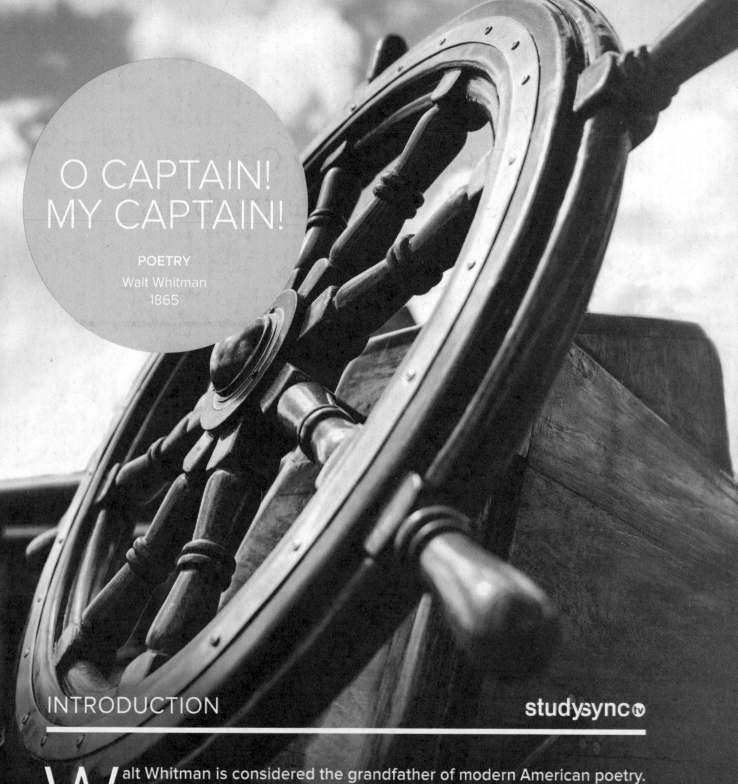

# O CAPTAIN! MY CAPTAIN!

POETRY
Walt Whitman
1865

## INTRODUCTION

Walt Whitman is considered the grandfather of modern American poetry. Largely self-taught, he broke from the traditional strictures of verse, writing long, robust lines brimming with populism, physicality, and personal content. Written to elegize the recently assassinated Abraham Lincoln, "O Captain! My Captain!" strikes a distinctly patriotic note, and marked a departure from Whitman's typical style with its conventional meter and rhyme. The poem was collected into *Leaves of Grass*, of which Whitman wrote, "This is no book; who touches this touches a man."

# "O Captain! my Captain! rise up and hear the bells"

## FIRST READ

1   O Captain! my Captain! our fearful trip is done,
2   The ship has **weather'd** every rack, the prize we sought is won,
3   The port is near, the bells I hear, the people all **exulting**,
4   While follow eyes the steady keel, the vessel grim and daring;
5      But O heart! heart! heart!
6        O the bleeding drops of red,
7         Where on the deck my Captain lies,
8          Fallen cold and dead.

9   O Captain! my Captain! rise up and hear the bells;
10  Rise up—for you the flag is flung—for you the bugle **trills**,
11  For you bouquets and ribbon'd wreaths—for you the shores a-crowding,
12  For you they call, the swaying mass, their eager faces turning;
13     Here Captain! dear father!
14      This arm beneath your head!
15       It is some dream that on the deck,
16        You've fallen cold and dead.

17  My Captain does not answer, his lips are pale and still,
18  My father does not feel my arm, he has no pulse nor will,
19  The ship is anchor'd safe and sound, its voyage closed and done,
20  From fearful trip the **victor** ship comes in with object won;
21     Exult O shores, and ring O bells!
22     But I with **mournful** tread,
23      Walk the deck my Captain lies,
24       Fallen cold and dead.

THINK QUESTIONS   CA-CCSS: CA.RL.8.1, CA.L.8.4a, CA.SL.8.1a, CA.SL.8.1b, CA.SL.8.1c, CA.SL.8.1d

1.  What clues does Walt Whitman provide in the opening stanza of the poem that suggest the captain did not die a natural death? Use textual evidence to support your answer.

2.  Describe the details Whitman provides in the second stanza that indicate the fallen Captain was a hero. Use textual evidence to support your answer.

3.  In what way does the narrator feel different from the crowds that line the shore waiting for the ship to arrive? Cite details from the text to explain your answer.

4.  Use context to determine the meaning of the word **trills** as it is used in "O Captain! My Captain!" Write your definition of *trills* and explain how you arrived at it.

5.  Use context to determine the meaning of the word **exulting** as it is used in "O Captain! My Captain!" Write your definition of *exulting* and explain how you arrived at it. Then explain what the port represents in the poem.

Please note that excerpts and passages in the StudySync® library and this workbook are intended as touchstones to generate interest in an author's work. The excerpts and passages do not substitute for the reading of entire texts, and StudySync® strongly recommends that students seek out and purchase the whole literary or informational work in order to experience it as the author intended. Links to online resellers are available in our digital library. In addition, complete works may be ordered through an authorized reseller by filling out and returning to StudySync® the order form enclosed in this workbook.

Reading & Writing Companion   **443**

# CLOSE READ

CA-CCSS: CA.RL.8.1, CA.RL.8.4, CA.RL.8.5, CA.L.8.5c, CA.W.8.4, CA.W.8.5, CA.W.8.6, CA.W.8.10

Reread the poem "Oh Captain! My Captain!" As you reread, complete the Focus Questions below. Then use your answers and annotations from the questions to help you complete the Writing Prompt.

 FOCUS QUESTIONS

1. Reread the four indented lines at the end of each stanza in "O Captain! My Captain!". How does each of these show a progression, from the fact of Lincoln's death, the initial disbelief, to the final reluctant acceptance that the "Captain," or president, is dead? What are some of the words, phrases, and poetic devices that Whitman uses to show this progression? Use the annotation tool to paraphrase your responses.

2. Highlight evidence that Walt Whitman uses the metaphor of a captain steering a ship through rough and dangerous weather to explore the idea of a commander-in-chief guiding a nation through a war. Make annotations to explain why this is or is not an effective metaphor.

3. Reread "O Captain! My Captain!", paying close attention to the way Whitman has structured each stanza. Highlight where the structure changes in the poem, and how Whitman shifts

between celebration and loss. What effect does this have on the reader? Make annotations to describe how the focus shifts.

4. Reread the first stanza of "O Captain! My Captain!" and highlight the words *exulting* and *vessel*. Use a dictionary to find the denotation of each word. Ask yourself how *exulting* and *vessel* fit into the larger meaning of the poem. What do these words connote in this context? Make annotations to record your reasoning.

5. How does Whitman's use of an apostrophe in the last four lines of the poem connect with his references to both bells and shores earlier in the poem? How do these final four lines in the last stanza fully reveal the narrator's feelings about the poem's events, and indirectly the effects of the Civil War on the country? Use textual evidence to support your answer.

## WRITING PROMPT

Walt Whitman uses an extended metaphor in "O Captain! My Captain!" to compare a ship and its captain to a nation and its head of state. Use your understanding of extended metaphor to write a short narrative about an event or a person that you feel deserves a tribute, and how you might use an extended metaphor to write it. Then write one or two stanzas of a poem using this metaphor. Decide on a poetic structure that suits your topic, and use your understanding of connotation and denotation to highlight and emphasize the meaning of the poem.

# NARRATIVE OF THE LIFE OF ADA LEE, AN AMERICAN FARM GIRL

English Language
Development

**FICTION**

# INTRODUCTION

"Narrative of the Life of Ada Lee, an American Farm Girl" is a historical fiction story of a young woman doing everything in her power to achieve her goals even though the law and culture of the time are working against her. Ada Lee's relentless pursuit of an equal education reveals what it can take to change minds and fight for what is right.

# "I wished that women could do anything we wanted to, and I set out to find a way to change the law..."

## FIRST READ

1   I lowered myself down onto the stool and dug my heels into the barn's dirt floor. "You know I love you, Bessie," I whispered dreamily to our prized dairy cow, "but I'm not going to be with you for much longer. I am going to college." A **secret** grin spread slowly across my face. It was the first time I had said my plan out loud. "I know what you're thinking, Bessie," I continued, patting her gently. Women could not go to college, but I had heard about a college on the east coast that would accept female students. Even though the school was far away and the workload might be too hard for me given my limited education, I was determined to **enroll**. After all, I had taught myself to read. Learning from a teacher couldn't be harder than that. "It's going to be hard, Bessie, but I will go to college and become a lawyer."

2   Life on the east coast was different than I had expected it to be. I missed my life on the farm terribly, and the pile of law books that rested on my desk practically reached the ceiling. They were filled with **incomprehensible** legal **terminology** that I hadn't much use for when I was back home. I knew I needed to get some help if I were going to succeed. There was a young man in the law program with me who came from a long line of lawyers. His name was John Wilson. I flashed him a wide smile and cleverly told him I'd exchange home-cooked meals for some tutoring. He gladly accepted.

3   John and I worked together intensely from then on. By the time we had earned our law degrees, we had grown quite close. We were married the day after graduation. It was my **earnest** desire that we would open a law office together and continue working side by side. The state legislature, however, had other plans. Even though I had earned a law degree, the state stubbornly would not grant me a license to actually practice law because I was a woman.

4   My husband was not bothered by this turn of events. He had loved studying with me, but he was happy to provide for his family while I ran our home. I was devastated. I didn't have to go to college to be a homemaker. I spent my days bored, **grieving** for the career I'd never have. I wished that I had never heard of the college, because then I'd be a happy wife. But then I wished something else. I wished that women could do anything we wanted to, and I set out to find a way to change the law so we could.

 USING LANGUAGE   CA-CCSS: ELD.PI.8.1.Ex

Complete the sentences by filling in the blanks.

1.  Find the sentence in paragraph 1 that tells what Ada did with her plan.

    It was the first time I _____ my plan out loud.

2.  Find the sentence in paragraph 1 that tells about women's ability to go to college.

    Women _____ to college, but I had heard about a college on the east coast that _____ female students.

3.  Find the sentence in paragraph 1 that tells why Ada might struggle in college.

    Even though the school _____ far away and the workload _____ too hard for me given my limited education, I was determined to enroll.

4.  Find the sentence in paragraph 1 that tells how Ada learned to read.

    After all, I _____ myself _____.

5.  Find the sentence in paragraph 1 that tells what Ada will do.

    "It's going to be hard, Bessie, but I _____ to college and _____ a lawyer."

Please note that excerpts and passages in the StudySync® library and this workbook are intended as touchstones to generate interest in an author's work. The excerpts and passages do not substitute for the reading of entire texts, and StudySync® strongly recommends that students seek out and purchase the whole literary or informational work in order to experience it as the author intended. Links to online resellers are available in our digital library. In addition, complete works may be ordered through an authorized reseller by filling out and returning to StudySync® the order form enclosed in this workbook.

Reading & Writing
Companion   **447**

## MEANINGFUL INTERACTIONS CA-CCSS: ELD.PI.8.1.Ex

Work with your group to discuss your first impressions of the text. First, summarize the major events of the story. Then, discuss what you think of Ada and her struggle. Use the speaking frames to ask and answer relevant questions during your discussion. Last, use the self-assessment rubric to evaluate your participation in the discussion.

- What happens at the beginning of the story?
  At the beginning of the story, Ada . . .

- Where does Ada go?
  Ada goes to . . .

- Who does Ada meet in college? What happens between them?
  Ada meets . . . They . . .

- Why does Ada . . . ?

- What do you think about . . . ?

- I think you said . . . Why do you think that . . . ?

- I agree/disagree because . . .

## SELF-ASSESSMENT RUBRIC CA-CCSS: ELD.PI.8.1.Ex

| | 4 I did this well. | 3 I did this pretty well. | 2 I did this a little bit. | 1 I did not do this. |
|---|---|---|---|---|
| I took an active part with others in doing the assigned task. | | | | |
| I contributed effectively to the group's discussion. | | | | |
| I asked relevant questions that helped the group understand the story. | | | | |
| I asked group members relevant questions about what they thought of the story. | | | | |
| I answered questions clearly. | | | | |

# REREAD

Reread paragraphs 1 and 2 of "Narrative of the Life of Ada Lee, an American Farm Girl." After you reread, complete the Using Language and Meaningful Interactions activities.

## USING LANGUAGE   CA-CCSS: ELD.PII.8.2.a.Ex

Read each quotation from the text and note the referring word in bold. Then complete the chart by choosing the type of referring word from the options and determining the noun that the bolded word refers to.

| Type of Referring Word Options | |
|---|---|
| pronoun | synonym |

| Quotation | Type of Referring Word | Noun |
|---|---|---|
| "I know what you're thinking, Bessie," I continued, patting **her** gently. | | |
| Women could not go to college, but I had heard about a college on the east coast that would accept female students. Even though the **school** was far away and the workload might be too hard for me given my limited education, I was determined to enroll. | | |
| There was a young man in the law program with me **who** came from a long line of lawyers. | | |
| His name was John Wilson. I flashed **him** a wide smile and cleverly told **him** I'd exchange home-cooked meals for some tutoring. | | |

## MEANINGFUL INTERACTIONS   CA-CCSS: ELD.PI.8.1.Ex, ELD.PII.8.1.Ex

Work with your group to paraphrase the key ideas and events of the text. Use the speaking frames to guide your discussion. Then complete the structure chart by filling in the major events of the story. Some events have been filled in for you. Last, use the self-assessment rubric to evaluate your participation in the discussion.

- What other words could you use to say . . . ?

- What other words or phrases mean the same as . . . ?

- When did . . . happen?

- Did . . . happen before or after . . . ?

| First | Then | Last |
|---|---|---|
| Ada sits in the barn. | | Ada worries college might be hard. |
| | | |
| | | |

## SELF-ASSESSMENT RUBRIC   CA-CCSS: ELD.PI.8.1.Ex

| | 4<br>I did this well. | 3<br>I did this pretty well. | 2<br>I did this a little bit. | 1<br>I did not do this. |
|---|---|---|---|---|
| I took an active part with others in doing the assigned task. | | | | |
| I contributed effectively to the group's decisions. | | | | |
| I was able to put events in the right order. | | | | |
| I paraphrased the key ideas from the text concisely and accurately. | | | | |

# REREAD

Reread paragraphs 3 and 4 of "Narrative of the Life of Ada Lee, an American Farm Girl." After you reread, complete the Using Language and Meaningful Interactions activities.

## USING LANGUAGE   CA-CCSS: ELD.PII.8.2.b.Ex

Read each sentence about the text. Choose the connecting word or phrase that best completes the sentence.

1. _____ Ada and John worked hard, they earned their degrees.

   ○ Because
   ○ While

2. Ada and John graduated _____ they got married.

   ○ before
   ○ therefore

3. Ada hoped they would open a law office _____ continue working together.

   ○ or
   ○ and

4. _____ Ada earned a degree, the state would not give her a license to practice law.

   ○ Even though
   ○ Until

5. John was not bothered, _____ Ada was disappointed.

   ○ since
   ○ but

6. Ada was upset; _____ she set out to change the law.

   ○ likewise
   ○ as a result

MEANINGFUL INTERACTIONS  CA-CCSS: ELD.PI.8.10.b.Ex, ELD.PII.8.2.b.Ex

Work with a small group to prepare and practice presenting a summary of "Narrative of the Life of Ada Lee, an American Farm Girl." Use the connecting words chart and writing frames that follow to plan your summary. Then, on a separate piece of paper, write your final summary. Write at least three sentences and use at least one connecting word or phrase.

| Relationship | Examples |
|---|---|
| time | as, before, since, finally, meanwhile, when, while, until |
| sequence | after, first, later, last, next, second, then, third |
| conclusion | so, in conclusion |
| contrast | although, but, despite, however, even though, on the other hand |
| compare | in other words, likewise, similarly |
| cause | because, due to, for, in order to, since |
| effect | as a result, if, so, therefore, thus |
| additional information | also, and, furthermore, in addition |
| an example | for example, for instance |

- First, Ada _____

_____

- Ada felt this way because _____

_____

- After Ada went to college, _____

_____

- Even though Ada worked hard, _____

_____

- John felt _____

On the other hand, Ada felt _____

- Finally, _____

_____

# CATHERINE'S CALLING

English Language
Development

**FICTION**

## INTRODUCTION

How can we stay brave in the face of danger? That is the question faced by a kind young woman who decides to be a nurse during the Civil War. "Catherine's Calling" tells the story of her struggle to persevere as she experiences war's violence.

# "She imagined herself fighting bravely to preserve the Union."

## FIRST READ

1 A young woman listened with **eager** ears to the words of President Abraham Lincoln. "The world will little note, nor long remember what we say here, but it can never forget what they did here. It is for us, the living, rather to be dedicated here to the unfinished work which they who fought here have thus far so nobly advanced." Catherine looked at the families gathered in the **graveyard** at Gettysburg to hear the president's address. Death touched each of them. The war had affected every American family. She **yearned** to give them comfort, but she did not know how. She needed to be alone with her thoughts.

2 Catherine closed herself into the small bedroom she shared with her younger sisters. She thought of the men who had given their lives in the battle. Surely if she were a man, she would have joined the army. She imagined herself fighting bravely to preserve the Union. **Patriotism** burned in her chest. She longed to seek honor and glory alongside her countrymen. Her daydream was interrupted when her little sister Sara noisily burst into the room. Sara had fallen and scraped her knee. Catherine carefully wrapped a bandage around the wound. Sara offered a sweet smile. Catherine's heart filled with pride. She realized she did have a way to serve her country. She could volunteer to be a nurse.

3 Safe at home, Catherine had heard cannons in the distance. But she had never heard musket fire that sounded as close as her own heartbeat. Now that she had begun work at the field hospital, gunfire thundered around her. The **barrage** was interrupted only by screams. Catherine tried to stay focused. Her first patient lay before her. The war didn't care that she was scared. It raged on. This man needed help. Catherine reached for a bandage. Suddenly, a bullet tore through the hospital tent. Catherine's feet took flight. It wasn't until she had tucked herself under a nearby weeping willow tree that she realized she had run. She had fled when the soldiers needed her most.

4    Catherine tried to tell herself that it was a **noble** act. If she were killed, there would be one less nurse to tend to the soldiers' wounds. She would return when the **siege** was over. But then she realized something else. She was alone under the tree. None of the other nurses had fled. What would they think of her when she returned? Would they pity her? Would they ever trust her again? Maybe it would be better if she just walked away. Maybe she did not have what it takes to serve after all. Catherine sunk to her knees and wept in the tree's warm embrace.

## ⚙ USING LANGUAGE   CA-CCSS: ELD.PI.8.6.c.Ex

Read each excerpt from "Catherine's Calling" and note the bold word or phrase. Then use context to choose the correct meaning.

1.    Catherine looked at the families gathered in the graveyard at Gettysburg to hear the president's address. Death **touched each of them**.

○ had lost family in the war
○ would be killed

2.    She imagined herself fighting bravely to preserve the Union. Patriotism **burned** in her chest.

○ felt a strong feeling
○ felt pain from a wound

3.    Safe at home, Catherine had heard cannons in the distance. But she had never heard musket fire that **sounded** as close as her own heartbeat

○ made the same noise as
○ made a noise

4.    Catherine's feet **took flight**. It wasn't until she had tucked herself under a nearby weeping willow tree that she realized she had run.

○ flew away
○ started to move very quickly

5.    Catherine **sunk** to her knees and wept in the tree's warm embrace.

○ went underwater
○ lowered down

## MEANINGFUL INTERACTIONS  CA-CCSS: ELD.PI.8.1.Ex

What does Catherine think war will be like? How well does Catherine's experience as a nurse match up to her expectations? Work in small groups to discuss these questions, using the speaking frames below. Listen carefully to your peers' ideas and respond thoughtfully. Then, use the self-assessment rubric to evaluate your participation in the discussion.

- Before she goes to the war, Catherine imagines . . .

- At the field hospital, Catherine sees . . . and hears . . .

- How does that compare to what Catherine expected . . . ?

- The war is similar to/different than what Catherine expected because . . .

- What did you mean when you said . . . ?

- I agree/disagree because . . .

- You said that . . . I want to add that . . .

## SELF-ASSESSMENT RUBRIC  CA-CCSS: ELD.PI.8.1.Ex

|  | 4 I did this well. | 3 I did this pretty well. | 2 I did this a little bit. | 1 I did not do this. |
|---|---|---|---|---|
| I took an active part with others in doing the activity. | | | | |
| I contributed effectively to the group's decisions. | | | | |
| I listened carefully to my peers' ideas. | | | | |
| I asked appropriate and helpful questions. | | | | |
| I built on my peers' responses to contribute my own ideas. | | | | |

# REREAD

Reread paragraphs 1 and 2 of "Catherine's Calling." After you reread, complete the Using Language and Meaningful Interactions activities.

## USING LANGUAGE  CA-CCSS: ELD.PII.8.5.Ex

Complete the sentences by filling in the blanks.

1. Find the sentence in paragraph 1 that tells where Catherine and the families are.

   Catherine looked at the families gathered _____
   to hear the president's address.

2. Find the sentence in paragraph 2 that tells how the men lost their lives.

   She thought of the men who had given their lives _____.

3. Find the sentence in paragraph 2 that tells how Catherine imagines herself.

   She imagined herself fighting _____ to preserve the Union.

4. Find the sentence in paragraph 2 that tells how Sara appeared.

   Her daydream was interrupted when her little sister Sara _____ burst _____.

5. Find the sentence in paragraph 2 that tells how Catherine wrapped the bandage.

   Catherine _____ wrapped a bandage _____.

Please note that excerpts and passages in the StudySync® library and this workbook are intended as touchstones to generate interest in an author's work. The excerpts and passages do not substitute for the reading of entire texts, and StudySync® strongly recommends that students seek out and purchase the whole literary or informational work in order to experience it as the author intended. Links to online resellers are available in our digital library. In addition, complete works may be ordered through an authorized reseller by filling out and returning to StudySync® the order form enclosed in this workbook.

Reading & Writing Companion  **457**

MEANINGFUL INTERACTIONS  CA-CCSS: ELD.PI.8.1.Ex

Based on what you have read in the first two paragraphs of "Catherine's Calling," do you think she will do well as a Civil War nurse? Consider what you know about her skills and personality. Work in small groups to practice stating your opinion and offering helpful feedback to your peers, using the speaking frames. Then, use the self-assessment rubric to evaluate your participation in the discussion.

- In my opinion, Catherine will/will not do well as a nurse because . . .

- The text shows Catherine is . . . because she . . .

- Why do you think Catherine is . . . ?

- I think you said that . . .

- I think you made a good point that . . .

- I agree / don't agree that . . .

 SELF-ASSESSMENT RUBRIC  CA-CCSS: ELD.PI.8.1.Ex

|  | 4<br>I did this<br>well. | 3<br>I did this<br>pretty well. | 2<br>I did this<br>a little bit. | 1<br>I did not<br>do this. |
|---|---|---|---|---|
| I expressed my opinion clearly. |  |  |  |  |
| I listened carefully to others' opinions. |  |  |  |  |
| I offered useful feedback about other people's opinions. |  |  |  |  |
| I was courteous when disagreeing with other people's opinions. |  |  |  |  |

# REREAD

Reread paragraphs 3 and 4 of "Catherine's Calling." After you reread, complete the Using Language and Meaningful Interactions activities.

## USING LANGUAGE CA-CCSS: ELD.PI.8.12.a.Ex

Read each sentence from "Catherine's Calling" and note the bold word. Then complete the chart by filling in the correct synonyms and antonyms from the options.

| Synonym | | | Antonym | | |
|---|---|---|---|---|---|
| boomed | run away | near | stayed | far | whispered |

| Sentence | Synonym | Antonym |
|---|---|---|
| But she had never heard musket fire that sounded as **close** as her own heartbeat. | | |
| Gunfire **thundered** around her. | | |
| She had **fled** when the soldiers needed her most. | | |

## MEANINGFUL INTERACTIONS   CA-CCSS: ELD.PI.8.12.a.Ex

Do you think Catherine should return to the field hospital or go home? What evidence from the text supports your opinion? Read the antonym pairs below and complete the chart by adding your own in the two empty spaces. Work in small groups to practice sharing and discussing your opinions, using the speaking frames. Use the word pairs in your answer.

| | |
|---|---|
| brave | cowardly |
| helpful | hurtful |
| safe | dangerous |
| planned | |
| intelligent | |

- I think Catherine is . . . and the field hospital is . . .

- The text describes Catherine/the war as . . .

- This evidence shows that . . .

- It would be . . . to return to the field hospital.

- My opinion is that Catherine should/not return to the field hospital. My opinion is based on . . .

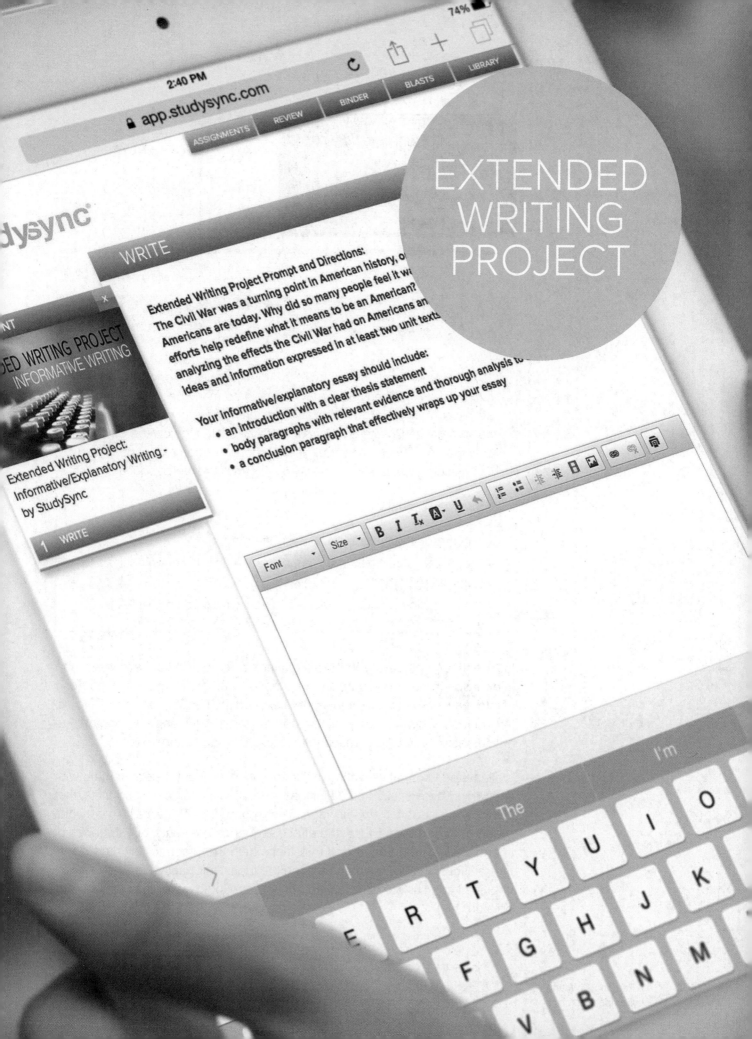

EXTENDED
WRITING
PROJECT

# INFORMATIVE/ EXPLANATORY WRITING

## WRITING PROMPT

The Civil War was a turning point in American history, one that helped define who Americans are today. Why did so many people feel it was necessary to fight? How did their efforts help redefine what it means to be an American? Write an informative essay analyzing how the Civil War changed Americans and their ideas about freedom. Use ideas and information expressed in at least two unit texts to reinforce your analysis.

Your essay should include:

- an introduction with a clear thesis statement
- body paragraphs with relevant evidence and thorough analysis to support your thesis
- a conclusion paragraph that effectively wraps up your essay

**Informative/explanatory writing** examines a topic and conveys ideas and information through comparisons, description, and explanation. The purpose of informative writing is to help readers expand their understanding of a topic. Informative writing examples include reports, newspaper or magazine articles, scientific studies, research papers, and non-fiction texts.

Well-crafted informative writing includes a main idea or thesis statement with supporting details, such as definitions, quotations, examples, and facts, that clarify and support the main idea. The informative piece has an obvious organization, such as cause and effect, sequence of events, or categories of information. Varied and strong transitions help the piece to flow and clarify the relationships between and among the ideas. Informative pieces draw an unbiased conclusion that is based on facts and logic rather than the author's opinion.

**The features of informative/explanatory writing include:**

- an introduction with a clear central idea or thesis statement
- details that support the central idea or thesis.
- a clear and logical organizational structure
- a formal style characterized by specific, precise language and domain-specific vocabulary
- citations of sources
- a concluding statement

During this extended writing project, you will be given more instructions and have opportunities to practice each of the elements of informative writing as you develop your own essay.

 STUDENT MODEL

As you prepare to create your own informative essay, start by reading this essay that one student wrote in response to the writing prompt. Examine this Student Model as you read, locating, highlighting, and making notes about each feature of informative writing that the student used.

### The Meaning of Freedom

*The Civil War was a turning point in American history that reshaped American ideas about freedom because it brought a resolution to the question of slavery. Prior to the Civil War, the issue of slavery divided Americans. Some were concerned that most African American people were kept as slaves. These people could not enjoy the freedom that white Americans took for granted. Others felt this situation was not only right, but also vital to the economy. This division was at the heart of the Civil War. Its resolution forever altered what it means to be an American. Many passages from the period explore these ideas of freedom. Abraham Lincoln's "Gettysburg Address" and Narrative of the Life of Frederick Douglass, An American Slave by Frederick Douglass are good examples. Both pieces discuss American views on freedom before and during the Civil War, as well as the necessity for change.*

Please note that excerpts and passages in the StudySync® library and this workbook are intended as touchstones to generate interest in an author's work. The excerpts and passages do not substitute for the reading of entire texts, and StudySync® strongly recommends that students seek out and purchase the whole literary or informational work in order to experience it as the author intended. Links to online resellers are available in our digital library. In addition, complete works may be ordered through an authorized reseller by filling out and returning to StudySync® the order form enclosed in this workbook.

Reading & Writing Companion **463**

In the excerpt from Douglass' memoir, *Narrative of the Life of Frederick Douglass, An American Slave*, he tells the story of how he learned to read in spite of being forbidden to do so. In fact, the idea of helping a slave learn to read in that time and place was so strictly forbidden that Douglass refrained from naming the young white boys he had befriended, and who shared their lessons with him. He said, ". . . for it is almost an unpardonable offence to teach slaves to read in this Christian country" (Douglass). To Douglass, the books he read "gave tongue to interesting thoughts" in his own soul (Douglass). The concerns of the white masters who had not allowed slaves to learn how to read came true. The books Douglass read gave him the words to express the truth that he had always felt: Slavery contradicted human rights on all levels. How could a country, said to be based on freedom, allow it? In fact it could not, because the contradiction made one part of the country stand against the other in war.

Almost 20 years after Douglass published his memoir, Abraham Lincoln gave a speech in the middle of the Civil War that said much the same thing and stirred much of the nation. Unlike Douglass, Lincoln did not have first-hand knowledge of slavery, and for him learning to read was not a forbidden activity. But he worked on the Mississippi river as a young man, and he saw the slave markets in New Orleans. He knew about the evils of slavery.

In "The Gettysburg Address," Lincoln acknowledged the same division that Douglass had written about. The Civil War had created a landscape on which fathers were fighting sons and brothers were fighting brothers. Families were torn apart and the nation was ripped in two. On one side stood the Abolitionists, who believed in freedom for all, and on the other side stood the slave-owners, who were in danger of losing their entire way of life. Those in favor of slavery were fighting to maintain the economic and social structure of America, and those against it were fighting for one of the strongest ideals upon which our country stands: freedom. Speaking to the crowd gathered at Gettysburg, Lincoln said that this nation was "dedicated to the proposition that all men are created equal" (Lincoln), and now was being tested to determine "whether that nation, or any nation so conceived and so dedicated, can long endure" (Lincoln). Mr. Lincoln acknowledged the need for all citizens to stand up and fight for this ideal.

In his speech, Lincoln called the movement toward freedom for all "the unfinished work" (Lincoln). He called on his countrymen to "be dedicated" in the fight for freedom. By the end of the Civil War, America was committed to the idea that

Copyright © BookheadEd Learning, LLC

"all men are created equal" (Lincoln). The country soon found, however, that some deep-seated beliefs about the nature of equality would take time to change, through many generations of Americans to follow. Healing got off to a slow start at the end of the Civil War. It is only now starting to come to fruition. Now we can see that the efforts of oppressed men like Douglass and brave leaders like Lincoln have redefined what it means to be a free American.

The Civil War forever changed our country's laws regarding freedom and rights for all. It took decades of legal and social changes to fulfill the promises made after that war. African-American people are no longer owned by others, but discrimination still abounds in many areas, compromising economic and social justice. African Americans are no longer held in iron chains by oppressors, but there is still work to be done in the arena of equalizing opportunity and just treatment. The work that our forefathers began with the Civil War continues to this day. It will continue until all persons, no matter what their race or circumstance, have the same freedoms everywhere in this country, forever.

## THINK QUESTIONS

1. What is the central idea of the first paragraph of this essay, and where does it appear? Support your answer with textual evidence.

2. How is the text in "The Meaning of Freedom" organized? Did the writer use a cause and effect, compare and contrast, or a chronological text structure? Cite textual evidence to support your answer.

3. How does the writer use relevant, well-chosen examples and quotations to show that Frederick Douglass' writing reflected the national division over slavery? Cite textual evidence to support your answer.

4. In considering the writing prompt, what resources, references or other sources could you use in developing your own informative essay? What ideas would you like to explore? List your ideas and discuss them with a partner.

5. Based on your background knowledge, texts you have read, and ideas you have studied, how would you answer the question, "How did the war between the states redefine America?" Write your ideas in a paragraph and share them with a partner.

Please note that excerpts and passages in the StudySync® library and this workbook are intended as touchstones to generate interest in an author's work. The excerpts and passages do not substitute for the reading of entire texts, and StudySync® strongly recommends that students seek out and purchase the whole literary or informational work in order to experience it as the author intended. Links to online resellers are available in our digital library. In addition, complete works may be ordered through an authorized reseller by filling out and returning to StudySync® the order form enclosed in this workbook.

Reading & Writing
Companion

**465**

## PREWRITE

CA-CCSS: CA.RI.8.1, CA.RI.8.2, CA.RI.8.3, CA.W.8.5, CA.W.8.6, CA.W.8.9b, CA.W.8.10, CA.SL.8.1a

### WRITING PROMPT

The Civil War was a turning point in American history, one that helped define who Americans are today. Why did so many people feel it was necessary to fight? How did their efforts help redefine what it means to be an American? Write an informative essay analyzing how the Civil War changed Americans and their ideas about freedom. Use ideas and information expressed in at least two unit texts to reinforce your analysis.

Your essay should include:

- an introduction with a clear thesis statement
- body paragraphs with relevant evidence and thorough analysis to support your thesis
- a conclusion paragraph that effectively wraps up your essay

In addition to studying techniques and methods authors use to present information, you have been reading and examining passages related to the way that the Civil War changed American ideas about freedom. Now you will use the new techniques you have been learning to begin work on your informative essay.

The topic of your informative essay will have to do with the effects the Civil War had on Americans and their ideas about freedom, so you'll want to think about how the people and events you've read about had an impact on the events that led up to the war, and helped to redefine the way Americans thought about freedom. Consider what you read in *Narrative of the Life of Frederick Douglass, An American Slave* and how it addresses the following questions:

- How have American ideas about freedom changed since the time before the Civil War?

- Why was it important for American citizens to clarify their ideas about freedom?

- Who was instrumental in discussing the problem and its solutions?

Make a list of your answers to these questions for *Narrative of the Life of Frederick Douglass, An American Slave* and at least two other texts in this unit, in order to develop an informative essay based on this writing prompt. As you read, look for patterns that begin to emerge. Are there any central ideas that surface again and again? What connects these ideas? Look for similarities in the answers you have noted. Do any ideas occur again and again? When you find these commonalities, you will be able to decide which texts to use in your essay. Use this model to help you get started with your own prewriting:

**Text:** *Narrative of the Life of Frederick Douglass, An American Slave*

### Ideas About Freedom:

- As a child and slave, Douglass struggled with the idea that he would never be free like the white children he met, even upon reaching adulthood, and longed for an education.

- The white children consoled him with hopes that something would change that would allow him to be free.

- In voicing his concerns and frustrations, Douglass helped the white children to understand the unjustness of slavery and the differences between their freedom and his enslavement.

### What Happened:

- Douglass bribed the white children to share their lessons with him, and he taught himself to read.

- This act of rebellion both freed and further enslaved him, as he learned more about the institution of slavery through books, and he discovered that slavery contradicted the country's foundation of freedom.

- This knowledge caused Douglass to feel more desperate than ever to be free, and his writings shed important light on the evolution of American freedoms from the Civil War era to the present.

After you have completed your prewriting, consider your thoughts and ideas as you work through the following Skills lessons to help you map out your analysis.

Reading & Writing Companion

NOTES

SKILL:
THESIS
STATEMENT

## DEFINE

The foundation of informative/explanatory writing is the **thesis statement**. This is a single sentence that summarizes the central idea or position that the writer will develop in the body of the essay through organized facts, details, quotations, definitions and other pieces of textual evidence. It also briefly introduces what the writer plans to say about the topic. The thesis statement most often appears as the last sentence of the introductory paragraph of an essay.

## IDENTIFICATION AND APPLICATION

**A good thesis statement:**

- makes a clear statement about the central idea of the essay
- lets the reader know what to expect in the body of the essay
- is presented in the introductory paragraph
- responds completely to the writing prompt

## MODEL

The following is the introductory paragraph from the Student Model essay "The Meaning of Freedom":

> **The Civil War was a turning point in American history that reshaped American ideas about freedom because it brought a resolution to the question of slavery.** Prior to the Civil War, the issue of slavery divided Americans. Some were concerned that most African American people were kept as slaves. These people could not enjoy the freedom that white Americans took for granted. Others felt this situation was not only right,

but also vital to the economy. *This division was at the heart of the Civil War. Its resolution forever altered what it means to be an American. Many passages from the period explore these ideas of freedom. Abraham Lincoln's "Gettysburg Address" and Narrative of the Life of Frederick Douglass, An American Slave by Frederick Douglass are good examples. Both pieces discuss American views on freedom before and during the Civil War, as well as the necessity for change.*

Notice the bold-faced thesis statement. This student's thesis statement responds to the questions raised by the prompt and meets the requirements of an effective thesis statement. First, it reminds readers of the topic of the essay: that the Civil War was an important event in American history that changed Americans' views of slavery. Then it specifically states the writer's central or main idea about this topic: that the Civil War changed views of slavery by bringing resolution to a long outstanding question. A strong thesis will always have both of these two aspects, so when developing your own thesis continue to ask yourself these two questions:

- Have I clearly stated the topic of the essay?
- Have I clearly stated the central or main idea that I will explore in the body paragraphs to follow?

 PRACTICE

Write a thesis statement for your informative essay that articulates your central idea in relation to the essay prompt. When you are finished, trade with a partner and offer each other feedback. How clear was the writer's main point or idea? Is it obvious what this essay will focus on? Does it specifically address the prompt? Offer each other suggestions, and remember that they are most helpful when they are constructive.

Please note that excerpts and passages in the StudySync® library and this workbook are intended as touchstones to generate interest in an author's work. The excerpts and passages do not substitute for the reading of entire texts, and StudySync® strongly recommends that students seek out and purchase the whole literary or informational work in order to experience it as the author intended. Links to online resellers are available in our digital library. In addition, complete works may be ordered through an authorized reseller by filling out and returning to StudySync® the order form enclosed in this workbook.

Reading & Writing Companion **469**

NOTES

Organize
INFORMATIVE
WRITING

sync · Writing

# SKILL:
# ORGANIZE
# INFORMATIVE
# WRITING

 **DEFINE**

The purpose for writing an informative/explanatory text is to inform readers about a specific topic. To do this effectively, writers need to organize their ideas, facts, details, and other information in an organizational pattern, or text structure, that's easy to understand and that best suits their material.

For example, historians might use a sequential or a chronological structure, discussing events in the order they occurred. They may also employ a cause-and-effect text structure to show how one event can influence or cause another. Authors of scientific articles might choose a problem and solution text structure, which presents a problem or a series of problems and then offers or explains solutions on how to solve them. A social studies article that discusses immigration to the United States early in the twentieth century could use a compare and contrast text structure to compare these statistics to immigration today.

 **IDENTIFICATION AND APPLICATION**

- When selecting an organizational structure, writers must consider their purpose for writing. Often they ask themselves questions about the kind of information they are writing about. They might consider:
  › What is the main idea I'd like to convey to readers?
  › Would it make sense to present a series of events in sequential order?
  › Is there a problem with possible solutions?
  › What solutions seem likely answers to the problem?
  › Is there a natural cause and effect relationship in my information?
  › Can I compare and contrast different examples of my thesis statement?
  › Am I teaching readers how to do something?

- Writers often use words to alert readers to connections between details and hint at the organizational structure they are using. These words also act as transitions to create cohesion, or unity, and explain the relationships between ideas in the text:
  - › Sequential order: *first, next, then, finally, last, initially, ultimately*
  - › Cause and effect: *because, accordingly, as a result, effect, so*
  - › Compare and contrast: *like, unlike, also, both, similarly, although, while, but, however*
  - › Problem and Solution: *so, consequently, due to*

- Sometimes, authors may use more than one text structure or organizational pattern. For example, a text organized with information primarily presented in sequential order may also contain some cause-and-effect relationships in the text.

- Sometimes authors include headings to help organize the information in their texts into different sections.

 MODEL

The writer of the Student Model understood that by drawing on sources such as "The Gettysburg Address" and *Narrative of the Life of Frederick Douglass, An American Slave* he would be comparing and contrasting the feelings and ideas of two different figures in history.

In this sentence from the introductory paragraph of the Student Model, the writer makes the organizational structure clear:

> Abraham Lincoln's "Gettysburg Address" and *Narrative of the Life of Frederick Douglass, An American Slave* by Frederick Douglass are good examples. **Both** pieces discuss American views on freedom before and during the Civil War, as well as the necessity for change.

The writer uses the word "both" to identify something the two subjects, Douglass and Lincoln, have in common.

The writer of the Student Model informative essay, "The Meaning of Freedom," knew that he was comparing and contrasting crucial similarities and differences in the outlook of two famous historical figures. He used a two-column chart to organize his ideas during the prewriting process, color-coding the information so that it was clear what the figures had in common. What was unique to each individual is unmarked.

| FREDERICK DOUGLASS | ABRAHAM LINCOLN |
|---|---|
| Former slave | President of the United States |
| Prevented from learning to read or attending school when a slave | Was able to learn to read |
| Wrote about the contradiction of a country based on freedom having slaves | Wrote about how the nation could not endure half-free and half-slave |
| Felt slavery contradicted human rights on all levels | Said that the nation was "dedicated to the proposition that all men are created equal and was being tested to determine "whether that nation, or any nation so conceived and so dedicated, can long endure." |

 PRACTICE

Using an *Organize Informative/Explanatory Writing Two-Column Chart* graphic organizer like the one you have just studied and/or the *Organize Informative/Explanatory Writing Three-Section Web* graphic organizer, fill in the details you gathered for at least two texts in the Prewrite stage of writing your essay. Exchange your organizer with a partner and offer each other feedback.

SKILL:
SUPPORTING
DETAILS

## DEFINE

In informative writing, writers develop their main idea with relevant information called **supporting details.** Relevant information can be any fact, definition, concrete detail, example, or quotation that is important to a reader's understanding of the topic and closely related to the thesis, or main idea. Supporting details can be found in a variety of places, but only those that provide substance for the thesis should be included:

- Facts important to understanding the topic
- Research related to the main idea or thesis
- Quotations from experts, eyewitnesses, or other source material
- Conclusions of scientific findings and studies
- Definitions from reference material

Writers can choose supporting details from many sources. Encyclopedias, research papers, newspaper articles, graphs, memoirs, biographies, criticism, documentaries, and online references can all provide relevant information for source material. Though information is plentiful and the source material varied, the writer must be careful to evaluate the quality of information to determine what information is most important and most closely related to the thesis. If the information doesn't support the topic or if the information doesn't strengthen the writer's point, it is not relevant.

## IDENTIFICATION AND APPLICATION

**Step 1:**

Review your thesis statement. To identify relevant supporting details, ask this question: What is my main idea about this topic? Here is the thesis statement of the Student Model, "The Meaning of Freedom":

> *The Civil War was a turning point in American history that reshaped American ideas about freedom because it brought a resolution to the question of slavery.*

## Step 2:

Ask what a reader needs to know about the topic in order to understand the main idea. What details will support your thesis? Consider how the writer of the Student Model follows the thesis statement with an explanation of *why* the Civil War was a pivotal moment in American history:

> **Prior to the Civil War, the issue of slavery divided Americans. Some were concerned that most African American people were kept as slaves. These people could not enjoy the freedom that white Americans took for granted. Others felt this situation was not only right, but also vital to the economy.**

But how has the Civil War reshaped American ideas about freedom? The writer provides more information to tie these details to the thesis statement:

> **This division was at the heart of the Civil War. Its resolution forever altered what it means to be an American.**

## Step 3:

Search for facts, quotations, research, and the conclusions of others to help strengthen and support your thesis statement. As you search for details, carefully evaluate their relevance to your main idea. Ask yourself:

- Is this information necessary to the reader's understanding of the topic?
- Does this information help to develop and refine my key concept?
- Does this information relate closely to my thesis?
- Where can I find better evidence that will provide stronger support for my point?

 MODEL

In the following excerpt from Frederick Douglass's *Narrative of the Life of Frederick Douglass, An American Slave*, Douglass develops the idea that learning to read helped him understand important aspects of the institution of slavery that had been unclear to him before.

> I was now about twelve years old, and the thought of being a slave for life began to bear heavily upon my heart. Just about this time, I got hold of **a book entitled "The Columbian Orator."** Every opportunity I got, I used to read this book. Among much of other interesting matter, I found in it **a dialogue between a master and his slave.** The slave was represented as having run away from his master three times. The dialogue represented the conversation which took place between them,

NOTES

when the slave was retaken the third time. In this dialogue, the whole argument in behalf of slavery was brought forward by the master, all of which was disposed of by the slave. The slave was made to say some very **smart** as well as **impressive** things in reply to his master — things which had the desired though unexpected effect; for **the conversation resulted in the voluntary emancipation of the slave on the part of the master.**

In the same book, I met with one of **Sheridan's mighty speeches** on and in behalf of Catholic emancipation. These were choice documents to me. I read them over and over again with unabated interest. They **gave tongue to interesting thoughts of my own soul,** which had frequently flashed through my mind, and died away for want of utterance. The moral which I gained from the dialogue was the power of truth over the conscience of even a slaveholder. **What I got from Sheridan was a bold denunciation of slavery, and a powerful vindication of human rights.**

In the first paragraph, Douglass reveals the source of his newfound knowledge: a book entitled "The Columbian Orator." He then provides details from the book to help the reader understand how learning to read helped him see important aspects of the institution of slavery. First, he describes reading "a dialogue between a master and his slave," in which the master argues for slavery and the slave argues against it. Douglass reveals that the details of the slave's argument against slavery were so "smart" and "impressive" that "the conversation resulted in the voluntary emancipation of the slave on the part of the master."

Next Douglass introduces another selection from "The Columbian Orator," a speech by Richard Sheridan. Douglass offers details about how these readings affected him and "gave tongue to interesting thoughts of my own soul," an enlightening process for Douglass. He then concludes by revealing the most important detail of all: "What I got from Sheridan was a bold denunciation of slavery, and a powerful vindication of human rights." With this concluding detail, Douglass shows how learning to read helped him understand important aspects of the institution of slavery that he had not fully understood before.

 PRACTICE

Review a text you plan to include in your informative/explanatory essay. Then choose a fact, definition, concrete detail, quotation, or other piece of information from the text that supports your thesis. Write three or four sentences that explain why this specific detail constitutes relevant evidence for your thesis.

Copyright © BookheadEd Learning, LLC

PLAN

CA-CCSS: CA.W.8.2a, CA.W.8.2b, CA.W.8.5, CA.W.8.6, CA.W.8.10, CA.SL.8.1a

## WRITING PROMPT

The Civil War was a turning point in American history, one that helped define who Americans are today. Why did so many people feel it was necessary to fight? How did their efforts help redefine what it means to be an American? Write an informative essay analyzing how the Civil War changed Americans and their ideas about freedom. Use ideas and information expressed in at least two unit texts to reinforce your analysis.

Your essay should include:

- an introduction with a clear thesis statement
- body paragraphs with relevant evidence and thorough analysis to support your thesis
- a conclusion paragraph that effectively wraps up your essay

In this step, you will apply the skills you learned in the Thesis Statement lesson, the Organize Informative Writing lesson, and the Supporting Details lesson. You will also consider what information best suits your purpose and the needs of your audience.

Begin by looking again at the information you gathered from the source texts. If you have not done so already, complete the *Organize Informative/Explanatory Writing Three-Section Web* graphic organizer to categorize your ideas into three groups and sort details according to the ideas they support. If you have already begun to fill in this organizer, expand upon the existing information. Be sure to find at least two supporting details for each idea. If there are missing details, return to your resource texts to find additional support. If you cannot find enough support, you may need to adjust some of your main ideas.

The organized information on the web that you created will guide you in crafting a thesis statement. Make your thesis statement broad enough to cover all three groups of ideas, but also narrow enough so your information

addresses all of the points you want to make adequately. Remember that your thesis statement should clearly state not only the topic of your essay but also your stance on that topic.

The organized information and your thesis statement will allow you to create a roadmap for your essay. Consider the following questions as you develop your roadmap:

- What themes, patterns, or commonalities did you find in your survey of texts about changing ideas of freedom?
- Why is it important for American citizens to consider how our ideas of freedom have changed?
- How were the men and women who expressed these ideas instrumental in changing our understanding of freedom in America?
- What was the connection between the Civil War and our understanding of freedom?
- How do people who wrote about freedom both before and during the Civil War era speak to us in the present time?
- How are those changes apparent in our society today?

Use this model to get started with your road map:

**Essay Road Map**

    Thesis statement:

        Introduction/Paragraph 1:
            Supporting Detail #1:
            Supporting Detail #2:

        Body/Paragraph 2 Topic:
            Supporting Detail #1:
            Supporting Detail #2:

        Body/Paragraph 3 Topic:
            Supporting Detail #1:
            Supporting Detail #2:

        Body/Paragraph 4 Topic:
            Supporting Detail #1:
            Supporting Detail #2:

        Conclusion/Paragraph 5:
            Restated supporting idea #1:
            Restated supporting idea #2:
            Restated supporting idea #3:
            Restated thesis or concluding statement:

# SKILL:
# INTRODUCTIONS

 ## DEFINE

The **introduction** is the opening paragraph or section of a nonfiction text. In an informative/explanatory text, the introduction provides readers with important information by **introducing the topic** and **stating the thesis** that will be developed in the body of the text. A strong introduction also generates interest in the topic by engaging readers in an interesting or attentive way.

 ## IDENTIFICATION AND APPLICATION

- In informative or explanatory writing, the introduction identifies the topic of the writing by stating what the text will be about.

- A writer may provide necessary background information about the topic in the introduction to help the reader understand the topic.

- The introduction also contains the main idea or **thesis** of the essay.

- An essay's introduction often contains a **"hook,"** or an element that grabs the reader's attention and piques reader curiosity to encourage the reader to keep reading. Examples of effective hooks include emotional language, open-ended questions, and surprising facts

 ## MODEL

Look at the introduction of Abraham Lincoln's "Gettysburg Address" speech:

> Four score and seven years ago our fathers brought forth on this continent, **a new nation, conceived in Liberty, and dedicated to the proposition that all men are created equal.**

This introductory sentence of Lincoln's speech has several functions. First, it alerts readers to the topic Lincoln will discuss in his speech: America as "a new nation, conceived in Liberty, and dedicated to the proposition that all men are created equal." Second, this sentence also serves as the thesis for Lincoln's speech. Readers know that Lincoln believes that America is dedicated to the proposition that all men are created equal. Third, the opening line of the speech acts as a hook. Lincoln's use of emotion-laden words such as "conceived" and "dedicated" create interest and compel us to keep reading.

Because the first paragraph of the speech is only one sentence, the second paragraph provides more information about the main topic of the speech:

> Now **we are engaged in a great civil war,** testing whether that nation, or any nation so conceived and so dedicated, can long endure. We are met on a great battle-field of that war. We have come to dedicate a portion of that field, as a final resting place for those **who here gave their lives that that nation might live.** It is altogether fitting and proper that we should do this.

Here Lincoln has developed his main idea. Because the nation was conceived with these ideals, "we are engaged in a great civil war" and must honor the soldiers "who here gave their lives that that nation might live." Lincoln's thesis in this introduction might be summarized as follows: *We are fighting the Civil War to protect our ideals of liberty and equality for all, and we must honor the soldiers who have died fighting for this cause.* This important idea is designed to compel the audience's attention by creating a sense of patriotism, duty, and obligation.

 ## PRACTICE

Write an introduction for your essay that alerts readers to the topic, includes the thesis you have written and revised, and contains a hook to capture readers' interest. When you are finished, trade with a peer review partner and offer helpful and constructive feedback on your peer's introduction.

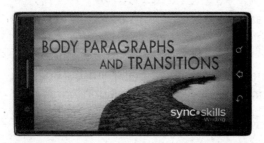

SKILL: BODY
PARAGRAPHS
AND
TRANSITIONS

 DEFINE

**Body paragraphs** are the section of an essay that fall between the introductory and concluding paragraphs. This is where you support your thesis statement through analysis and by developing your main points with evidence from the text. Typically, each body paragraph focuses on one important idea to avoid confusing readers. The main point discussed in each body paragraph must support the thesis statement.

It's important to organize the paragraphs that make up the body of your text in such a way that the information is clear. Here is one strategy to use when structuring the body paragraph for an informational essay:

> **Topic sentence:** The topic sentence is usually the first sentence of your introductory paragraph. It can also come at the end. It clearly states the main point of the paragraph. It's important that your topic sentence develop the main statement or point you made in your thesis statement.
> **Evidence #1:** It's important to support your topic sentence with evidence. Evidence can be relevant facts, definitions, concrete details, quotations, or other information and examples.
> **Analysis/Explanation #1:** After presenting evidence to support your topic sentence, you will need to analyze the evidence and explain how it supports your topic sentence and your thesis.
> **Evidence #2:** Continue to develop your topic sentence with a second piece of evidence.
> **Analysis/Explanation #2:** Analyze this second piece of evidence and explain how it supports your topic sentence and your thesis.
> **Concluding sentence:** After presenting your evidence you need to wrap up your main idea and transition to the next paragraph in your concluding sentence.

**Transitions** are connecting words and phrases that explain and clarify the relationships among ideas in a text. Good transitions can connect paragraphs and turn choppy, disconnected writing into a complete whole. Instead of treating paragraphs as separate ideas, transitions can help readers

Copyright © BookheadEd Learning, LLC

understand how the information in two paragraphs works together, and builds to a larger point.

The key to writing good transitions is making connections between paragraphs. By making a reference in one paragraph to related material from a previous paragraph, writers can develop important points for their readers.

> **Example:** After escaping from slavery, Frederick Douglass became a leader of the abolitionist movement, and also a well-known speaker. There are other things to note about Frederick Douglass as well. Douglass also actively supported women's rights.

> **Revision:** After escaping from slavery, Frederick Douglass became a leader of the abolitionist movement, and also a well-known speaker.
> - Though his stand against slavery is well known, however, his work on behalf of women's rights has received less notice from historians.

Authors of informative/explanatory texts use transitions to help readers make connections among ideas within and across sentences and paragraphs. Also, by adding transition words or phrases to the beginning or end of a paragraph, authors guide readers smoothly through the text.

Transitional words and phrases can also help authors make connections between words within a sentence. Conjunctions such as *and, or*, and *but* and prepositions such as *with, beyond,* and *inside* show the relationships between words. In this way, transitions can help readers understand how words fit together to make meaning.

##  IDENTIFICATION AND APPLICATION

- Body paragraphs are the parts of an essay between the introductory and concluding paragraphs. The body paragraphs provide the evidence and analysis/explanation needed to support the thesis statement. Typically, writers develop one main idea per body paragraph.
  - › Topic sentences clearly state the main idea of a paragraph.
  - › Evidence consists of relevant facts, definitions, concrete details, quotations, or other information and examples.
  - › Analysis and explanation are needed to explain how the evidence supports the topic sentence.
  - › The conclusion sentence in each body paragraph wraps up the main point and transitions to the next body paragraph.
- Transitions are a necessary element of a successful piece of informative writing.

Please note that excerpts and passages in the StudySync® library and this workbook are intended as touchstones to generate interest in an author's work. The excerpts and passages do not substitute for the reading of entire texts, and StudySync® strongly recommends that students seek out and purchase the whole literary or informational work in order to experience it as the author intended. Links to online resellers are available in our digital library. In addition, complete works may be ordered through an authorized reseller by filling out and returning to StudySync® the order form enclosed in this workbook.

Reading & Writing Companion    **481**

NOTES

- Transitional words and phrases help readers understand the flow of ideas and concepts in a text. Some of the most useful transitions are words that indicate that the ideas in one paragraph are building on or adding to those in another:

| To show: | Consider using transition words such as: |
| --- | --- |
| similarities | likewise, also, in the same way |
| compare and contrast | however, in spite of, on the other hand, on the contrary, yet, still, unlike, same, similarly |
| example | namely, to illustrate, for instance |
| added evidence | as well, besides, furthermore, moreover |
| sequence or time order | after, afterward, later, during, meanwhile, recently, first, next, then |
| cause and effect | therefore, because, so, accordingly, as a result |
| conclusion | briefly, on the whole, to sum up, finally |

- The strongest transitions often restate the idea that you want to connect to the next idea.
- By the end of the essay, the reader should be able to look back on a clear path of support for the thesis statement that leads to the conclusion in the closing paragraph.

 MODEL

The Student Model uses a body paragraph structure to develop the main ideas presented in the thesis statement and transitions to help the reader understand the relationship between ideas in the text.

Read the body paragraphs from the Student Model essay "The Meaning of Freedom." Look closely at the structure and note the transition words in bold. Think about the purpose of the information presented. How do the transition words help you to connect the information presented in the essay?

In the excerpt from Douglass' memoir, *Narrative of the Life of Frederick Douglass, An American Slave,* he tells the story of how he learned to read in spite of being forbidden to do so. In fact, the idea of helping a slave learn to read in that time and place was so strictly forbidden that Douglass refrained from naming the young white boys he had befriended, and who shared their lessons with him. He said, ". . . for it is almost an unpardonable offence to teach slaves to read in this Christian country" (Douglass). To Douglass, the books he read "gave tongue to interesting thoughts" in his own soul (Douglass). The concerns of the white masters who had not allowed slaves to learn how to read came true. The books Douglass read gave him the words to express the truth that he had always felt: Slavery contradicted human rights on all levels. How could a country, said to be based on freedom, allow it? In fact it could not, because the contradiction made one part of the country stand against the other in war.

**Almost 20 years** after Douglass published his memoir, Abraham Lincoln gave a speech in the middle of the Civil War that said much the **same** thing and stirred much of the nation. **Unlike Douglass,** Lincoln did not have first-hand knowledge of slavery, and for him learning to read was not a forbidden activity. But he worked on the Mississippi river as a young man, and he saw the slave markets in New Orleans. He knew about the evils of slavery.

In "The Gettysburg Address," **Lincoln acknowledged the same division** that Douglass had written about. The Civil War had created a landscape on which fathers were fighting sons and brothers were fighting brothers. Families were torn apart and the nation was ripped in two. On one side stood the Abolitionists, who believed in freedom for all, and on the other side stood the slave-owners, who were in danger of losing their entire way of life. Those in favor of slavery were fighting to maintain the economic and social structure of America, and those against it were fighting for one of the strongest ideals upon which our country stands: freedom. Speaking to the crowd gathered at Gettysburg, Lincoln said that this nation was "dedicated to the proposition that all men are created equal" (Lincoln), and now was being tested to determine "whether that nation, or any nation so conceived and so dedicated, can long endure" (Lincoln). Mr. Lincoln acknowledged the need for all citizens to stand up and fight for this ideal.

In his speech, Lincoln called the movement toward freedom for all "the unfinished work" (Lincoln). He called on his countrymen to "be dedicated" in the fight for freedom. By the end of the Civil War, America was committed to the idea that "all men are created equal" (Lincoln). The country soon found, **however,** that changing some deep-seated beliefs about the nature of equality would take time to change, through many generations of Americans to follow. Healing got off to a slow start at the end of the Civil War. It is only now starting to come to fruition. Now we can see that the efforts of oppressed men like Douglass and brave leaders like Lincoln have redefined what it means to be a free American.

The Civil War forever changed our country's laws regarding freedom and rights for all. It took decades of legal and social changes to fulfill the promises made after that war. African-American people are no longer owned by others, but discrimination still abounds in many areas, compromising economic and social justice. African Americans are no longer held in iron chains by oppressors, but there is still work to be done in the arena of equalizing opportunity and just treatment. The work that our forefathers began with the Civil War continues to this day. It will continue until all persons, no matter what their race or circumstance, have the same freedoms everywhere in this country, forever.

The first paragraph in this excerpt from the Student Model begins by stating, "In the excerpt from Douglass' memoir, *Narrative of the Life of Frederick Douglass, An American Slave,* he tells the story of how he learned to read in spite of being forbidden to do so." This **topic sentence** clearly establishes the main idea this body paragraph will develop. The writer will attempt to show how Douglass taught himself how to read.

This topic sentence is immediately followed by details. The writer explains that Douglass learned to read from the white boys in his neighborhood, who "shared their lessons with him." The author then states that the books Douglass read gave him the words to express the truth that he had always felt: Slavery contradicted human rights on all levels.

Copyright © BookheadEd Learning, LLC

Directly after this, the writer opens the next paragraph with the phrase "Almost 20 years after Douglass published his memoir . . ." Then he provides information about Abraham Lincoln's speech at Gettysburg and how Lincoln's message was similar to Douglass's message even though his experience was different. The word "after" shows a transitional link between Douglass and Lincoln.

All three body paragraphs use **transitional words** to show relationships between the main points in each paragraph. Words like "however", "unlike", and "same" within the body paragraphs help guide the reader as they transition from one sentence to the next.

 ## PRACTICE

Write one body paragraph for your informative essay that follows the suggested format. When you are finished, trade with a partner and offer each other feedback. How effective is the topic sentence at stating the main point of the paragraph? How strong is the evidence used to support the topic sentence? Did the analysis thoroughly support the topic sentence? Offer each other suggestions, and remember that they are most helpful when they are constructive.

# SKILL:
# CONCLUSIONS

## ⭐ DEFINE

The **conclusion** is the final paragraph or section of a nonfiction text. In an informative/explanatory text, the conclusion brings the discussion of the topic to a close. A conclusion should reiterate the thesis statement and summarize the main ideas covered in the body of the text. Depending on the type of text, a conclusion might also include a recommendation or solution, a call to action, or an insightful or memorable statement. A conclusion should leave a lasting impression on a reader.

## ⋯ IDENTIFICATION AND APPLICATION

- An effective informative conclusion reinforces the thesis statement.
- An effective informative conclusion briefly reviews or summarizes the strongest supporting facts or details. This reminds readers of the most relevant information and evidence in the work.
- The conclusion leaves the reader with a final thought. In informative writing, this final thought may:
  › Answer a question posed by the introduction
  › Ask a question on which the reader can reflect
  › Ask the reader to take action on an issue
  › Convey a memorable or inspiring message
  › Spark curiosity and encourage readers to learn more

## ◎ MODEL

In the concluding paragraph of the Student Model "The Meaning of Freedom," the writer reinforces the thesis statement, reminds the reader of relevant details, and ends with a concluding thought.

NOTES

*The Civil War forever changed our country's laws regarding freedom and rights for all. It took **decades of legal and social changes to fulfill the promises made after that war.** African-American people are no longer owned by others, but **discrimination still abounds in many areas,** compromising economic and social justice. African Americans are no longer held in iron chains by oppressors, but **there is still work to be done in the arena of equalizing opportunity and just treatment.** The work that our forefathers began with the Civil War continues to this day. **It will continue until all persons, no matter what their race or circumstance, have the same freedoms everywhere in this country, forever.***

According to the thesis statement, the Civil War resulted in decades of changes to America's laws to ensure freedom and rights for all citizens. The writer then addresses the significance of these changes, which have resulted in freedom for African Americans. The writer also introduces two concluding ideas: "discrimination still abounds in many areas" and "there is still work to be done in the arena of equalizing opportunity and just treatment." These ideas emphasize the point that though the Civil War caused great change regarding the freedom of American citizens, there is still a need for further change to reach the goals of equalizing opportunity and fair treatment of all citizens.

Finally, the writer presents a concluding statement about the changes that began after the Civil War: "It will continue until all persons, no matter what their race or circumstance, have the same freedoms everywhere in this country, forever." With this final thought, the writer has presented an inspiring message and has created a strong conclusion for the claims made in this essay. Readers may be inspired to examine other texts from the Civil War era, to dig deeper into the issue of how the Civil War forever changed America's views on freedom.

 PRACTICE

Write a conclusion for your informative essay. When you are finished, trade with a partner and offer each other feedback. Use these questions as the basis of your peer review: How effectively did the writer restate the main points of the essay in the conclusion? What final thought did the writer leave you with, and how did this create a lasting impression? Offer each other suggestions, and remember that they are most helpful when they are constructive.

DRAFT

CA-CCSS: CA.W.8.2a, CA.W.8.2b, CA.W.8.2c, CA.W.8.2f, CA.W.8.4, CA.W.8.5, CA.W.8.6, CA.W.8.10, CA.SL.8.1a, CA.SL.8.1c, CA.L.8.1a

## WRITING PROMPT

The Civil War was a turning point in American history, one that helped define who Americans are today. Why did so many people feel it was necessary to fight? How did their efforts help redefine what it means to be an American? Write an informative essay analyzing how the Civil War changed Americans and their ideas about freedom. Use ideas and information expressed in at least two unit texts to reinforce your analysis.

Your essay should include:

- an introduction with a clear thesis statement
- body paragraphs with relevant evidence and thorough analysis to support your thesis
- a conclusion paragraph that effectively wraps up your essay

You have already completed several important steps for writing an informative essay. Most of the difficult work is done! Now use the information that you gathered during the Prewriting step. Combine it with the organizational structure that you worked out in the Plan step. Recall what you have learned about audience and purpose, an introduction that contains a thesis statement, body paragraphs with supporting details and transitions, and a conclusion that wraps up your essay, and you're ready to write the first draft of your essay.

Use your roadmap and other prewriting materials to help you as you write. Remember that informative/explanatory writing begins with an introduction and presents a clear thesis statement in the first paragraph. Body paragraphs develop the thesis statement with strong supporting ideas, details, quotations, and other relevant information drawn from the texts you have chosen. Transitional words between paragraphs and ideas help readers understand how different facts and events are related. They also help readers follow the information you present to a logical conclusion. Then the concluding paragraph restates or reinforces your thesis statement and leaves a lasting impression on your readers.

When drafting, ask yourself these questions:

- How can I improve my introductory paragraph to make it more appealing and grab readers' attention right away?

- What can I do to clarify my thesis statement?

- What textual evidence—including well-chosen facts, definitions, concrete details, quotations, and other information and examples—supports the thesis statement?

- Have all my sources been cited properly, both within the text of my essay and in a Works Cited page?

- Would more precise language or different details about my topic make the text more exciting and vivid?

- How well have I communicated how Americans changed their ideas about freedom?

- What final thought do I want to leave with my readers in my conclusion paragraph?

Before you submit your draft, read it over carefully for any spelling or grammatical errors. You also want to be sure that you've responded to all aspects of the prompt.

REVISE

**CA-CCSS:** CA.W.8.2a, CA.W.8.2b, CA.W.8.2c, CA.W.8.2d, CA.W.8.2e, CA.W.8.2f, CA.W.8.4, CA.W.8.5, CA.W.8.6, CA.W.8.10, CA.SL.8.1a, CA.L.8.1b, CA.L.8.1d, CA.L.8.3a

## WRITING PROMPT

The Civil War was a turning point in American history, one that helped define who Americans are today. Why did so many people feel it was necessary to fight? How did their efforts help redefine what it means to be an American? Write an informative essay analyzing how the Civil War changed Americans and their ideas about freedom. Use ideas and information expressed in at least two unit texts to reinforce your analysis.

Your essay should include:

- an introduction with a clear thesis statement
- body paragraphs with relevant evidence and thorough analysis to support your thesis
- a conclusion paragraph that effectively wraps up your essay

You have written the first draft of your informative essay and have received feedback on your work from at least two peers. The next step is to revise your draft to incorporate the suggestions and improvements you have been considering. Be sure to consider all that you have learned about constructing strong, logically organized introductions, body paragraphs, and conclusions that support thesis statements by providing evidence drawn from sources. Always keep your audience and purpose in mind.

Here are some ideas to consider as you revise:

- Review the suggestions you received from your peers.
- Focus on maintaining a formal style, which means your essay should be written in a serious tone. Your subject is important and your audience is reading the piece to fully understand the topic. Here are a few suggestions:
  › Review your piece for slang and remove any that you find.

> › Be sure the entire piece is written in the third person. If you find words such as "I," "me," or "mine," remove them. Also watch for addressing readers as "you." These words give your essay an informal, conversational feel which is not appropriate for an informative essay.
>
> › Read carefully to see if you accidentally included any personal opinions. Informative essays are unbiased. They provide information, but they do not try to influence or convince readers.

- Once you have revised for style, read your essay again and focus on the content and organization. How can it be improved?

  > › What details are missing to support your ideas? How can you clarify the development of America's ideas about freedom since the Civil War?
  >
  > › Do you need to add any new textual evidence to fully support your thesis statement or engage the interest of readers?
  >
  > › Think about the exact words you have used. Can you substitute a more vivid verb or a more specific noun to clarify a point?
  >
  > › How can you strengthen the transitions to improve the flow of the essay? Make sure each transition correctly highlights the relationships between ideas.

- Evaluate your introduction, your thesis statement, and your conclusion. It is easy to edit parts of the body of your essay and to accidentally move away from your original idea as you do so. Be sure that any revisions do not move away from your thesis statement.

Please note that excerpts and passages in the StudySync® library and this workbook are intended as touchstones to generate interest in an author's work. The excerpts and passages do not substitute for the reading of entire texts, and StudySync® strongly recommends that students seek out and purchase the whole literary or informational work in order to experience it as the author intended. Links to online resellers are available in our digital library. In addition, complete works may be ordered through an authorized reseller by filling out and returning to StudySync® the order form enclosed in this workbook.

Reading & Writing Companion **491**

# SKILL: SOURCES AND CITATIONS

## DEFINE

**Sources** are the documents and information that an author uses to research his or her writing. Some sources are **primary sources**. A primary source is a first-hand account of events by the individual who experienced them. Other sources are **secondary sources**. A secondary source analyzes and interprets primary sources. These sources are one or more steps removed from the actual event. Some secondary sources, however, may have pictures, quotations, or graphics from primary sources in them.

**Reliable sources** are those that are known to be accurate and trustworthy. Books and magazines that have been fact-checked, such as journals or encyclopedias, are considered reliable. Websites that are developed and maintained by a knowledgeable source, such as a university or the government, are also considered reliable. Today, however, it is possible for nearly anyone to develop a website or to publish a book without the benefit of others checking their work. Personal websites and information coming from the general public are not, usually, considered reliable sources.

Writers study their sources before writing to learn about the topic and the way in which others have treated it. However, it is not acceptable to take another person's ideas and call them your own. This would be plagiarism. Instead, give credit to the source where the idea or quotation came from using a **citation.** These are notes that give information about the sources an author used in his or her writing. Citations let readers know who originally came up with those words and ideas.

## IDENTIFICATION AND APPLICATION

- Sources can be primary or secondary in nature. Primary sources are first-hand accounts, artifacts, or other original materials. Examples of primary sources include:
  - › Letters or another correspondence

Copyright © BookheadEd Learning, LLC

- › Photographs
- › Official documents
- › Diaries or journals
- › Autobiographies or memoirs
- › Eyewitness accounts and interviews
- › Audio recordings and radio broadcasts
- › Works of art
- › Interviews

- Secondary sources are usually text. Some examples include:
  - › Encyclopedia articles
  - › Textbooks
  - › Commentary or criticisms
  - › Histories
  - › Documentary films
  - › News analyses

- Writers of informative/explanatory texts look for sources from experts in the topic they are writing about. When researching online, they look for URLs that contain ".gov" (government agencies), ".edu" (colleges and universities), and ".org" (museums and other non-profit organizations)

- A writer includes a citation to give credit to any source, whether primary or secondary, that is quoted word for word. There are several different ways to cite a source.
  - › One way is to put the author's last name in parenthesis at the end of the sentence in which the quote appears. This is what the writer of the Student Model essay does after every quotation. For print sources, the author's name should be followed by the page number on which the text of the quotation appears.
  - › Your citations can also appear as a list at the end of your essay. In the body of your essay, place a number after each reference to a primary or secondary source. At the back of your essay, list the numbers and identify the source that goes with each number.

- Citations are also necessary when a writer borrows ideas from another source, even if the writer paraphrases, or puts those ideas in his or her own words. Citations credit the source, but they also help readers discover where they can learn more.

 ## MODEL

In the introductory paragraph of the Student Model, "The Meaning of Freedom," the author introduces the sources that will be discussed in the essay:

NOTES

*The Civil War was a turning point in American history that reshaped American ideas about freedom because it brought a resolution to the question of slavery. Prior to the Civil War, the issue of slavery divided Americans. Some were concerned that most African American people were kept as slaves. These people could not enjoy the freedom that white Americans took for granted. Others felt this situation was not only right, but also vital to the economy. This division was at the heart of the Civil War. Its resolution forever altered what it means to be an American. Many passages from the period explore these ideas of freedom.* **Abraham Lincoln's "Gettysburg Address"** *and* **Narrative of the Life of Frederick Douglass, An American Slave by Frederick Douglass** *are good examples. Both pieces discuss American views on freedom before and during the Civil War, as well as the necessity for change.*

By listing these texts in the first paragraph, the student has explained to readers which two texts the essay will discuss.

In this second paragraph of the essay, the student has included direct quotations from the first text, *Narrative of the Life of Frederick Douglass, An American Slave*, to support his claim that this text discusses American views on freedom before and during the Civil War:

*In* **the excerpt from Douglass' memoir,** *Narrative of the Life of Frederick Douglass, An American Slave,* *he tells the story of how he learned to read in spite of being forbidden to do so. In fact, the idea of helping a slave learn to read in that time and place was so strictly forbidden that Douglass refrained from naming the young white boys he had befriended, and who shared their lessons with him. He said, "...* **for it is almost an unpardonable offence to teach slaves to read in this Christian country"** *(Douglass). To Douglass, the books he read* **"gave tongue to interesting thoughts"** *in his own soul* **(Douglass).** *The concerns of the white masters who had not allowed slaves to learn how to read came true. The books Douglass read gave him the words to express the truth that he had always felt: Slavery contradicted human rights on all levels. How could a country, said to be based on freedom, allow it? In fact it could not, because the contradiction made one part of the country stand against the other in war.*

Here, the introductory clause "In the excerpt from Douglass' memoir, *Narrative of the Life of Frederick Douglass, An American Slave*," lets readers know which text will be discussed in this paragraph. The student also gives credit to Douglass for his ideas by including parenthetical citations after the quoted material from the text: "He said, '... for it is almost an unpardonable offence to teach slaves to read in this Christian country' (Douglass)." A writer must always use quotation marks around words taken directly from a text. Note, too, that the writer uses ellipses to indicate where he omitted words in the original text. Writers sometimes omit less relevant words from quotations in order to be succinct. However, they must be careful not to omit words in such a way as to alter the original meaning of the material.

Including quotations and citations in an informative essay helps readers understand which ideas have originated with the writer, and which ideas belong to the author of the source material. Writers can also lend credibility to their claims by showing readers how information in reliable sources supports the writer's ideas.

The next step the writer of the Student Model must take to fully give credit for his sources is to provide full bibliographic information for *Narrative of the Life of Frederick Douglass, An American Slave* and "The Gettysburg Address" in a Works Cited page. This Works Cited page should appear at the end of the essay and include, for each work cited in the essay, the author's name, the title of the work, the place of publication, the publisher, and the date of publication. If the work is in a collection, sometimes the name of the editor will also be included. According to Modern Language Association (MLA) style, commas are used to set off elements within each of these general groupings, but each grouping ends with a period. If a source is electronic, the last element of the citation indicates that the item is from the "Web."

It is common practice to present the titles of full-length works such as books, plays, and movies in italics. Shorter works, such as titles of articles, chapters, speeches, short stories, poems, and songs are presented within quotation marks. When citing a speech, the writer must include the date on which the speech was given and where he or she found the speech. Consider the following example:

Lincoln, Abraham. "The Gettysburg Address." 19 November 1863. *The Collected Works of Abraham Lincoln.* Ed. Roy P. Basler. New Brunswick, NJ: Rutgers UP, 1955.

You will need to search online for each text you cite in your essay and gather its complete bibliographic information. Then use this information to create a Works Cited page to accompany your essay.

 ## PRACTICE

Write in-text citations for quoted information in your informative essay. When you are finished, trade with a partner and offer each other feedback. How successful was the writer in citing sources for the essay? Offer each other suggestions, and remember that they are most helpful when they are constructive.

# EDIT, PROOFREAD, AND PUBLISH

**CA-CCSS:** CA.W.8.2a, CA.W.8.2b, CA.W.8.2c, CA.W.8.2d, CA.W.8.2e, CA.W.8.2f, CA.W.8.4, CA.W.8.5, CA.W.8.6, CA.W.8.10, CA.SL.8.1a, CA.SL.8.1c, CA.L.8.1a, CA.L.8.1b, CA.L.8.1d, CA.L.8.2a, CA.L.8.2b, CA.L.8.2c, CA.L.8.3a

## WRITING PROMPT

The Civil War was a turning point in American history, one that helped define who Americans are today. Why did so many people feel it was necessary to fight? How did their efforts help redefine what it means to be an American? Write an informative essay analyzing how the Civil War changed Americans and their ideas about freedom. Use ideas and information expressed in at least two unit texts to reinforce your analysis.

Your essay should include:

- an introduction with a clear thesis statement
- body paragraphs with relevant evidence and thorough analysis to support your thesis
- a conclusion paragraph that effectively wraps up your essay

Now that you have revised your informative/explanatory essay and received input from your peers on the revision, it's time to edit and proofread your essay in order to produce a final version. As you review your work, ask yourself the following questions:

- Does my essay follow the basic structure of an informative/explanatory essay (introduction, body paragraphs, conclusion)?
- Does my introduction grab the readers' attention in an interesting yet relevant way? Is my thesis statement part of my introduction as well as my conclusion? Does it respond to the prompt clearly and effectively?
- Have I included strong main ideas, supporting details, and relevant evidence to support my thesis and create a cohesive, vivid presentation of what I want to say?
- Have all of my sources been cited properly both within the body of my essay and in a Works Cited page at the end of my essay?

- Do I use appropriate and smooth transitions to connect ideas and details within paragraphs as well as between paragraphs?
- Have I presented my readers with a conclusion that summarizes my purpose and intent as well as coherently restates my thesis?
- Have I established a formal tone through the use of precise language and academic, domain-specific words?
- Have I incorporated all the valuable suggestions from my peers?

When you are satisfied with your work, move on to proofread it for errors. For example, check that you have used the correct punctuation for quotations, citations, and restrictive/nonrestrictive phrases and clauses. Have you used ellipses to indicate where in direct quotations you have omitted material? Have you used verbals correctly? Are commas used appropriately? Be sure to correct any misspelled words.

Once you have made all your corrections, you are ready to submit and publish your work. You can distribute your writing to family and friends, hang it on a bulletin board, or post it on your blog. If you publish online, create links to your sources and citations. That way, readers can follow-up on what they've learned from your essay and read more on their own. You might also consider using headings to organize your information or graphics to enhance readers' comprehension of your material.

# Text Fulfillment
# Through StudySync

If you are interested in specific titles, please fill out the form below and we will check availability through our partners.

## ORDER DETAILS

Date:

| TITLE | AUTHOR | Paperback/ Hardcover | Specific Edition *If Applicable* | Quantity |
|-------|--------|---------------------|----------------------------------|----------|
|       |        |                     |                                  |          |
|       |        |                     |                                  |          |
|       |        |                     |                                  |          |
|       |        |                     |                                  |          |
|       |        |                     |                                  |          |
|       |        |                     |                                  |          |
|       |        |                     |                                  |          |

### SHIPPING INFORMATION

Contact:

Title:

School/District:

Address Line 1:

Address Line 2:

Zip or Postal Code:

Phone:

Mobile:

Email:

### BILLING INFORMATION ☐ SAME AS SHIPPING

Contact:

Title:

School/District:

Address Line 1:

Address Line 2:

Zip or Postal Code:

Phone:

Mobile:

Email:

### PAYMENT INFORMATION

☐ CREDIT CARD

Name on Card:

Card Number:          Expiration Date:          Security Code:

☐ PO

Purchase Order Number:

StudySync Text Fulfillment, BookheadEd Learning, LLC
610 Daniel Young Drive | Sonoma, CA 95476